NOVEL TO FILM

Novel To Film

An Introduction to the
Theory of Adaptation

BRIAN McFARLANE

CLARENDON PRESS · OXFORD

OXFORD
UNIVERSITY PRESS

Great Clarendon Street, Oxford OX2 6DP

Oxford University Press is a department of the University of Oxford.
It furthers the University's objective of excellence in research, scholarship,
and education by publishing worldwide in

Oxford New York

Athens Auckland Bangkok Bogotá Buenos Aires Calcutta
Cape Town Chennai Dar es Salaam Delhi Florence Hong Kong Istanbul
Karachi Kuala Lumpur Madrid Melbourne Mexico City Mumbai
Nairobi Paris São Paulo Singapore Taipei Tokyo Toronto Warsaw

with associated companies in Berlin Ibadan

Oxford is a registered trade mark of Oxford University Press
in the UK and in certain other countries

Published in the United States
by Oxford University Press Inc., New York

© Brian McFarlane 1996

First published 1996

British Library Cataloguing in Publication Data

Data available

Library of Congress Cataloging in Publication Data

McFarlane, Brian, 1934–
Novel to film: an introduction to the theory of adaptation / Brian McFarlane.
Includes bibliographical references.
1. Film adaptations. I. Title.
PN 1997-85-M338 1996 791-43—dc20 95-50525

ISBN 0-19-871151-4
ISBN 0-19-871150-6 (pbk.)

5 7 9 10 8 6 4

Printed in Great Britain
on acid-free paper by
Biddles Ltd,
Guildford and King's Lynn

For Charles Barr and Thomas Elsaesser,
with thanks

Preface

IN surveying the broader film-and-literature field, then focusing more narrowly on adaptation, the first part of this book suggests the pervasive nature of the interest in this confluence of two art-forms. Partly, this is a matter of sketching a history of the way film has seemed to draw towards the novel, assuming through its own practices the narrative complexity and mimetic richness of the earlier medium, until it might be claimed that film has displaced the novel as the twentieth century's most popular narrative form. Some writers have argued convincingly for a continuing process of convergence among the arts as a site for discussing novel–film affinities; others have drawn attention to film's indebtedness to particular Victorian novelists; and there is no end to attempts to establish correspondences between various aspects of narrative and enunciation as they are manifested in the two media. Only in more recent years, and by no means consistently even then, is there any attempt to examine rigorously, to conceptualize, the relations between the media. Modern theoretical work from writers such as Roland Barthes and Christian Metz (their emphases fall on, respectively, literature and film) has suggested new and more productive ways of confronting some of the issues raised by a comparison of the two media, though none has been primarily concerned with adaptation.

The aim of this book is to offer and test a methodology for studying the process of transposition from novel to film, with a view not to evaluating one in relation to the other but to establishing the *kind* of relation a film might bear to the novel it is based on. In pursuing this goal, I shall set up procedures for distinguishing between that which can be transferred from one medium to another (essentially, narrative) and that which, being dependent on different signifying systems, cannot be transferred (essentially, enunciation). The distinction is not as boldly simple as the previous sentence makes it sound, but it *is* simple enough to make one wonder why it has not been pursued in adaptation studies. This study is an exercise in applied theory; its originality lies in the application of theoretical insights to situations and purposes other than those that gave rise to them. The aim is, through the use of certain theoretical concepts, to offer an alternative to the more subjective, impressionistic comparisons endemic in discussions on the phenomenon of adaptation.

In choosing the texts for case-study, an explicit rationale for which is given in the Introduction to Part II of this book, I have restricted myself to 'realist' novels in English. This no doubt reflects personal preference, but the choice is also based on my sense that mainstream cinema has owed much of its popularity to representational tendencies it shares with the nineteenth-century English novel. However, nothing in my analysis of the texts chosen suggests that the methodology used would be unsuited to other kinds of novel—to, say, modernist or post-modernist fiction—though the results yielded might exhibit different emphases.

I have limited the scope of this book in other ways, too, and thereby, reluctantly, marginalized several other potentially productive—and certainly interesting—approaches to adaptation. These include the much-debated question of authorship in relation to film, a question which becomes even more complex in the case of adaptation, and the influence of the industrial and cultural context in which the film is made on how the original novel is adapted. In the case-studies I have drawn attention to such matters only when they appear to have been explicitly responsible for major shifts of narrative emphasis or for certain elements in the film's enunciatory procedures. Also, the problems and issues associated with television serial adaptation are different in many respects from those confronted by the film-maker, and a full discussion of such differences is outside the scope of the present study, tempting though some comparisons may be.

In spite of efforts to deal as objectively and systematically as possible with the issues raised by adaptation, I am aware that there is a good deal in our response to novels and films that resists such an approach. It is one thing to identify and categorize certain key narrative functions, another to account for how we respond to them aesthetically and affectively, and I hope my accounts of the film–novel pairs chosen for case-studies do not suggest otherwise. However, without wishing to raise the study of adaptation to the level of a science, I believe it is possible to apply to it analytical methods more rigorous than has commonly been the case. In the light of this belief, Part I of this book will survey the field and propose an agenda for such an approach, and Part II will test such an approach in relation to the five chosen case-studies.

Some aspects of the chapters on *Random Harvest*, *Great Expectations*, and *Daisy Miller* have provided the basis for articles published in the *Literature/Film Quarterly*. I am grateful for permission to reprint here extracts from these. My thanks are also due to colleagues at Monash University and the University of East Anglia, to Eleni Naoumidis for her expert and patient typing of the manuscript, and to my wife Geraldine for her support throughout.

B. M.

Melbourne,
December 1994

Contents

Part I

Backgrounds, Issues, and a New Agenda

EVERYONE who sees films based on novels feels able to comment, at levels ranging from the gossipy to the erudite, on the nature and success of the adaptation involved. That is, the interest in adaptation, unlike many other matters to do with film (e.g. questions of authorship), is not a rarefied one. And it ranges backwards and forwards from those who talk of novels as being 'betrayed' by boorish film-makers to those who regard the practice of comparing film and novel as a waste of time.

The film-makers themselves have been drawing on literary sources, and especially novels of varying degrees of cultural prestige, since film first established itself as pre-eminently a narrative medium. In view of this fact, and given that there has been a long-running discourse on the nature of the connections between film and literature, it is surprising how little systematic, sustained attention has been given to the processes of adaptation. This is the more surprising since the issue of adaptation has attracted critical attention for more than sixty years in a way that few other film-related issues have. Writers across a wide critical spectrum have found the subject fascinating: newspaper and journal reviews almost invariably offer comparison between a film and its literary precursor; from fan magazines to more or less scholarly books, one finds reflections on the incidence of adaptation; works serious and trivial, complex and simple, early and recent, address themselves to various aspects of this phenomenon almost as old as the institution of the cinema.

In considering the issues here, I want to begin by drawing attention to some of the most commonly recurring discussions of the connections between the film and the novel.

BACKGROUNDS

Conrad, Griffith, and 'Seeing'

Commentators in the field are fond of quoting Joseph Conrad's famous statement of his novelistic intention: 'My task which I am trying to achieve is, by the powers of the written word, to make you hear, to make you feel— it is, before all, to make to see'.[1] This remark of 1897 is echoed, consciously

---

[1] Joseph Conrad, Preface to *The Nigger of the Narcissus* (J. M. Dent and Sons: London, 1945), 5.

or otherwise, sixteen years later by D. W. Griffith, whose cinematic intention is recorded as: 'The task I am trying to achieve is above all to make you
see'.[2] George Bluestone's all-but-pioneering work in the film-literature field,
Novels into Film, draws attention to the similarity of the remarks at the start
of his study of 'The Two Ways of Seeing', claiming that 'between the percept
of the visual image and the concept of the mental image lies the root
difference between the two media'.[3] In this way he acknowledges the connecting link of 'seeing' in his use of the word 'image'. At the same time, he
points to the fundamental difference between the way images are produced
in the two media and how they are received. Finally, though, he claims that
'conceptual images evoked by verbal stimuli can scarcely be distinguished in
the end from those evoked by non-verbal stimuli',[4] and, in this respect, he
shares common ground with several other writers concerned to establish
links between the two media.

By this, I mean those commentaries which address themselves to crucial
changes in the (mainly English) novel towards the end of the nineteenth
century; changes which led to a stress on showing rather than on telling and
which, as a result, reduced the element of authorial intervention in its more
overt manifestations. Two of the most impressive of such accounts, both of
them concerned with ongoing processes of transmutation among the arts,
notably between literature and film, are Alan Spiegel's *Fiction and the Camera
Eye*[5] and Keith Cohen's *Film and Fiction*.[6] Spiegel's avowed purpose is to
investigate 'the common body of thought and feeling that unites film form
with the modern novel',[7] taking as his starting-point Flaubert, whom he sees
as the first great nineteenth-century exemplar of 'concretized form', a form
dependent on supplying a great deal of visual information. His line of en-
quiry leads him to James Joyce who, like Flaubert, respects 'the integrity of
the seen object and . . . gives it palpable presence apart from the presence of
the observer'.[8] This line is pursued by way of Henry James who attempts 'a
balanced distribution of emphasis in the rendering of what is looked at, who
is looking, and what the looker makes of what she [i.e. Maisie in *What Maisie
Knew*] sees',[9] and by way of the Conrad–Griffith comparison. Spiegel presses
this comparison harder than Bluestone, stressing that though both may have
aimed at the same point—a congruence of image and concept—they did so
from opposite directions. Whereas Griffith used his images to tell a story, as
means to understanding, Conrad (Spiegel claims) wanted the reader to

[2] Quoted in Lewis Jacobs, *The Rise of the American Film* (Harcourt, Brace: New York, 1939), 119.
[3] George Bluestone, *Novels into Film* (University of California Press: Berkeley and Los Angeles, 1957), 1.
[4] Ibid. 47.
[5] Alan Spiegel, *Fiction and the Camera Eye: Visual Consciousness in Film and the Modern Novel* (University Press of Virginia: Charlottesville, 1976).
[6] Keith Cohen, *Film and Fiction: The Dynamics of Exchange* (Yale University Press: New Haven, 1979).
[7] Spiegel, *Fiction and the Camera Eye*, p. xiii.
[8] Ibid. 63.   [9] Ibid. 55.

' "see" in and through and finally past his language and his narrative concept to the hard, clear bedrock of images'.[10]

One effect of this stress on the physical surfaces and behaviours of objects and figures is to de-emphasize the author's personal narrating voice so that we learn to read the ostensibly unmediated visual language of the later nineteenth-century novel in a way that anticipates the viewer's experience of film which necessarily presents those physical surfaces. Conrad and James further anticipate the cinema in their capacity for 'decomposing' a scene, for altering point of view so as to focus more sharply on various aspects of an object, for exploring a visual field by fragmenting it rather than by presenting it scenographically (i.e. as if it were a scene from a stage presentation).

Cohen, concerned with the 'process of convergence' between art-forms, also sees Conrad and James as significant in a comparison of novels and film. These authors he sees as breaking with the representational novels of the earlier nineteenth century and ushering in a new emphasis on '*showing* how the events unfold dramatically rather than recounting them'.[11] The analogy with film's narrative procedures will be clear and there seems no doubt that film, in turn, has been highly influential on the modern novel. Cohen uses passages from Proust and Virginia Woolf to suggest how the modern novel, influenced by techniques of Eisensteinian montage cinema, draws attention to its encoding processes in ways that the Victorian novel tends not to.

Dickens, Griffith, and Story-Telling

The other comparison that trails through the writing about film and literature is that between Griffith and Dickens, who was said to be the director's favourite novelist. The most famous account is, of course, that of Eisenstein, who compares their 'spontaneous childlike skill for story-telling',[12] a quality he finds in American cinema at large, their capacity for vivifying 'bit' characters, the visual power of each, their immense popular success, and above all their rendering of parallel action, for which Griffith cited Dickens as his source. On the face of it, there now seems nothing so remarkable in these formulations to justify their being so frequently paraded as examples of the ties that bind cinema and the Victorian novel. In fact Eisenstein's discussion of Dickens's 'cinematic techniques', including anticipation of such phenomena as frame composition and the close-up, is really not far removed from those many works which talk about film language, striking similar analogical poses, without giving adequate consideration to the qualitative differences enjoined by the two media.

Later commentators have readily embraced Eisenstein's account:

[10] Ibid. pp. xi–xii.   [11] Cohen, *Film and Fiction*, 5

[12] Sergei Eisenstein, *Film Form*, ed. and trans. Jan Leyda (Harcourt, Brace: New York, 1949), 196.

Bluestone, for instance, states boldly that: 'Griffith found in Dickens hints for every one of his major innovations',[13] and Cohen, going further, points to 'the more or less blatant appropriation of the themes and content of the nineteenth-century bourgeois novel'.[14] However, in spite of the frequency of reference to the Dickens–Griffith connection, and apart from the historical importance of parallel editing in the development of film narrative, the influence of Dickens has perhaps been overestimated and under-scrutinized. One gets the impression that critics steeped in a literary culture have fallen on the Dickens–Griffith comparison with a certain relief, perhaps as a way of arguing the cinema's respectability. They have tended to concentrate on the thematic interests and the large, formal narrative patterns and strategies the two great narrative-makers shared, rather than to address themselves, as a film-oriented writer might, to detailed questions of enunciation, of possible parallels and disparities between the two different signifying systems, of the range of 'functional equivalents'[15] available to each within the parameters of the classical style as evinced in each medium.

As film came to replace in popularity the representational novel of the earlier nineteenth century, it did so through the application of techniques practised by writers at the latter end of the century. Conrad with his insistence on making the reader 'see' and James with his technique of 'restricted consciousness', both playing down obvious authorial mediation in favour of limiting the point of view from which actions and objects are observed, provide clear examples. In this way they may be said to have broken with the tradition of 'transparency' in relation to the novel's referential world so that the mode and angle of vision were as much a part of the novel's content as what was viewed. The comparisons with cinematic technique are clear but, paradoxically, the modern novel has not shown itself very adaptable to film. However persuasively it may be demonstrated that the likes of Joyce, Faulkner, and Hemingway have drawn on cinematic techniques, the fact is that the cinema has been more at home with novels from—or descended from—an earlier period. Similarly, certain modern plays, such as *Death of a Salesman*, *Equus*, or M. *Butterfly*, which seem to owe something to cinematic techniques, have lost a good deal of their fluid representations of time and space when transferred to the screen.

Adaptation: The Phenomenon

As soon as the cinema began to see itself as a narrative entertainment, the idea of ransacking the novel—that already established repository of narrative fiction—for source material got underway, and the process has continued

---

[13] Bluestone, *Novels into Film*, 2.   [14] Cohen, *Film and Fiction*, 4.

[15] David Bordwell's term, in *The Classical Hollywood Cinema* (Routledge and Kegan Paul: London, 1985), 13.

more or less unabated for ninety years. Film-makers' reasons for this continuing phenomenon appear to move between the poles of crass commercialism and high-minded respect for literary works. No doubt there is the lure of a pre-sold title, the expectation that respectability or popularity achieved in one medium might infect the work created in another. The notion of a potentially lucrative 'property' has clearly been at least one major influence in the filming of novels, and perhaps film-makers, as Frederic Raphael scathingly claims, 'like known quantities . . . they would sooner buy the rights of an expensive book than develop an original subject'.[16] Nevertheless most of the film-makers on record profess loftier attitudes than these. DeWitt Bodeen, co-author of the screenplay for Peter Ustinov's *Billy Budd* (1962), claims that: 'Adapting literary works to film is, without a doubt, a creative undertaking, but the task requires a kind of selective interpretation, along with the ability to recreate and sustain an established mood'.[17] That is, the adaptor should see himself as owing allegiance to the source work. Despite Peter Bogdanovich's disclaimer about filming Henry James's *Daisy Miller* ('I don't think it's a great classic story. I don't treat it with that kind of reverence'[18]), for much of the time the film is a conscientious visual transliteration of the original. One does not find film-makers asserting a bold approach to their source material, any more than announcing crude financial motives.

As to audiences, whatever their complaints about this or that violation of the original, they have continued to want to see what the books 'look like'. Constantly creating their own mental images of the world of a novel and its people, they are interested in comparing their images with those created by the film-maker. But, as Christian Metz says, the reader 'will not always find *his* film, since what he has before him in the actual film is now somebody else's phantasy'.[19] Despite the uncertainty of gratification, of finding audiovisual images that will coincide with their conceptual images, reader-viewers persist in providing audiences for 'somebody else's phantasy'. There is also a curious sense that the verbal account of the people, places, and ideas that make up much of the appeal of novels is simply *one* rendering of a set of existents which might just as easily be rendered in another. In this regard, one is reminded of Anthony Burgess's cynical view that 'Every best-selling novel *has* to be turned into a film, the assumption being that the book itself whets an appetite for the true fulfilment—the verbal shadow turned into light, the word made flesh.'[20] And perhaps there is a parallel with that late

---

[16] Frederic Raphael, 'Introduction', *Two for the Road* (Jonathan Cape: London, 1967).

[17] DeWitt Bodeen, 'The Adapting Art', *Films in Review*, 14/6 (June–July 1963), 349.

[18] Jan Dawson, 'The Continental Divide: Filming Henry James', *Sight and Sound*, 43/1 (Winter 1973–4), 14; repr. in part as 'An Interview with Peter Bogdanovich' in G. Peary and R. Shatzkin (eds.), *The Classic American Novel and the Movies* (Frederick Ungar Publishing: New York, 1977).

[19] Christian Metz, *The Imaginary Signifier* (Indiana University Press: Bloomingdale, 1977), 12.

[20] Anthony Burgess, 'On the Hopelessness of Turning Good Books into Films', *New York Times*, 20 Apr. 1975, p. 15.

nineteenth-century phenomenon, described by Michael Chanan in *The Dream that Kicks*, of illustrated editions of literary works and illustrated magazines in which great novels first appeared as serials. There is, it seems, an urge to have verbal concepts bodied forth in perceptual concreteness.

Whatever it is that makes film-goers want to see adaptations of novels, and film-makers to produce them, and whatever hazards lie in the path for both, there is no denying the facts. For instance, Morris Beja reports that, since the inception of the Academy Awards in 1927–8, 'more than three-fourths of the awards for "best picture" have gone to adaptations . . . [and that] the all-time box-office successes favour novels even more'.[21] Given that the novel and the film have been the most popular narrative modes of the nineteenth and twentieth centuries respectively, it is perhaps not surprising that film-makers have sought to exploit the kinds of response excited by the novel and have seen in it a source of ready-made material, in the crude sense of pre-tested stories and characters, without too much concern for how much of the original's popularity is intransigently tied to its verbal mode.

The Discourse on Adaptation

On being faithful

Is it really 'Jamesian'? Is it 'true to Lawrence'? Does it 'capture the spirit of Dickens'? At every level from newspaper reviews to longer essays in critical anthologies and journals, the adducing of fidelity to the original novel as a major criterion for judging the film adaptation is pervasive. No critical line is in greater need of re-examination—and devaluation.

Discussion of adaptation has been bedevilled by the fidelity issue, no doubt ascribable in part to the novel's coming first, in part to the ingrained sense of literature's greater respectability in traditional critical circles. As long ago as the mid-1940s James Agee complained of a debilitating reverence in even such superior transpositions to the screen as David Lean's *Great Expectations*. It seemed to him that the really serious-minded film-goer's idea of art would be 'a good faithful adaptation of *Adam Bede* in sepia, with the entire text read offscreen by Herbert Marshall'.[22] However, voices such as Agee's, querulously insisting that the cinema make its own art and to hell with tasteful allegiance, have generally cried in the wilderness.

Fidelity criticism depends on a notion of the text as having and rendering up to the (intelligent) reader a single, correct 'meaning' which the film-maker has either adhered to or in some sense violated or tampered with. There will often be a distinction between being faithful to the 'letter', an

[21] Morris Beja, *Film and Literature* (Longman: New York, 1979), 78.
[22] *Agee on Film* (McDowell Oblonsky: New York, 1958), 216.

approach which the more sophisticated writer may suggest is no way to ensure a 'successful' adaptation, and to the 'spirit' or 'essence' of the work. The latter is of course very much more difficult to determine since it involves not merely a parallelism between novel and film but between two or more readings of a novel, since any given film version is able only to aim at reproducing the film-maker's reading of the original and to hope that it will coincide with that of many other readers / viewers. Since such coincidence is unlikely, the fidelity approach seems a doomed enterprise and fidelity criticism unilluminating. That is, the critic who quibbles at failures of fidelity is really saying no more than: 'This reading of the original does not tally with mine in these and these ways.'

Few writers on adaptation have specifically questioned the possibility of fidelity; though some have claimed not to embrace it, they still regard it as a viable choice for the film-maker and a criterion for the critic. Beja is one exception. In asking whether there are 'guiding principles' for film-makers adapting literature, he asks: 'What relationship should a film have to the original source? Should it be "faithful"? Can it be? To what?'[23]

When Beja asks 'To what' should a film-maker be faithful in adapting a novel, one is led to recall those efforts at fidelity to times and places remote from present-day life. In 'period' films, one often senses exhaustive attempts to create an impression of fidelity to, say Dickens's London or to Jane Austen's village life, the result of which, so far from ensuring fidelity to the text, is to produce a distracting quaintness. What was a contemporary work for the author, who could take a good deal relating to time and place for granted, as requiring little or no scene-setting for his readers, has become a period piece for the film-maker. As early as 1928, M. Willson Disher picked up the scent of this misplaced fidelity in writing about a version of *Robinson Crusoe*: 'Mr Wetherell [director, producer, writer and star] went all the way to Tobago to shoot the right kinds of creeks and caves, but he should have travelled not westwards, but backwards, to reach "the island", and then he would have arrived with the right sort of luggage.'[24] Disher is not speaking against fidelity to the original as such but against a misconstrued notion of how it might be achieved. A more recent example is Peter Bogdanovich's use of the thermal baths sequence in his film of *Daisy Miller*: 'The mixed bathing is authentically of the period', he claims in an interview with Jan Dawson.[25] Authentically of the period, perhaps, but not so of Henry James, so that it is only a tangential, possibly irrelevant fidelity that is arrived at. The issue of fidelity is a complex one but it is not too gross a simplification to suggest that critics have encouraged film-makers to see it as a desirable goal in the adaptation of literary works. As Christopher Orr has noted: 'The concern

[23] Beja, *Film and Literature*, 80.

[24] M. Willson Disher, 'Classics into Films', *Fortnightly Review*, NS 124 (Dec. 1928), 789.

[25] Dawson, 'The Continental Divide', 14.

with the fidelity of the adapted film in letter and spirit to its literary source has unquestionably dominated the discourse on adaptation.'[26] The issue is inevitably raised in each of the succeeding Case-Studies, and is the object of a Special Focus in the study of *Daisy Miller*, which offers revealing insights into the limits of fidelity, especially from the film-maker's point of view.

Obscuring other issues

The insistence on fidelity has led to a suppression of potentially more rewarding approaches to the phenomenon of adaptation. It tends to ignore the idea of adaptation as an example of convergence among the arts, perhaps a desirable—even inevitable—process in a rich culture; it fails to take into serious account what may be transferred from novel to film as distinct from what will require more complex processes of adaptation; and it marginalizes those production determinants which have nothing to do with the novel but may be powerfully influential upon the film. Awareness of such issues would be more useful than those many accounts of how films 'reduce' great novels.

Modern critical notions of *intertextuality* represent a more sophisticated approach, in relation to adaptation, to the idea of the original novel as a 'resource'. As Christopher Orr remarks: 'Within this critical context [i.e. of intertextuality], the issue is not whether the adapted film is faithful to its source, but rather how the choice of a specific source and how the approach to that source serve the film's ideology.'[27] When, for instance, MGM filmed James Hilton's 1941 bestseller, *Random Harvest*, in the following year, its images of an unchanging England had as much to do with Hollywood anti-isolationism with regard to World War II as with finding visual equivalents for anything in Hilton. The film belongs to a rich context created by notions of Hollywood's England, by MGM's reputation for prestigious literary adaptation and for a glossy 'house style', by the genre of romantic melodrama (cf. *Rebecca*, 1940, *This Above All*, 1942), and by the idea of the star vehicle. Hilton's popular but, in truth, undistinguished romance is but one element of the film's intertextuality.

Some writers have proposed strategies which seek to categorize adaptations so that fidelity to the original loses some of its privileged position. Geoffrey Wagner suggests three possible categories which are open to the film-maker and to the critic assessing his adaptation: he calls these (*a*) *transposition*, 'in which a novel is given directly on the screen with a minimum of apparent interference';[28] (*b*) *commentary*, 'where an original is taken and either purposely or inadvertently altered in some respect . . . when there has

[26] Christopher Orr, 'The Discourse on Adaptation', *Wide Angle*, 6/2 (1984), 72.   [27] Ibid.

[28] Geoffrey Wagner, *The Novel and the Cinema* (Fairleigh Dickinson University Press: Rutherford, NJ, 1975), 222.

been a different intention on the part of the film-maker, rather than infidelity or outright violation';[29] and (c) *analogy*, 'which must represent a fairly considerable departure for the sake of making another work of art'.[30] The critic, he implies, will need to understand which kind of adaptation he is dealing with if his commentary on an individual film is to be valuable. Dudley Andrew also reduces the modes of relation between the film and its source novel to three, which correspond roughly (but in reverse order of adherence to the original) to Wagner's categories: 'Borrowing, intersection, and fidelity of transformation'.[31] And there is a third comparable classification system put forward by Michael Klein and Gillian Parker: first, 'fidelity to the main thrust of the narrative'; second, the approach which 'retains the core of the structure of the narrative while significantly reinterpreting or, in some cases, deconstructing the source text'; and, third, regarding 'the source merely as raw material, as simply the occasion for an original work'.[32] The parallel with Wagner's categories is clear.

There is nothing definitive about these attempts at classification but at least they represent some heartening challenges to the primacy of fidelity as a critical criterion. Further, they imply that, unless the kind of adaptation is identified, critical evaluation may well be wide of the mark. The faithful adaptation (e.g. *Daisy Miller* or James Ivory's *Howard's End*, 1992) can certainly be intelligent and attractive, but is not necessarily to be preferred to the film which sees the original as 'raw material' to be reworked, as Hitchcock so persistently did, from, say, *Sabotage* (1936) to *The Birds* (1963). Who, indeed, ever thinks of Hitchcock as primarily an adaptor of other people's fictions? At a further extreme, it is possible to think of a film as providing a commentary on a literary text, as Welles does on three Shakespearian plays in *Chimes at Midnight* (1966), or as Gus Van Sant does in *My Own Private Idaho* (1992), drawing on both Shakespeare and Welles. There are many kinds of relations which may exist between film and literature, and fidelity is only one—and rarely the most exciting.

REDEFINING ISSUES AND A NEW APPROACH

The Centrality of Narrative

The more one considers the phenomenon of adaptation of novel into film— the whole history of the reliance on the novel as source material for the fiction film—the more one is drawn to consider the central importance of

---

[29] Ibid. 224.   [30] Ibid. 226.

[31] Dudley Andrew, 'The Well-Worn Muse: Adaptation in Film History and Theory', in Syndy Conger and Janice R. Welsch (eds.), *Narrative Strategies* (West Illinois University Press: Macomb, Ill., 1980), 10.

[32] Michael Klein and Gillian Parker (eds.), *The English Novel and the Movies* (Frederick Ungar Publishing: New York, 1981), 9–10.

narrative to both. Whatever the cinema's sources—as an invention, as a leisure pursuit, or as a means of expression—and whatever uncertainties about its development attend its earliest years, its huge and durable popularity is owed to what it most obviously shares with the novel. That is, its capacity for narrative. By the time of Edwin Porter's *The Great Train Robbery* (1903), in which scenes set in different locations are spliced together to tell a story, the cinema's future as a narrative art was settled, and no subsequent development of its techniques has threatened the supremacy of that function.

Christian Metz, discussing film narrativity, writes: 'Film tells us continuous stories; it "says" things that could be conveyed also in the language of words; yet it says them differently. There is a reason for the possibility as well as for the necessity of adaptations.'[33] He goes on to consider the '*demand*' for the feature-length fiction film, 'which was only one of the many conceivable genres',[34] but which has dominated film production. 'The basic formula, which has never changed, is the one that consists in making a large continuous unit that tells a story and calling it a "movie". "Going to the movies" is going to see this type of story.'[35] Whatever other uses the cinema might have found, it is, as Metz suggests, as a story-teller that it found its greatest power and its largest audience. Its *embourgeoisement* inevitably led it away from trick shows, the recording of music halls acts and the like, towards that narrative representationalism which had reached a peak in the classic nineteenth-century novel. If film did not grow *out* of the latter, it grew *towards* it; and what novels and films most strikingly have in common is the potential and propensity for narrative. And narrative, at certain levels, is undeniably not only the chief factor novels and the films based on them have in common but is the chief transferable element.

If one describes a narrative as a series of events, causally linked, involving a continuing set of characters which influence and are influenced by the course of events, one realizes that such a description might apply equally to a narrative displayed in a literary text and to one in a filmic text. Nevertheless, much of the dissatisfaction which accompanies the writing about films adapted from novels tends to spring from perceptions of 'tampering' with the original narrative. Words like 'tampering' and 'interference', and even 'violation', give the whole process an air of deeply sinister molestation, perhaps springing from the viewer's thwarted expectations relating to both character and event. Such dissatisfactions resonate with a complex set of misapprehensions about the workings of narrative in the two media, about the irreducible differences between the two, and from a failure to distinguish what can from what cannot be transferred.

---

[33] Christian Metz, *Film Language: A Semiotics of the Cinema*, trans. Michael Taylor (Oxford University Press: New York, 1974), 44.
[34] Ibid.   [35] Ibid. 45.

To begin with the last point: there is a distinction to be made between what may be *transferred* from one narrative medium to another and what necessarily requires *adaptation proper*. Throughout the rest of this study, 'transfer' will be used to denote the process whereby certain narrative elements of novels are revealed as amenable to display in film, whereas the widely used term 'adaptation' will refer to the processes by which other novelistic elements must find quite different equivalences in the film medium, when such equivalences are sought or are available at all.

Narrative Functions: Novel and Film

Roland Barthes has defined the essence of a narrative function as 'the seed that it sows in the narrative, planting an element that will come to fruition later—either on the same [narrative] level or elsewhere, on another level',[36] going on to claim that, 'A narrative is never made up of anything other than functions: in differing degrees, everything in it signifies.' He distinguishes two main groups of narrative functions: *distributional* and *integrational* and, though he is not concerned with cinema in this discussion, this distinction is valuable in sorting out what may be tranferred (i.e. from novel to film) from that which may only be adapted. To distributional functions, Barthes gives the name of *functions proper*; integrational functions he calls *indices*. The former refer to actions and events; they are 'horizontal' in nature, and they are strung together linearly throughout the text; they have to do with 'operations'; they refer to a functionality of *doing*. *Indices* denotes a 'more or less diffuse concept which is nevertheless necessary to the meaning of the story'.[37] This concept embraces, for instance, psychological information relating to characters, data regarding their identity, notations of atmosphere and representations of place. Indices are 'vertical' in nature, influencing our reading of narrative in a pervasive rather than a linear way; they do not refer to operations but to a functionality of *being*.

The most important kinds of transfer possible from novel to film are located in the category of functions proper, rather than that of indices, though some elements of the latter will also be seen to be (partly) transferable. Barthes further subdivides functions to include *cardinal functions* (or *nuclei*) and *catalysers*. *Cardinal functions* are the 'hinge-points' of narrative: that is, the actions they refer to open up alternatives of consequence to the development of the story; they create 'risky' moments in the narrative and it is crucial to narrativity ('the processes through which the reader . . . constructs the meaning of the text'[38]) that the reader recognizes the possibility of

---

[36] Roland Barthes, 'Introduction to the Structural Analysis of Narratives' (1966), in *Image-Music-Text*, trans. Stephen Heath (Fontana/Collins: Glasgow, 1977), 89.
[37] Ibid. 92.   [38] Orr, 'The Discourse on Adaptation', 73.

such alternative consequences. The linking together of cardinal functions provides the irreducible bare bones of the narrative, and this linking, this 'tie between two cardinal functions, is invested with a double functionality, at once chronological and logical'.[39] These cardinal functions, or, in Seymour Chatman's terms, *kernels* ('narrative moments that give rise to cruxes in the direction taken by events'[40]), are, as I shall show, transferable: when a major cardinal function is deleted or altered in the film version of a novel (e.g. to provide a happy rather than a sombre ending), this is apt to occasion critical outrage and popular disaffection. The film-maker bent on 'faithful' adaptation must, as a basis for such an enterprise, seek to preserve the major cardinal functions.

However, even if the latter are preserved in the filming process, they can be 'deformed' by varying the catalysers which surround them. Catalysers (in Chatman's term, *satellites*) work in ways which are complementary to and supportive of the cardinal functions. They denote small actions (e.g. the laying of the table for a meal which may in turn give rise to action of cardinal importance to the story); their role is to root the cardinal functions in a particular kind of reality, to enrich the texture of those functions: 'their functionality is attenuated, unilateral, parasitic: it is a question of a purely chronological functionality',[41] in Barthes's words. Unlike the 'risky moments' created by cardinal functions, the catalysers 'lay out areas of safety, rests, luxuries';[42] they account for the moment-to-moment minutiae of narrative.

In so far as these functions, whether cardinal or catalysing, are not dependent on language, in the sense that they denote aspects of story content (actions and happenings) which may be displayed verbally or audio-visually, they are directly transferable from one medium to the other. Among the integrational functions, which Barthes subdivides into *indices proper* and *informants*, only the latter may be directly transferred. Whereas the former relate to concepts such as character and atmosphere, are more diffuse than the functions proper, and are therefore more broadly open to adaptation rather than to the comparative directness of transfer, informants 'are pure data with immediate signification'.[43] They include 'ready-made knowledge' such as the names, ages, and professions of characters, certain details of the physical setting, and, in these senses and in their own ways, share the authenticating and individuating functions performed in other respects by catalysers, and they are often amenable to transfer from one medium to another. What Barthes designates as cardinal functions and catalysers consti-

[39] Barthes, 'Introduction to the Structural Analysis of Narratives', 94.

[40] Seymour Chatman, *Story and Discourse: Narrative Structure in Fiction and Film* (Cornell University Press: Ithaca, NY, 1978), 53.

[41] Barthes, 'Introduction to the Structural Analysis of Narratives', 94.

[42] Ibid. 95.   [43] Ibid. 96.

tutes the formal content of narrative which may be considered independently of what Chatman calls 'its manifesting substance' (e.g. novel or film), and informants, in their objective name-ability, help to embed this formal content in a realized world, giving specificity to its abstraction. Perhaps informants may be seen as a first, small step towards mimesis in novel and film, the full mimetic process relying heavily on the functioning of the indices proper, to which I shall return shortly.

I should note at this point that Barthes has subsequently modified the structural taxonomy set up here with his designation of the five narrative codes which structure all classical narrative in *S/Z*, his reading of Balzac's *Sarrasine*. For my purposes, the earlier distinction between *distributional* and *integrational* functions, with the metaphors implied in their characterization, provides a more accessible and usable taxonomy in establishing what may be transferred from a long, complex work in one medium to a long, complex work in another. Barthes was not, of course, concerned with cinematic narrative when he wrote his 'Structural Analysis' essay, but, in Robin Wood's words, 'the critic has the right to appropriate whatever s/he needs from wherever it can be found, and use it for purposes somewhat different from the original ones'.[44]

Kinds of Narration and their Cinematic Potential

The distinctions to be drawn between various narrational modes as they appear in the novel are difficult to sustain in film narrative. The novels chosen as case-studies in this book exhibit notably different approaches to the question of narrative point of view: for example, first-person, omniscient, a mixture of both, the use of 'restricted consciousness'. However, these different approaches are considerably elided in the narrational procedures adopted by the films, a matter to be investigated in detail in Part II of this study. It is sufficient to draw attention at this point to the varying amenability to cinematic practice of these kinds of literary narration.

The first-person narration

There is only a precarious analogy between the attempts at first-person narration offered by films and the novel's first-person narration, comprising the individual discourses of each character surrounded by a continuing (generally past-tense) discourse which is attributed to a known and named narrator who may or may not be an active participant in the events of the novel. These attempts will usually be one of two kinds.

---

[44] Robin Wood, 'Notes for a Reading of *I Walked with a Zombie*', *CineAction!*, 3–4 (Winter 1986), 9.

(*a*) *The subjective cinema*   The subjective cinema on the scale of *The Lady in the Lake* (1946) has scarcely been tried since, in mainstream film-making at least, and has the status of a curiosity rather than of a major contribution to screen practice. Of its more localized manifestations (e.g. the point-of-view shot or succession of shots), screen narration has clearly made much use, as in Alan Bridges' film version of Rebecca West's novella *The Return of the Soldier* (1982), in which the first-person narration of the original is reduced to allowing the novel's narrator a preponderance of point-of-view shots. However, a 'preponderance' is by no means equivalent to the *continuing* shaping, analysing, directing consciousness of a first-person narrator. Further, as Thomas Elsaesser has noted, 'The *subjective perception*—what the characters themselves see and how they experience it—is integrated with an objective presentation of these individual points of view and what they signify inside the same narrative movement and the continuous action.'[45] While cinema may be more agile and flexible in changing the physical point of view from which an event or object is seen, it is much less amenable to the presentation of a consistent psychological viewpoint derived from one character.

(*b*) *Oral narration or voice-over*   The device of oral narration, or voice-over, may serve important narrative functions in film (e.g. reinforcing a sense of past tense) but, by virtual necessity, it cannot be more than intermittent as distinct from the continuing nature of the novelistic first-person narration. (Woody Allen's *Radio Days* (1987) is one of the few films that would be incomprehensible without its voice-over.) In usual film practice, the narrating voice-over may be dropped for sequences at a time: in fact, a sustained, non-diegetic oral accompaniment to visually presented action is scarcely feasible in relation to the feature films with which this study (like most cinema audiences) is concerned. Those words spoken in voice-over accompany images which necessarily take on an objective life of their own. One no longer has the sense of everything's being filtered through the consciousness of the protagonist-speaker: even in a film such as David Lean's *Great Expectations*, which goes to unusual lengths to retain the novel's 'first-person' approach, the grotesques who people Pip's world are no longer presented to the viewer as an individual's subjective impressions. One now sees everything the camera 'sees', not just what impressed itself on the hero-narrator's imaginative responsiveness. In relation to those films which employ the voice-over technique, one's sense of the character to whom it is attributed is more likely to be the product of his involvement in the action directly presented than of his occasional comment upon it, whereas this is frequently not the case in the first-person novel.

---

[45] Thomas Elsaesser, 'Film and the Novel: Reality and Realism of the Cinema', *Twentieth Century Studies* 9 (Sept. 1973), 61.

The omniscient novel

The narrative in such a novel is conveyed through two kinds of discourses: those attributed to various characters in direct speech (Colin MacCabe's 'object language'[46]) and that of the narrative (I should prefer 'narrating') prose, the apparently authoritative 'metalanguage' which surrounds them. It is this latter which guides our reading of the direct speech of the characters. MacCabe goes on to construct an analogy between these two kinds of discourse as they appear in the novel and in the film:

The narrative prose achieves its position of dominance because it is in the position of knowledge and this function of knowledge is taken up in the cinema by the narration of events. Through the knowledge we gain from the narrative we can split the discourses of the various characters from their situation and compare what is said in those discourses with what has been revealed to us through narration. The camera shows us what happens—it tells the truth against which we can measure the discourses.[47]

'The camera shows us what happens . . .'. David Bordwell has taken issue with MacCabe's hierarchy of discourses, both for its oversimplification of the classic realist novel and for the way in which it 'reduce[s] the range of filmic narration'. He particularly challenges MacCabe's 'privileging of camera work . . . over other film techniques', claiming that 'all materials of cinema function narrationally—not only camera but speech, gesture, written language, music, color, optical processes, lighting, costume, even offscreen space and offscreen sound'.[48] There is a certain captiousness in Bordwell's response since, it seems to me at least, MacCabe's use of 'the camera' is a shorthand way of referring to all those narrational materials which the camera *can* show or imply: that is, all from Bordwell's list except those which relate to soundtrack, which can, of course, initiate a tension with the visual image. Clearly, certain functions of the narrating prose, such as establishing setting and physical appearance of characters, can be achieved through the film's mise-en-scène. Other functions, such as those which enable us, through the writer's tone, to evaluate a character's speech, seem less immediately amenable to the camera's eye. The camera in this sense becomes the narrator by, for instance, focusing on such aspects of mise-en-scène as the way actors look, move, gesture, or are costumed, or on the ways in which they are positioned in a scene or on how they are photographed: in these ways the camera may catch a 'truth' which comments on and qualifies what the characters actually say.

It is, however, too simple to suggest that the mise-en-scène, or its deployment by the cinematic codes (notably that of montage), can effortlessly

---

[46] Colin MacCabe, 'Realism and the Cinema: Notes on Some Brechtian Theses', *Screen* 15/2 (Summer 1974), 10.

[47] Ibid.   [48] David Bordwell, *Narration in the Fiction Film* (Methuen: London, 1985), 20.

appropriate the role of the omniscient, inaudible narrator, or that the camera (to interpret MacCabe more narrowly), by 'show[ing] what happens', replaces such a narrator. For one thing (and a very obvious one) the camera—here used metonymically to denote its operator *and* whoever is telling him what to aim it at, and how—is outside the total discourse of the film, whereas the omniscient narrator is inextricably a part of the novel's. Or perhaps it is truer to say that the omniscient *narration* is inextricably part of the novel's total discourse, as much so as the spoken words of the characters. (However, whereas the latter—the spoken words—can, if a film-maker wants them to, be rendered word for word by the characters in the film, clearly no such possibility exists for the narration: for that narrational prose to which, in most novels, we allow a privileged position of knowledge about characters, periods, places; knowledge which may in fact be concealed from characters in the novel.) By exercising control over the mise-en-scène and soundtrack or through the manipulations of editing, the film-maker can *adapt* some of the functions of this narrational prose. The latter may indicate adverbially the tone of voice in which a remark is made by a character; the camera, on the other hand, may register a similar effect through attention to the actor's facial expression or posture (i.e. aspects of the mise-en-scène), or by cutting so as to reveal a response to such a remark (i.e. through montage) which will guide the viewer's perception of the remark, as well as through the actor's vocal inflection (i.e. through sound-track).

In regard to rendering on film the descriptive functions of narrating prose, relating to places, objects, activities, there is perhaps a stronger possibility of the new (cinematic) reality at once displacing the earlier (verbally created) reality; in matters relating to character and to the psychological action involving characters, the situation is more complex. There is, in film, no such instantly apparent, instantly available commentary on the action unfolding as the novel's narrating prose habitually offers. In the omniscient novel, in which this prose is not 'suspect' in the sense of belonging to a first-person narrator, the continuing mediation between the reader and the action of the novel is, by virtue of its privileged status as 'knowledge', the reader's guarantee of the 'truth' of the proceedings. In a sense, all films are omniscient: even when they employ a voice-over technique as a means of simulating the first-person novelistic approach, the viewer is aware, as indicated earlier, of a level of objectivity in what is shown, which may include what the protagonist sees but cannot help including a great deal else as well.

The mode of 'restricted consciousness'

In broad terms, it appears that neither first-person nor omniscient narration is, of its nature, amenable to cinematic narrative. Both seem always to know too much, or at least to know more than we feel is known in advance by the more directly experienced film narrative; and this sense of foreknowledge is no doubt intimately connected to the characteristic past-tense rendering of the prose narrative as opposed to the perceptual immediacy of the film. The novelistic form of the *restricted consciousness* (as in *Daisy Miller*) perhaps approximates most closely to the cinematic narrative mode. Cohen, in discussing the techniques of Conrad and James, and making comparisons with impressionist painters, writes:

The indirect approach of these novelists [Conrad and Ford Madox Ford] is not fully comprehensible without reference to their unconventional handling of point of view. . . . The reader, one might say, is constantly forced to pass through several foregrounds before he can make out clearly what is looming in the background. . . . The same basic mechanism is operative with James's 'central reflectors' through whom all or nearly all of the action takes place.[49]

Such 'central reflectors'—for example, Strether in *The Ambassadors*, Winterbourne in *Daisy Miller*—provide a point of identification for the reader, not necessarily in the affective sense but as a more or less consistently placed vantage-point from which to observe the action of the narrative. One is conscious always that there is a more comprehensive point of view than that available to such protagonists; that there is, as it were, a narrator looking over their shoulder, in the way that the camera may view an action over the shoulder of a character in the foreground of a shot, giving the viewer both the character's point of view and a slightly wider point of view which includes the character. The Jamesian concept of the 'centre of consciousness', by no means to be confused with narrational omniscience or the latter's obliteration by first-person narration, is perhaps the nearest that film may come in the direction of either first- or third-person narration. Its use will be examined in more detail in the case-study of *Daisy Miller*.

A Note on Terminology

The foregoing distinctions considered under the headings of 'Narrative Functions' and 'Kinds of Narration' may be summarized as those between a series of events sequentially and *con*sequentially arranged and the modes (more easily distinguishable in literary terms) of their presentation. This distinction between *narrative* and *narration* finds rough parallels in that between *story* and *discourse*. The latter pair—*histoire* and *discours* in modern French poetics—derives from the Russian Formalist distinction of the 1920s 'between *fabula*—the story-material as pure chronological sequence—and *suzet*, the plot as arranged and edited by the shaping of a story-teller, i.e. the finished narrative work as we experience it in a text; no longer pure story but

---

[49] Cohen, *Film and Fiction*, 35.

a selective narrative act',[50] in Roger Fowler's words. *Histoire* and *discours* he goes on to define as 'story-matter and its manner of delivery'.[51]

In the proliferating terminology of film theory, a further parallel frequently subsumes the categories referred to above in discussions of *enunciated* and *enunciation*. Of these terms, originating with the linguist Émile Benveniste, the former designates the 'utterance' (*l'énoncé*) as manifested in 'a stretch of text'[52] (David Bordwell's phrase), as a coherent set of events enacted in a series of syntagmatic units, as the sum of its narrative functions. The latter, the enunciation (*l'énonciation*), characterizes the process that creates, releases, shapes (I am aware of groping for exactly the right word) the 'utterance'. Enunciation, that is, refers to the ways in which the utterance is mediated, and, as such, obviously shares common ground with narration, *suzet*, and discourse. Neither film nor novel is 'transparent', however much either seeks to suppress signs of its enunciation, such 'suppression' being much more marked in the case of film. Film may lack those literary marks of enunciation such as person and tense, but in the ways in which, for example, shots are angled and framed and related to each other (i.e. in matters relating to mise-en-scène and montage) the enunciatory processes are inscribed. The institutional codes and their often highly individual deployment by different film-makers can either minimize or foreground the processes of cinematic enunciation but they cannot eradicate them, even when, as Metz writes, 'films give us the feeling that we are witnessing almost a real spectacle'.[53] Film enunciation, in relation to the transposition of novels to the screen, is a matter of adaptation proper, not of transfer. In the case-studies offered below, it will be considered in relation to how far the films concerned exhibit the interaction of cinema-specific and extra-cinematic codes, and to what extent they provide—or seek to provide—equivalences for the enunciatory procedures of the novels on which they are based.

An essential function of this study will be to distinguish between:

(i) those elements of the original novel which are transferable because not tied to one or other semiotic system—that is, essentially, *narrative*; and

(ii) those which involve intricate processes of adaptation because their effects are closely tied to the semiotic system in which they are manifested—that is, *enunciation*.

I have preferred 'enunciation', finally, to 'narration' because the latter is too often attached, in a limiting way, to matters of person and tense. By enunciation, I mean the whole expressive apparatus that governs the presentation—and reception—of the narrative.

[50] Roger Fowler, *Linguistics and the Novel* (Methuen: London, 1977), 78–9.
[51] Ibid. 79.
[52] Bordwell, *Narration in the Fiction Film*, 21.   [53] Metz, *Imaginary Signifier*, 4.

What is Understood by Adaptation

The 'distinctive feature' of adaptation, asserts Dudley Andrew, is 'the matching of the cinematic sign system to a prior achievement in some other system'. He claims that 'Every representational film adapts a prior conception . . . [but that] Adaptation delimits representation by insisting on the cultural status of the model . . . in a strong sense adaptation is the appropriation of a meaning from a prior text'.[54] The 'matching' and the 'appropriation' referred to are in the interests of replacing one illusion of reality by another. Whatever claims of fidelity and authenticity are made by film-makers, what these essentially amount to are the effacement of the memory derived from reading the novel by another experience—an audio-visual-verbal one—which will seem, as little as possible, to jar with that collective memory. It seeks, with one concretized response to a written work, to coincide with a great multiplicity of responses to the original. Its aim is to offer a perceptual experience that corresponds with one arrived at conceptually. The kinds of complaints directed at film adaptations of classic or popular novels, across a wide range of critical levels, indicate how rarely the 'appropriation of meaning from a prior text' is fully achieved—even when it is sought. Underlying the processes suggested here, in the manufacture of the more or less faithful film version at least, are those of *transferring* the novel's narrative basis and of *adapting* those aspects of its enunciation which are held to be important to retain, but which resist transfer, so as to achieve, through quite different means of signification and reception, affective responses that evoke the viewer's memory of the original text without doing violence to it.

The preceding paragraph of course suggests (wrongly) that the film adaptation will reach only viewers who are familiar with the novel. The very fact that this is not the case ought to be a deterrent to the fidelity-seeking critics, indicating that there is a varying, but large, segment of the audience to whom an adaptation is of no more consequence or interest *as such* than any other film. The stress on fidelity to the original undervalues other aspects of the film's intertextuality. By this, I mean those non-literary, non-novelistic influences at work on any film, whether or not it is based on a novel. To say that a film is based on a novel is to draw attention to one—and, for many people, a crucial—element of its intertextuality, but it can never be the only one. Conditions within the film industry and the prevailing cultural and social climate at the time of the film's making (especially when the film version does not follow hot upon the novel's publication) are two major determinants in shaping any film, adaptation or not. Among the former (i.e. conditions within the industry) one might include the effect of certain star personae, or, in the days of the studios' dominance, a particular studio's 'house style', or a director's predilections or genre conventions, or the pre-

[54] Andrew, 'Well-Worn Muse', 9.

vailing parameters of cinematic practice. As to the latter (i.e. the climate of
the times) it is difficult to set up a regular methodology for investigating how
far cultural conditions (e.g. the exigencies of wartime or changing sexual
mores) might lead to a shift in emphasis in a film as compared with the novel
on which it is based. However, it is necessary to make allowance in individual cases of adaptation for the nature of such influences, and this matter
will be looked at more closely in the Special Focus section of the chapter on
Cape Fear.

Perhaps, indeed, it is just because questions of narrativity *can* be formal-
ized that so much attention is paid to the original text's contribution to the
film. And certainly, in raising the issue of intertextuality, I am not denying
how powerfully formative the source work is in shaping the response of
many people to the film version. Consequently two lines of investigation
seem worthwhile: (*a*) in the transposition process, just what is it *possible* to
transfer or adapt from novel to film; and (*b*) what key factors other than the
source novel have exercised an influence on the film version of the novel?
For those who know and/or value the novel, the process of narrativity in
regard to the film version will necessarily differ from that of the spectator
unfamiliar with it: in either case, a true reading of the film will depend on a
response to how the cinematic codes and aspects of the mise-en-scène work
to create this particular version of the text.

What Kind of Adaptation?

While the fidelity criterion may seem misguided in *any* circumstances, it is
also true that many film-makers are on record as being reverently disposed
towards reproducing the original novel on film. It is equally clear, however,
that many adaptations have chosen paths other than that of the literal-
minded visualization of the original or even of 'spiritual fidelity', making
quite obvious departures from the original. Such departures may be seen
in the light of offering a *commentary* on or, in more extreme cases, a
deconstruction ('bring[ing] to light the internal contradictions in seemingly
perfectly coherent systems of thought'[55]) of the original. While I do not wish
to propose a hierarchy of valuableness among such approaches, it does seem
important in evaluating the film version of a novel to try to assess the *kind* of
adaptation the film aims to be. Such an assessment would at least preclude
the critical reflex that takes a film to task for not being something it does not
aim to be. Given the precariousness of the concept of fidelity in relation to
novels made from films, it seems wiser to drop terms like 'violation', 'distortion', 'travesty', and those others which, like them, imply the primacy of the
printed text.

[55] John Sturrock, 'Introduction' to Sturrock (ed.), *Structuralism and Since* (Oxford University Press:
Oxford, 1979), 14.

AGENDA FOR FURTHER STUDY

Nothing is likely to stop the interest of the general film-viewer in comparing films with their source novels, usually to the film's disadvantage. The aim of the present study is to use such concepts and methods as permit the most objective and systematic appraisal of what has happened in the process of transposition from one text to another. Given the prevalence of the process, and given that interpretations and memories of the source novel are powerful determining elements in the film's intertextuality, there is little value in merely saying that the film should stand autonomously. So it should, but it is also valuable to consider the kinds of transmutation that have taken place, to distinguish what the film-maker has sought to retain from the original and the kinds of use to which he has put it.

Transfer and Adaptation Proper

This distinction, elaborated earlier in this chapter, is central to the procedures of the following case-studies and, I believe, to any systematic study of what happens in the transposing of novel into film.

Transfer

In considering what can be transferred from novel to film, one begins to lay the theoretical basis for a study of the phenomenon of turning novels into films as well as a basis for what has been transferred in any particular case (i.e. how far the film-maker has chosen to transfer what is possible to do so). In broad terms, this involves a distinction between *narrative* (which can be transferred) and *enunciation* (which cannot, involving as it does quite separate systems of signification). Some potentially valuable strategies for considering the idea of transfer are outlined below.

The story/plot distinction

Terence Hawkes, drawing on Viktor Shklovsky's work on the nature of narrative, makes the following distinction: ' "Story" is simply the basic succession of events, the raw material which confronts the artist. Plot represents the distinctive way in which the "story" is made strange, creatively deformed and defamiliarized.'[56] Novel and film can share the same story, the same 'raw materials', but are distinguished by means of different plot strategies which alter sequence, highlight different emphases, which—in a word—defamiliarize the story. In this respect, of course, the use of two separate systems of signification will also play a crucial distinguishing role.

[56] Terence Hawkes, *Structuralism and Semiotics* (Methuen: London, 1977), 65–6.

The distinction between 'distributional' and 'integrational' functions

As discussed earlier, Barthes's 'distributional functions', those which he designates as 'functions proper', are those most directly susceptible to transfer
to film. This classification is further subdivided into *cardinal functions*, those
narrative actions which open up alternatives with direct consequences for
the subsequent development of the story ('the risky moments of a narrative'
in Barthes's term), supported, given a richer texture, by elements characterized by a different order of functionality. This 'different order' may be either
'lesser' (in the case of *catalysers*) or 'vertically functioning' (in the case of
distributional functions) as opposed to the essential horizontality of the cardinal functions. The first level of 'fidelity' in relation to the film version of a
novel could be determined by the extent to which the film-maker has chosen
to transfer the cardinal functions of the precursor narrative.

Identification of character functions and fields of action

If we take V. Propp's notion 'that the all-important and unifying element is
found . . . in the characters' *functions*, the part they play in the plot',[57] that
these functions[58] are distributed among a limited number of 'spheres of
action',[59] and that the 'discernible and repeated *structures* which, if they
are characteristic of so deeply rooted a form of narrative expression,
may . . . have implications for *all* narrative[60] (i.e. not just for folk-tales), then
we may see a further way of systematizing what happens in the transposition
of novel into film. No doubt the character functions are more clearly displayed in a Russian folk-tale than in a complex nineteenth-century English
novel or a feature-length film; nevertheless, some of Propp's formulations
point to underlying, transferable components of narrative. (Barthes's concept of *cardinal functions* is partly based on Propp's work, as Barthes acknowledges.[61]) To Propp, 'Function is understood as an act of character, defined
from the point of view of its significance for the course of the action.'[62] It is
not that he fails to allow for other narrative elements as having their roles to
play; he, in fact, pays special attention to the question of motivations, which
'often add to a tale a completely distinctive, vivid colouring';[63] but he finds
those elements other than character functions and their connectives 'less
precise and definite'.[64]

---

[57] Terence Hawkes, 68.

[58] V. Propp, *Morphology of the Folktale* (1927), trans. Laurence Scott (University of Texas: Austin, 1968), 22–63.

[59] Ibid. 79.

[60] Ibid. 21.

[61] Barthes, 'Introduction to the Structural Analysis of Narratives', 92.

[62] Propp, *Morphology of the Folktale*, 21.

[63] Ibid. 75.   [64] Ibid. 43.

I am suggesting here that, in considering what kind of adaptation has been made, one might isolate the chief character functions of the original and observe how far these are retained in the film version. (Peter Wollen's Proppian analysis of Hitchcock's *North by Northwest*[65] suggests that a sophisticated narrative is susceptible to procedures and categorizations derived from the study of much simpler modes.) By observing these functions, distributed among seven 'spheres of action' (named for their performers— 'villain', 'helper', etc.), one could determine whether the film-maker has aimed to preserve the underlying structure of the original or radically to rework it. Such a study would give a firmer basis for comparison by sorting out what functions are crucial to the narrative: i.e. to the *plot* which organizes the raw materials of the story.

Identification of mythic and/or psychological patterns

In relation to those myths which encapsulate in narrative form certain universal aspects of human experience, Lévi-Strauss has claimed that 'the mythical value of the myth is preserved even through the worst translation . . . [Unlike poetry, its] substance does not lie in its style, its original music, or its syntax, but in the *story* it tells'.[66] By extension, then, it is not too much to expect that the mythic elements at work in a novel seem likely to be transferable to the screen since their life is independent of whatever manifestation they are found in, resistant as they are to even 'the worst translation'. Intimately connected with the idea of myth, such Freudian concepts as the Oedipus complex so profoundly underlie human experience, and, therefore, the narrative renderings of that experience, that their nature remains unchanged through varying representations. The denotative material which provides the vehicle for these patterns may change from novel to film without affecting the connotations of the mythic and psychological motifs themselves. It is clear that these patterns exercise a powerfully organizing effect on narratives: one could propose, for example, that the Freudian notion that: 'An action by the ego is as it should be if it satisfies simultaneously the demands of the id, of the super-ego and of reality'[67] provides a way of classifying the narrative elements and their motivations in a story—whether on page or screen.

What the approaches outlined above have in common are:

(*a*) they all refer to elements which exist at 'deep levels' of the text;

(*b*) they address narrative elements which are not tied to a particular mode of expression (i.e. those which may be found at work in verbal or other sign systems); and

---

[65] Peter Wollen, '*North by North-West*: A Morphological Analysis', *Film Form*, 1 (1976), 20–34.

[66] Claude Lévi-Strauss, *Structural Anthropology* (Penguin Books: Harmondsworth, 1972), 210.

[67] David Stafford-Clark, *What Freud 'Really' Said* (Penguin Books: Harmondsworth, 1967), 112.

(c) all are susceptible to that more or less objective treatment that eludes less stable elements (e.g. character motivation or atmosphere).

They relate to the level of *narrative*, to areas in which *transfer* from one medium to another is possible, and to isolate them is to clear the way for examination of those elements that resist transfer and call for adaptation proper.

Adaptation Proper

Those elements of the novel which require *adaptation proper* may be loosely grouped as (in Barthes's term) *indices*, as the *signifiers of narrativity*, and as *the writing*, or, more comprehensively, as *enunciation*, to use the term now commonly employed in film theory. The film version of a novel may retain all the major cardinal functions of a novel, all its chief character functions, its most important psychological patterns, and yet, at both micro- and macro-levels or articulation, set up in the viewer acquainted with the novel quite different responses. The extent to which this is so can be determined by how far the film-maker has sought to create his own work in those areas where transfer is not possible. He can, of course, put his own stamp on the work by omitting or reordering those narrative elements which are transferable or by inventing new ones of his own: my point is that, even if he has chosen to adhere to the novel in these respects, he can still make a film that offers a markedly different affective and / or intellectual experience. Some key differ-ences which need to be considered in relation to areas of adaptation proper are summarized below. Essentially they refer to distinctions between enunciatory modes.

Two signifying systems

The full treatment of such a topic is of course beyond the scope of this study; at this point I want merely to draw attention to some matters centrally important here. The novel draws on a wholly *verbal* sign system, the film variously, and sometimes simultaneously, on *visual, aural,* and *verbal* signifiers. Even the apparently overlapping verbal signs (the words on the novel's page, the written or printed words used in the film, e.g. letters, street signs, newspaper headlines), while they may give the same information, function differently in each case. In the examples given, the letter, the street sign, and the newspaper headline will each resemble their real-life referents in ways that are customarily beyond the novel's capacity for iconic represen-tation. And this semi-exception to the rule of difference between the two systems points to a major distinction between them: the verbal sign, with its low iconicity and high symbolic function, works *conceptually*, whereas cinematic sign, with its high iconicity and uncertain symbolic functi works directly, sensuously, *perceptually*. Such a distinction is all but axiomatic but failure to concede its pervasive importance leads to a good deal of impressionistic, dissatisfied, and unsatisfying comparison of novel and film. Comparisons of this kind grow out of a sense of the film-maker's having failed to find satisfactory visual representations of key verbal signs (e.g. those relating to places or persons), and of a sense that, because of its high iconicity, the cinema has left no scope for that imaginative activity necessary to the reader's visualization of what he reads. In the study of adaptation, one may consider to what extent the film-maker has picked up visual suggestions from the novel in his representation of key verbal signs—and how the visual representation affects one's 'reading' of the film text.

The novel's linearity and the film's spatiality

We construct meaning from a novel by taking in words and groups of words sequentially as they appear on the page. In order, say, to grasp a scene, a physical setting, we have no choice but to follow linearly that arrangement of arbitrary symbols set out, for the most part, in horizontal rows which enjoin the linearity of the experience. The relentless linearity associated with the usual reading of a novel favours the gradual accretion of information about action, characters, atmosphere, ideas, and this mode of presentation, of itself, contributes to the impression received. At first glance, it may seem that the relentless movement of film through the projector offers an analogy to this situation. (And, of course, classic narrative cinema is posited on a powerful, forward-thrusting linearity, the product of causality and motivation.) However, though viewing time (and, thus sequentiality) is controlled much more rigorously than reading time, frame-following-frame is not analogous to the word-following-word experience of the novel. There are at least two significant differences to be noted: (i) the frame instantly, and at any given moment, provides information of at least visual complexity (sometimes increased by the input of aural and verbal signifiers) beyond that of any given word because of the *spatial* impact of the frame; and (ii) the frame is never registered as a discrete entity in the way that a word is. We do not ordinarily view a film frame by frame as we read a novel word by word.

The fact that we are always being exposed to the multiplicity of signifiers contained within the space of a frame or series of frames has implication for the adaptation of verbal material; for example, as it relates to the representation of characters and settings. What we receive as information from the mise-en-scène may be less susceptible to the film-maker's control (because of the strongly spatial orientation of film and because of the simultaneous bombardment by several kinds of claims on our attention) than what we receive from the linear presentation of words on the page. Dickens, for instance, may force us to 'see' Miss Havisham in the interior of Satis House in the order he has chosen in *Great Expectations*; as we watch her visual representation in David Lean's film we may be struck first, not by the yellow-whiteness of her apparel, but by the sense of her physical presence's being dwarfed by the decaying grandeur of the room. In the form which stresses spatiality rather than linearity, the eye may not always choose to see next what, in any particular frame, the film-maker wants it to fasten on. The challenge to the film-maker's control of the mise-en-scène is obvious.

Cinematic enunciation has two other approaches, specific to its medium, relating to the disposition of space and, hence, to the generation of aspects of narrative in ways closed to the novel. They are: (i) Noel Burch's theory of *a dialectic between on-screen and off-screen space* (he identifies six 'segments' of off-screen space, four determined by the borders of the frame, the others 'an off-screen space behind the camera' and 'the space existing behind the set or some object in it'[68]); and (ii) Raymond Bellour's proposal of *alternation*[69] (e.g. between long shot and close-up, between seeing and being seen) as a key cinematic practice, operating on levels of both code and diegesis. Both of these concepts advert to enunciatory techniques peculiar to the unfolding of cinematic narrative, and both will be considered in relation to particular case-studies in this book. Neither has any real equivalent in the verbal narrative, except in the much broader sense of alternation offered by a novel's moving between two major strands of narrative. The 'spacelessness' of the novel's linear procedures precludes the setting up of spatial tension achieved by (i) and the spatial mobility required by (ii).

Codes

If film, unlike verbal language, has no vocabulary (its images, unlike words, are non-finite), it also lacks a structuring syntax, instead of which it has conventions in relation to the operation of its codes. In so far as these codes enable us to 'read' film narratives, in so far as we learn to ascribe meanings to them (e.g. to assume that 'fade out/fade in', as an editing procedure, denotes a major lapse of time), it is through frequent exposure to their deployment in a particular way, without there being any guarantee that they will always be used in this way. There is, for instance, nothing corresponding to the comparatively fixed usage of full-stop and comma as punctuational signs denoting the longest and shortest pauses respectively, or to those rules which signify tenses, in the written work.

[68] Noel Burch, *The Theory of Film Practice* (Cinema Two/Secker and Warburg: London, 1973), 20.

[69] Janet Bergstrom, 'Alternation, Segmentation, Hypnosis: Interview with Raymond Bellour', *Camera Obscura*, 3–4 (1979), 76–8.

Further, in 'reading' a film, we must understand other, *extra-cinematic* codes as well. These include:

(*a*) *language codes* (involving response to particular accents or tones of voice and what these might mean socially or temperamentally);

(*b*) *visual codes* (response to these goes beyond mere 'seeing' to include the interpretative and the selective);

(*c*) *non-linguistic sound codes* (comprising both musical and other aural codes);

(*d*) *cultural codes* (involving all that information which has to do with how people live, or lived, at particular times and places).

In a sense, the cinematic codes may be seen as integrating the preceding four in ways that no other art-form does. When we witness a film, we share with the film's maker a basic assumption that we know the codes: i.e. a general cinematic code which, as Christian Metz has shown, can be broken down into subcodes, such as those to do with editing, or those to do with particular genres, and the extra-cinematic codes referred to above. Failure to recognize—or, at least, to pay adequate attention to—the differences between the operation of these codes in film and the novel's reliance on the written representation of language codes has been a key element in accounting for the fuzzy impressionism of so much writing about adaptation.

Stories told and stories presented

In moving from novel to film, we are moving from a purely representational mode to 'an order of the operable',[70] to use Barthes's distinction (which has not, to my knowledge, been pursued in film studies but which offers a broad statement of intermedial disparity). This distinction relates partly to earlier points about:

(i) differences between two 'language' systems, one of which works wholly symbolically, the other through an interaction of codes, including codes of execution;

(ii) tense: film cannot present action in the past as novels chiefly do; and

(iii) film's spatial (as well as temporal) orientation which gives it a physical presence denied to the novel's linearity.

Another aspect of the distinction between telling and presenting is located in the way in which the novel's metalanguage (the vehicle of its telling) is replaced, at least in part, by the film's mise-en-scène. In a sense, the film's story does not have to be told *because* it is presented. Against the gains in immediacy, the loss of the narrational voice may, however, be felt as the chief casualty of the novel's enunciation.

---

[70] Barthes, 'Introduction to the Structural Analysis of Narratives', 80.

   The enunciatory matters discussed above refer to crucially important novelistic elements which offer challenges to the film-maker, especially if he does not wish the experience of his film to shatter a pre-existing reality (i.e. of the novel) but, rather, to displace it.

Part II

The Case-Studies

Introduction

THE choice of five texts which exist as novels and as films obviously cannot in any exhaustive sense be regarded as seriously representative. My aim has been to look closely at what has happened to five sufficiently diverse literary texts (four novels and one novella) in the process of transposition to film. Further, the choice was governed by the films' showing sufficiently diverse approaches to this process and by their deriving from different contexts.

All five novels may be broadly categorized as 'realist' but within that range they display some clearly divergent responses to problems of narrative and enunciation. They exhibit important differences in length, in narrational modes, and in cultural status: the novella-length *Daisy Miller* poses different challenges from those offered by a long Victorian novel such as *Great Expectations*; the narrating 'voices' are variously omniscient, first-person, and the product of a restricted consciousness; and *Random Harvest*, a once-popular fiction, and *Cape Fear* are clearly of a cultural order remote from that of the other three. That is, they offer enough variety to test whether the proposed agenda for examining the processes of adaptation might be profitably applied across a certain literary range. In a study of this length, it has not been possible to include every kind of novelistic procedure. A further volume might well focus on the extent to which modernist or post-modernist texts have shown themselves susceptible to film adaptation. Novels such as *Ulysses*, *Orlando*, *Lolita*, and *A Clockwork Orange* come to mind in such a connection; they are, however, outside the range of the present study, in which the focus is on the processes of transposition rather than on the enormous range of fiction available for adaptation. So long as novels are concerned—in any degree—with a series of events happening to and/or caused by a continuing set of characters, I believe my methodology will prove efficacious in articulating the inescapable processes at work in *any* adaptation.

As to the films, they derive from strikingly different *contexts*. *The Scarlet Letter* (1926) as a *silent* film version of a classic American novel enables a historical perspective on the phenomenon of adaptation. The lack of spoken dialogue and other diegetic sound (musical accompaniment of silent films was, we know, standard practice) makes demands on other means of presenting a narrative; as my analysis will show, the classical Hollywood narrative was very firmly established by the end of the silent era, to which period *The Scarlet Letter* belongs. It also belongs to a moral climate in which Hollywood was striving at least superficially for moral as well as cultural respectability.

Random Harvest (1942) is an archetypal studio product, in which the MGM house style overlays a fascinating conjunction of Freud, the star system, World War II, and Hollywood's view of England. What emerges is a powerful romantic melodrama structurally altering and psychologically deepening the narrative contours of Hilton's best-seller. Unlike the other three case-studies, with *Random Harvest* there is little more than a year's time-lapse between book and film, so that one is not concerned with a major shift in prevailing ideology between the two.

Great Expectations (1946) is a work clearly conscious of Dickens as belonging to Britain's cultural heritage and the publicity surrounding the film's production stresses its respect for its source. The film has acquired its own cultural status: it is a critically lauded high-point in a rich period of British film-making. In recent years, it has been read as a potent fable for post-war Britain and for its film industry, as well as a key early film in director David Lean's *œuvre*.

More than a quarter of a century later, *Daisy Miller* (1974) is a post-studio-era film, making highly conscious use of its authentic settings and reflecting a much closer adherence to the original text than any of the preceding three does. While knowingly adverting, as it seems, to certain Hollywood traditions, it nevertheless bears none of the strongly marked influences of the industrial and cultural conditions surrounding its production that the preceding case-studies do.

Cape Fear (1991) is a remake of the 1961 version of John D. MacDonald's thriller, *The Executioners*. It makes a fascinating study in intertextuality and in the ways in which lapse of time may lead to shifts in emphases and narrational modes. It derives from a period in which melodrama as a mode has been rehabilitated and in which the representation of violence has been radically liberated. It bears the name of a well-known studio, but it is more properly regarded as the product of its director, a man powerfully placed in the contemporary Hollywood hierarchy. There is clearly more at stake in the intertextuality of a film derived from a novel than the precursor novel itself. Contextual matters, whether relating to other films made by the directors involved in the case-study films chosen, or to the characteristic products of the studios or periods from which they emanated, or the phenomenon of the star system's influence on how we read films, to suggest but three variables beyond the narrowest novel–film comparisons, are always important—and tend to defy easy quantification. My study draws attention to such matters representatively: for example, the star system is not discussed in every case-study, but its treatment in the chapter on *Random Harvest* is meant to imply that this is a matter worth considering in relation to many / most adaptations. Naturally, if one were studying the latest adaptation of *Cape Fear*, it would be fruitful to consider in what ways Nick Nolte's star persona, or his status as an actor, points one in a direction other than that of Gregory Peck's characteristically embattled liberal in the earlier film version of John MacDonald's novel.

The issue of *authorship*, always complex in film, is especially so in relation to the film version of a literary work. Not only will the directorial signature inscribe itself with varying degrees of forcefulness on adapted material; not only will the spectre of the novel's author, especially in the case of the classic or best-selling novel, hover over the spectator and critic's reading of the film; also, the status of the author(s) of the screenplay will intervene between the former two.

In the case-studies I have chosen, two of the films—*Random Harvest* and *Great Expectations*—have been written by what might be termed scripting committees, so that the assessment of authorial input is more difficult to arrive at. Writing credits for *Random Harvest* are shared by Arthur Wimperis, Claudine West, and George Froeschel, whose names appear in various collaborations on the writing credits for many MGM films, most often derived from literary sources.

The scripting committee for *Great Expectations* consists of David Lean (the film's director), Ronald Neame (producer), and Anthony Havelock-Allan (executive producer), 'with Kay Walsh and Cecil McGivern'. The points to be noted here are that the screenplay is written chiefly by three men intimately involved with the whole production, Lean was then married to Kay Walsh, and Havelock-Allan to the film's female star, Valerie Hobson. How far such an intricate network of personal and scriptwriting relationships bears on the authorship of the film is outside the scope of this study, but it does at least suggest a significant intervention between Dickens and the final film. The kinds of omission enjoined upon the film version of so long a novel almost go without saying; Kay Walsh told me that she, for example, particularly regretted the loss of Trabb's boy,[1] less crucial to the narrative events than to the thematic texture of the story and therefore more likely to be excised.

The screenplay for *The Scarlet Letter* is the work of Frances Marion, described by Ephraim Katz as 'one of Hollywood's busiest and highest-paid screenwriters and . . . credited with nearly 150 scenarios, original stories, and adaptations for some of the industry's top directors and stars'.[2] By 1926, the year of *The Scarlet Letter*, hers was already a name to inspire critical respect, and would remain so for more than another decade. Also, Lillian Gish claimed in a 1932 biography that she 'worked with Frances Marion on the

---

[1] Interview with Kay Walsh, London, June 1991.

[2] Ephraim Katz, *The International Film Encyclopedia* (Macmillan: London, 1979), 776.

story'.[3] Though there is no clear account of her contribution, the kind of influence she suggests ('Hester as the victim of hard circumstance', etc.) is apparent in the film.

Whereas these three case-studies all seem to embody certain strong impulses of Hollywood or British cinema at the time of their making, *Daisy Miller* exhibits a much more consciously intellectual approach to its material and to the *verbal* primacy of the novel. It is tempting to attribute this, in large part, to the fact that the author of its screenplay is Frederic Raphael. Among the five case-studies, he is the only author who is a novelist as well as a screenwriter. His credentials suggest a stronger determining influence on the film than in the other three case-studies, and such a view is encouraged by his own forcefully expressed opinions on the writer's place in a film's authorship, railing against critics who cling 'with a touching monotheism to the idea that all the visual content of a film is thought up by the director after the writer has supplied the words'.[4]

The screenplay for *Cape Fear* (1991) is credited to Wesley Strick, with the gloss that it is 'Based on a screenplay by James R Webb and the novel *The Executioners* by John D MacDonald.' In doing so, it acknowledges its double inheritance, from both the precursor novel and the 1961 film version, to which it also makes reference in its casting and in its musical credits.

My five case-studies represent a range of authorial possibilities as well as a diversity of contextual possibilities. In the face of this, I shall want to see how far my methods of approaching the case-studies' text can cut across such diversity. To this end, each case-study will examine in detail the extent to which narrative elements of the novels (e.g. major cardinal functions, underlying psychological and/or mythic elements, large structural movements) have been *transferred* and aspects of enunciation have been *adapted*.

Further, each case-study will have as its final section a Special Focus which is appropriate to the particular pair of texts involved. The chapter on *The Scarlet Letter* takes as its Special Focus the application of Raymond Bellour's notion of *alternation*, as a narrative principle of (at least) classical Hollywood cinema, to the film version of a novel structured about striking oppositions on a number of levels. The Special Focus for *Random Harvest* is the way in which certain elements of Freudian psychology suffuse the narrative borrowed from a popular novel in such a way as to satisfy audience demand for dreamlike experience and to exploit nostalgic, Utopian longings in a time of political upheaval. In *Great Expectations*, I examine in closer detail than elsewhere the possibility of creating a visual style that matches a highly distinctive literary style, often regarded as having a powerful visual element, and, in doing so, raise questions relating to the figurative possibilities of each. In

---

[3] Albert Bigelow Paine, *Life and Lillian Gish* (Macmillan: New York, 1932), 224.

[4] Frederic Raphael, Introduction to the screenplay for *Two for the Road* (Jonathan Cape: London, 1967), 24.

Daisy Miller, the Special Focus section confronts the issue of fidelity, much the most pervasive distraction in the writing about adaptation, and one rarely subjected to close scrutiny. Very often the 'fidelity argument' is used to denigrate the film; the aim of this book is to shy away from such unrewarding comparisons. They are unrewarding usually because their roots lie deep in a subjective impressionism, not exposed to the kind of detailed, rigorous examination of both texts which can alone reveal the nature of the adaptive enterprise. In *Cape Fear*, I shall examine closely the influence of time-lapse between the novel's publication and the film's release. This will always be a significant factor in the ascribing of diverse responses, affective and intellectual, to two related texts in different media; it is highlighted when the novel at stake has been adapted twice, once shortly after the novel's publication, and then thirty years later.

Though the Special Focus is governed in each case by important elements of each pair of texts, the issue raised in each of course surfaces in discussion of the other pairs. The concluding section of each case-study is a way of highlighting such elements without undue repetition. The overall aim of the case-studies is to discover whether a more objective approach to adaptation will throw more light on its processes, problems, and possibilities than has generally followed from more subjective accounts.

Lillian Gish as Hester Prynne in Victor Sjöström's *The Scarlet Letter*

I

The Scarlet Letter (1926)

I F the Puritan values of seventeenth-century Boston, scrutinized by Hawthorne in *The Scarlet Letter* in 1850, seem remote from readers today, so too does the Hollywood of 1926 when the novel was 'on the black list',[1] in Louis B. Mayer's words. In spite of its being 'an American classic, often required reading in the classroom', as Lillian Gish 'retorted',[2] and, though there had been at least five short silent screen versions of the novel before the MGM adaptation in 1926, at that time the Protestant Church (especially the Methodist) opposed its filming. Hollywood had been much shaken by widely publicized scandals in the early 1920s, involving some of its key names. Its subsequent deference to accepted morality, institutionalized in the Hays Office, reflects its concern to project a more wholesome image. In this climate, it required Lillian Gish's persuasion to induce Metro-Goldwyn-Mayer to make the film and the Hays Office to drop its objections, giving in to her pleas, 'Partly because she was Miss Gish, and partly because she pointed out that it was a classic'.[3] This account is corroborated by Lillian Gish herself, who says she 'took the matter up with Will Hays and prominent members of the clergy. When I told them how I proposed to present it, they gave their sanction. When they saw the picture, by and by, they recommended it.'[4] If such objections to Hawthorne's novel now seem quaint, they are worth remembering when one considers how the novel's narrative structure was altered for the film and, as I shall suggest, its emphasis shifts from symbolic romance to romantic melodrama.

That Victor Sjöström's[5] film version of *The Scarlet Letter* takes the form it does—structurally and emotionally—no doubt owes much to Lillian Gish's presence in it, to her influence as perhaps the major silent screen star of the period, and to the nature of her star persona. In films such as *Broken Blossoms* (1919), *Way Down East* (1920), and *Orphans of the Storm* (1921), she had revealed, if not a wide emotional range, an extraordinary intensity and a capacity for rendering innocence resourceful and resilient in the face of

[1] Quoted in Lillian Gish and Ann Pinchot, *Mr Griffith, the Movies and Me* (W. H. Allen: London, 1969), 285.

[2] Ibid.

[3] David Shipman, *The Story of Cinema*, i (Hodder and Stoughton: London, 1982), 169.

[4] Quoted in Albert Bigelow Paine, *Life and Lillian Gish* (Macmillan: New York, 1932), 224.

[5] Sjöström's name was changed to Seastrom for his Hollywood credits.

threat. By her own accounts, she was crucially influential in not merely
clearing obstacles from the path of the film's production and in the choice of
its Swedish director and leading man (Lars Hanson), but in determining the
tone and emphasis of the production: 'My idea was to present Hester as the
victim of hard circumstances, swept off her feet by love. . . . that was what
she was, but her innate innocence must be apparent.'[6] 'Victim', 'innocence':
here are two of the key terms which help to account for the long opening
movement of the film leading up to Hester's public shame. Much of the
defiance of Hawthorne's Hester, who acquires a certain pride in wearing the
scarlet letter, is replaced with aspects of Lillian Gish's star persona. The film's
Hester is created at first as a fun-loving girl, devoted to harmless pleasures,
made more interesting, however, by a suggestion of assertiveness in her
pursuit of the young minister. The film's narrative thus steers a line between
presenting Hester-as-victim and showing her as much more active in propel-
ling the narrative than is Hawthorne's Hester. This balance is partly a result
of the invented opening movement of the film, which may be seen as the
result of a need to acknowledge Gish's 'star power' and the nature of her
public image.

   In the Hays-influenced moral climate of the mid-1920s (a sort of parody of
the Puritanical rigour of seventeenth-century Boston, already seen by
Hawthorne in 1850 as antiquated, so that he writes of it as history), the victim
element and the essential innocence of Hester are stressed. The film's commercial success and its emotional power may be seen to derive from the
perfect choice of star and a skilful manipulation of the moral standards by
which the industry had chosen to be guided.

NARRATIVE AND TRANSFER

Structural Patterns: The Novel

Basic events

The basic events of the story (corresponding to Barthes's 'cardinal functions') have almost the simplicity of ballad or fable. Baldly stated, the narrative may be summarized as telling the moral fall of the secretly married
Hester Prynne; her giving birth to a daughter Pearl, the result of a passionate
liaison with the minister, Dimmesdale; her public punishment and subsequent life of blameless expiation while Dimmesdale bears his part in her guilt
in private agony; the thwarting of their plans to escape through the insidious
malevolence of Chillingworth, the husband Hester was forced to marry and

---

[6] Gish, quoted in Paine, ibid. 224.

who returns after many years to wreak subtle revenges; the public confession and death of Dimmesdale; and Hester's final acquiescence—for life—in her role of the woman with the scarlet letter. As will be seen shortly, the novel's complexity exists less at this level than at the level of enunciation.

Story and plot order

The Scarlet Letter is a novel with a *'repressed flashback'*;[7] it is structured so that 'story' and 'plot', in Shklovsky's distinction, do not coincide chronologically. The novel begins, as it were, in the middle: that is, with Hester's punishment for her sin. She is presented as the victim of a harsh code: she is to be exhibited in the pillory in reparation of the adultery that has led to the birth of an illegitimate child, and she is to wear always the scarlet letter 'A' as a reminder of her sin. At this stage the novel's two other protagonists are introduced: in chapter 3, Chillingworth, an as-yet-unnamed stranger, who asks one of the crowd witnessing Hester's shame 'what has brought her to yonder scaffold'[8] and in chapter 4, the Reverend Dimmesdale, a young clergyman whose 'eloquence and religious fervour had already given the earnest of high eminence to his profession' (p. 72). Chillingworth's question provides the occasion for answering some of the reader's curiosity about past events, so that we begin to fill in the 'repressed flashback', though we, like Chillingworth, are denied the crucial answer: the name of the father of Hester's child. We can only infer the passionate relationship that once existed between Dimmesdale and Hester and the knowledge creeps almost imperceptibly upon the reader, rather than as a melodramatic revelation. We are presented with the results of the passion—the child and the badge of shame—but the relationship of which these were the culmination is indeed repressed.

A symmetrical structure

Broadly speaking, the novel may be seen as structured about three symmetrically placed scenes at the scaffold, scenes which occur in the second, central, and second-last chapters. In the first of these scenes, Dimmesdale pleads with Hester as she stands branded, before the crowd, to name her 'fellow sinner and fellow sufferer'; in the second, on the occasion of his night vigil there (joined by Hester and Pearl), he releases his guilt in a great cry to the empty sky; and, in the third, he reveals his guilt—and perhaps his own letter of shame on his breast—to the assembled crowd. Dimmesdale's is an

---

[7] Helen McNeil, lecture on *The Scarlet Letter*, Silent Cinema Conference, University of East Anglia, Dec. 1983.

[8] Nathaniel Hawthorne, *The Scarlet Letter* (Signet Classic edition: New York, 1959), 68. (Subsequent page references given in brackets as they occur.)

opposite movement from that of Hester's own life in the same period: hers begins with exposure and ends with a curious mixture of acceptance and respect (the film's altered structure denies itself this telling symmetry). What shapes Dimmesdale's life, cowardly and tortured as it is, is a longing for his own scarlet letter, for the chief inner fact of his life, to be as manifest as Hester's emblem of shame. The novel's narrative then moves towards the convergence of the opposite actions of their lives in the penultimate chapter which, symmetrically, offers the public display of Dimmesdale's guilt on the same scaffold on which, in the second chapter, Hester's shame was displayed.

Structuring oppositions

This is a novel obviously and overtly preoccupied with and, indeed, structured about such contrasting abstractions as suppression / expiation, display / concealment, appearance / reality, and the public / the private. Its spare narrative moves between—and causes the reader to weigh the claims of—these oppositions. My point is that Hawthorne has chosen to embody these notions and abstractions in a narrative whose meaning is chiefly effected through the complex use of powerfully resonant visual symbols. I shall return to this matter when discussing the novel's enunciatory procedures and, in the Special Focus for this chapter, how the film responds to a narrative presented in terms of such stark oppositions. Most crucially, the opposing symbols of the letter and its absence offer a paradigm for those structuring oppositions referred to above, oppositions dramatized at every level of the narrative.

Structural Patterns: The Film

Basic events

The essential 'story' of Hawthorne's novel is retained (clandestine affair, birth of child, thwarting of escape, etc.) but in terms of 'plot' the film has chosen to begin at a period about a year anterior to the time of the novel's opening chapter. For a variety of reasons about which one may speculate (to do with Gish and the industry, with censorship?), the film has chosen to present its protagonists in a happier, more conventionally romantic light before (as well as) addressing itself to the novel's central preoccupations. I say 'as well as' because the film's opening movement does more than merely introduce Dimmesdale and Hester as romantic lovers. Dimmesdale's attempts to suppress his feeling for Hester at this stage anticipate the concealment of guilt which harrows him until his final disclosure of his own self-inflicted brand of shame.

'Linearization'

The film's major restructuring of the basic events of the novel involves the disappearance of the sense of a repressed flashback, in so far as such a term relates to the nature of Hester's relationship with Dimmesdale. Instead of gradually and obliquely implying Hester and Dimmesdale's former passion, as the novel does, the film presents their love directly, as firmly in the *present tense* as anything else in the film. Frances Marion has created the film's first 'movement' (lasting over one-third of the running time) by taking the fact of the passion, indicated in the novel only by its results, and imagining a background and context for it. One sees the growth of their relationship before one sees its outcome; the film begins, as it were, at the beginning, whereas the novel may be said to plunge us into the middle.

Implications of 'linearization'

This change in structure, necessitating as it does the invention of the film's first movement, has a number of significant implications for the film. Above all, it foregrounds the love between Hester and Dimmesdale, giving it a different order of importance from that it enjoys in the novel's hierarchy of interests. It dominates the first third (or more) of the film. They are presented as lovers borne away on a single tide of passion (the extent of their affair in the novel is not specified). The venerated minister is seen: (*a*) as trying to resist his feeling for her (cf. his sternness in reproving her, first in church, later in the woods); and (*b*) also as humanely sympathetic towards her when she is treated unkindly by the community. A film in 1926 (and for many subsequent years) would be unlikely to risk with its audience a hero as weak and cowardly as Hawthorne's Dimmesdale; and Sjöström's male star, Lars Hanson, is given opportunities to appear handsome, virile, and sympathetic. Further, his is presented as a passion for a woman who has been established: (*a*) as essentially innocent and playful, filled with a delight in life which is at odds with the community; and (*b*) as actively, if innocently, the pursuer in the situation. In fact, she literally pursues him in the forest scene where, we assume, they finally make love. Such was the effect of Lillian Gish's persona that, in structural terms, the film can afford to present her as the pursuer without any danger of a loss of sympathy for *her*, and this reduces Dimmesdale's guilt in the matter. He becomes a strong man beguiled by love in the form of a girl whose innocently beguiling qualities audiences could be counted on to endorse.

The film's linear treatment of the basic plot events, bringing the narrative more firmly into line with classic Hollywood style,[9] involves a major re-

---

[9] David Bordwell and Kristin Thompson summarize the characteristics of this style in *Film Art: An Introduction*, 4th edn. (McGraw Hill: New York, 1993), 82–4.

arrangement of the novel's structure, but two points should be noted. First, it does not lose any of the novel's essential events (the novel's striking tableau of Dimmesdale on the scaffold at midnight has a primarily symbolic rather than narrative significance); and, second, the rearrangement may well be a function of the new medium. The linearization obviates the need for explanations which may have been peculiarly difficult to effect in a silent adaptation. The use of intertitles for long passages of explanation would have appeared dangerously disruptive in what was a wholly visual medium. It is hard to see how the use of a single long flashback would have been more effective than the film's first movement, which establishes the community and the protagonists in relationship to each other in such a way as to ensure the dramatic effectiveness of the public announcement of Hester's guilt. In arguing for the effectiveness of the film's opening movement, I would claim that:

(*a*) it has been constructed from information gradually leaked in the novel, in relation to its chief events;

(*b*) its details, the inventions of the script (the escaped bird, the comedy involving Giles, the communal laundry) serve the purpose of visualizing abstractions clearly present in the novel (e.g. the effects of a stern community on natural liveliness); and

(*c*) it throws the ensuing grim events into sharper relief.

That the film chooses a different narrative structure inevitably points to a different emphasis and preoccupation from the novel's: the latter starts with the public revelation of Hester's guilt and ends with Dimmesdale's public confession, while its geographically central scene is the extraordinary one of Dimmesdale's midnight vigil on the scaffold. At these crucial, symmetrically placed moments of the novel, our attention is fastened on the abstract notion which underlies the whole novel. The central scene reflects backward on to the opening scene (with its mystery about Hester's love) and forward on to the closing one (with Dimmesdale's overcoming of the urge to concealment). It is an unmissably clear dramatic structure, and it shapes our reading of the text. The film's structure works differently upon us, but not necessarily less powerfully: the linear presentation permits and acquires a deepening emotional power, which is intensified by the lighter tone of the beginning and by the invention of the comic 'sub-plot' centring on Giles.

Structuring oppositions

It is a commonplace of writing about literature and film that the latter is much less able to render the symbolic than the former and that film adaptations of novels which rely much on processes of symbolization are like to founder both as films and adaptations. Hawthorne's novel is intensely, not to say explicitly, symbolic but the abstractions—guilt concealed vs. guilt revealed, individual passion vs. communal repressiveness, for example—are so vividly rendered in concrete terms as to cause one to doubt the conventional wisdom on the subject. In the case of *The Scarlet Letter*, it was not a matter of the film-maker's having to flesh out a stripped-down symbolic fable with the perhaps distracting particularities of visual representation; whatever symbolic power Hawthorne's novel exerts, it is firmly rooted in the actual and the detailed. Those large binarisms I referred to in relation to the novel find their place in the film, the product at several levels of its enunciatory system. (See Special Focus.)

The comic sub-plot

This sub-plot is, along with the opening movement, the film's major narrative invention and calls for some comment. It contains three main elements:

   (i) Giles's sneezing in church and punishment for this;
   (ii) his frustrated courtship; and
   (iii) his heckling and tricking of Mistress Hibbins for her malice against Hester.

Giles, a character invented for the film, is a vehicle for expanding on the idea, chiefly embodied in Hester, of the 'natural man'. When he sneezes in church, he is hit on the head by a churchwarden (with his staff of office) and warned to 'Control thy wanton sneezing, Master Giles'. His violation of Puritan sobriety and his punishment for it in this early scene anticipates and parallels Hester's breathless late arrival at church and her subsequent (and more serious) punishment for running and playing on the Sabbath. Giles, whose words, appearance, actions, and facial expressions are signifiers of an atypical good nature and kindness, is repeatedly used as a means of—comically—highlighting Hester's situation in the community. For instance, they are both punished early in the film for minor transgressions; and, later, Giles's comic courtship is sandwiched between the implied passion of Hester and Dimmesdale in the woods and their subsequent anguished meeting at the cottage. Giles is used to coalesce and intensify the suggestions in the novel of touches of compassion at work in this grim community. It is perhaps misleading to speak of the events which cluster round him as a sub-plot, since they have a continuity of tone and purpose that imbues them with a thematic coherence which is more important than their function in the narrative.

It is impossible to miss the parallel between the woodland passion of Dimmesdale and Hester and Giles's courtship of his prim fiancée. The correspondences are reinforced in these ways:

   (i) each segment (8 and 10, see Appendix 1) begins with a page of writing
        from the colony's statutes and ends with an embrace at odds with
        such attempts to regulate conduct;
  (ii) each makes explicit use of off-screen space to build the drama of the
        scene (the camera lingers on an empty sunlit clearing as Hester and
        Dimmesdale go further into the forest; Giles and his fiancée are
        forced to talk through a long speaking-tube, the camera panning from
        the on-screen one to the other, and revealing that her parents have
        been there all along); and
 (iii) each ends with an act of passion, mutual in Dimmesdale and Hester's
        embrace ('Hester, I have fought against it—but I love thee'), rebuffed
        in Giles's case by his outraged fiancée ('Father! I will not be wed to a
        man of such unbridled passions'). In each case the embrace is regis-
        tered as 'forbidden'; Giles knowingly and willingly flouts the code,
        and Dimmesdale's giving way is obscured by a bush.

In the surrender of Hester and Dimmesdale, the mildness of Giles's offence
and the wildness of his fiancée's response, is further evidence—serious and
comic—that the Puritan code can go only so far in the matter of suppression.
That one is intended to draw such parallels is further emphasized by the
scene immediately following that of Giles's courtship: that in which
Dimmesdale stumbles out into the snow, reeling from the revelation of
Hester's marriage. The previous scene ends with Giles's being thrown into
the snow by his fiancée's father, and in both cases the town crier's announcement that all's well (in parallel exterior shots) is ironically undercut. Such
narrative parallels become in fact part of the film's enunciatory procedures:
of its way, that is, of providing a commentary on the central narrative.

   The sustained heckling by Giles of Mistress Hibbins ('tabby-cat', 'wood-
pussy', 'cockroach', 'old crow', etc.), for her vindictive gossip against Hester
and her self-righteous satisfaction at Hester's punishment, reaches its climax
in the public ducking she receives at Giles's hands. In ignoring the novel's
clear indications that she practises witchcraft, the film shows itself more
interested in the social persecution of Hester by a smug, austere community
at odds with normal human feelings, than in the darker repressions that such
a rigid regime may enjoin. (It also reduces the resonance of the novel's
symbolic use of the forest: no longer the scene of witches' gatherings, in the
film it becomes more simply a symbol of freedom from restraint.) Hibbins's
ducking, ordered by the Governor, who believes she has insulted him and
the Beadle, though it was actually Giles disguised as her, is a comic precursor
to the film's final scene. In the ducking segment, the crowd enjoys watching
Hibbins get her come-uppance, and the fact that Giles is its executor suggests
that, even in this community, openness and generosity may sometimes have
their hour. In this way, the scene prepares the viewer for the crowd's

response to the final scene: Dimmesdale's self-disclosure and Hester's joining him on the platform.

Transfer of Narrative Functions

Cardinal functions

As a starting-point for considering how closely the film-makers have sought to reproduce the original novel in film terms, it is revealing to note the extent to which they have chosen to transfer those narrative functions not dependent on language. Essentially these are the major cardinal functions or nuclei, defined by Barthes as 'constitut[ing] real hinge-points of narrative'.[10]

(a) *Novel* In Hawthorne's novel, the following are the cardinal functions crucial in determining the overall movement of the narrative:

1. Hester Prynne and unknown lover have been guilty of adultery.
2. Hester has become pregnant.
3. She gives birth to an illegitimate child (Pearl).
4. She is publicly punished (appearance on scaffold, the scarlet letter, ostracism).
5. The Reverend Dimmesdale urges her to name her lover.
6. She refuses to do so.
7. A stranger to the colony (Hester's husband, Chillingworth) learns of her 'sin'.
8. He desires to know her lover's name.
9. She again refuses to name him.
10. Chillingworth pledges her to secrecy about his own identity.
11. He becomes aware that Dimmesdale is Hester's guilty partner.
12. He becomes Dimmesdale's mentor.
13. Dimmesdale's private anguish increases.
14. He intervenes (with the Governor) to enable Hester to keep their child.
15. Hester urges Dimmesdale to go away with her and Pearl.
16. Chillingworth thwarts their escape plans.
17. Dimmesdale makes public confession then dies.
18. Hester leads life of lonely, respected spinsterhood.

Comments

- Each of these is a *major* cardinal function, in Barthes's terms, a 'dispatcher', offering a 'risky', moment in the narrative, risky in the sense

[10] Roland Barthes, 'Introduction to the Structural Analysis of Narratives', *Image-Music-Text* trans. Stephen Heath (Fontana/Collins: Glasgow, 1977), 93.

that alternative outcomes are available. (e.g. Hester's adultery may or may not have led to pregnancy.)

- Like true cardinal functions, they work both *sequentially* and *consequentially*. Each of the cardinal functions listed above clearly leads to a further development in the story, either to another action (e.g. 5) or to a changed situation (e.g. 13).

- The element of consequentiality is sometimes blurred locally (i.e. within a particular syntagma or between two successive syntagmas) by the intervention of other functions and by our awareness of the *vertical* 'functionality of being' (i.e. paradigmatic relations) which meshes with the *horizontal* 'functionality of doing'.[11] Whereas the latter refers to the functions proper, the former, more or less diffusely, provides us with information about, for example, character or atmosphere. In my list, the sense of the community's role in Hester's drama looks minimal; in fact, its influence is chiefly felt in a more pervasive contribution to the suppression/expression binarism which persists throughout the novel. In this matter, less crucial to the *structure* of the narrative, a film version, in so far as it seeks to render a comparable notion of community, will do so through its manipulation of various aspects of the mise-en-scène (costume, settings, facial expression, etc.).

- Functions (1), (2), and (3) have taken place at a time anterior to the starting-point of the novel's plot: they are part of its 'repressed flashback', though the result (Hester's public punishment) of the third is dramatized in the novel's course. In a sense, they—(1), (2), and (3)—are functions only by (necessary) implication.

(b) *Film* The major cardinal functions of the film's narrative may be listed as follows:

1. Hester commits a minor transgression.
2. She is reproached by Dimmesdale and punished by the Committee.
3. Hester and Dimmesdale fall in love.
4. Their love is consummated.
5. Hester gives birth to an illegitimate child.
6. She is publicly punished (appearance on scaffold, scarlet letter, ostracism).
7. Dimmesdale urges her to name her lover.
8. She refuses to do so.
9. Dimmesdale suffers private anguish.
10. He intervenes (via baptizing) to enable Hester to keep their child.
11. A stranger to the colony (Hester's husband, Chillingworth) discovers her 'sin' and her lover's name.

[11] Roland Barthes, 'Introduction to the Structural Analysis of Narratives', *Image-Music-Text* trans. Stephen Heath (Fontana/Collins: Glasgow, 1977), 93.

12. Hester urges Dimmesdale to go away with her and Pearl.
13. Chillingworth thwarts their escape plans.
14. Dimmesdale makes public confession and dies in Hester's arms.
15. The crowd is subdued.

Comments

- Functions (1) and (2) are inventions for the film to help provide a background to the relationship between Hester and Dimmesdale which must be inferred in reading the novel.
- Function (3) is explicitly present in the film whereas it is merely implied in the novel's function (1).
- Function (10), leading to Dimmesdale's intervention so that Hester may keep their child, has the same effect in both film and novel, but occurs much earlier in the film's narrative chain than in the novel's (where it is function 14).
- Function (8)—Hester's refusal to name her lover—does not lead to the same immediate effect as in the novel, because her husband's return, function (11) in the film, comes considerably later than in the novel, though that return leads to the same result—thwarting of the escape plan.
- Function (14) corresponds with the novel's function (17) but its effect is different: whereas the film ends on a pietà-like tableau, surrounded by the crowd moved to silence, the novel adds a coda summarizing Hester's life after Dimmesdale's death, a life she chooses to live in Boston, the scene of her 'sin'. The novel, that is, ends on a note of lifelong expiation of sin, the film on a moment's transcendence.
- The major cardinal function of the novel which is not transferred to the film is (12): in the film, Chillingworth's role is reduced and simplified, perhaps because a silent film would be at a disadvantage in showing his gradually becoming Dimmesdale's mentor. The novel makes much use of both dialogue and discursive prose to establish this.

In general, there is considerable correspondence between the major cardinal functions (i.e. those responsible for the overall narrative development as distinct from those at work within a given segment) in novel and film. They do not necessarily appear in the same order in each, but on the level of 'story', it is clear the Sjöström has been concerned to adhere closely to Hawthorne's original. On the level of 'plot' ('the distinctive way in which the "story" is made strange, creatively deformed and defamiliarized'),[12] he has chosen to rearrange the order of some of the cardinal functions identified and to invent function (1) in order to promote the situation with which the novel opens. I have not listed any of the invented material relating to Giles as major cardinal functions, in the sense of influencing the central succession

---

[12] Terence Hawkes, *Structuralism and Semiotics* (Methuen: London, 1977), 65.

of events concerning Hester and Dimmesdale. They contribute, rather, to our general sense of what the atmosphere of the community is like and from that point of view they may be seen as *indices* rather than functions.

Character functions

In so far as Sjöström's film offers a qualitatively different experience from Hawthorne's novel, it will do so chiefly on a level other than that of cardinal functions or 'story'. Partly it will do so because of the film's inventions as noted above; but the difference has not been created by the radical introduction of a new function. Hester, Dimmesdale, and Chillingworth retain, in Proppian terms, their functions as heroes and villain: I do not mean that the film, as a whole, is necessarily susceptible to a full Proppian reading, nor am I interested in pursuing such a possibility here: I want merely to suggest that, on this basic level, the film can and does effect a transfer from, rather than a major transformation of, the original. The hero function is split between Hester, whose strength grows in adversity, and Dimmesdale, whose strength declines. The disparities between them are rendered with striking symmetry in the novel. In the film, he carries out his role as preacher winning the same kind of adulation as in the novel but his moral weakness in regard to his affair with Hester is de-emphasized. The film's Hester, while allowed some of the defiant strength of the novel's, is not seen as gradually settling into respected citizenship following her one indiscretion. However, essentially their *functions* in the narrative remain unchanged: it is their function to love clandestinely, for Hester to bear the outer shame and punishment for doing so, for Dimmesdale to suffer privately, and for him to join her at the end in a public confession and a display of unity. Chillingworth's role may be reduced in the film but his function remains that of villain, satisfying in both film and novel such Proppian functions as:

IV. The Villain Makes an Attempt at Reconnaissance. (He seeks information about Hester's 'sin'.)

V. The Villain Receives Information about his Victim. (Slowly in the novel, quickly in the film, he discovers that Dimmesdale has been Hester's lover—they both share the Victim function in relation to him.)

VI. The Villain Attempts to Deceive his Victim in Order to take Possession of Him or His Belongings. (In both novel and film, he misrepresents Dimmesdale and Hester to the Spanish Captain on whose ship they plan to escape, thereby thwarting their plans.)[13]

Obviously not all of Propp's 31 functions can be seen at work in *The Scarlet Letter* (though one might note that XVII reads, 'The Hero is

---

[13] Functions quoted from headings in V. Propp, *Morphology of the Folktale* (1928), trans. Laurence Scott (University of Texas Press: Austin, 1968), 28–9.

Branded',[14] true for both Hester and Dimmesdale), but, if one examines the dramatis personae from a point of view of the functions they perform, one finds a striking correspondence between novel and film. A function remains a function whether it is conveyed verbally or audio-visually, or in the case of *The Scarlet Letter* verbally and visually.

ENUNCIATION AND ADAPTATION

Narrational Mode: The Novel

The Manuscript in the Custom House

Hawthorne wrote *The Scarlet Letter* at great speed in the latter half of 1849 and, when he had finished it, 'he realized that it was too long to include in a volume of tales as he planned. But it was not quite long enough to stand alone. Hence the introductory chapter, "The Custom House"'.[15] Hawthorne himself says that this introductory sketch 'created an unprecedented excitement in the respectable community immediately around him' (Preface to the Second Edition of *The Scarlet Letter*, Signet p. xiii), but this is not my chief interest in it. Nor is most of its intrinsic content. However, since 'The Custom House' *was* in fact published with the novel, we should consider the effect it has on the way we receive the narrative.

The Custom House, at which the author/narrator (i.e. Hawthorne the writer *and* the owner of the authorial voice) worked for three years, is established as a repository of 'true' records: 'On some shelves, [there were] a score or two of volumes of the Acts of Congress and a bulky Digest of the Revenue Laws' (p. 19). As a result, by the time we read: 'I chanced to lay my hand on a small package, carefully done up in a piece of ancient parchment' (p. 39), we have been prepared to accept *its* comments as 'true'. The package encloses the scarlet letter itself and 'several foolscap sheets, containing many particulars respecting the life and conversation of one Hester Prynne' (p. 42). It procures for the novel that impression of 'reality', of reporting things that have really happened. In the sense, then, of presenting a document, Hawthorne's *The Scarlet Letter* is heavily dependent on its introductory chapter; omit this chapter and one is left with a conventionally 'told' tale.

The narrating voice

If we take the work to consist of 'The Custom House' plus the twenty-four chapters of *The Scarlet Letter*, the latter may be received as 'presented' in

---

[14] Ibid. 52.   [15] Leo Marx, Introduction to the Signet edition, p. xii.

relation to the context provided by the former. However, the entire discourse, including both, recalls the eighteenth-century novel's habit of drawing, for an illusion of authenticity, on first-person narration (e.g. on the appearance of the novel's being an exchange of letters, as in *Evelina*, or a journal, as in *Robinson Crusoe*). 'The Custom House' manuscript is used to establish the essential authenticity of Hester Prynne's story, but it also establishes the narrator's voice which carries over from the introductory section to the tale proper. The first-person voice of 'The Custom House' becomes unobtrusive in *The Scarlet Letter*, surfacing only as a generalized 'we' as it comments on the action, but sufficient to remind us that the story is being 'told' as well as being 'presented' as a species of document. This unobtrusive first person is sufficient also to remind us that *The Scarlet Letter* is a novel with a 'repressed flashback', that it is being *told* in a particular way. Story and plot do not coincide chronologically and the narrating voice is aware of the discrepancy. However, *The Scarlet Letter* proper reads much more like an omniscient novel (e.g. *Pride and Prejudice*) than a first-person one (i.e. *Great Expectations*); its 'I' or 'we' is not merely rare but has in no sense the status of a character.

Abstractions enunciated

If the events and characters of the novel (passionate heroine, weak-kneed hero, and vengeful villain) may recall the large simplicities of ballad or fable, they are rendered complex by two processes: first, by the weight of *particularization* that is brought to bear on them, and, second, by the *symbolic* functions they are required to discharge.

These two processes—particularization and symbolization—would seem to be working in contrary directions. The former is aimed at that peculiarly novelistic quality described by Ian Watt as 'the production of what purports to be an authentic account of the actual experience of individuals'.[16] Hawthorne offers a sharply visual rendering of his protagonists and their world and uses the discursive mode of the novel form to scrutinize and record the inner lives of his characters in a way that distinguishes and begins with the nineteenth-century novel. The clearly symbolic aspects of the novel inhere in those resonances of meaning that ripple out from the individuation of person and place; from, for example, what Hester's response to the severities of seventeenth-century Boston may mean in more general terms, or what the concrete physicalities of forest and community may embody about the moral systems in which the novel is clearly interested. The richness of the novel's texture derives chiefly from the tension generated by these processes.

---

[16] Ian Watt, *The Rise of the Novel* (Chatto and Windus: London, 1957), 27.

Not all novels insist on their symbolic intentions as explicitly as *The Scarlet Letter* does; nor, having alerted the reader to these, is it then common to find such vivid particularization. The brief opening chapter draws attention to the rose bush which grows by the prison door: it is at once 'a wild rose bush, covered, in this month of June, with its delicate gems' and offered to us 'to symbolize some sweet moral blossom that may be found along the track, or relieve the darkening close of a tale of human frailty and sorrow' (p. 56). And there it grows, adjacent to 'the black flower of civilized society, a prison'. The forest which edges the colony is both the real forest, black and dense and fitfully lit, and the repository of conflicting symbolic functions: it may be free from the cruel subjugations of human law, but it is also a 'moral wilderness' (p. 175). Hawthorne's symbols are first imbued with a concrete reality, which they retain whatever other significances they accrete. And the same is true of the protagonists, who have each an individual complexity that anchors them in the 'real world' of the novel, a physical and psychological reality that goes well beyond the emblematic role that the ballad or fable usually requires of its dramatis personae.

There is, in fact, at work in *The Scarlet Letter* a process of intense concretization with regard to place and person which helps to suggest why this essentially symbolic novel might make so strong an appeal to the film-maker working in a medium (in this case, the silent film) in which symbolic intentions must be realized wholly through the representation of physical surface. The novel's imagistic power most often derives from the complexity of resonance set up by the image, and it is, of course, the eponymous image which reverberates most variously and tellingly through the novel. It is the sign that sets Hester apart as a creature found guilty by her society, but it is as much a sign of that society's puritanical harshness as it is of her guilt. In its sheer visibility, it becomes almost a performer in the central moral drama of the novel: in the exploration of contrasting ways of dealing with guilt: in the contrast between that guilt which finds expiation and even a curious sort of pride in the wearing of a badge that proclaims it and the kind which, not outwardly apparent, eats away within. The scarlet letter is, further, a focus for Pearl's curiosity about her mother ('. . . the first object of which Pearl seemed to become aware was—shall we say it?—the scarlet letter on Hester's bosom!' p. 98), and the basis of a comparison with Pearl's 'whole appearance [which] irresistibly and inevitably reminded the beholder of the token which Hester Prynne was doomed to wear upon her bosom. It was the scarlet letter . . . endowed with life' (p. 103). And, finally, when Hester need no longer wear the letter, when Pearl is married and living abroad, and Dimmesdale is dead, she 'resumed—of her own free will, for not the sternest magistrate of that iron period would have imposed it—resumed the symbol of which we have related so dark a tale . . . the scarlet letter ceased to be a stigma which attracted the world's scorn and bitterness, and became a type of something to be sorrowed over, and looked upon with awe, yet reverence too' (p. 244). In the complex chain of signification set up by the scarlet letter, it has become a crucial element in Hester's identity; it ends by conferring on her a kind of dignity. And the contrast with the *absence* of such a symbol in Dimmesdale's life underpins the narrative's central structural principle.

Narrational Mode: The Film

'The Custom House', the manuscript, and the first-person narrator

Sjöström's film dispenses with 'The Custom House' and the manuscript and in doing so removes any need for a first-person narrator. The screen has in general resisted the idea of subjective narration (except in the limited, intermittent sense of voice-over and the point-of-view shot) in favour of the presented document, as if to erase traces of its enunciation. The first-person voice of Hawthorne's narrator is unobtrusive, compared with, say, the rhetorical significance of Pip's first-person voice in *Great Expectations*. Not to have sought to retain a sense of Pip's narrational presence in filming the latter would have been to declare a crucial departure from the original; in the film of *The Scarlet Letter*, one scarcely notices its absence.

What happens to the novel's discursive prose?

In the case of *The Scarlet Letter*, the novel's 'metalanguage', in Colin MacCabe's use of the term, constitutes a discursive commentary on the protagonists' behaviour, speech, and appearance, and on the community which is their context. This element of a novel's discourse must always suffer the most radical etiolations in adaptation, its functions to some extent subsumed in the mise-en-scène. Dialogue may be maintained more or less intact, but the metalanguage which teaches us how to 'read' the dialogue (MacCabe's 'object language') is inevitably less susceptible to film. Certain kinds of descriptive prose can find visual correspondences on the screen (e.g. Sjöström's opening image of the rose bush by the prison door is a visual adaptation of Hawthorne's description), but that which analyses inner states, or reflects on abstract matters, or summarizes recurrent or habitual experience, is likely to be lost in a screen adaptation.

(a) *Intertitles*   The discursive mode is reduced to negligible fragments in the film's intertitles. If the talking film is likely to make short shrift of the novelist's commentary, in any explicit way, then the silent film is under even greater pressure to reduce it. It seems unlikely that it was acceptable to a silent film audience to have the narrative too much interrupted by intertitles, most of which were required (certainly in *The Scarlet Letter*) for the recording of spoken dialogue. The reflective element, which looms so large in the texture of Hawthorne's novel, is, in terms of intertitles, reduced to only a handful of bold comments. There are 123 intertitles in Sjöström's film, only ten of which are not words spoken by one of the characters, and four of these ten merely announce time and place ('Puritan Boston on a Sabbath Day in June', 'It was summer again . . .') or person ('The Reverend Arthur Dimmesdale', 'His Worship, the Governor of the Colony'). The remaining six come closest to a literal transferring of the novel's discursive element, but to quote them indicates how little the film can do in this matter. These six intertitles (numbered according to their place in the film—see Appendix 1) are as follows:

No. 1 'Here is recorded a stark episode in the lives of a stern, unforgiving people; a story of bigotry uncurbed and its train of sorrow, shame and tragedy.'

No. 71 'Outcasts—shunned and despised. But Hester's happy child reflected the hope that still lay in the mother's heart.'

No. 80 'The tortured heart—doubly tortured by the love and veneration of his people' (i.e. Dimmesdale).

No. 81 'And Hester—never in all the bitter, lonely years had she felt so helpless' (i.e. when Pearl is ill).

No. 99 'Days of indecision—and wretchedness—At last a way seemed open—' (preceding escape plans).

No. 108 'On the morrow—Election Day—the one day in the Puritan's year when gaiety was not an offence.'

There is no attempt here (as there is in the dialogue titles which draw quite heavily on the original) to use Hawthorne's words or to emulate his tone, though one recognizes in their diction a felt need to encapsulate large areas of the novel's narrative and enunciation. Numbers 1 and 108 elide a great deal of descriptive writing which brings the seventeenth-century Boston community to a more complex life in the novel than the film's—perhaps necessary—insistence on its protagonists can allow. Numbers 71, 80, 81, and 99 work towards summarizing states of mind dramatized at leisure in the novel's prose, through that kind of 'psychological' exegesis open to the novelist whom we allow to have an omniscient view of his characters.

(b) *Diegetic writing*   As well as the sparse use of such intertitles as those quoted above, the film uses several examples of diegetic writing, perhaps as a sort of shorthand for the novel's descriptive prose, particularly in establishing the community. These include:

(a) Wooden plaques saying, respectively, 'DRUNK' and 'A WANTON GOSPEL-LER'[17] worn round the necks of transgressors against the Puritan code;

---

[17] The film has borrowed the latter from Hawthorne's tale, 'Endicott and the Red Cross' (1830), reprinted in *The Scarlet Letter*, Signet edition, 248.

    (*b*) the sign which introduces the heroine—'Heſter Prynne, Ye Seamſtreſs';

    (*c*) the embroidered sampler in Hester's cottage announcing 'VANITY IS AN EVIL DISEASE';

    (*d*) the notice nailed above the stocks where Hester is punished 'FOR RUNNING & PLAYING ON YE SABBATH';

    (*e*) two close-ups of pages of writing from 'YE RECORDS of YE LAWS & STATUTES of YE COLONIE'.

The first, third, and fourth of these remind us, tersely, that this is a community in which punishment enjoys a high visibility. The fourth also offers a comment on the community made ironic by Hester's lifting the sampler to reveal a mirror. The second is perhaps no more than one of Barthes's 'informants', 'serving to identify, to locate in time and space';[18] but it is an unusually 'charged' informant. The comparative delicacy of the writing prefigures the distinction to be drawn between Hester and her community, and it establishes the place, the name, and the occupation of the heroine in a way that saves explanatory dialogue or titles. Further, the archaism of the long 'ſ' and 'Ye' helps to reinforce the sense of a remote time. Two important segments are introduced by the close-ups of the pages of writing. On the first occasion, the page revealed gives laws for the secluded washing of female undergarments; on the second are revealed 'Laws of Ye Courtship'. The segment following the first page ends with Hester and Dimmesdale embracing; that following the second ends with Giles snatching a kiss from his fiancée, in a comic echo of the protagonists. Each segment ends with an expression of feeling at odds with the regulatory tone that ushered it in. Most of this diegetic writing is an invention of the film; in its laconic way, it performs some of the functions of the novel's discursive prose, though essentially this has disappeared along with the first-person narration.

(*c*) *Sub-plot as enunciation*   The events which make up the sub-plot, involving Giles and his fiancée, have already been referred to. I refer to them here to make only one point: as inventions for the film, they exercise an enunciatory function more important than their narrative role. By this I mean the way in which Sjöström uses them to provide a kind of commentary on the Hester–Dimmesdale story. They guide us in how to read the latter by offering in comic terms a critique of those severely repressive mores which cause censure for Hester and anguish for Dimmesdale. The community's strictures on relationships are made to look absurd in the light of Giles's frustrated courtship, and his fiancée's final gesture of understanding makes a claim for a more humane approach to the love between men and women.

---

[18] Barthes, 'Introduction to the Structural Analysis of Narratives', 96.

Adaptation and the codes

At this point I want to consider how the film works at one level of adaptation proper: that is, the level either at which it must seek visual equivalents for novelistic effects intransigently dependent upon the linguistic medium, or, more importantly, at which it manipulates the specifically cinematic codes in presenting its version of the story. This will refer chiefly to two matters: what is within the individual shot (i.e. the product of mise-en-scène and camera movement) and how the shots are joined (i.e. the product of montage). From my shot-by-shot analysis of the film, certain cinematic procedures emerge clearly.

(*a*) *Codes relating to mise-en-scène*   In responding perceptually to the information the film offers from shot to shot, we construct our sense of its narrative. In so far as mise-en-scène is a crucial, perhaps *the* crucial, element governing our perceptions, it does so through its meshing of a number of codes, some of them specifically cinematic (e.g. lighting, figure arrangement, effects produced by distance and angle and movement of camera), some of them extra-cinematic, more broadly cultural (e.g. relating to matters of costume and setting). In regard to *The Scarlet Letter*, aspects of the mise-en-scène important in considering how enunciation is effected (i.e. through processes of adaptation proper) include the following:

Lighting   This is a film of bold contrasts in lighting, one of the codes which most forcefully articulates the oppositions which are at the heart of the film. Two examples:

(i) Hester is characteristically presented as the centre of light in scenes otherwise notably dim and gloomy. For example, our first glimpse of her, in medium close-up, in a lacy white dress which emphasizes the radiant innocence of the character, is presented against the dimly neutral background of her cottage walls.

(ii) The warmth of interior lighting is frequently contrasted with dark exteriors, enunciating the idea of domesticity under threat of various kinds. For example, Hester in her cottage with her sick child is expecting Dimmesdale to visit and comfort her and the intercut exterior shows the approach of Chillingworth.

Figure arrangement and posture   Position in the frame (foreground/background; left/right; alone/in group) and posture (standing/sitting; sitting/lying; gesturing/still; moving/still) are codes which are invoked to govern our response to particular shots and, thereby, to make us aware of how power is disposed among the film's actants. In doing so, they fulfil some of the functions of the novel's discursive prose.

(i) *Foreground/background distinctions* are less crucial in *The Scarlet Letter* than they would be in a film which made greater use of the long take or depth of field. Nevertheless, there are some striking moments such as when a long shot of a crowd suddenly highlights individual censoriousness by foregrounding a smugly pontificating Puritan and his wife, without, however, losing the sense of the crowd behind them from which they draw the strength of their unattractive opinions.

(ii) *Left/right distinctions.* Typically, in the many two-shots of Dimmesdale and Hester, he is in the left-hand side of the frame; this would not be a meaningful distinction if it were not for the fact that, at certain crucial points in the film, positions are reversed or one invades the other's space, as it were. When Dimmesdale first falls under Hester's spell (i.e. when releasing her from the stocks), or when he is reduced to speechless misery on Chillingworth's learning his and Hester's secret and she goes to comfort him, or most notably, in the film's last moments when she takes him in her arms, pulling him into her space: in each of these moments, when a sense of Hester's superior power in relation to Dimmesdale is at issue, the break with the usual spatial dispositions makes the dramatic point more forcibly.

(iii) *Alone/in group.* The individual's relation to a difficult community being one of the key thematic elements, it is not surprising that the mise-en-scène should register it through a distinction such as this. Examples abound. Pearl, with her doll, on the cottage doorstep watches the jeering village children, separated in the frame by the physical space of the cottage garden, an analogue for the psychological separation of Pearl's outcast innocence and their respectable spite. Most strikingly, Hester and Pearl, on Election Day, stand alone by the scaffold, the empty space that separates them from the crowd making its point about the diminished but still operative obloquy in which they are held. The grouping in this shot establishes the by now almost unconscious way the community leaves a gap around Hester and Pearl.

(iv) *Postural distinctions.* Frequently the nature of a relationship is enacted in distinctions between: (*a*) one character standing while another sits or crouches or lies down (e.g. Hester looms confidently over Dimmesdale in the forest as she envisages their escape from the colony while Dimmesdale lies down, head in hands, bewailing: 'I am too ill—too broken. I lack the courage to venture alone'; Chillingworth stands, preparing medicine, while Hester crouches protectively over Pearl's bed: in each case the relative posture indicates who is in control of the scene); or (*b*) one character standing still while the other gestures wildly or moves about (e.g. Dimmesdale, gesturing, pleading with Hester, in the prison, to allow him to share her punishment, and meeting with her calm resistance). The *placement* of the figures in the frame in relation to each other makes clear, in purely cinematic terms, how things stand between them at this moment. It suggests one way in which the process of adaptation, as distinct from transfer of cardinal functions, may work.

Distance from camera, angle of shot, camera movement within shot   If often
not regarded as, strictly speaking, aspects of the mise-en-scène, the choices
made in these matters (long shot, medium shot, or close-up; high or low
angle, etc.) inevitably influence how *we receive* the information of the mise-
en-scène. Film does not offer an innocent window on a (piece of the) world:
the choices considered here help to determine way the narration is to be
effected. In *The Scarlet Letter*, it is worth noting that:

(i) Out of the film's more than 950 shots (See Appendix 1), there are no
more than 25 long shots, and these are usually limited by sets representing,
for example, the interior of the church, the town square, a clearing in the
forest. Their function is either to show one of the protagonists set apart from
the community or to suggest a larger area than is actually shown. There is a
marked preponderance of close-ups and medium close-ups and the effect is
to intensify the sense of *The Scarlet Letter*'s being an intimate personal drama.
So is Hawthorne's novel at its narrative core but its symbolist and discursive
practices give it an expansiveness that is, for the most part, absent from the
film.

(ii) This is a film which places a good deal of trust in its faces and
Sjöström's reliance on close-up views of his protagonists' face particularly in
highly emotional moments and often against neutrally undistracting backgrounds, is a choice well made in interests of intimacy and intensity.

(iii) There is not much use of unusual camera angles, but when they do
occur their presence is felt as meaningful. In the opening segment, there is a
low-angled shot of the church bell tolling, followed by the camera's tilting
down to the pillory and the barred enclosure beneath it, to reveal a man
wearing a wooden plaque saying DRUNK. The movement of the camera
establishes a hierarchical interconnectedness in the life of the colony.

(iv) There is relatively little use of the panning shot but on at least two
occasions it enables Sjöström to make dramatically effective use of off-screen
space. Segment 8 ends as Hester and Dimmesdale, hand in hand, leave the
frame right, and the camera stays eloquently on the empty sunlit space as
they make for the concealment of the forest. The camera then pans left to
rest on Hester's panties left hanging on a bush, reminders of the joyous
Hester who, we anticipate, is about to embark on a darker aspect of her
drama. A little later, in segment 10, the courtship of Giles and his fiancée is
conducted, in accordance with statutes, via a speaking-tube. The camera
pans slowly between Giles and the girl, comically exploiting the off-screen
space as the camera solemnly pans the length of the tube to reveal the
response of the speaker at the other end. Neither of these episodes is found
in the novel, but the former grows out of obvious suggestions in it, and the
latter has its function in helping to present the absurdity of some of the
community's regulations.

Settings and costumes   These two important aspects of the mise-en-scène draw for their effectiveness on our awareness of certain cultural codes: certain kinds of place and dress will connote for us certain attitudes to life. Two examples will make this point: (i) the film very unobtrusively makes Hester's outcast state clear by the fact that the cottage she lives in after her disgrace is on the edge of the community (tree stumps are visible, suggesting that the land has only recently been cleared), whereas prior to it she has lived in a cottage near the centre of the village; (ii) Hester's dress, characteristically white and rather lacy in the first movement of the film, contrasts with both the severities of the Puritan garb (black with white collar) and with the sombre grey of her own dress when the scarlet letter has become its only adornment.

(b) *Codes of cinematic punctuation*   The overall effect of *The Scarlet Letter* is of remarkable cinematic fluency and of a speed in the unfolding of its narrative that contrasts with the somewhat leisurely pace of Hawthorne's novel. This effect is partly the result of relationships possible within the frame or shot (i.e. as distinct from what is possible in language where all our knowledge is derived linearly, film can economically 'fuse' subject and predicate, in a single frame, as Bluestone noted nearly forty years ago[19]). It is also partly the result of the film's use of the codes of punctuation. Figures are revealing here: there are 957 shots in the film (i.e. each shot averages 5.75 seconds, a figure almost at the centre of the range for American films of the period[20]), and in all but 28 cases the punctuation is that of the cut. By this time—1926— classical editing of the seamless cut had been perfected; the film moves fluently from shot to shot, cutting on eye-line match or on action. The pre-eminence of the cut has several effects. Along with the shot-length, it promotes the illusion of a speedy narrative unfolding. Secondly, it throws into relief those occasions when another punctuational device is used. For instance, in the opening segment (a Metzian descriptive syntagma 'in which the relationship between *all* the motifs successively presented on the screen is one of simultaneity'[21]), there are dissolves from people walking to church, to the bell tolling, to children in Puritan garb, then a cut to adults similarly dressed, and a further dissolve to a long shot of the procession. The effect of the dissolves is to relate the children, the adults, the church bell in a fluid evocation of community. Elsewhere, the dissolve is used to draw more reflective attention to a distinction between the communal and the indi-

[19] George Bluestone, *Novels into Film* (University of California Press: Berkeley and Los Angeles, 1957), 59.

[20] See Barry Salt's figures in *Film Style and Technology: History and Analysis* (Starwood: London, 1983), 211–12.

[21] Christian Metz, *Film Lanaguage: A Semiotics of the Cinema*, trans. Michael Taylor (Oxford University Press: New York, 1974), 127.

vidual: e.g. in the clothes-washing segment, two dissolves are used to move from the communal washing, to a medium close-up of three women washing, to one of Hester at a slight remove from the others. In their more obvious 'visibility' (i.e. compared with the seamless cut), dissolves seem to serve narrational purposes which recall a novel's linking narration. Fades, used several times to mark a clear temporal break, often seem to correspond to a novel's break between episodes or chapters. Thirdly, the predominance of the cut works most effectively in scenes of emotional intensity where it sets up a powerful sense of the reliance on those processes of alternation which I see as the film's chief means of rendering the oppositions centrally important to the novel and which will be discussed in the final section.

A 'Silent' Film Adaptation

The discursive element

The necessary loss in virtually all film adaptations of the novel's discursive prose, at least in any obvious sense, is intensified in the silent screen adaptation. However, the film medium may, in its manipulation of space, through its use of camera angle, focus, distance from its object, through the quality of its lighting, and through its editing procedures, provide a kind of cinematic equivalent to the novelistic capacity for commenting on its action. The fact that *The Scarlet Letter* ends on a long shot (comparatively rare in this film) which isolates its protagonists, both by position and by lighting, from the subdued, watching crowd, may be read as Sjöström's using his mise-en-scène, the distance of his camera from the central action, and the lighting design to make a commentary on that action. That is, Hester, victim of an inhumanly oppressive system, and Dimmesdale, at last freed from the chains of suppressed guilt, are not merely united publicly in their love but the quality of their feeling is seen to have an effect on the watching crowd. The silent film, if it wishes to reflect upon inner states or abstract concepts, must do so through primarily visual means.

Dialogue titles

In his account of early cinema history, Barry Salt writes:

The introduction of dialogue titles was far from being a trivial matter, for they entirely transformed the nature of the film narrative. Not only does a dialogue title take less time to read than the narrative title it replaces, but when it is cut into the point at which it is spoken, it interrupts the flow of the narrative far less, and it may also permit a more complex story to be told within the same running time.[22]

---

[22] Salt, *Film Style and Technology*, 121.

Salt is here writing about a period more than a decade earlier than *The Scarlet Letter* but it is worth noting here since the use of dialogue titles is a key element in the film's narrational procedures. *The Scarlet Letter* has, in fact, a good deal of dialogue by silent film standards:[23] there are 123 dialogue titles (see Appendix 1) in the 90 minutes of the film's running time, but this is obviously still sparse compared with the dialogue of a talking film of comparable length. Several points about these dialogue titles and their distribution are instructive to note in relation to the adaptation process:

(i) Hester and Dimmesdale, with 30 and 31 titles respectively, have more than twice as many allocated to them than has anyone else; the film focuses on their relationship much more insistently than the novel does. Chillingworth comes next with only 12.

(ii) Hester herself does not speak until the 19th title. Following her innocent misdemeanour (chasing her singing bird), she is in the stocks and Dimmesdale is shocked to find her there. She says: 'It matters not—since the order came not from thee'. Significantly, her first title indicates both her semi-outsider's relation with the community and her feeling for Dimmesdale.

(iii) On several important occasions, the three protagonists have an unbroken *series* of titles. For example, Hester has four titles uninterrupted by replies on three occasions: when she is explaining to Dimmesdale the story of her marriage; when, in prison, she persuades him not to reveal his role in her present shame; and when, in the forest, she urges him out of despair, this last occasion interrupted only once—feebly—by his protests. Dimmesdale has three long uninterrupted titles as he tries to persuade Hester on the scaffold to name her 'fellow sinner', and Chillingworth has four terse utterances, culminating in 'My revenge will be infinite', when he realizes the nature of Hester and Dimmesdale's relationship. At moments of intense emotion, that is, the film tends to allow the chief character involved unbroken access to the titles.

(iv) Pearl's words are given only three times and she is much more simply a symbol of hopeful vitality in the film, shorn of the novel's suggestions of a darker, more capricious waywardness.

(v) It is difficult to assign clear-cut functional categories to the dialogue titles but the following allocations may be discerned:

(*a*) asking for or giving narrative information: 54 titles (e.g. 'Go for the minister! Tell him my child is dying!')

(*b*) direct expressions of feeling: 28 titles (e.g. 'Hester, I have fought against it—but I love thee.')

(*c*) cultural / religious / social information, of a kind likely to be found in

[23] Cf. Ernst Lubitsch's 1925 adaptation of *Lady Windermere's Fan* and Alfred Hitchcock's 1926 version of *The Lodger*, which have less than half the number of *The Scarlet Letter*.

the novel's metalanguage, and relating to the film's thematic patterning: 30 titles (e.g. 'Every time I pass the house I put a curse upon that child of sin.')

The Scarlet Letter needs nearly half of its dialogue titles, plus four of the non-dialogue ones, to work as bearers of crucial narrative information. No surprise, then, that it has comparatively little scope for the kind of reflective activity and subtlety of comment which are so much a part of the novel. What *is* surprising is how much sense of community attitudes and of the binary oppositions central to the novel's conceptual framework is retained, chiefly through visual images but also partly through Frances Marion's dialogue.

(vi) One of the challenges to the silent film's fluidity is to insert the dialogue titles with as little disruptive effect as possible. In *The Scarlet Letter*, the narrative titles offer little problem since they usually introduce a new segment of the film. As to dialogue titles, Sjöström sometimes achieves the opposite of disruption by establishing a rapid alternation between speakers and titles (cf. segment II, titles 33–8). In general, he avoids undue disruption by cutting from the actor starting to speak (this was common silent cinema practice from around 1915[24]) and returning, after giving the titles, to the identical composition or to one in which the speaker still appears prominently even if he or she has been joined by others, in either case re-establishing the context of the remark. This is true for 102 of the 123 dialogue titles. Only on ten occasions, and always for reasons of particular dramatic effect, does the shot following the title not include the speaker. For example, title 66, spoken by Mistress Hibbins in medium close-up, 'Wouldst thou protect the brat of the devil, un-baptized and damned?', is followed by a medium close-up of Hester and Dimmesdale: the effect is to dramatize Dimmesdale's ignoring of Hibbins's vindictive hypocrisy.

(vii) My final point relating to the film's dialogue is that it draws closely on Hawthorne's: surprisingly, in view of the different emphasis the film adopts: and the divergences are themselves instructive. Title 60 is a revealing case in point: titles 57, 58, 59, and 61 are taken almost verbatim from the scene in the novel in which Dimmesdale pleads with Hester on the scaffold to name her fellow-sinner. These four titles reorder the sentences of the original but retain their sense and, largely, letter (e.g. title 59—'It would be far better for him to stand on thy pedestal of shame than hide a guilty heart through life'—is a key sentence in novel and film); title 60 is, 'I will never betray him. I love him—and I will always love him'. In the novel she replies simply, 'Never!' and follows it, looking into Dimmesdale's 'deep and troubled eyes', with 'It [the scarlet letter] is too deeply branded. Ye cannot take it off' (i.e. by the kind of naming and repentance to which she is exhorted).

---

[24] Salt, *Film Style and Technology*, 12.

Her next sentence is 'And would that I might endure his agony, as well as mine' which provides title 61. That is, at this crucial moment in the novel there is no talk of love, though that last line may be said to grow out of love, but the film's explicitness, at almost exactly its chronological centre, points to and is symptomatic of its pervasive preoccupation with the tragic love affair.

Intertitles will inevitably offer no more than a sketchy adumbration of the novel's prose. The film may *transfer* the novel's essential narrative functions (as, for the most part, *The Scarlet Letter* does) but, lacking the diegetic element of spoken and heard dialogue, it must crucially rely on its images—their composition and juxtapositions—in establishing its emotional and intellectual resonance. The process of *adaptation*—the making over of the original story into a new medium—is correspondingly more total in its demands. The silent film version of a novel is, in this sense, freer than a sound version which, having spoken dialogue at its disposal, has felt an increasing impulse/need to adhere closely to the letter of the original, sometimes with results of inhibiting 'literariness'.

SPECIAL FOCUS: THE PROCESSES OF ALTERNATION

Sjöström's film offers a notable example of Raymond Bellour's notion of *alternation* as a structuring technique in cinematic narrative. Bellour's work on alternation traces its development back to silent cinema. Defining it as 'the extension of an opposition a/b which is continued through a more or less prolonged process of serialization (a1/b1, a2/b2, etc.) until it breaks off',[25] Bellour claims that the 'classical cinema . . . uses alternation very specifically as a kind of formal basic principle which is constantly and organically at work in the film . . . as the generalized form of narrative'.[26] If it may be argued that the process can be found at work in all or most film narratives, it can be more emphatically claimed to work structurally in a narrative based firmly on such bold oppositions as underlie *The Scarlet Letter*. Losses of complexity (*vis-à-vis* the novel) are considerably compensated for by the dramatic immediacy the process achieves. The discursive aspects of Hawthorne's novel may be largely resistant to film but the major structural concepts of the novel find a new expression through the working out of alternations. Some of these, operating on the macro-level, may be seen as transferred from the

[25] Janet Bergstrom, 'Alternation, Segmentation, Hypnosis: Interview with Raymond Bellour', *Camera Obscura*, 3–4 (1979), 76.
[26] Ibid. 80.

Hawthorne novel; these large-scale oppositions are then given a detailed articulation through the micro-level of filmic alternations. It is at this level the process of adaptation, as distinct from transfer, may be said to occur.

Macro-Level Oppositions

In large terms, it may be said that Sjöström has perceived the way in which Hawthorne's novel is structured around a series of binarisms such as the following:

(a) publicly acknowledged and punished guilt (Hester) — privately experienced guilt and inner anguish (Dimmesdale)

(b) public contumely (Hester) → rejection and solitariness — public adulation (Dimmesdale) → acceptance

(c) strength (Hester) — weakness (Dimmesdale)

(d) natural passion (Hester, Giles) — repressed feeling (Dimmesdale, Giles's fiancée)

(e) the individual — the community

(f) the forest (= freedom from constraint of man's laws) — civilization (= constraint of man's laws)

(g) woman and woman's role — man and man's role

(h) love/compassion/forgiveness — hatred/vindictiveness/vengeance

All of these are to be found at work in the novel but there they make their presences felt through varied uses of the novel's dramatic and discursive capacities; in the film they are quite explicitly felt in the operation of the process of alternation. Perhaps the revealed/concealed binarism—(a) above—is the one that works most pervasively in structuring the novel, and the film reflects this emphasis in the emblematic significance it gives to Hester's scarlet letter and to Dimmesdale's hand on his heart, concealing, as it were, the *absence* of his public branding.

On the macro-level, the film's diegesis develops further alternations such as those between the following pairs:

(a) Interior scenes (cottage, council chamber, prison) — exterior scenes (village square, forest, roads)

(b) private places and experiences (both interior and exterior in setting) — public places and experiences (both interior and exterior in setting)

(c) gaiety (Hester's harmless fun-loving and vanity) — sobriety/sternness (Puritan disapproval)

    (d) the comic (Giles's comic and   the serious/tragic (Hester's more
         comically treated transgressions)   gravely treated transgressions)

    (e) handsome or beautiful faces   harsh, ugly faces (most of the
         (Dimmesdale, Hester)   Puritan community)

The above lists, not intended as exhaustive, are sufficient to indicate the central insistence of the film's narrative in compelling attention to the oppositions which regulate its structure and its meaning.

If in some ways the film seems to simplify Hawthorne's concepts (e.g. in presenting particular characters,[27] or in certain thematic notions), consideration of the above oppositions, and how they are woven into the film's texture, will lead to a claim for a still impressive complexity—as a brief look at the structure of segments 2 to 7 (from opening until Dimmesdale's departure from Hester) will suggest:

> Segment 2 (the Boston Sabbath) alternates between representations of law and punishment on the one hand and of religion on the other.
>
> Segment 3 (Hester's cottage) establishes the relation of contrast between high-spirited Hester and censorious community.
>
> Segment 4 is constructed as an alternating syntagma which cuts between Hester running in the woods (place of dappled light and freedom, her floating hair matched to a sparkling waterfall) and the church interior (Puritans complaining to Dimmesdale about Hester).
>
> Segment 5 (in church) contrasts Giles's 'natural' sneezing and the repressive action of the church warden who punishes him for such 'wanton' behaviour.
>
> Segment 6 (in church) alternates between Hester as contrite transgressor and Dimmesdale as reproving minister.
>
> Segment 7 (Hester in the stocks) contrasts Giles's compassion and Hibbins's vindictiveness, public punishment and private feeling as Dimmesdale releases Hester from the stocks.

It would tedious to go through the whole film in this way but I believe it is true to say that, in its large movements, its meaning is essentially established through the play of alternation between contrasting ambiences (e.g. church/woods), psychologies (e.g. gaiety/sobriety), emotions (e.g. compassion/vindictiveness), and so on. Bellour has claimed that 'the extraordinary power of alternation lies in that it can work simultaneously and in complementary fashion both on the level of diegesis and the level of specific codes, and that it can do so on multiple dimensions of the textual system going from the smallest to the largest elements'.[28] I have suggested above how the process

---

[27] cf. Mark Estrin's comment on how Chillingworth, in the forest scene, is 'used solely for purposes of turning the plot'. '"Triumphant Ignominy" on the Screen', in Gerald Peary and Roger Shatzkin (eds.), *The Classic American Novel and the Movies* (Frederick Ungar Publishing: New York, 1977), 24.

[28] Bellour in Bergstrom, 'Alternation, Segmentation, Hypnosis', 79.

may be seen at work on the level of diegesis, and as centrally significant to the shaping of each of the film's main movements and to the film as a whole. It shares with the novel a concern for such contrasts, but its alternating processes present them with a peculiarly cinematic directness. Whereas Hawthorne's discursive prose can take us inside the minds of his characters (a convention allowed the novelist), the film-maker, denied this ease of access, can exercise 'the extraordinary power of alternation' with an agility beyond the novelist's scope in presenting contrasting points of view and contrasting physical representations.

Micro-Level Alternations

On the micro-level, one finds the cinematic codes working to articulate the major oppositions through alternations such as those between:

close-up	and	long shot
shot	and	reverse shot
subjective (p.o.v.) shot	and	objective shot
tracking shot	and	still shot
on-screen space	and	off-screen space
light	and	dark

In a silent film where the exchange of spoken dialogue is virtually impossible (intertitles must be too sparingly used for such an effect) and in one which makes little or no use of the long take, such alternations are of pressing importance. Each segment is composed of many shots, characteristically edited to emphasize the dualities and oppositions I have been referring to. In several segments from the second 'movement' of the film (from Hester's punishment to the baptism of the child), Sjöström cuts insistently between Hester and Dimmesdale, the shot–reverse shot alternation establishing firmly the oppositions between man and woman, private guilt and public guilt, agitation and composure.

In segment 14 he visits her in prison just before she is due to mount the scaffold: there are eighteen shots alternating between Hester, composed, strong, her guilt known, and Dimmesdale in postures of increasing distraughtness before they are held in the two-shot ushered in by Hester's words: 'We may never see each other again but I will have comfort in beholding thy life of devotion & service.' The movement is clear: the drama is created in the rapid alternation between the two, reaching a sort of resolution in the two-shot. The drama is not just in the cutting, though, but in the interplay of contrasting facial expression and posture. Whereas Dimmesdale is increasingly wild-eyed in his pleading to share Hester's shame and is in profile towards her in most of his shots, she is typically photographed frontally, her gaze steady, achieving a kind of radiance as she urges him to, 'Atone! Atone for both of us with thy good works!'

In the latter half of segment 16, in which Dimmesdale baptizes the child in the prison cell, Sjöström cuts regularly between Dimmesdale and/or Hester, on the one hand, here united in purpose (i.e. to secure the child for Hester), and Mistress Hibbins and flanking crones or the Beadle, on the other. Here the process of alternation serves to oppose the loving aspect of religion (the baptism, wanted—out of love—by both Hester and Dimmesdale) and the censorious, vindictive face of it as practised in Boston (Hibbins etc. have come to remove the child to be 'brought up by a Christian woman'). The force of the alternation is stressed by a persistent use of medium close-ups for both sides of the opposition, except for: (*a*) the close-up of Dimmesdale actually pronouncing the baptism, and (*b*) the final medium long shot which shows the Puritans forced to bow their heads at the left of the frame, Hester, Dimmesdale, and child at the right: i.e. the drama is again created in the rapid alternation and resolved in a different kind of shot and camera set-up. In a sense, the alternation in time (through the cuts) comes to rest in an alternation in space, as its effect is visible within a single frame.

These two examples, from crucial moments, could easily be multiplied throughout the film. Sometimes the process is used to set up a tension between exterior and interior scenes (e.g. in segment 23, where Hester watches anxiously over her sick child inside the cottage and the audience is shown in four exterior shots the approach of Chillingworth, the returned husband whose approach she is unaware of—involving a further alternation of medium close-ups and long shots). Sometimes it is used to comic effect (e.g. in segment 10 where Giles's courtship is conducted through an alternation of off-screen/on-screen suggestions; or in segment 27 when Giles, pretending to be Mistress Hibbins, insults the passing Governor and Beadle: here the alternations are between close-up and medium shot, interior and exterior, liveliness and sternness, the ludicrous and the dignified). And in the very last part of the final segment 31, the film alternates movingly between Hester and Dimmesdale on the scaffold and the crowd below, between individual and community, between close-up and long shot, settling at the end for an objective long shot (rare in the film) of the scaffold small and brightly lit in the centre of the frame, surrounded by the crowd.

The novel's chief events make their impact through their comparative sparseness, interleaved with Hawthorne's ruminative commentary. The film, while generally maintaining the chief events, gives them a rich dramatic texture through the process of alternation, which is also its chief way of cinematizing the contrastive elements it has transferred from the novel.

Greer Garson as Paula and Ronald Colman as Smithy in a publicity still for Mervyn Le Roy's *Random Harvest*.

2

Random Harvest (1942)

Random Harvest is a useful case-study in that it represents best-selling popular fiction worked upon by the procedures of classic Hollywood film narrative. James Hilton, not much read now, was undoubtedly one of the most popular British authors of the 1930s and 1940s, and a film version of one of his novels would have attracted attention on those grounds alone. *Lost Horizon* (1973) and *Goodbye Mr Chips* (1939) were immensely successful films adapted from Hilton, who himself shared the screenwriter's credit for MGM's *Mrs Miniver* (1942). By the time of *Random Harvest*, published in 1941 and filmed a year later, he was at the peak of his popularity and a film adaptation would be likely to avoid doing violence to his novel. However, there are other perhaps more powerfully influential factors at work in ensuring that the film is as it is: it is a quintessential studio product from MGM, which specialized in prestige adaptations; it was made at a time when Hollywood's England was probably more vivid to the world at large than the real thing; and it starred Ronald Colman and Greer Garson, both at the height of their considerable fame. To even moderately knowledgeable film-goers in 1942, *Random Harvest* resonated with expectations that went well beyond those of simply seeing the film-of-the-book. The book has not worn well, but the film nevertheless continues to exert an extraordinary power that derives partly from the determinants referred to above, partly from the way it restructures the events of the original, causing it to yield compelling psychological and emotional patterns. It offers an excellent case for not over-privileging the precursor novel at the expense of other elements of the film's intertextuality: MGM, Freud, and 1942 are as important as Hilton in shaping the film of *Random Harvest*.

NARRATIVE AND TRANSFER

Structural Patterns: The Novel

A novel in five parts

As one of the major interests in the adaptation of *Random Harvest* derives from the film's need for a radical reordering of the novel's events, I shall

begin abruptly with a summary of the novel's structure. It is divided into five
'parts', each of which contains a number of sections. Parts One, Three, and
Five are set in the novel's present, covering a period from Armistice Day 1937
to the outbreak of World War II, and each of these parts is narrated by
Harrison, private secretary to Charles Rainier, successful upper-class busi-
nessman and, later, politician, who confides what he can remember of his
past history to Harrison. Part Two deals with the period December 1919–
1929, Part Four with the year from Armistice Day 1918 to December 1919—
that is, with the crucial 'missing' year in Rainier's life. Parts Two and Four
are told in the third person.

Part One opens with the meeting between Harrison and Rainier on a
train heading for Cambridge where Rainier is to be guest of honour at a
dinner, after which he tells Harrison about his war experience (including
shell-shock and memory loss), an accident in Liverpool, which brought on
his second memory loss while restoring his pre-shell-shock identity, and his
return to his family home, Stourton. As well as establishing the novel's
central mystery—what happened in the 'lost' year?—Part One also provides
intimations of the nature of Rainier's marriage: both Rainier and his wife,
Harrison comes to feel, are suppressing something, a part of themselves.
Harrison becomes Rainier's secretary (a post once held by Mrs Rainier) and
his confidant.

The main function of Part Two, occupying nearly a hundred pages, is to
clarify Rainier's post-Liverpool history. Having no notion of what brought
him to Liverpool, he returns unannounced to Stourton for an edgy reunion
with his upper-middle-class family, gathered for the imminent death of
Rainier's father. Following family squabbles and mismanagement of the
firm, he is invited to take over; under his management it flourishes, and he
becomes an 'industrial prince', without finding real satisfaction in the work.
Nor does his growing relationship with Kitty, stepdaughter of his oldest
sister Jill, expel the sense of there being something crucially 'missing' at his
core. This relationship comes to a head in 1929 when Rainier and Kitty
become engaged, following a holiday in Switzerland, but the engagement is
broken by Kitty, in a letter she leaves for him: 'I'm not the one for you,
though God knows the mistake was excusable for both of us, because I'm
nearly the one'.[1]

Part Three shows Rainier still emotionally adrift, despite the 'saga of
success'. There is also a further insight into his marriage to Miss Hanslett, the
quiet efficient secretary who has become a brilliant political hostess. That the
blank spot in his past is still a worry to him is dramatized in the way a mere
hint of enlightenment is enough to send him off again in search of an answer:

[1] James Hilton, *Random Harvest* (Grosset and Dunlap: New York, 1941), 293. (Subsequent references
will be given in brackets as they occur.)

a music hall performance, *Salute the Flag*, stirs a memory in Rainier so that he and Harrison drive off to Melbury that night. At the end of Part Three, in Melbury, a policeman replies to Rainier's question about the hospital, 'You wouldn't be meaning the *asylum* would you, sir?', thus leading into Part Four, which recalls his escape from the asylum, fills the gap in his memory from Armistice Night 1918 to December 1919. This part, much the longest, is crowded with incident: Rainier (then Smithy) meets the actress Paula on Armistice Night; she rescues him, looks after him during the flu epidemic, rescues him again when the asylum men come looking for him; he joins her theatre company as a handyman, runs away after a disastrous stage performance; she finds him again and they marry; Paula becomes pregnant; Smithy goes to Liverpool about a newspaper job and is knocked down in a street accident. Part Four, that is, recounts the missing year.

Part Five: Harrison reports Rainier's pleasure in the recollection. To Harrison's suggestion that, now the memory gap is closed, he is 'completely cured', Rainier replies:

'You don't *really* think that's all it amounts to? You must know there's only one thing that matters—only one thing left for me to do.'
   'And that is?'
   'I must find her.' (p. 298)

As Rainier goes off on his search, Harrison and Mrs Rainier drive to the country, and past and present converge, closing the gap, so as to secure the future, the novel's last page revealing that Mrs Rainier and Paula are one and the same.

Overall structuring pattern

Essentially Hilton's novel is concerned with one man's search for his full identity. That his knowledge of himself is partial derives from the missing year in his life, during which, he is dimly aware, he was emotionally engaged in ways that subsequently make it impossible to commit himself to a relationship. When the memory of this year returns, he commits himself to re-finding the girl who was so crucially a part of it. The narrative is structured upon a series of losses and (re-)findings, and its time-scheme, moving between present and past, reflects this.

Structural Patterns: The Film

A radical reordering of the novel's plot

The film radically reorders the novel's plot while retaining much of its story. Dictated largely by the constraints of the cinema, it retains the novel's underlying patterns of loss and finding, despite a quite different structural procedure. Perhaps the crucial reason for the film's structural change is its need to show rather than to tell, for, on film, it will be apparent from the first appearance of the secretary who later marries Rainier (Colman) that she and Paula (Garson), the wife of his missing years, are the same person. The fact that 'both' roles must be represented by the same actress, that she must have a physical, visual presence, as distinct from being merely named and described on the page, has implications for the structuring and emphasis of the film. In the novel, neither Rainier nor the reader (nor anyone else) knows that Mrs Rainier is Paula until the last page; in the film, the remarkable panning shot that introduces the secretary allows (indeed, forces) the audience to know at once, and establishes how complete is Rainier's memory blank for the missing years at the end of the war. What is a mysterious search in the novel, a search for a past which would hold a key to Rainier's emotional life, acquires in the film a different sort of tension. In the novel, we know only what Rainier knows, and as it is told to Harrison; in the film, we share the camera's knowledge, which is very much greater that Rainier's. Put crudely, in reading the novel, we wonder what Rainier will do if and when he rediscovers Paula; in watching the film, we wonder when he will discover that he has found her long ago.

A film in three parts

Hilton's novel spans twenty-one years from Armistice Night 1918 to just after the declaration of World War II in 1939. The film linearizes the story's events, moving from Armistice Night to 1935, this date glimpsed on an invitation card for a reception given by Sir Charles and Lady Rainier for the Prime Minister. The film's structure suggests two roughly parallel parts with a brief final movement. The first part (from 11 November 1918 to 14 November 1920) represents Smithy/Rainier's (Smithy's) escape from the Melbridge Asylum, his meeting with and marriage to Paula, and the accident in Liverpool which restores his earlier, pre-1917 memory. The second part (from November 1920 to 1935) traces his return to his family home, his near-marriage to his step-niece Kitty (Susan Peters), his successful career, and his marriage to his secretary. The third, very short part involves the separate returns of Rainier and his wife to the scene of their past happiness and the reunion which closes the gap in Rainier's past by revealing his wife to him as Paula.

Apart from this short final section, which I have called Part Three, the film really divides into two halves which exhibit a very striking sense of balance and parallelism, summarized below:

PART ONE	PART TWO
Paula—confident, successful	Rainier (Smithy)—confident, successful
Smithy—oppressed by loss of identity	Margaret (Paula)—oppressed by concealment of identity
Smithy finds helper in Paula	Margaret seeks help from psychiatrist Benet
Smithy longs to be recognized, to belong (e.g. to the Lloyds at the asylum)	Margaret longs to be recognized by, to belong to, Smithy
Marriage followed by success	Marriage followed by (qualified) success

Essentially this balance is a matter of Paula's command of the situation in Part One being replaced by Rainier's in Part Two. However, the film does not end with Part Two because neither the marriage nor the political success brings fulfilment for the protagonists. Hence, the brief final movement:

PART THREE
Rainier returns to Melbridge.
Margaret returns to Mrs Deventer's Inn.
They re-meet at the country cottage of their earlier married idyll.

The reunion in Part Three is a surrendering of the 'command' referred to above in the rediscovery of the 'perfect love', which the sound-track celebrates, between two people who are now able to be wholly themselves: he because he now knows what that whole self *is*, she because she now no longer need suppress one part of herself.

The narrative parallelism between the film's first and second parts is a very powerful element in its construction, reinforced through corresponding narrative detail and the use of parallel signs (visual and aural) to highlight either comparison or contrast. These will be considered in relation to the film's enunciatory procedures.

The novel's structure works to make the present more meaningful by interspersing it with dips into the past, but its awkwardness in managing its mixture of narrative techniques and, perhaps, its author's less imaginatively powerful command of the detail that draws attention to basic structures, as compared with the film-makers' command of the resources of *their* medium, keeps it from generating the emotional tension of the film. In one sense the film works more simply than the novel: that is, in its linearization of the chronology of events; also, it shears away many of the novel's characters and incidents, and most of its discursive concern with social and political life. Working then on a clarified and streamlined version of the narrative (the 'summary' in Barthes's term, which 'preserves the individuality of the message [and . . .] is *translatable* without fundamental damage',[2] it invests its transferred 'cardinal functions' with an extraordinarily rich and suggestive set of 'catalysers' and 'indices' (see below), to strengthen the meaning of those functions by powerful cross-referencing between the two halves of the film.

Transfer of Narrative Functions

Major cardinal functions

Despite the film's simplified narrative mode, it is clear that certain crucial narrative functions have been transferred from novel to film, though not necessarily in the same order. The *story* in both film and novel depends from three narrative 'facts':

  (i) the hero's loss of memory (the result of war—this has happened before the film or novel begins);
  (ii) the first return of memory (December 1919 in the novel, November 1920 in the film);
  (iii) the second return of memory (September 1939 in the novel, 1935 in the film).

In both texts, these constitute the most important of Barthes's 'cardinal functions'. In each, despite key differences in their chronological presentation, in plot terms, the major cardinal functions could be summarized as follows:

  (i) *Loss of memory* which leads to
    (a) Institutionalization of the hero →
    (b) His longing for identity and a sense of belonging →
    (c) His escape from the institution (catalysed by Armistice Night excitement and attendant's negligence) →
    (d) His rescue by and help from the girl, Paula →
    (e) His acquiring a new identity (as Smithy) and new roles of husband, father, and writer →
    (f) A journey of separation and his accident →
  (ii) *The first return of memory* which leads to
    (a) Hero (in new-old identity of Charles Rainier) returning to his pre-shell-shock home →
    (b) Reunion with family, reimmersion in family affairs, and his rise as 'industrial prince' →
    (c) Growth of relationship with and near-marriage to Kitty (as part of his search for fulfilment) →

---

[2] Roland Barthes, 'Introduction to the Structural Analysis of Narratives', in *Image-Music-Text*, trans. Stephen Heath (Fontana/Collins: Glasgow, 1977), 121.

(d) His throwing himself into business and political life →

(e) Marriage of convenience to his secretary who becomes a brilliant hostess →

(f) A period of qualified happiness/satisfaction for both, which does not wholly repress →

(g) Rainier's need to pursue his full identity which *now* includes the shell-shock years.

(iii) *The second return of memory* which leads to

(a) The hero's return to the crucial location of the missing years →

(b) His recognition that the secretary-wife and actress-wife are the same →

(c) The closing of the gap with reconciliation.

Though the film's surface (the product of its mise-en-scène and its editing procedures, i.e. of its enunciation) may be very different from the novel's (the product, obviously, of the 'writing'), at the level of crucial narrative functions which I am discussing here there is virtually complete transfer. These functions could be tersely labelled 'Loss', 'Searching', and 'Finding' and, though at any given point in the narrative they and the hierarchy of cardinal functions they give rise to may be surrounded by markedly different 'catalysers', both film and novel offer essentially the same permutations on these three key functions. This holds true even allowing for the necessary structural change enjoined by the visual medium relating to the identity of Paula/Margaret. For example, Rainier, in losing his memory, 'loses' the first 20–30 years (Ronald Colman appears older than the novel's Rainier) of his life; in searching for these, he at first finds, not those earlier years and the identity that went with them, but a new life and a new identity (= husband, father, writer). With the accident in the Liverpool street, he loses this new identity but finds again his old one. And both novel and film end on a finding: in finding who he wholly is (i.e. Rainier is also Smithy), he realizes who his wife wholly is (i.e. Margaret is also Paula).

The film preserves the novel's essential story-material, but each adopts a different plot order for the *display* of this material. Both may be structured around the same major cardinal functions, but the changes in narrative procedures, especially in regard to plot chronology, are crucial to their overall affective impact. Despite narrative reliance on the same cardinal functions, there are certain crucial shifts in emphasis. For instance, the film gives much more time and dramatic weight to the parallel sequences (segments 12 and 22—see Appendix 2) of Smithy's marriage to Paula and the marriage 'rehearsal' of Rainier and Kitty. Their order is of course reversed by the film's linear chronology, and the church scene on the day before Rainier is due to marry Kitty gains immensely in emotional resonance through signifiers which recall the earlier sequence. The cancellation of the wedding in the novel is effected in a single sentence at the end of Part Two: 'It [a letter from Kitty to Rainier] had been delivered by hand early that morning, and contained, in effect, the breaking of their engagement and an announcement that she was leaving immediately to join her stepmother in Luxor' (p. 154). The text of the letter referred to is given in Part Five (dated 30 September 1929) and only then is it clear why Kitty has broken the engagement: 'Sometimes, especially when we've been closest, I've had a curious feeling that *I remind you of someone else*'—and her awareness of being *'nearly* the one' (p. 294).

When Kitty makes these remarks, about being nearly the one and feeling like 'an intrusive stranger, trying to take the place of someone else', in the film, the viewer has the dramatic advantage over the reader of knowing exactly with whom to compare her. And Rainier's yearning for what he has lost is reinforced by aspects of the soundtrack and the mise-en-scène: by the use of the same hymn tune, a similarly benign organist, by Rainier's words to Kitty ('Don't leave me Kitty. I need you. I'm trying to make a life') recalling words he, as Smithy, had spoken to Paula just before their marriage ('Never let me out of your sight again . . . I can't imagine the future without you'). Aural echoes like these and the visual reminders of place—the two churches—invest the later scene in the film with a romantic power which the novel's narrative procedures, almost necessarily, deny it. His psychological withdrawal from the marriage preparations, in spite of his need for Kitty, is charged for the viewer with the aural and visual recall of the earlier scene.

The novel records Smithy's marriage to Paula in a sentence: 'So they were married at St. Clement's, Vale Street, London, N.W., and as they left the church after the ceremony newsboys were racing down the street offering extra editions—"Peace Treaty Signed at Versailles"' (p. 259). Like the news of the broken engagement, it has the effect of historical record, in contrast with the *dramatic* presentation of each in the film's present tense. The two episodes assume a dramatic centrality in their respective halves of the film, their comparable importances highlighted by the parallelisms in their mise-en-scène. That is, aspects of the film's enunciation, as well as of narrative detail, work to stress the parallelism. What has happened in each case is that the film has retained a major cardinal function—Smithy marries Paula, Rainier nearly marries Kitty—from the novel, but has clustered around it a whole range of different minor cardinal functions and catalysers from those which obtain at comparable points in the novel.

Character functions

There is some redistribution of character functions, in the Proppian sense. However, the film can accommodate such shifts while not rearranging the novel's structure. For instance, the 'helper', in Proppian terms, is in *Random*

Harvest also 'the sought-for person', or perhaps it would be better to say that the 'sought-for person' is one of the 'helpers' since there are others in the latter category. This is true of both texts, though there are changes of identity, in some cases, between novel and film: for example, though Paula/ Margaret remains both 'helper' and 'sought-for' in each, Blampied the clergyman (one of the novel's key helpers) disappears from the film version, whereas an unnamed doctor/psychiatrist in the novel becomes Benet, an important 'helper' in the film. The *function* of 'helper' is crucial in both, though it is distributed among a different set of characters in each.

On this basic level—of cardinal narrative functions (in Barthes's terms), of character functions and spheres of action (in Propp's term)—the MGM film and the Hilton novel correspond.[3] If we are to look for changes, for what is adapted as distinct from what is transferred, for what gives the film its peculiar 'cinematicity', it will not be at the level of major narrative or character functions. MGM in 1942, no doubt mindful of a devoted reading public[4] for *Random Harvest*, has not sought to make radical alterations at these levels.

Modified transfer

At levels less crucial to the structure of the story, there are other transfers from novel to film which help to minimize for the audience of the time (in so far as it overlaps the novel's audience) the sense of jarring as the story is transposed from one medium to another. Apart from the underlying narrative and character functions, one may speak of 'transfer' in relation to such matters as the following, in which, however, important elements of 'adaptation' have begun to make themselves felt. The following are, in a sense, 'grey areas' in which transfer is not as clear-cut as is the case with, say, cardinal functions because, in them, the enunciatory procedures which effect the adaptation are crucial, depending on the new signifying system for the element of transfer to be recognized.

(*a*) *Some of the data relating to the characters and their lives*, apart from those crucial character functions which propel narrative. Take, for example, Rainier's social background (trade risen to the ranks of gentry and large country house); his academic predilections and their frustration by the demands of the family business, which he proves the most efficient at running; his 'gentlemanliness', apparent even when he doesn't know who he is: in details of Ronald Colman's screen persona and the collaboration of his

---

[3] So, too, do such Propp-designated functions as Absentation, Violation, Lack, Counteraction, Recognition, etc.

[4] In England, its popularity lasted well beyond the 1940s; there were five Modern Fiction Library reprints between 1954 and 1965. In the United States, there were three separate editions in 1941 alone, including an 'Editions for the Armed Services' printing.

performance with other aspects of the mise-en-scène, the film transfers these details of Rainier's character first created by Hilton.

(b) *The details of some episodes* in which the major cardinal functions are developed through lesser ones and clustered about by catalysers *and* by Barthes's 'indices' of atmosphere and character. For instance, the details of Armistice Night 1918, with Smithy's escape from Melbury (Melbridge) County Asylum, and his rescue by Paula from the excited crowds, or of the Rainier family breakfast reunion with its tensions and selfish impulses at work, involve significant transfer from the novel, though the film's reliance on aural and visual signs, as opposed to purely verbal, means that the line between transference and adaptation has notably blurred.

(c) *A general sense of class differences.* The 'lower orders' are seen as either warmer or more comic than their social superiors. Compare for instance, the tobacconist, Biffer, Mrs Deventer, and Sheldon with Rainier's siblings, Benet and Harrison: these differences preserve the novel's sense of a layered society. In each, Smithy/Rainier's 'gentlemanliness' is insisted on.

However, when one says that these elements (*a*)–(*c*) have been 'transferred' from novel to film, it is important to note what is implied by the word: it means visual and aural signifiers have been found to produce data corresponding to those produced by the verbal signifiers of the novel; and it means paying attention to the way the specifically cinematic codes—for example, those relating to camera movement and editing, lighting, and music—take what is transferred and adapt it to the screen. And at this point, one is clearly talking about enunciation, about transforming what has been transferred into another signifying system. It is at the level of enunciation, not of narrative, that the most important discrepancies between film and novel are found.

ENUNCIATION AND ADAPTATION

Narrational Mode: The Novel

Shifts in narrating voice

As indicated earlier, the novel moves between first- and third-person narration.

The first-person voice belongs to Harrison, who becomes Rainier's secretary and confidant. It is a polite, educated, upper-middle-class voice, a product of Harrison's background; and it is this voice which narrates Parts One, Three, and Five. For all Harrison's importance as a repository for and recorder of other people's information (a role crucial to the kind of narrative offered here), he remains himself a somewhat nebulous figure. However, it is through him that the reader receives his sense of the 'lack' at the centre of Rainier's life and the curious nature of his marriage to his former secretary.

Third-person narration takes over in Parts Two and Four, in both of which large slabs of Rainier's past are revealed. The change to third-person narrative in Part Two is introduced by the last sentence of Part One when Harrison writes, 'So he began, and as it makes a fairly long story it goes better in the third person' (p. 57). Part Four simply shifts into third person with no explanation. Not until the start of Part Five is an explanation offered for this reversion, when Harrison again takes over with: 'Rainier began to tell me most of this during the drive back from Melbury that night; a few minor details obtained from other sources, I have since fitted in' (p. 279). The very long Part Four reads like a slab of omniscient story-telling. It is not perfectly clear how Rainier comes to remember all the information contained in Part Four or, having done so, why he still does not fit all the pieces together. How, one wonders, did the Melbury visit set all this memory in train? It is hard not to see the film's conjunction of resonant signifiers, visual and aural, as by contrast a model of economic story-telling. Part Four is cluttered with characters, sympathetic or unsympathetic to Rainier and Paula's romance and marriage. Harrison resumes the narration for Part Five, reporting on the preceding narrative and on Rainier's pleasure in the recollection.

Despite the novel's awkward narrational procedures and the flatness of much of the writing, there is no denying the emotional power of its conclusion or the skill with which the resolution is concealed until the end. This power derives from concealing until the last possible moment what Rainier's amnesia has repressed: the fact that the object of his full sexual and emotional commitment and the object of his restrained respect and affection (that is, his wife) are the same person. The sense of repression is central to our understanding of Rainier and of the novel's structure. The concealment which contributes significantly to the impact of the ending is of course a function of the narrational mode: the reader's knowledge is limited to Harrison's, the final moments a revelation to both.

The discursive element

Because of the shifts between first- and third-person narration, there is no consistently functioning discursive prose to instruct in the reading of—to provide a context for—the individual character discourses. Colin MacCabe's notion of a 'metalanguage', which performs these functions, in relation to the direct discourse of characters, 'those words held in inverted commas',[5] may perhaps be applied to Parts Two and Four. However, as David Bordwell

[5] Colin MacCabe, 'Realism and the Cinema: Notes on Some Brechtian Theses', *Screen*, 15/2 (Summer 1974), 8.

points out: 'Many novels frame characters' speeches not within a "transparent" metalanguage but within the writing or speech of a narrator, either that of a character in the fiction . . . or a more or less personified speaker or writer'.[6] The three parts narrated by Harrison clearly fall into this category: he is 'a character in the fiction'. *Random Harvest*, then, exhibits—theoretically—two different kinds of metalanguage. In practice, however, the distinction is scarcely worth noting. Harrison's narrating voice is so little coloured by his lightly sketched personality that it seems scarcely more characterized than the supposedly impersonal, third-person narration of the two parts set in the past.

There are of course differences in the kind of information recorded by the two voices. What Harrison records is predominantly the result of his observation of Rainier (and, to a lesser extent, of Mrs Rainier). On the other hand, the anonymous narration of Parts Two and Four (allegedly pieced together from Rainier's own accounts) is much more likely to contain slabs of potted social and political history against which Rainier's return to health and his industrial rise take place, or to compress various sections of his personal history. The kind of social/political history sketched in the section of Part Two dealing with changes wrought during the years 1921 to 1924 (pp. 130–1) is scarcely digested in the novel and the film, at least overtly, never aims to replicate it. The film is also much terser in suggesting the changing circumstances of Rainier's personal history. As to the kind of commentary offered by Harrison's 'metalanguage' ('But his appearance was slightly disconcerting; there was a twitch about his mouth and eyes as he spoke, and a general impression of intense nervous energy in desperate need of relaxation'), the film will either ignore it or seek to achieve comparable ends through manipulations of mise-en-scène.

Narrational Mode: The Film

Narrating voice

The film dispenses with the novel's first-person narrator. Harrison (Branwell Fletcher) is reduced to a very minor role and, though he is present in the Melbridge scenes near the end, he is in no sense specially privileged in relation to narrative knowledge. There is, therefore, no sense of the novel's movement between first- and third-person narration. The film's straightforwardly linear treatment is in the classic Hollywood narrative style which stresses showing rather than telling. The 'narrator' is essentially the camera, which begins its work with a slow forward tracking shot down a flagged path, lined with bare trees, to a barred door set in a wall, with a figure visible

---

⁶ David Bordwell, *Narration in the Fiction Film* (Methuen: London, 1985), 19.

behind the glass of the door. The camera then pans slowly left to settle on
the large iron gates and plaque announcing Melbridge County Asylum.
During this long, graceful shot, an unidentified voice[7] on the sound-track
announces:

Our story takes you down this shadowed path to a remote and guarded building in
the English Midlands—the Melbridge County Asylum, grimly proud of its new
military wing which barely suffices in this autumn of 1918.

The diction and intonation of this voice-over and the accompanying images
at once raise expectations of a particular kind of film narrative: of the Hollywood romantic melodrama of which *Rebecca* (1940) was an earlier striking
example. Generic expectations have been established which provide a guide
as to how the film is to be read. After this opening shot, however, the film
dispenses with the voice-over, adopting the classic Hollywood narrative
mode in which the narrator is invisible and inaudible; in which, as I have
suggested, the camera seems to be the narrator.

What becomes of the discursive element?

In referring to elements of 'Modified Transfer' (above), I cited some of the
'data relating to characters and their lives' and 'a general sense of class
differences'. In the novel these are very often the product of the discursive
prose, though of course such information may well be revealed in dialogue
as well. In fact Hilton's metalanguage, whether it belongs to Harrison or to
the third-person narrator, predominantly fulfils these functions, functions
which are essentially assumed by the film's mise-en-scène.

As to *data relating to characters*, the film transfers Paula's professions of
actress then of secretary, and, later, of society hostess, in all of which she
performs the functions of 'helper'. These three 'roles' are derived from the
novel certainly, but the film characterizes them in ways not open to the
novel, or, at least, not so readily open to it. For instance, in matters of facial
expression and dress, the film is clearly able to go much further in visual
specificity, even when it is working on suggestions contained in the novel. In
the first half of the film, Paula appears bright-eyed, open-faced, with hair
creating almost an aureole effect (produced by a manipulation of lighting); in
the latter half, there is a sense of banked-down feeling in her expression
which is characteristically unsmiling, the eyes consciously blank. 'Figure
expression and movement', in Bordwell and Thompson's phrase,[8] are powerful elements of mise-en-scène at work in creating this contrast: the ways in

---

[7] Mervyn LeRoy identifies its owner as James Hilton himself, in his autobiography *Mervyn LeRoy: Take
One* (W. H. Allen: London, 1974), 151.

[8] David Bordwell and Kristin Thompson, *Film Art: An Introduction* (4th edn.) (McGraw Hill, Inc.: New
York, 1993), 157–63.

which Greer Garson sits, stands, moves; the ways she is lit and framed; and
the facial expressions so often caught in close-up are crucial elements in
distinguishing the two personae of this character. And in that other revealing
aspect of the mise-en-scène—costumes—the film distinguishes clearly between Paula and Miss Hanson/Lady Rainier. In the first half of the film,
Paula's dress at once announces a freer, more outgoing personality (vivid
checked coat, light skirt, and frilly blouse) compared later with the severities
of Miss Hanson's secretarial garb, and the hostess's *haute couture* which
characterizes Lady Rainier. These are simple examples of the way purely
visual signs not so much transfer actual verbal descriptions of dress (in
fact the film rather oddly ignores one of the few such notations from the
novel, relating to the 'long mackintosh and a little fur hat, like a fez' which
both Paula—p. 186—and Kitty—p. 145—wear) but effect specific adaptations
of generalized elements in Paula's life, largely recorded in the novel's
metalanguage.

A clear sense of class differences: the film drops most of the overt social/
political comment of the novel, but it nevertheless sets its story in a firmly
realized representation of England. One of the film's chief signifiers of Englishness is in the clear sense of class differences. The small but crucial scene
in the tobacconist's shop on Armistice Night offers a case in point. Hilton's
metalanguage describes the tobacconist as 'an old woman watching from
behind the counter—thin-faced, gray-haired, rather baleful' (p. 185). The film
uses Una O'Connor to display these characteristics (except that 'gray-haired'
is saved for her second appearance, years later, when Rainier returns to
Melbridge). Like the book, it establishes her as distinctly lower class. Hilton
writes that she 'said nothing in answer, but after a longer scrutiny began
sidling away,' the word 'sidling' implying an undignified furtiveness one
might expect of the proprietress of 'a small neglected general store' (certainly
not of the assured upper-middle class to which Rainier's family belongs). The
film establishes her lower-classness by a visual gesture: as she says, 'I haven't
got all day', she pats her hair in a way that reveals some of the film's attitude
to the lower orders: that is, it makes her a recognizable comic stereotype of
genteel aspirations.

The film as a whole supports its (much-criticized) physical representation
of England (see below) with a clear notation of class differences: the tobacconist, the pub-keeper (Reginald Owen), the landlady (Margaret Wycherly),
Paula, the actress and, later, the secretary, Harrison, the psychiatrist (Philip
Dorn), the Rainier family and servants are all clearly placed on a social
spectrum which may or may not be authentic from an Englishman's point of
view, but which functions in the film to provide recognizable signs about
class structure. These signs are very revealing about the ways in which
Hollywood, and especially MGM, represented England in films of this period: it is a country in which people have and know their place, though
occasionally a successful transition may be effected (e.g. Paula's).

One may speculate that this sort of structure posits something stable about the society which contains it: not a view for more egalitarian times, but perhaps very much a view for wartime, a view to be promoted in a country—USA—whose support for Britain was crucial. The film's discourse on class, less explicit than some of the novel's social commentary, is both built into the narrative (Paula's progress) and the product of a signifying system that uses faces, voices, and body language, as well as other elements of mise-en-scène (costume, setting) to enunciate a stable, clearly layered social structure. In the film, such information is often received simultaneously with that relating to the narrative's progress, whereas the two kinds of activity are apt to be more distinct in the novel.

Adaptation and the Codes

What is achieved in the processes of adaptation is a remarkable fluidity of movement, partly the result of the linearization and parallelisms of the narrative as previously discussed, and partly the result of its manipulation of various codes. Some of these are cinematic (e.g. codes of montage), some of them more broadly based (e.g. cultural codes).

Cultural codes

In relation to these, I shall consider one very specific example and one more pervasive in its effects.

(a) *Jewellery*   Jewellery, as a subset of the costume code, is strikingly used to reinforce the parallelism between the film's two halves: the expensive necklace Rainier gives his wife after she has successfully entertained the Prime Minister recalls at once (for her and for us) the cheap glass beads he had given her after the birth of their child, the value of the gifts to Paula in inverse relation to their costs. Such a point is made in the film not simply through the visual codes which enable us to identify the physical differences between the two necklaces, but also through the exercise of narrative codes (by which we grasp the structure of a story—how the near-repetition of a gesture highlights the differences between the occasions that give rise to it), linguistic codes (the dialogue accompanying the two gestures is notably different in spontaneity and emotional content), and cultural codes (the second gift clearly denotes a socially more imposing level than the first).

(b) *An idea of Englishness*   My second example is the way various cultural codes at work in the film's mise-en-scène and on its sound-track contrive to produce an idea of Englishness. Hilton's novel is characterized by some very English aspirations and values, by affection for English institutions, by an indulgent wryness towards English idiosyncrasy, and by its picture of a society founded on class discriminations. MGM, several thousand miles from the setting of the story, makes clear from the film's opening credits that, in matters of physical presentation, *Random Harvest* will be in line with the studio's notion of a 'prestige' adaptation of an English novel. Even the credits themselves encode intimations of 'Englishness'. On a satiny background with a sprig of apple blossom and a well-known English hymn on the sound-track, they announce expensive stars and a largely English cast, as well as gifted off-screen contributors who, to the cognoscenti at least, set up expectations of superior attention to the film's physical attributes.

In the early 1940s, with a large number of English artistes (especially actors) in Hollywood, and as a symptom of a strongly felt urge to stimulate American interest in the war in Europe, there was a marked increase in films set in England. MGM was perhaps the leader in this field (cf. also *The White Cliffs of Dover* (1944) and *Mrs Miniver* (1942) both anti-isolationist films), though the trend was by no means limited to one studio. The more or less standardized representation of England in these Hollywood films is that of a world of stately homes, of cobbled streets with quaint bow-fronted shops and cosy pubs, of the gaslit squares of an earlier era, of urban elegance and rural serenity, except when threatened by war which provided the opportunity for displays of quiet English courage. Critics, English critics in particular, were frequently scathing about what they detected as the false notes in such representations. What is interesting now is the persistence of these images of England and why Hollywood studios should have elected to present England in the particular ways that they did.

Random Harvest is a typical specimen of Hollywood's England and it elicited some of the same sorts of critical carping about authenticity that later films like *Lassie Come Home* (1943) and *The White Cliffs of Dover* attracted. The *Monthly Film Bulletin* contended that: 'Though Hollywood has tried to take every precaution to reproduce the English scene, some small error of detail or behaviour frequently obtrudes itself upon the senses and jars.'[9] And William Whitebait, who liked this 'Hollywood-English drama', felt that 'it reeks of the studio, and every landscape looks as though one could put one's foot through it. Devonshire, especially, is precarious.'[10] A more recent commentator on the English in Hollywood and Hollywood's England, Sheridan Morley, writes sneeringly of the 'plastic attempts by Hollywood to create a never-never England about as phoney as the tweed-raincoat ads seen occasionally in *The New Yorker*'.[11] None of these comments attempts to account for the images of England offered by such films as *Random Harvest*.

There are two key representations of England in the film: (i) the country

---

[9] *Monthly Film Bulletin* of the British Film Institute, 10/109 (31 Jan. 1943).

[10] *New Statesman*, 30 Jan. 1943.

[11] Sheridan Morley, *Tales from the Hollywood Raj* (Weidenfeld and Nicolson: London, 1983), 178.

cottage with blossom tree, picket fence, nearby stream and rustic bridge, and, inside, the usual 'rural antique' look of gate-legged table, chintz, low-beamed ceiling, and carefully rustic doors; and (ii) Random Hall (Stourton in the novel), the family seat of the Rainiers, with large ballroom, imposing entrance hall and staircase, breakfast room with mullioned windows, and landscaped garden. It may be argued that there is a chocolate-box prettiness about the cottage set, but it may also be claimed that it offers an ideal of romantic love, spatially and temporally dissociated from, insulated from, the pressures and anxieties of the real world. The fact that exteriors are always viewed from the same angle suggests not so much studio economy as the steadiness with which the protagonists view it. Its centrality to the emotional core of their lives is underlined when it reappears in the film's last scene, shot from exactly the point of view of, and apparently at the same time of year (spring) as, its first appearance. If one chooses not to make realism the ultimate criterion, the apparently unchanged image serves a profound narrative purpose: it is a symbol of what Rainier/Smithy has repressed, and Lady Rainier/Paula has had to suppress. Such an interpretation seems to be moving some distance from the idea of the cottage as representing an aspect of English life dear to the heart of Hollywood's England,[12] but in fact the two are linked in so far as, in each, the cottage embodies a desired ideal. And, in 1942, the very *unchangingness* of the cottage may be seen to have yet another function: it is not just the symbol of Paula and Smithy's 'perfect love', but also of a society in which certain elements retain their character while everything around them is in danger or is being called into question.

Random Hall, despite the breakfast table snipings of Rainier's family, offers a complementary idealization of English country house life. (Only rarely, as in *Rebecca*, or, decades later, *Remains of the Day* (1993), was the basis of this gracious façade exposed to serious scrutiny.) It is the sort of house which announces itself with a plaque on its impressive gateway pillar, which has a lodge and lodge-keeper at some distance from the house itself, which is run with unobtrusive efficiency by the butler Sheldon (Aubrey Mather), a faithful family retainer. In its representation of the house, the film does not in fact outdo the suggestions of the novel: Harrison 'hadn't expected Stourton to be quite so overwhelming' as they 'swooped into the final half-mile stretch that ended in a wide Palladian portico' (p. 44). Most of its use is discreet, as if it is being saved for the grandeur of the reception of the Prime Minister. Whatever criticisms may be implied or expressed about the people involved (as in the breakfast bickerings of Rainier's family), there is

---

[12] Hollywood may most memorably have enshrined this idealized view of England but it is interesting to note its being echoed in the leading article in the *New York Times*, 24 July 1940, evoking Britain under threat in these words: 'The old, old towns of Britain, the hills and cliffs and shores and meadows rich with history, the homes and lives of forty million people, the great British traditions of human worth and dignity, the folk-sayings, the deep wisdom and long-suffering hopes of a race . . .' Quoted in Collie Knox (ed.), *For Ever England* (Cassell: London, 1943), 69.

barely a suggestion that the way of life metonymically rendered by such
scenes is other than gracious and dignified.

If the cottage and Random Hall are the twin poles of the film's representation of England, there are several other importantly contributing factors.
The music hall in which Paula is seen performing on Armistice Night to a
rowdy, appreciative audience and the noisy, jostling camaraderie of the
Melbridge Arms and the adjacent streets flesh out the notion that, beneath
the surface reserve of English life, true at least of upper- and middle-class life,
there is a warmth of feeling that may require a crisis or a celebration to
manifest itself. All these physical representations of Englishness are powerfully reinforced by the casting. The only significant members of the cast
without a British background are Susan Peters (Kitty) and Philip Dorn (Dr
Benet), respectively American and Dutch. Garson (Irish-born, English-edu-
cated) and Colman were firmly identified as British star presences, and
supporting players such as Una O'Connor, Jill Esmond, Reginald Owen, and
Alan Napier all signified, visually and vocally, instantly recognizable levels of
Hollywood's version of the English class system. Hollywood's England, a
product of such players and of a characteristic mise-en-scène, must be seen as
a key element in the film's enunciation. In this regard, Jeffrey Richards
summarizes perceptively some key aspects of the film's power in accounting
for its popularity: it is 'artificial and unreal, perhaps, but utterly believable
and hypnotic because it is entirely created and played out in that corner of
MGM that is forever England. It is a world which has never existed and yet
has always existed, an idealized amalgam of elements half-remembered, half-
imagined in the mind of the expatriate.'[13]

The cinematic codes

If the film is 'utterly believable and hypnotic', this is at least partly due to the
supremely confident exercise of the cinematic codes. These codes—the use
of certain kinds of shots and certain ways of suturing them—are 'inseparable
from the material of expression proper to what is called cinema', 'general
cinematic codes . . . being systems of signifier; without signified.'[14] Metz
offers the 'lap dissolve' as an example of what he means here, and it is on the
codes relating to cinematic punctuation I wish to concentrate in suggesting
how *Random Harvest*, having transferred a series of narrative functions and
reordered them to provide a new and powerful structure, achieves the
process of adaptation in major part through its command of this code. The
dissolve is the most strikingly invoked manifestation of the code.

I have divided the film into 32 segments (see Appendix 2), to use Metz's
general term for an autonomous cinematic unit. These are each character-

---

[13] Jeffrey Richards, *Visions of Yesterday* (Routledge and Kegan Paul: London, 1973), 110.
[14] Christian Metz, *Language and Cinema*, trans. D. J. Umiker-Sebeok (Mouton: The Hague, 1974), 136.

ized by a change in location and / or time, varying in length from a single shot (e.g. No. 27, the close-up insert of an invitation) to a complex episodic sequence (e.g. No. 13, which depicts the married life of Paula and Smithy, using seven dissolves and eighteen cuts). The 'punctuation' separating these segments breaks down as follows: 21 dissolves, 7 fades, and 3 cuts.

Also, there are 52 further dissolves *within* segments (not counting the 12 during the unfolding of the credits); for example, when Rainier arrives at Random Hall for the first time, the shot dissolves from that of the train, to one of the plaque announcing the name of the house, to one of the car arriving, to one of Rainier's knocking at the lodge-keeper's door. I stress the use of the dissolve because it contributes so markedly to the film's fluidity of movement and to the romantic 'look' of the film. The entire film (unlike the novel with its intrusive narration) has something of the seamless, hypnotic quality of a dream, broken for viewer and protagonist only with the latter's final discovery of his whole self. The use of the dissolve is powerfully instrumental in creating this oneiric effect. Consider some of its usages:

1. The entire episodic sequence (segment 3) of Smithy's time in Melbridge Asylum and his escape from it on Armistice Night, until he takes refuge in the tobacconist's shop, consists of eight parts each linked by a dissolve. The effect is of Smithy's disorientation, of living below a level of full consciousness, and of being impelled, in his escape, by a scarcely understood purpose. Naturally, it is not the dissolves alone which produce this effect: they work in conjunction with other cinematic codes (e.g. of camera movement, notably in the slow, smooth tracking shots down the asylum path to the barred door and following Smithy as he leaves; of the subdued lighting, both indoors and out; of the musical sound-track), with the acting, particularly of Colman's almost-somnambulist Smithy, and with the visual codes that register the fog and the figures behind translucent glass.

2. The three shots (exterior-interior-exterior) which comprise segment 8, of the train speeding through the countryside by night and carrying Paula and Smithy away to safety. Whereas cutting between these shots might have communicated urgency, the use of dissolves renders a sense of rapid, dreamlike retreat to safety, which seems confirmed by the dissolve to the next shot of Paula and Smithy as they stand observing a mist-swathed hill.

3. The entire depiction of their married life (segment 13) in a nine-minute episodic sequence of nine parts, linked by seven dissolves and one cut as Smithy moves from one room to another. The segment is introduced by a dissolve as they arrive from the church in which they are married to the idealized cottage in which they will live until Smithy leaves for the fateful journey to Liverpool. The dissolves in this segment effect a transition from exterior to interior, from season to season, from night to day. The result is the creation of an idyll, a trance of happiness. The one scene away from the

cottage—Smithy's registering the birth of his son with a laconic clerk—both fails to disrupt the sequence (*because* it is enclosed by dissolves) and acts as a perhaps necessary comment on its insulation from the larger world.

4. The use of dissolves, not merely in the interests of narrative fluidity and of the film's romantic look, but often as a means of ensuring simultaneous consideration of two narrative elements. For example, the segment in which Paula, first at a lawyer's office, then in a judge's chambers, has her marriage to Smithy terminated dissolves into a shot of Rainier and Kitty walking in the garden of Random Hall on the eve of their wedding. Their apparent happiness, superimposed on Paula's face in the dissolve, seems thus to derive from her sacrifice of her own happiness; once again, and as always, the cinematic code works in conjunction with the narrative, visual, and acting codes to create a complex response.

The power of the dissolve as the film's chief link between segments and between parts of segments is reinforced by:

   (i) the sparing use of the cut in this capacity;

  (ii) the fade-out/fade-in technique used to mark the most important breaks between segments; and

 (iii) the graceful tracks and pans which characterize the camera's movements within segments.

   (i) *Cuts* are used to divide segments or parts of segments when there is a sense of urgency or anxiety in the narrative shifts. The cut between segments 3 and 4, between Smithy's bewilderment among the crowds on Armistice Night and his taking refuge in the tobacconist's shop, is a clear example of its use for this purpose. Sometimes, too, there are cuts between the brief 'scenes' which compose an episodic sequence; for example, in segment 28, there is a cut between the scene in Paula's sitting-room (after the successful reception for the Prime Minister) to the next as she leaves Rainier to go to her bedroom. There is clearly a tension between them here which a dissolve would undermine.

  (ii) The *fade-out/fade-in* technique is used, generally, to usher in such major narrative events as Smithy's arrival in Liverpool, or Paula's interview with the lawyer to arrange the dissolution of her marriage to Smithy, or Paula's railway departure for Devon. In these instances, there is a decisive turning-point in the narrative, the shot fading in on a situation which will profoundly influence narrative direction.

 (iii) The *tracks* and *pans* contribute significantly to this film's narrative elegance and fluidity. An example of each will suffice to make the point. The forward track with which the film opens, immediately following the credits, is accompanied by a voice-over intoning, 'Our story takes you down this shadowed path . . .'; and the effect of the smooth tracking shot (which gives way to an equally smooth pan to the asylum's gates) and these words is to draw the spectator irresistibly forward into the film's world. The pair of panning shots which introduce Greer Garson into each half of the film offers a prime instance of the cinematic code's capacity—in alliance with aspects of the mise-en-scène—to make a dramatic point. First, in the tobacconist's shop (segment 4), Smithy has failed to speak clearly to the proprietress who has gone to telephone the asylum, when a voice is heard saying: 'You are from the asylum, aren't you?' and the camera pans to reveal the sympathetic face of Garson in her role as Paula. Second, in Rainier's office (segment 20), he asks through an inter-office telephone for his secretary to bring in a file. Oddly, as it seems, the camera pans from Rainier's desk to rest on a closed door which is then opened to reveal Garson in her role of Miss Hanson. This pan is the film's equivalent of the novel's last-page revelation that the two women are one and the same and, in its way and in its place, it is quite as powerful.

To sum up, the reorganization of the novel's major cardinal functions into a linear chronological progression and the employment of cinematic codes which emphasize such a progression have led to a remarkable sense of an effortlessly unfolding narrative, moving with the inner consistency of a dream. The processes of transfer and of adaptation have worked together to create an illusion of timeless romantic melodrama, and the film's structural parallelism is reinforced through visual and aural detail. The following lists are not exhaustive but enough to suggest how the film's control of narrative detail and its use of parallel signs (visual and aural) highlight either comparison or contrast between the film's two main parts.

PART ONE	PART TWO
(*a*) MELBRIDGE COUNTY ASYLUM: Large iron gates, with name noted in close-up of plaque on pillar	RANDOM HALL: Large iron gates, with name noted in close-up of plaque on pillar.
(*b*) Dr Benet warns Smithy not to count too much on Mr and Mrs Lloyd's recognizing him.	Benet warns Paula not to count on Rainier's recognizing her at any particular time.
(*c*) Excited crowds by arched gate of Melbridge Cable Works on Armistice night.	Excited crowds at same place when Rainier averts strike.
(*d*) Paula is introduced by panning shot *after* her voice is heard (in tobacconist's).	Miss Hanson (Paula) is introduced by panning shot *after* her voice has been heard (on Rainier's intercom).
(*e*) Paula exercises initiative in entering Smithy's life.	Miss Hanson takes initiative in entering Rainier's (Smithy's) life.
(*f*) Paula is performer at theatre.	Lady Rainier is spectator at theatre.

PART ONE	PART TWO
(g) Theatre company provides sense of family for Paula, whereas Smithy is alone.	Rainier has family background of Random Hall, whereas Miss Hanson is alone.
(h) Paula and Smithy's train journey to 'somewhere quiet and lovely' and subsequent explanations to Mrs Deventer (landlady).	Rainier's train journey to Random Hall and subsequent explanations to gate-keeper.
(i) Paula asks Smithy to kiss her after proposal.	Kitty asks Rainier to kiss her after proposal.
(j) Use of 'O perfect love' at Paula–Smithy marriage. (Benevolent organist—lady.)	Use of same hymn at rehearsal for Kitty–Rainier marriage. (Benevolent organist—man.)
(k) Cottage (always viewed from same angle) as symbol of ideal happiness.	Random Hall as symbol of remote grandeur.
(l) Intimacy of Smithy's and Paula's married life —bedroom as chief setting for these scenes.	Lack of intimacy of the Rainiers' married life—separate bedrooms.
(m) Smithy gives Paula a glass necklace as present on birth of child.	Rainier gives wife emerald necklace as present after successfully entertaining the Prime Minister.
(n) Smithy's separate train journey to Liverpool.	(Start of Part Three) Lady Rainier's separate train journey to what was formerly Mrs Deventer's inn.

These lists, in order of occurrence in Part One, suggest the multiplicity of narrative and enunciatory levels on which the film works to reinforce its underlying structural parallel, which, in turn, accounts for much of its power and for the way it foregrounds those psychological patterns considered in the next section.

SPECIAL FOCUS

Random Harvest has attracted surprisingly little serious criticism. Leslie Halliwell describes it as 'Sheer hokum with roses round the door, but persuasively produced in M-G-M's best manner';[15] Kingsley Canham's factually

---

[15] Leslie Halliwell, *The Filmgoer's Companion* (Granada: London, 1977), 596.

inaccurate account of the film describes how 'The natural co-incidences of soap opera build up . . . and all live happily ever after';[16] John Douglas Eames in *The M-G-M Story* wrote that Colman and Garson 'were guided by Mervyn LeRoy through the wonderful land of Amnesia, whose paths were paved with gold for moviemakers';[17] and Laurence J. Quirk, in one of the longest accounts of the film, claimed that it 'was just the ticket for 1942–3 audiences confronted daily with tragic war news'. While allowing 'its sympathetic treatment' and 'the restrained eloquent performances of the principals and supporting cast', he considered that, 'The coincidences and happenstances are worked up too patly, the psychology is shaky'.[18] And Hilton Tims writes of the 'fond remembrances [of audiences] which transcend the ludicrous contrivances of its plot and production'.[19] Even Jeffrey Richards, who writes persuasively of how the film projects an image of an ideal England,[20] does not explore in detail the psychological underpinning of the story, which, in the main, the film transfers from the novel, but stylizes and concentrates its manifestations in ways more compelling than the novel chooses.

Contemporary reviews tend to regard amnesia as a somewhat arbitrary plot device in furthering the affairs of what was seen as essentially a 'woman's film'. Lionel Collier in *Picturegoer* warned his readers not to 'try to analyse the plot of this picture';[21] *Today's Cinema*, noting that 'the amnesia theme has had a long screen innings', allows that, in this case, 'its appealing romantic by-play and near-tragic detail make for absorbing entertainment';[22] while the unnamed reviewer in *Kinematograph Weekly* finds it a 'gentle and appealing romantic drama' though 'the actual plot is not far removed from the novelette'.[23] These less pretentious sources were in fact less patronizing and obtuse than 'quality' critics like James Agee in America and C. A. Lejeune in England, whose dismissals of the film now seem curiously imperceptive in the face of what is offered, as well as offensively mandarin.[24]

One needs to remember that it is in the early 1940s that Freudian psychology begins to make its presence felt in Hollywood films. However, no one at the time (or later) seems to have considered *Random Harvest* seriously from such a potentially productive viewpoint. Later in the decade, Parker Tyler, believing that 'movies are dreamlike', assumes '(a) the existence of the

---

[16] Kingsley Canham, *The Hollywood Professionals*, vol. v (Tantivy Press: London, 1976), 159.

[17] John Douglas Eames, *The M-G-M Story* (Octopus: London, 1979), 177.

[18] Lawrence J. Quirk, *The Great Romantic Films* (Citadel Press: Secaucus, NJ, 1974), 107.

[19] Hilton Tims, *Emotion Pictures: The 'Women's Picture', 1930–55* (Columbus Books: London, 1987), 149.

[20] Richards, *Visions of Yesterday*, 110.

[21] Lionel Collier, 'Random Harvest', *Picturegoer*, 12/575 (6 Mar. 1943), 12.

[22] C.A.W., 'Random Harvest', *Today's Cinema*, 1 Jan. 1943, p. 2.

[23] *Kinematograph Weekly*, Jan. 1943.

[24] Agee recommended the film to 'those who can stay interested in Ronald Colman's amnesia for two hours and who could with pleasure eat a bowl of Yardley's shaving soap for breakfast' (*The Nation*, 26 Dec. 1942, in *Agee on Film* (McDowell, Oblonsky: New York, 1958), 24). C. A. Lejeune, relentlessly witty, thought it a 'Chips off Mrs. Henry Wood' (*The Observer*, 21 Jan. 1943).

unconscious mind as a dynamic factor in human action and (b) the tendency of screen stories to emphasize—unintentionally—neuroses and psycho-pathic traits discovered and formulated by psychoanalysis'.[25] When, a page further on, he writes of Hollywood's response to the mythic, to 'the basic vestigial patterns surviving in popular imagination and reflecting the uncon-scious desires', one can only regret that he did not address himself to *Random Harvest*. The 1940s Hollywood output offers a rich field for the investigation of psychological patterns at work in mainstream film and in recent years has begun to receive it. So far it has not yielded a full account of *Random Harvest*, though Barbara Deming's 1969 book, *Running away from Myself*,[26] in spite of an irritating facetiousness, does consider the film in ways that draw attention to its psychological structuring. Freud hovers over many key films of the 1940s in their concern with repression as a narrative generator and in their anxious search for reassurance. It will be clear how such an account might apply to *Random Harvest*.

My purpose here is not to offer the sort of detailed psychoanalytic reading which more recent feminist criticism has brought to bear on Hollywood melodrama,[27] particularly on 'women's films' such as *Now Voyager*. Instead, I want to show that the *psychological patterns* which exist at the deepest levels of 'story' in novel and film constitute an important element of potential transfer in the processes of transposition. They are not tied to 'the writing'; and one would expect them to be transferable in the way that the major cardinal functions are, albeit acquiring a different mode of signification. In order to explore the degree of transfer at this level in *Random Harvest*, I have chosen to comment briefly on:

1. the search for identity;
2. patterns of sexual differentiation and relationship;
3. variations on motifs of suppression and repression; and
4. Utopian dreams.

The Search for Identity

In both novel and film, Rainier's amnesia is the central narrative fact. His search for his full identity requires him to find the answer to that portion of his life between being shell-shocked and being knocked down by a car in a Liverpool street. If the search for identity may be seen as inextricably bound

[25] Parker Tyler, 'Preface to First American Edition', *Magic and Myth of the Movies* (1947; repr. Secker and Warburg: London, 1971), 28.

[26] Barbara Deming, *Running away from Myself* (Grossman Publishers: New York, 1969). Its provocative subtitle is 'A dream portrait of America drawn from the films of the forties'; *Random Harvest* is discussed in ch. 4.

[27] See, for instance, Christine Gledhill (ed.), *Home is Where the Heart is: Studies in Melodrama and the Woman's Film* (BFI Publishing: London, 1987).

up with the normal processes of maturation in every human being, a coming
to terms with the forces at work within one and with the awareness of the
world around one, the amnesiac's search is complicated by the formidable
obstacle of the knowledge of a missing period in his life. In Rainier's case, the
missing period has included the events most distressing and most perfectly
happy in his life.

In the asylum from which he escapes on Armistice night 1918, Rainier had
been given the name Smith, one of the commonest of all English names, as
a first step towards establishing—or manufacturing—an identity for him.
Both novel and film use this means of identification and in both he tells Paula
that this is not his real name; in the final moment of each text, in the present
tense of each, as it were, he responds to Paula's calling him Smithy in a way
that completes his sense of identity. Ironically, to respond to that false name
clinches for him the full truth about himself. And in both novel and film, as
if to stress that a name is no more than a label, though one to which a person
may attach a sense of self, Paula in telling Smithy *her* name, says, 'It's not my
real name, though.'

Tied to Smithy's search for identity is a seeking to *belong*. The following
exchange of dialogue from the novel, in which Paula speaks to Smithy,
comes from Part Four:

'Isn't there some way of tracing any of your relatives and friends? Advertising for
them, or something like that?'
'They've tried. Some people did come to see me at the hospital once, but—I
wasn't their son.'
'I'll bet they were disappointed. You'd make a nice son for somebody.'
'Well, *I* was disappointed too. I'd like to have belonged to them—to have had a
home somewhere.' (p. 191)

The film picks up the idea contained here and very movingly dramatizes the
suggestions in segment 2 in its opening sequence set in the asylum. Benet the
psychiatrist discusses with an elderly couple, Mr and Mrs Lloyd, the possibility that one of the shell-shocked patients may be their son. In a waiting-
room, Smithy sits in uniform, saying the name Lloyd to himself, as Benet and
the Lloyds appear first through frosted-glass windows, then in the doorway.
The camera cuts between the Lloyds and Smith, who is not their son, and
Mrs Lloyd is led off in tears. Smithy later, in Paula's dressing-room, tells her,
'I'd like to have belonged to them', in an exact echo from the novel.

The notion of belonging is pursued through his association with the
theatre company (much more fully developed in the novel than in the film)
and through his return to Random Hall (the novel's 'Stourton'). Restored to
his pre-shell-shock identity, he finds he belongs—effortlessly but without
much sense of warmth or pleasure—to a large, squabbling family. The novel
records that he decided to leave Stourton, because 'he felt that he was

causing a disturbance, and the disturbance disturbed him just as much as the others' (p. 83): the disturbance is the result of his not being able to explain the missing period in his life. The film is more explicit about his incapacity fully to belong to the life of Random Hall when he shows the family the key he carries:

> 'The key to your house?' Kitty asks.
> 'If I knew that, I'd know where I belonged.'
> 'You belong here Uncle Charles.' (Segment 18)

It thus makes clear that the issue of belonging is caught up with the knowledge of his full identity, which now includes the lost years as Smithy; and when the family has gone he is left looking isolated in the empty house.

Patterns of Sexual Differentiation and Relationship

Connection with the search for identity

Smithy's wish to belong is a key element in his search for identity. When he meets Paula, there is a strong sense that he, with no memory of parents and having failed to find them in the Lloyds, finds in her at first both mother and father. Both novel and film are very clear about the strongly protective, *parental* element in Paula's growing love for Smithy and the element of the grateful child in his response to and reliance upon her. Through the security which she offers him, he learns to talk again; when this is threatened by the arrival at the pub of the warden from the asylum and by the suggestion that Paula may leave him, he regresses at once, unable to form his words. The novel is in fact more explicit about the parental aspect of her early feeling for him:

Without undressing, except to slip off her shoes, she lifted the blankets and lay down beside him. He felt her nearness slowly, luxuriously, a relaxation of every nerve. 'Tell you what, old boy, I'm just like a mother tonight, so cuddle up close as you like and keep warm . . . Good night, Smithy.'
. . . Presently, as he lay listening, he fell asleep in her arms. (pp. 200–1)

In the early stages of their acquaintance, theirs is clearly a parent–child relationship.

Towards an equal relationship

Both texts record their flight to safety. The film shears away a good deal of the novel's detail in leading up to an acknowledgment of mutual love, and in doing so highlights the pattern of its development which the novel records in this sentence: 'And he knew, too, that his feeling for Paula was no longer an eagerness to submit, like a child; but something positive, strong enough to demand equality, if there were ever to be any further relationship between them at all' (p. 214). The film postpones the declaration of his love until he has received his first cheque as a writer: the confidence that this gives him confers a sufficient sense of equality to enable him to propose. The happiness of the marriage that follows may, in psychological terms, be seen as the product of a healthy ego ('whose business it . . . is to discover the most favourable and least perilous method of obtaining satisfaction, taking the external world into account'[28]) working harmoniously with the id, uninhibited by the superego of his upper-middle-class background and training. The film's structure stresses the idyllic nature of this period of his life through the contrasting occasions of his marriage to Paula and the wedding rehearsal with Kitty. As Paula enters the church, he turns to look at her with a love born of perfect confidence, and the recollection of this movement creates a powerful emotional resonance in the blank lost look he turns on Kitty in the chapel.

The rupture of an idyll

'And d'you know, I don't *want* to remember anything now—anything I've forgotten. It would be so—so unimportant. My life began with you, and my future goes on with you—there's nothing else, Paula.' (p. 278)

Smithy speaks these words to Paula at the end of Part Four of the novel just before setting out for Liverpool. In the novel, he knows Paula is pregnant; in the film, as if to underline Smithy's new maturity, their son has been born before he leaves. From the role of dependent child, he has been nurtured back into physical and psychic health, has adjusted again to the external world, has found in Paula a focus for a full sexual love, and the idyll is completed by fatherhood and the prospect of a profession that will draw on his talents. When this idyll is shattered by the Liverpool accident and he returns to Stourton/Random Hall, he is returned to a number of roles: to upper-middle-class gentleman, brother, and son to a father who, in the novel, is dying, in the film has just died. The film, that is, ruptures the idyll more decisively by wrenching Smithy away from Paula and his child to return him to the role of son to a just-dead father. In this setting the demands of the superego assume their old force and the idyll of sexual and familial bliss with Paula and the child is utterly repressed.

Parents and children

From himself being full of pride in the birth of his son, the film's Rainier is returned to the role of the son who asks the butler as they stand before the father's portrait:

---

[28] Sigmund Freud, *An Outline of Psycho-analysis*, trans. and ed. James Strachy (Hogarth Press: London, 1973), 5.

'I wonder what he would have liked us to do?'

'I think he'd have liked you to carry on where he left off'

replies Sheldon. Smithy/Rainier has lost his new life at the point of father-hood and regained the old in which his own wishes must be subservient to what his father might have liked. In this sense his return to his pre-shell-shock identity constitutes a regression from the level of maturity he has reached in his relationship with Paula. And, as if to stress the loss of equality of relationship, the film has Rainier come close to marriage with a girl young enough to be his daughter (Colman was in fact 51, Susan Peters, who played Kitty, was 21), whereas in the novel the disparity is only eleven years. In the matter of parent–child relationships the film recognizes the tightness of patterns suggested by the novel.

Symbols and sexuality

Rainier's recurrent playing with the *key*, the door for which he doesn't know, is a clear symbolic representation of a phallic search. He is married to someone with whom he does not have a sexual relationship because he is dimly but disturbingly aware of a prior emotional and sexual commitment to someone now lost, someone who, if he could find her again, would open to him as the right door will to the key. The novel dramatizes the same sense of sexual suppression, of a conserving of the sexual self, until the proper object for its expression is refound. The novel uses an image of landscape—of two hills in the hollow between which lay a little pool in which Smithy had once bathed and to which he returns—to represent the missing portion of Smithy and Paula's lives. It is a less direct image than the film's but there is no mistaking the same psychological action at work in the two images. In the novel, this image of landscape is shared by Paula and Smithy; in Freudian terms, *landscapes* are referred to as 'representing the female genitals [but] *hills* and *rocks* are symbols of the male organ'.[29] The film uses the image of the key as the symbol of Smithy's search and longing, and the image of jewellery as the symbol of Paula's lost happiness. There is the pretty, cheap necklace Smithy gives her in the first glow of paternity and the once-royal emerald pendant Rainier gives her as a reward for her hostessing skills. Whether MGM had Freud in mind or not is irrelevant: the power of the image—the *double* image in this case—remains; and it seems almost too neat to find Freud writing in his chapter on 'Symbolism in Dreams': 'Another symbol of the female genitals which deserves mention is a *jewel-case*. *Jewel* and *treasure* are used in dreams as well as in waking life to describe someone who is loved.'[30]

[29] Sigmund Freud, *Introductory Lectures on Psychoanalysis* (Penguin: Harmondsworth, 1974), 192.
[30] Ibid. 190.

In the period of 'perfect love', the id is comparatively unconstrained by the superego. The period in which Rainier's 'old' memory returns, and during which he shoulders responsibility for the family company, engages in political life, suppresses sexual instinct while contracting a marriage of convenience, may be seen as one in which the superego is dominant, the id denied appropriate expression. In the final scene, when the key causes the door of the ideal cottage to swing open, when a mature, permitted, wholly mutual love is recognized, it could be said that the ego is satisfying simultaneously the demands of the id, of the superego, and of reality. What superior critics may dismiss as 'hokum' is, for such reasons, received unconsciously by the mass andience as profoundly satisfactory.

Patterns of Repression and Suppression

Suppression normally refers to conscious, voluntary inhibition of activity in contrast to repression, which is unconscious, automatic, and instigated by anxiety, not by an act of will.[31]

Whereas Freud used the term 'repression' to define 'a mental process arising from the conflict between the pleasure principle and the reality principle',[32] without distinguishing between conscious and unconscious processes, most later psychological writing reserves 'repression' to refer to the unconscious process, 'suppression' to the conscious. Both seem to me clearly at work in *Random Harvest* and these later glosses on the term 'repression' are particularly useful in distinguishing the patterns of behaviour exhibited by Paula and Smithy/Rainier.

Repression, then, seems the more accurate term to use in relation to the amnesiac who has no control over what knowledge of his past is denied to his consciousness, and Smithy is twice its victim. In both novel and film, sometimes a word or an object or a voice will fleetingly strike a responsive chord. For example, hearing the psychiatrist's voice in the restaurant in which Rainier proposes to Kitty, or the organist's playing the hymn, 'O perfect love', at their wedding rehearsal, distracts him from the present with its unplaceable echo of the past. No amount of conscious cerebration, however, can arrest the fleetingness of the impression or place it in relation to the context in which he first heard either voice or hymn. The film times these two intimations of what Rainier has repressed in such a way as to draw attention to the inappropriateness of his proposed marriage to Kitty, as if to suggest that he is dimly aware of a deeper emotional commitment in his repressed past.

[31] Charles Ryecroft, *A Critical Dictionary of Psycho-analysis* (Nelson: London, 1968), 161.
[32] David Stafford-Clark, *What Freud 'Really' Said* (Penguin: Harmondsworth, 1967), 211.

Because 'what cinema needs is external action, not introspective psychology',[33] the film must find visual correlatives for the kinds of suppression and repression which underlie its—and the novel's—story. In Rainier's case, it picks up this sentence from the novel in which Harrison says: 'I felt that one thing Miss Hobbs had said about him *was* true—the look in his eyes as if he were searching for something and couldn't find it' (p. 27). The key, attached to his watch-chain, is an externalization of his sense of inner loss, and one of the excellences of Colman's performance is the worried remoteness of expression which at certain crucial moments suggests a mind striving—vainly—to call up what is repressed.

In Paula's case, the *suppression* she has found necessary to cope with her life—as secretary, as wife to Rainier, the industrial prince—is externalized in matters of dress and facial expression. Further, her background as an actress is peculiarly well chosen: to succeed as an actress requires suppression of self in the interests of creating a new sense of character. The novel draws specific attention to this aspect of her function: for instance, Woburn, the librarian, comments on her social skill of remembering names when she introduces people (p. 52). Mrs Rainier (MGM characteristically gives Rainier a knighthood so that Paula's hurdling of social barriers from actress to *Lady* Rainier becomes the more striking), it is made clear, is playing her role with consummate skill. In doing so, she suppresses the truth of her connection with Rainier. The film renders the process of suppression through: (i) costumes which contrast with the actress's frilly garb, first in the secretarial suits, then in Lady Rainier's sumptuous *décolletage*; and (ii) facial expressions and posture that suggest cool efficiency and, later, social facility, both in contrast with the openness and warmth of the actress, but no doubt in part deriving from the actress's skill. These latter permit the externalization of the processes of suppression: one is aware of the performance and of what it overlays. And part of Garson's skill is to keep one aware of this performance-within-a-performance, as it were.

In the film's final scene, where id and superego are in happy relation to reality, it may also be said that what is suppressed and what is repressed are both brought simultaneously to an open expression.

Utopian Dreams

How can I help loving England? England with the quiet lawns and the great trees in which the roots are *always* restless; England whose summer is *eternal* April, whose winter is a *sleep* broken with distant laughter.[34]

---

[33] Christopher Williams, *Realism and the Cinema* (Routledge and Kegan Paul/BFI: London, 1980), 169.
[34] Beverley Nichols, 'All these I Love', *Cry Havoc*, quoted in Knox (ed.), *For Ever England*, 86.

Part of the immense appeal of *Random Harvest* in 1941 (novel) and 1943 (film)
may perhaps be attributed to its seeming to posit the existence of an attain-
able Utopia *where nothing changes*. Beverley Nichols's vision of England,
quoted above, significantly stresses its unchanging beauties, not as facts but
as symbols of a longing for a secure Utopia located in a pre-war past. By 1943
certainly, there was a strongly nostalgic element in MGM's view of an
England of rustic streams, friendly pubs, cheery music hall, and stately
home, and that is precisely the point. This England, epitomized above all in
the blossom-wreathed cottage, stands for something stable, threatened by
intervening disorders both personal and national, but ultimately not inacces-
sible. In the early 1940s this image, no less powerful for being idealized,
represented a time before the war, a way of life threatened by the present
strife. My point here is not so much a sociological as a psychological
one: whether one is English or not, there is, the film (especially) suggests,
'somewhere quiet and lovely' (Paula's words) to which we can all return
if we can only find the door to which the key belongs. That is, we can
bear chaos and disorder as long as we can believe in the existence of such an
ideal.

An amnesiac's elusively apprehended sense of a world of perfect happiness, of freedom from the harassing or numbing constraints of everyday life,
becomes a perfect analogue for a mass audience's longing for a dream world.
In this film—and the film dramatizes this notion much more powerfully and
explicitly than the novel, perhaps because it *is* American rather than English—this dream world is equated with a mythic view of England. An England where nothing ever changes, an England also celebrated in verse and
song[35] at the time, becomes a symbol of Utopian yearning. This yearning is
there in Hilton's novel; it has been transferred to *and* adapted for the film. At
one point in the film, Colman's Rainier says, 'Why should I have a sense of
loss so acute—' and Garson finishes the line with, 'That it's spoiling your
life?' Rainier's sense of 'loss', which the film represents by a missing memory
of idyllic happiness, must have been especially resonant in the early 1940s,
offering an objective correlative for everyman's longing for the simple joy he
associates with times past. The amnesiac's retrieval of that piece of his past
that makes him whole again offers a profound, analogical reassurance to
audiences fearing that a loved past—or at least a past gentled by time and the
contrast of present discord—may be lost.

Jeffrey Richards is sociologically right when he says, 'Ironically, it is the
war which finally destroys it [the dream]'[36] but the film's continued power to
engross and move the spectator depends on its reaching layers of perhaps

---

[35] cf. Alice Duer Miller's enormously popular verse novella, *The White Cliffs* (eleven editions in 1941
alone), and songs, popularized by Vera Lynn, such as 'There'll always be an England'.
[36] Richards, *Visions of Yesterday*, 110.

only semi-conscious yearning for 'perfect love' (the film's hymn tune is shrewdly chosen) and freedom from everyday inadequacies.

Though there is a touch of flippancy elsewhere in Richard's account of the MGM version of Hilton, hardly anyone else has been as shrewd about this remarkable film. As an adaptation, it is utterly confident and streamlined; it is an example *par excellence* of MGM's 'prestige' production factory, providing a very limousine among star vehicles; its structural felicities reveal a striking psychological patterning; and its version of Hollywood's England is magisterial.

Pip (Anthony Wager) and Miss Havisham (Martita Hunt) in David Lean's *Great Expectations.*

3

Great Expectations (1946)

THE idea of Dickens's amenability to the film medium dies hard. It has had almost mythic status since Eisenstein all but enshrined Dickens as the fore-father of cinematic narrative. One sees in a general way some of his points (e.g. that he found in Dickens the basis for Griffith's idea of parallel editing) but closer scrutiny of aspects of Dickens's style suggests that many of his effects are indissolubly linked to the verbal medium. However, there is no denying that Dickens has been the most often filmed of the classic authors. *Great Expectations* alone has been filmed five times (two silent, three sound) but only David Lean's 1946 version for Cineguild has acquired anything like classic status as a film and as an adaptation of Dickens. My particular interest in *Great Expectations* as a case-study of adaptation lies in: (*a*) its way of addressing itself to the problem of the novel's first-person narration; and (*b*) how far Lean has sought to find a visual stylistic verve that may be compared to the novel's peculiar rhetorical power.

NARRATIVE AND TRANSFER

Structural Patterns: The Novel

Serial form

Great Expectations was first published in serial form. It appeared in thirty-six weekly instalments of *All the Year Round* from December 1860 to August 1861, each instalment consisting of one or, more commonly, two chapters of the novel as it was finally published. No doubt there are implications for the novelist who must retain a grip on his readers' interest from instalment to instalment: for example, the plotting of climactic moments to ensure a focus for each instalment, and the need to leave the reader at the end of one instalment with a narrative question to be answered in the next. However, as Julian Poole has noted, *Great Expectations* is structurally 'a much more accomplished piece of engineering' than *Oliver Twist*, in which 'the cliff-hanger endings of many of the . . . instalments are obtrusive, owing some-thing to the immaturity of Dickens's writing at this stage and to the fact that each instalment had to bridge a month's gap'.[1] The serial form in which *Great Expectations* first appeared has, as a result partly of the weekly continuity, partly of the integrating presence of Pip as narrator, much less of the episodic in its structure than the earlier novel which Lean also filmed.

Pip's education: a drama in three parts

As the drama of Pip's moral education, *Great Expectations* is divided into three virtually equal parts:

Part I—the childhood and youth leading up to the acquiring of his expectations;

Part II—learning to live up to these expectations;

Part III—adjusting to the dissipation of his expectations.

In the serialization of the novel, each of these parts occupied twelve instalments of, respectively, 19, 20, and 21 chapters, the figures pointing to the extremely careful structuring which underpins the novels and is manifested at many levels.

Part I ends with Pip's departure for London with its potential for the enlargement of his life, a notion expressed in the final sentence of chapter 19: 'And the mists had all solemnly risen now, and the world lay spread before me' (p. 162).[2] The influences at work on Pip's life in Part I are of two kinds: those pushing him, urging him to break away from his present constricting circumstances; and those large, sometimes vaguely alluring forces which draw him on. This distinction is not intended to make the structuring impulses sound too clear-cut and diagrammatic; the two kinds of forces too obviously interrelate for that to be the case. The forge and Satis House work together—one pushing, one pulling—to promote Pip's growth: what he sees in Satis House, specifically Estella, but, more generally, intimations of passion and imagination, helps tighten the oppressive sense of confinement the forge has come to be in his view. Further, whereas Satis House leads out towards London, the forge is tied to the marshes and to the chief basis of Pip's childhood guilt: his association with the convict Magwitch. It is a powerful irony that Pip believes it is Satis House which causes his removal to London, thus extending the new world it has opened up to him, whereas it is in fact the forge world, including the convict on the marshes, which is the true source of his great expectations and his London life.

Part II intensifies the novel's ironic structuring procedures. The opening out that London was to mean in Pip's life proves to be the scene of his moral slackening, though that is not to say that Dickens is nostalgic for the old

[1] Julian Poole 'Novel–Film; Dickens–Lean: A study of *Great Expectations* and *Oliver Twist*'. Unpublished thesis (University of East Anglia, 1979), 29.

[2] Charles Dickens, *Great Expectations* (1860) (Thomas Nelson & Sons: Edinburgh, no publication date given but approx. 1960), 162. (Subsequent references given in brackets as they occur.)

village simplicities ('Dickens holds no brief for village life,'[3] writes Mrs Leavis with terse accuracy). The London Pip comes to know is built on an abattoir and a gaol, on the seedy paraphernalia of the law, on the oppressed lives of many subsisting beneath and supporting a foolish 'Society'. Pip's life here is one of the footling accomplishments which pass for a gentleman's education, of snobbery, absurd extravagance, and 'an inability to settle to anything' (p. 317). The illusoriness of Pip's idea of the gentleman's life is painfully felt. Further, in Part II, despite Pip's having risen in the world, Estella has become not more but less available: Pip escorts her about the fashionable world but makes no inroad upon her feelings. His love for her does not constitute an opening out or enrichment of his life; increasingly, it is a source of oppressive unhappiness for him.

The pervasive taint of guilt and shame which Pip feels is intensified by his dealings with the lawyer Jaggers, but most of all by the return of Magwitch at the end of Part II. It is his childhood meeting with Magwitch that has awakened him to guilt (he *has* stolen for Magwitch, whatever his motives) and his entire upbringing has reinforced a sense of his being unwanted and unworthy. Satis House and Estella have added shame to guilt, and the return of Magwitch brings the guilt to the surface again and gives Pip his most powerful reason yet for shame in relation to Estella. The irony that the source of this shame is Estella's convict father awaits disclosure, but at this point, at the end of Part II, Pip is only aware of the lesser irony: that the source of his becoming a gentleman can only succeed in separating him farther from Estella, the reason for his aspirations. Part II ends, as Part I does, on a note in which the realistic notation of time and place imperceptibly blends with the symbolic. The scene—inner as well as outer—is set for Pip's descent into a maelstrom of suffering which must be endured before regeneration is effected.

Part III moves from 'groping around in the darkness' (p. 329) to the sober optimism of the novel's last sentence in which the narrator records: 'as the morning mists had risen long ago when I first left the forge, so the evening mists were rising now, and in all the broad expanse of tranquil light they showed to me, I saw no shadow of another parting from her' (p. 491). There is no need to labour the structural purpose of the three parts with their endings which so invite comparison. Part III is centred on the disappearance of Pip's expectations when he decides he can no longer use Magwitch's money and the moral reclamation that follows in the wake of that decision. Magwitch comes to the forefront of the novel here as the major influence of Pip's life: in overcoming his abhorrence of Magwitch and the origin of his expectations, Pip acquires a new purposiveness. He must lose almost everything—wealth, happiness, nearly life itself—before he can acquire a sense of

---

[3] Q. D. Leavis, 'How We Must Read *Great Expectations*', in F. R. Leavis and Q. D. Leavis, *Dickens the Novelist* (Penguin: Harmondsworth, 1972), 392.

earnt competence. Expectations have been replaced by the solid bourgeois virtue of honest industry and by true appraisals of the people who have influenced his life.

The ending

Bulwer Lytton persuaded Dickens to alter the original, bleaker ending to the novel,[4] and there has been controversy about the decision. Humphry House believes it is 'artistically wrong'[5] whereas Mrs Leavis argues for its being 'a true symbol of the successful end of Pip's pilgrimage'.[6] It strikes a note of tentative reconciliation between two people who have been so sobered by experience as only now truly to understand each other.

The idea of the three parts, with their clear patterns, their parallels and contrasts, may sound unduly schematic, but this is not the effect in reading. The deployment of what Barthes designates as 'integrational' functions,[7] diffusively pervasive in their effects on the narrative, ensures that tight thematic and structural organization does not become merely diagrammatic.

Parallels and contrasts

Any narrative is likely to make use of repetition and variation through the sort of parallelism which highlights both similarity and dissimilarity. The drama of Pip's great expectations is heightened by the comparison it offers with that of the expectations of other characters in the novel. Pip's career as the village boy catapulted into metropolitan society contrasts with those of:

(a) Herbert, who, with no expectations, succeeds by effort and some discreetly applied financial support;
(b) Estella, who, like Pip, is used as the object of someone else's ambition;
(c) Mr Wopsle, the village parish-clerk, who vainly seeks fame on the London stage;
(d) Bentley Drummle, born to upper-class expectations, but achieving nothing but a sneering boorishness;
(e) Orlick, the blacksmith's assistant, whose attempt to change his position is thwarted by Pip, and who exacts near-fatal vengeance.

The parallelism between Pip and Estella, each the victim of someone else's aspirations, is of course the most important. Herbert, unlike them, is the object of benign interference in the course of his life; the interference which

---

[4] See John Forster's account of this in his *The Life of Dickens* (1872–4) (J. M. Dent: London, 1966), 289.
[5] Humphry House, *The Dickens World* (Oxford University Press: London, 1976), 157.
[6] Leavis, 'How We Must Read *Great Expectations*', 427.
[7] Roland Barthes, 'Introduction to the Structural Analysis of Narratives', *Image-Music-Text*, trans. Stephen Heath (Fontana Paperbacks: Glasgow, 1977), 92.

renders Pip and Estella mere puppets threatens their entire development as human beings. By comparison with Pip, Estella remains a shadowy figure, a conception rather than a fully imagined character. Mrs Leavis claims that Estella 'has gone through a process comparable with Pip's self-knowledge and humiliation so that they can truly come together at last'.[8] However, despite the correspondences Dickens creates between the two characters, and their situations, I think we are a good deal required to take on trust that Estella is as she is and that Miss Havisham's upbringing has been able to educate all feeling out of her.

A full account of the narrative structure of *Great Expectations* would include discussion of such matters as: the relation of children to parents and surrogate parents; the impact of childish guilt on subsequent development; the continuing discourse on the relations between expectations and effort, between wealth and true gentility. These thematic concerns are bodied forth in one of Dickens's most maturely structured, ironically controlled narratives.

Structural Patterns: The Film

Pip's education: a drama in three 'parts'

The film does not make the same clear division into three parts that the novel does, though it is still plain that it retains the overall movement of the novel. That is, the childhood and youth leading up to the acquiring of his expectations and departure for London (cf. novel's Part I) gives way to Pip's London life, in which he learns to live up to his expectations until their source is revealed (cf. novel's Part II), after which he adjusts to the dissipation of his expectations (cf. novel's Part III). The end of 'Part II' in the film (the return of Magwitch) is marked by a quite long fade but so are several other important sequences, and the end of 'Part I', Pip's departure for London, is marked only by a dissolve, a technique common throughout the film. In fact, continuity rather than break is stressed here by means of a montage depicting Pip's journey to London.

In rendering a novel of approximately 500 pages in a film of a little under two hours, it will be obvious that a good deal of selection and compression is necessary. These processes are not, however, spread evenly over the film, the most striking shift in emphasis lying in the truncation of Part II of the novel. In terms of running time, the film's 'Part I' takes 39 per cent, 'Part II' only 27 per cent, and 'Part III' takes 34 per cent. In reducing the length of the film's central section, Lean has greatly compressed the processes of Pip's education as a gentleman. These are reduced to a few comments on table manners by Herbert Pocket during their first dinner together at Barnard's

---

[8] Leavis, 'How We Must Read *Great Expectations*', 426.

Inn (segment 24, see Appendix 3) and a series of fifteen rapid shots (51 seconds altogether) in which we see Pip's lessons in dancing, fencing, and boxing. Ten seconds later, after a shot of Pip's asking for more money in Jaggers's office, there is a brief segment (45 seconds) of Pip and Herbert's 'At Home' in Barnard's Inn, followed by their adding up their debts. Pip, by ironic implication, has completed his education as a gentleman. The adding up of the debts works as a metonymic representation of Pip's foolish, spendthrift London life.

'Part I' of the film most nearly replicates the action of the corresponding section of the novel, though even here are several omissions (the characters of Orlick and Trabb's boy, particularly) and Mrs Joe dies much earlier than in the novel, and by natural causes. This change is linked with the omission of Orlick, who attacks her (in Part I) and tries to murder Pip (in Part III). Orlick, it may be argued, represents certain darker, repressed impulses at work in Pip, who might like to abuse his shrewish sister if he dared. Indeed, the narrating Pip says: 'I was at first disposed to believe that I must have had some hand in the attack on my sister . . .' (p. 120). To omit Orlick is seriously to deplete the working out of the theme of guilt and shame and the taint of prison, which so haunt the novel's Pip. Further, the film's London sequences, apart from brief shots of criminals being hanged and of the supplicants who loiter about Jaggers's door, also fail to develop the idea, so that the filmed Pip's motivations become correspondingly less complex.

The film's 'Part III' is concerned, like the novel's, with Pip's adjustment to the loss of his expectations, with his helping Magwitch to escape and the moral regeneration implied in his growing tenderness for the convict, his loss of Estella when she marries Bentley Drummle, and their final reconciliation. Such an account, however, elides certain important omissions and alterations. Without Orlick, there is no occasion for Pip's fight for his life in the deserted sluice house and he is thus not brought face to face with the extremity of evil represented by Orlick. By omitting Herbert's romance with Clara and Pip's secret help in financing Herbert, two elements are lost: a comparison with Pip's own unhappy love for Estella and one of the few acts of positive good he is shown to do. To some extent this latter omission is compensated for by the changes in the final sequence in which Pip plays a much more vigorously active role than in the novel.

The ending—and a new beginning?

Perhaps the film's major change in terms of narrative structure is that relating to the novel's ending. There is no suggestion that Pip might ever have considered marrying Biddy ('Much too old an actress—looks three times the age of Pip',[9] one critic noted about Eileen Erskine in the role), when he

---

[9] Julian Moynahan, 'Seeing the Book, Reading the Movie', in Michael Klein and Gillian Parker (eds.), *The English Novel and the Movies* (Frederick Ungar: New York, 1981), 48.

returns to Joe's house. Thus, his final reconciliation with Estella is not seen
in the context of his failed good intentions about Biddy. Whereas he and
Estella, in the novel, meet in the ruins of Satis House, as though shorn of
everything but devotion to each other (the benefactor of each is dead, their
benefactions now gone, Biddy married to Joe, Drummle dead), in the film
Pip comes upon Estella in the still-standing Satis House. She appears to have
taken up Miss Havisham's old position by the fireplace in the darkened
room. Pip savagely tears down the rotted curtains, opens the shutters, and,
as the light floods in, successfully exhorts Estella to leave this 'dead house'.
They run down the garden path and through the gates as the words 'GREAT
EXPECTATIONS' are superimposed over them. Though the film's ending has
been described as 'facile'[10] and as 'the one fatal flaw [which] is that of the
book itself—the happy ending',[11] it may be seen as a reconciliation of the
film's dramatization of the class conflict, its protagonists now having been
openly made equals in terms of background.

Now, it may be claimed that the film's more buoyant ending ('pure
movieland,'[12] chides Moynahan) merely rounds off in more conventional
terms a film which has chosen to stress the romantic at the expense of the
darker aspects of the lives of the central pair. Despite the loss of his inheritance, that is, Pip, who has overcome his snobbery and realized the warmth
and value of the lower orders (Joe, Magwitch), still wins the woman of his
dreams. As Raymond Durgnat writes: 'Estella will give Pip a cool, chastened,
grateful hand; his future is with the upper-middle-class image after all'.[13] The
orphan boy who eventually succeeds to a more prosperous future was
perhaps an apt hero for post-World War II Britain; and, with hindsight, it
does not seem fanciful to see the tearing down of the rotten drapes to let the
light into the gloom of Satis House, an invention for the film, as a metaphoric letting in of light on British life at large after the rigours of the war
years. In its scrutiny of class structure, in the significance of Satis House as
the symbol of an ossified attitude to wealth and class, of a structure that *needs*
dismantling, *Great Expectations* may be seen as very much a product of its
time and place. Fanciful or not, as Pip and Estella, both now aware of the
background to their gentrification, finally leave Satis House and the past it
represents, one is led to have more in mind than the famous novel whose
title Lean's film bears.

Parallels and contrasts

A good deal of the structural solidity and thematic coherence of Dickens's
novel depends on the exploitation of parallelism between Pip's situation and

---

[10] Gavin Lambert, 'British Films 1947: Survey and Prospect', *Sequence 2* (Winter 1947), 10.
[11] Ivan Butler, *Cinema in Britain: An Illustrated Survey* (A. S. Barnes: New York, 1973), 163.
[12] Moynahan, 'Seeing the Book', 151.
[13] Raymond Durgnat, *A Mirror for England* (Faber and Faber: London, 1970), 23.

that of several other characters. Inevitably, the film is forced to reduce the number of such parallels in the interests of narrative economy and clarity. In fact, the only one which is really maintained with any seriousness is that between Pip and Estella; it is perhaps even strengthened by having Estella realize in the end that her own history is no more elevated (actually, less so) than Pip's. There is certainly a structural narrowing involved here, perhaps dictated by the film's need to focus more firmly on the central 'romantic leads' rather than to retain the more complex moral and psychological overtones of the novel in which there are more developed parallels with Herbert, with Orlick and Wopsle (both omitted from the film, though Wopsle's name is given to Mr Hubble at the Christmas table), and with Drummle. The relations between expectations, or their absence, and morality reflect in various ways on Pip's drama, and in either deleting or minimizing these the film offers a thinner experience, particularly in regard to how Pip is presented. John Mills's performance has charm and authority but, with fewer surfaces for his Pip to be reflected in, there is less of him to be seen.

Those other thematic concerns which grow out of and enrich Pip's story—the relation of children to parents and surrogate parents, and the shifting relations between expectations and effort, for example—are almost invariably diminished in subtlety and complexity. By use of terms like 'reduce' and 'diminish', I do not intend to suggest that the film, as an adaptation, is entirely at a disadvantage vis-à-vis the source work. Later in this chapter, I shall consider the kinds of richness the film achieves and how far these derive from the novel.

Transfer of Narrative Functions

Of the novels chosen as case-studies to test the possibilities of a more rigorously objective approach to the study of films derived from novels, Great Expectations is considerably the most complex in its structure. It has a multiplicity of narrative strands and, consequently, of major cardinal functions. Sometimes, perhaps owing to its initial serial publication, a whole new location and set of characters, or a major break in time, will obscure the consequential connection of two actions.

Major cardinal functions

Listed below are those key cardinal functions which reverberate most significantly in the novel and, in an adjacent column, those which have been transferred to the film or omitted or altered in important ways. This will indicate how far Lean and his co-scriptwriters have chosen to adhere to the narrative line of the original. Despite the necessary truncating of a long and complex verbal narrative to produce a 113-minute[14] film, it will be seen that a surprising number of major cardinal functions have been retained. The *story* in both novel and film depends from two narrative 'facts': Pip's first terrified encounter with Magwitch in the churchyard; and his visit to Satis House where he meets Miss Havisham and her adopted child, Estella. In both novel and film, the essential narrative development is rooted in these two meetings.

In the two texts, the major cardinal functions may be summarized as follows:

NOVEL	FILM
1. Pip meets Magwitch in village churchyard.	As for novel.
2. Pip steals food and file for Magwitch.	As for novel.
3. Soldiers capture Magwitch and second convict, Compeyson.	As for novel.
4. Pip visits Satis House, meets Miss Havisham and Estella.	As for novel (+Death of Mrs Joe; Biddy's arrival)
5. Stranger at inn gives Pip a shilling wrapped in two pound notes, and stirs grog with Joe's file.	Not in film.
6. Pip returns to Satis House, meets Mr Jaggers, and fights Herbert Pocket.	As for novel.
7. Pip visits Satis House again.	Pip revisits Satis House.
8. Miss Havisham gives Joe £25 for Pip's indentures as blacksmith's apprentice.	Miss Havisham gives Pip money on his last visit before he goes to work.
9. Joe takes on Orlick as journeyman worker in forge.	Not in film.
10. Pip revisits Satis House. Estella has gone abroad.	Not in film.
11. Mrs Joe is brutally attacked (apparently with convict's leg-iron).	Not in film.
12. Biddy comes to live at the Gargery house.	See above—between 4 and 5.
13. Pip tells Biddy he wants to become a gentleman.	Ditto.
14. Jaggers brings news of Pip's 'great expectations'.	As for novel.
15. Pip goes to London.	As for novel.

[14] The version of the film I have used runs five minutes less than the original stated length. I have not been able to locate a 118-minute version.

NOVEL	FILM
16. He sets up house with Herbert Pocket at Barnard's Inn.	As for novel.
17. Herbert tells story of Miss Havisham's jilting.	As for novel.
18. Pip goes to Hammersmith, to be educated by Mr Pocket.	Not in film. (Pip's 'education' in bracket syntagma, segment 25)
19. Pip gets money from Jaggers to set himself up.	As for novel (+Pip and Herbert's 'At Home').
20. Pip dines with Jaggers (along with Herbert and Bentley Drummle).	Not in film.
21. Joe visits Pip at Barnard's Inn.	As for novel.
22. Pip visits Miss Havisham at her request (via Joe).	As for novel.
23. Pip re-meets Estella.	As for novel.
24. Pip secures Orlick's dismissal as gatekeeper at Satis House.	Not in film.
25. Pip and Herbert exchange their romantic secrets.	Not in film (Herbert's romance omitted).
26. Pip meets and escorts Estella in London.	As for novel.
27. Pip and Herbert fall into debt.	As for novel, but earlier (after 19, above) in film.
28. Mrs Joe dies.	Much earlier in film. (See 4 above.)
29. Pip returns to village for funeral.	Long before Pip leaves village.
30. Pip's income is fixed at £500 p.a. when he comes of age.	As for novel, but before 21 (above).
31. Pip takes Estella to Satis House.	Not in film.
32. She and Miss Havisham quarrel.	Not in film.
33. At Assembly Ball, Estella leads on Bentley Drummle.	As for novel.
34. Magwitch returns to reveal self as Pip's benefactor.	As for novel.
35. Pip verifies Magwitch's story with Jaggers.	As for novel.
36. Pip and Herbert make plans for Magwitch's escape.	As for novel.
37. Magwitch tells story of his past (involving Miss Havisham and Compeyson).	Fragments of story at 34 (above) and 41 (below).
38. Pip goes to farewell Miss Havisham and Estella.	As for novel.

NOVEL	FILM
39. Estella tells him she is to marry Drummle.	As for novel.
40. Wemmick warns Pip of being watched.	As for novel.
41. Pip, with help of Herbert and Wemmick, makes further plans for Magwitch's escape.	As for novel.
42. Pip visits Satis House to ask Miss Havisham to finance Herbert.	Not in film.
43. Pip tries to save Miss Havisham from burning.	As for novel, but combined with 38–9 (above).
44. Jaggers (reluctantly) tells Pip Estella's true story.	As for novel, but not until after 50 (below).
45. Pip goes to deserted sluice house.	Not in film.
46. Pip is saved from death at Orlick's hand by arrival of Herbert and others at sluice house.	Not in film.
47. The escape plan for Magwitch fails.	As for novel.
48. Pip loses fortune.	As for novel.
49. Magwitch is tried.	As for novel.
50. Magwitch dies in prison.	As for novel.
51. Pip becomes ill.	As for novel.
52. Joe looks after Pip.	As for novel.
53. Biddy and Joe get married.	Not clear when marriage has occurred.
54. Pip re-meets Estella in the ruins of Satis House.	As for novel but with altered circumstances and outcome.

Comments

1. In making the list above, I am aware of an inevitable degree of subjectivity in what I have selected as 'major cardinal functions'. However, all the above are what Barthes would call 'narrative hinge-points', in the senses that each is capable of alternative outcomes and is linked consequentially as well as sequentially to other events and actions in the narrative. For example, when Pip meets with Magwitch in the churchyard (1, above), he could subsequently have decided to tell Joe about the meeting, or simply tell no one and do nothing about Magwitch's request, or to do as in fact he does. That is, he steals the food and the file and takes them to the convict early next morning. The consequences of this act scarcely need alluding to: it is clear that they affect the rest of Pip's career in novel and film and their effects are palpable in other major cardinal functions (e.g. Pip's receiving his 'expectations').

Some of the other effects—especially the growth of Pip's sense of guilt, his 'taint of prison'—are more diffuse and (especially in the novel where there is much more pervasive attention to them) they belong to a different order of functionality, denoting character information rather than actions. If the film-maker wants to convey these effects, they will require adaptation proper as distinct from transfer.

2. Among the major cardinal functions lost in transition from novel to film, some of the most obvious are those relating to the violent assault on Mrs Joe and the jealous, threatening actions of Orlick. Their loss has the effect of removing certain influences on Pip's development and of rendering that development less complex.

3. In the interests of length and narrative clarity, the film omits those actions relating not merely to Orlick, but also to Herbert's romance, his career, and Pip's attempts to further this, and minimizes the material relating to Wemmick and Drummle. Wemmick's marriage, for instance, has an essentially symbolic function in the novel, as does his happy family life with its picture of filial devotion. The film's brief shot of Wemmick with his Aged P. and the happy marriage of Joe and Biddy perform some of the same functions.

4. If each visit Pip pays to Satis House constitutes a major cardinal function in the novel, the film cannot afford to be so expansive. On several occasions, it collapses the substance of a number of visits, either in a near-montage effect (e.g. segment 14) or by combining the matter of two or more into one visit (e.g. functions 38, 39, and 43 are combined in one visit in the film). The same kind of telescoping of a number of occasions applies to the plans for Magwitch's escape, in regard to which the film has to suggest a variety of preparations occurring over a long period.

5. My listing of the last of these major cardinal functions as 'Pip re-meets Estella in the ruins of Satis House', while true as far as it goes for novel and film, of course crucially obscures the essential differences between the two renderings. The adaptors have chosen to elaborate this final meeting with a series of much more vigorous actions by Pip, each in itself a minor cardinal function or catalyser in the process of letting in the light to Satis House and persuading Estella to leave. Dickens's changed version of the ending offers a more tentative suggestion of reconciliation than that enacted in the film's last, more exuberant shot.

In general, though, that chain of functions which accounts for the causal-ity in the narrative of Pip's career is essentially preserved, even if the effect is that noted by Charles Hopkins, who suggests that the scriptwriters

seem to have approached their task in the spirit of someone cutting a long play like *Hamlet* for presentation at normal length. The skeleton of the work has been altered very little, but the viewer familiar with the book may regret the absence of minor characters and secondary incidents whose existence the rest of the audience does not even suspect.[15]

Using a related metaphor, the *Observer* reviewer made a similar comment on 'the job of translation': 'Every bone of the original comes through, as if it were seen by an x-ray'.[16] My point is that it is this skeleton, a framework comprising the *transferable* functions of the narrative, which is most able to be retained in the film version of a novel because it is not tied to verbal language.

Character functions

Great Expectations is a novel which might well reward a full Proppian analysis and, in its necessarily selective way, the film has preserved to a striking degree those 'functions of characters which serve as stable, constant elements in a tale, independent of how and by whom they are fulfilled'.[17] Propp is writing about the recurrence of such character functions in successive tellings of fairy-tales; David Lean is on record as making the following comment: 'The characters were larger and more highly coloured than in life; and we deliberately kept them that way, because it was part of our intention to make a fairy tale.'[18] Aspects of character motivation and those traits that give distinctive colouring to this or that character are less susceptible to transfer from novel to film, being in general the products of their verbal display with its different order of precision about what is not *seen*. However, what the characters *do* (that is, their *function* in the narrative) is as amenable to audio-visual as to verbal manifestation. The key example, of course, is Pip who, as hero, inherits good fortune, loses it, and finds more modest and wholesome satisfaction. Tied to these processes is his longing to win the heroine, his losing her, and his final reconciliation with her. As A. L. Zambrano suggests, 'With this conclusion [Pip and Estella's running into the sunshine in the film's last scene], Lean creates more of the fairy tale quality than Dickens does, making Pip the classic hero who frees the princess from a magic spell.'[19] With this exception, the film's Pip performs those major functions attributed to him by Dickens.

Other character functions transferred include those of *helper* (e.g. Joe, Herbert), *donor* (e.g. Magwitch, Miss Havisham), and *villain* (e.g. Drummle

[15] Charles Hopkins, '*Great Expectations*', in *Magill's Survey of Cinema: English Language Films*, First Ser., vol. ii (Salem Press: Pasadena, Calif., 1980), 686.

[16] C. A. Lejeune, *Observer*, 15 Dec. 1946.

[17] V. Propp, *Morphology of the Folktale*, trans. Laurence Scott (University of Texas Press: Austin, 1968), 21.

[18] As quoted by C. A. Lejeune, 'Communiqués from the London Film Front', *New York Times*, 29 June 1947, s. 2, p. 5.

[19] A. L. Zambrano, '*Great Expectations*: Dickens and David Lean', *Literature/Film Quarterly*, 2/2 (1974), 161.

and Compeyson). Miss Havisham is particularly interesting in the distortion of the traditional role she exhibits. The apparent fairy godmother in the drama of Pip's career is revealed as being nearer to the ogre who inhibits it, a function which Magwitch at first appears to fulfil, whereas his intentions are later revealed as benign if misguided. Further, such Propp-designated functions ('spheres of action') as Absentation (Pip's leaving his early home), Lack (his lack of a gentleman's means and manners), and Interdiction (his being forbidden to enquire into the source of his expectations) are also clearly transferred.

Psychological patterns

In broader terms, underlying psychological patterns prove transferable. Such psychological patterns as the relation between children and parents (or surrogate parents), the concept of repression ('the dynamic, compulsive, but completely unconscious forgetting of unbearable, threatening or disturbing experiences'[20] such as Pip's terrifying childhood dealings with Magwitch), and the notion of young lives wrenched out of their natural courses (Pip's, Estella's) underpin the film's narrative action as they do the novel's.

Informants

Lean retains such informants as place-names (Richmond, Temple, etc., adding one by identifying the town near Pip's village as Rochester), the names of characters (though Hubble and Wopsle are confounded, retaining the latter's name and the former's marital status), the trades and professions of various characters, and data relating to place (e.g. the stopping of the clocks at Satis House at twenty minutes to nine). As always, though, the visual signification of such informants may set up resonances different from the verbal, so that the case for classifying informants as transferable remains dubious.

Dialogue

Much of the film's dialogue is transferred from the novel, notably in such key scenes as Pip's first meeting with Magwitch, his first visit to Satis House, and Joe's visit to London. There are, of course, major omissions, such as Pip's discussions about Joe with Biddy, even when the characters and their general situation have been transferred; there is wholesale change in the dialogue in the final scene between Pip and Estella;[21] Magwitch's account of his life to

---

[20] David Stafford-Clark, *What Freud 'Really' Said* (Penguin Books, Harmondsworth, 1967), 23.
[21] The effects of this have been analysed by Alain Silver, 'The Untranquil Light: David Lean's *Great Expectations*', *Literature/Film Quarterly*, 2/2 (1974), 149–52.

Pip and Herbert (chapter 42) is greatly truncated. However, most of the film's dialogue represents a judiciously selective transfer from Dickens; it sufficiently conveyed the impression of transfer to lead the reviewer Richard Winnington to write at the time: 'The original dialogue, left largely intact, is amazingly vivid.'[22]

Lean has not been able in a two-hour film to transfer all that can be transferred (whereas Peter Bogdanovich's film of *Daisy Miller* almost does achieve this), but the greater part of the 'bones' of his film is the result of a skilful selection of what can be transferred. Elisions and omissions are inevitable, but at this level invention is minimal.

ENUNCIATION AND ADAPTATION

Narrational Mode: The Novel

First-person narration

In her sometimes arrogant essay on *Great Expectations*, Q. D. Leavis claims that 'One of the principal reasons for the homogeneous tone of the novel is that it is told us by a narrator who is firmly kept before us as remote from the self who is the subject, a self that is seen in growth from childhood to adult status.'[23] This seems to me an accurate account of one of the novel's great strengths, and it offers a challenge to the would-be-faithful film-maker. Through this central sensibility everything we know—of places, events, people (including Pip himself)—is filtered. Despite the distance maintained between the narrating Pip and the Pip who is involved in the episodes which constitute the story, there is no sense of a clear 'objective' picture of those episodes. The mature Pip who is the narrator may seek to take us into the child's or the young man's mind but we are always aware that the younger mind is being re-imagined by the older narrator, giving a particular flavour to the events and perceptions being recorded. This flavour is apparent not only on those more obvious occasions when the middle-aged narrating Pip draws explicit attention to his earlier deficiencies (his snobbery, for example), but also in the way in which perceptions are encoded, not with realistic regard to how Pip at an early age may have articulated such perceptions, but shaped by an adult's superior understanding and often by a wit that does not seem ever to belong to the Pip who participates in the episodes of the plot. After his boyhood fight with Herbert Pocket, the youthful Pip fears retribution which the narrating Pip records as follows:

[22] Richard Winnington, '*Great Expectations*', *News Chronicle*, 11 Dec. 1946.
[23] Leavis, 'How We Must Read *Great Expectations*', 376.

Without having any definite ideas of the penalties I had incurred, it was clear to me that village boys could not go stalking about the country, ravaging the houses of gentlefolks and pitching into the studious youth of England, without laying themselves open to severe punishment. (p. 93)

This first-person narrator is a long way from the Pip who fought with young Herbert Pocket; he is also a long way from the experience-sobered Pip who is last glimpsed leaving Satis House with Estella; he is, as Mrs Leavis has said, 'remote from the self who is the subject'. All Pip's career, with its mistakes and illusions, its guilts, shames, and aspirations, is presented with a curious balance between a sense of immediacy and a sense of that critical scrutiny which derives from distance between the youthful protagonist and his own narrating self many years later.

So, the first-person narration enables (indeed, *enjoins*, especially when the time gap between the event and its recording is as considerable as it is here) the sustained illusion of the present contemplating the past. Our reading of the protagonist Pip, presented in an intricately connected series of episodes, is governed not just by how he seems to be conducting himself in these but also by his own mature perceptions of that conduct. We know what to make of Pip's changing attitudes towards, for example, Magwitch or Joe because we are encouraged to accept the mature Pip's evaluation of them. This narrator, not to be confused with Dickens himself, is the novel's guide to the reader's interpretation of events and of their role in the process of Pip's moral education, and he is often severely critical, either directly or with ironic obliqueness, of his own recollected earlier self. The narrator's tone is the means by which we measure the extent of Pip's moral decline and reclamation, maintaining a balance between involvement with and distance from that earlier Pip. As Booth says: 'The mature Pip . . . is presented as a generous man whose heart is where the reader's is supposed to be; he watches his young self move away from the reader, as it were, and then back again.'[24] As we watch Pip's behaviour, even at its least attractive, we are always aware, comfortingly, of the man he will grow into.

One further result of the narrator's young self's being the protagonist is that the novel is virtually free of sub-plots which do not substantially involve Pip himself. Since everything which happens in the novel must be known to Pip either because he is actually present at the time of a particular event or because he learns of it later, there is little scope for narrative digression. To a degree unusual in Dickens, the subsidiary characters are firmly integrated into the central action, through the ways in which their relationships and aspirations compare and contrast with those of the protagonist. Since the latter is also the highly aware first-person narrator, these are not lost on him, and overtly or covertly form part of his commentary on his own earlier self.

[24] Wayne C. Booth, *The Rhetoric of Fiction* (University of Chicago Press: Chicago, 1961), 176.

If the first-person narration can record only such perceptions as the narrator can reasonably have access to, one implication may be the different order of information it will offer in relation to the narrator and other characters respectively. In *Great Expectations*, there is virtually no physical description of Pip himself, except when another character makes direct reference to his appearance (e.g. Miss Havisham's 'This is a gay figure, Pip' when he comes to farewell her before leaving for London; or the boatman who comments on the blacksmith-like strength of Pip's arm). The novel's discursive prose is full of descriptive accounts of Pip's inner states as the narrator recalls them to have been—and of the physical appearance, the externals, of the other characters whom we see through Pip's eyes. But Pip's perceptions, unlike those of the omniscient author whom we allow to see into the inner lives of his characters, must stop at externals of appearance and behaviour, leaving us (as they leave Pip) to draw the appropriate conclusions about the lives within.

The passive element in Pip's presentation is perhaps unusually pervasive in a novel whose hero is also its narrator. Pip is often seen as victim: he is physically belaboured by Magwitch, Mrs Joe, and Orlick; humiliated by Estella; manipulated by Miss Havisham, Magwitch, and Jaggers; crudely mocked by Drummle; and threatened by Compeyson. He is frequently placed in situations where the element of choice is so small as to render him powerless (e.g. in the churchyard with Magwitch, in his first meeting with Miss Havisham and Estella, in the lime-kiln with Orlick). He is an *agent* in only two matters: the arranging of Herbert's business opportunity and the planning of Magwitch's escape, though in both of these matters he is ultimately impotent. Pip is not the only victim in the book, and victim is not all he is. I draw attention, though, to the peculiarly passive role he plays because it will be important to consider how the film—in which the character, rather than first-person narrator, dominates our awareness of Pip—renders this element through aspects of mise-en-scène and montage.

These aspects of the first-person narration have been touched on because of the kinds of challenge they offer the film-maker. Lean's *Great Expectations* is prepared to shear the original in a number of ways, but, as I shall show, he is plainly concerned to keep Pip's consciousness at the centre of the film.

Narrational Mode: The Film

David Lean and the first-person narrator: keeping Pip at the centre

Lean has, wisely, not attempted to make a first-person film. If he cannot ensure that Pip is able to exercise the moral or literal control over what is seen by the spectator in the way that Dickens's first-person narrator does, Lean as director (and, with others, as co-author of the screenplay) seems to have wanted to ensure that, as far as possible, the audience should share Pip's consciousness. Some of the means by which this is achieved are discussed below.

(*a*) *Voice-over*   The traditional cinematic equivalent of the novel's first-person narrative is the technique of voice-over, and, in *Great Expectations*, the voice of John Mills as the mature Pip is heard on the sound-track offering a commentary on events. Such commentary can never be more than intermittent, however, and is in fact reduced to no more than a dozen occasions, most often to indicate the passing of time or to accompany a change of location. These occasions and their functions are summarized below:

(i)   Pip's voice is heard reading aloud the novel's opening paragraph as the page appears on the screen; a wind then blows the pages over and they dissolve to a shot of a small boy, Pip (Anthony Wager), running along a path by the marshes. A connection is thus established at the outset by the voice heard on the sound-track, and the connection the spectator makes—an audio-visual perception of the link between voice and boy—is directly analogous to that of the mature narrator's 'voice' in the novel and the 'picturing' of the small boy in the graveyard. In this way, the film-maker announces that his story will have its roots in the same events as those of the novel.

(ii)   The most usual information conveyed by the voice-over is that time has elapsed. When it is next heard, it announces that: 'It was a year later . . .' and the scene is introduced by Mrs Joe (Freda Jackson) and Uncle Pumblechook (Hay Petrie) arriving by cart at the Gargery house. The next-but-one instance records (or 'recalls', because the fact that it is John Mills's voice well before he has begun to represent Pip visually reinforces our sense that the film's present really belongs to the past) that: 'Three months later my sister became ill and was laid to rest in the churchyard by the marshes'. A little later the voice-over announces: 'My boyhood had ended and my life as a blacksmith had begun. It was the sixth year of my apprenticeship . . .' and thereby justifies the replacement of the boy actor by Mills, seen at work with Joe (Bernard Miles) in the forge. This very important scene in the film's narrative development ushers in the eponymous expectations with Jaggers the lawyer (Francis L. Sullivan) suddenly appearing, as if from nowhere, in the forge doorway.

(iii)   Two later instances have more complex functions, being directly connected with Pip's moral growth. They begin and end the scene in which Joe comes to visit Pip at his rooms in Barnard's Inn, London, with a message asking Pip to visit Miss Havisham (Martita Hunt). Unlike the earlier ones (perhaps for the obvious reason that the spectator now associates the physical image of the actor on the screen with the voice on the sound-track), these are both accompanied by shots of Pip's standing silently. At first, by the window, he is observing Joe's arrival through the street below: 'As I watched

Joe that Tuesday morning . . . let me confess that, if I could have kept him away by paying money, I would have done so. In my efforts to become a gentleman, I had succeeded in becoming a snob.' This is the most explicit statement of the theme of class and it comes almost exactly half-way through the film. The film here creates the same double-view that the novel's first-person narrator achieves: that is, the voice-over, like the novel's narration, not merely gives the spectator a clear statement about Pip's having become a snob but places it clearly as an unattractive element of his *past*. It belongs to the younger Pip, the more mature voice of the narrating Pip, both in film and novel, having by implication recognized and outgrown the moral failure of that previous time. The sequence of Joe's visit, in which Joe appears gauche and foolish, concludes with the confrontation of his simple goodness and Pip's snobbery, followed by Pip's looking with dissatisfaction at his image in a handsome mirror while the voice-over recalls: 'All that day, Joe's simple dignity filled me with reproach . . .'. The film cannot spare the novel's time to create in full the sense of Pip's embarrassment and self-contempt, but it transposes the essential narrative function: that of bringing Pip to an awareness of the snobbery that his gentleman's progress has led him to.

(iv) The voice-over is used on several occasions to make explicit Pip's feeling for Estella (Jean Simmons and, later, Valerie Hobson) and the disruptive effect she has on his life. As he lies in bed on the night after his first visit to Satis House, the camera tracks in slowly to a close-up of Pip's face as the older Pip's voice is heard on the sound-track: 'Long after I'd gone to bed that night, I thought of Estella, and how common she would consider Joe, a mere blacksmith . . .', and later, after a sequence which compresses several visits to Satis House, the voice-over recalls: 'My admiration for her knew no bounds', and so, as Estella's face from the previous shot dissolves over that of Pip, now in bed, the voice-over says that, after these visits, Pip 'never went to sleep without the image of her pretty face' before him. The gap between protagonist and narrator is comparable to that between Dickens' young Pip and the mature narrator, and the voice-over on such occasions performs a function similar to that of the first-person narrator: to articulate what was intensely felt but difficult to express by the young protagonist.

(v) The last two voice-overs have simple narrative functions. Much later, Pip, having visited Satis House again and learnt that Estella is to marry Bentley Drummle, and having tried to rescue Miss Havisham from burning, records: 'Late that evening I left that room for the last time'. It is not, of course, the last time but at this stage Pip believes it to be so. The voice-over is not, on this occasion, claiming the full knowledge of hindsight which it usually implies. And shortly after, when it has become imperative to organize Magwitch's escape, the voice-over records: 'The following day I send Herbert to make some enquiries' (i.e. about sailing times). Pip is absent from this sequence and this draws attention to another way in which the film quite rigorously works to keep Pip as its centre of consciousness: that is . . .

(*b*) *Pip's near omnipresence*   There are virtually no scenes when Pip is not physically present on the screen or understood to be in the off-screen space. His near-continuous presence in the film's action ensures that, for the most part, the audience will know only what Pip knows. It is worth looking briefly at those few occasions when the spectator has access to visual information denied to Pip. They are:

(i) when Mrs Joe and Uncle Pumblechook return to the Gargery house in an open cart and dismount, Mrs Joe's shouts to Pip being drowned by bursts of non-diegetic music;

(ii) when the young Estella watches Pip and Herbert fight from a high window of Satis House;

(iii) when Estella and Miss Havisham are seen seated together by the fire before Pip knocks to enter;

(iv) the moment of Miss Havisham's catching fire after Pip has left the room (he hears her screams from the stairs);

(v) when Herbert goes to the shipping-office; and

(vi) a single shot of the scarred convict, Compeyson, as he watches events on the river, unseen by Pip.

Of (i), (iii), and (iv) (above), it could be said that they present audience-information which Pip could very quickly infer. These three occasions offer little impediment to the idea of the centrality of Pip's physical point of view on the action: if he wasn't there at the moment of the audience's being given a view, he was so a moment later and then his knowledge again equates with the audience's. On the second occasion, (ii), Estella years later tells Pip she has watched him and Herbert fight, and, given that the whole story is being recollected by Pip, it becomes reasonable for him to include a point of view he could not have shared at the time but with which he was subsequently acquainted. As to (v), Herbert's going to the ticket office is accompanied by Pip's voice-over; it is picturing of an action Pip has himself initiated. The brief glimpse of Compeyson in (vi) is a necessary bit of narrative shorthand: the audience needs to know how the authorities became aware of the plans for Magwitch's escape. It is, I believe, the only instance in the film when Pip is neither present nor able, in any specific sense, to have been aware of information to which the spectator has access. Even then, in a general way, he must realize later that by one means or other Compeyson has known of his plans.

The point of the above detail is to suggest that Lean has clearly felt a need to retain as far as possible a sense of the first-person narration which the novel employs. Lean's intermittent first-person narrator, physically present almost continuously, is in the end one who knows virtually everything, even if he did not do so at the time of the event's occurring. If Pip cannot be wholly a first-person narrator, Lean has made his perceptions and reflections, as far as possible, the focus for the spectator's perceptions and reflections.

(c) *Subjective camera work*   There is a great deal of subjective camera work that allows us literally to share Pip's point of view. This is notably true in certain key scenes such as the Christmas dinner party, Pip's first and final visits to Satis House, and his colloquy with Jaggers over Estella's parentage.

(i) Around the Gargerys' Christmas table is ranged an assortment of character actors briefly vivifying Dickensian caricatures and at first it seems that Pip is not present. As the shot is composed, his back towards the audience at the low left centre of the screen, all but hidden by the back of the chair, so unobtrusive compared to the vociferous adults ('Why is it the young are never grateful?' etc.), one is scarcely aware of him. The effect is twofold: first, the spectator is led to view the gaggle at the table from almost the same physical viewpoint as Pip; and, second, one is led to consider the kind of constricting idiocy from which Pip will eventually long to escape. (The shots of Mrs Joe, vainly searching for the pork pie in the pantry, are clearly from Pip's point of view.)

(ii) In the visit to Satis House three segments later, Pip is abandoned at the door by the imperious Estella. When he enters Miss Havisham's room, everything is seen over his shoulder, literally, and in some ways this kind of shot directs the spectator's point of view even more clearly along the same lines as Pip's than would a formal point-of-view shot. Both Pip and the spectator take in the decaying room as a whole before getting a clear view of its extraordinary occupant. In fact, Miss Havisham is not seen in close-up until Pip comes near enough to her to justify this; it is thus *his* view of her the spectator receives.

(iii) In the scene in Jaggers's office when Pip learns whose daughter Estella is (segment 49), the camera gives us Pip's view of Jaggers's hand-washing and stays on him as he 'puts a case' to Pip. During the rest of the scene, the filmic mode is that of alternation (between Pip and Jaggers) but it is Pip's view of Jaggers rather than the latter's of Pip that the spectator is likely to share. This is chiefly because it is Jaggers who is communicating the essential information and, like Pip, the spectator searches his countenance as he seeks to maintain an emotional detachment from the facts he displays. The other participant in this sequence is Molly, Jaggers's housekeeper, and the spectator—like Pip—for the first time views her face in medium close-up, and is struck by her resemblance to Estella. (She is played by the same actress, Valerie Hobson, though, as Molly, she is uncredited on the cast list.) Until now, neither the spectator nor Pip has had any particular reason to observe such a likeness.

(iv) On his last visit to Satis House, unaware, like the spectator, that Estella is inside, Pip looks up at the high mullioned window from which, on his first visit years before, the young Estella had insolently enquired his and Pumblechook's business. As Pip looks up, the camera takes in the object of his gaze—the high window—and on the sound-track Estella's words on that earlier occasion are heard again. The shot is, with the omission of the image of Estella, a replica of the earlier one, and its effect on Pip—and the spectator—is to make him poignantly aware of time past and the time that has passed. The subjective camera's alignment of the audience's conscious receptivity with Pip's own is felt again and again both in fleeting moments and on occasions of considerable importance.

(*d*) *Composition of screen space*   Again and again Lean organizes screen space so as to ensure our sympathetic alignment with Pip. One of the most striking symptoms of this is in the repeated shots in which Pip is seen dwarfed by large, looming, sometimes menacing adult presences. Perhaps the most memorable examples are those involving Magwitch.

(i) Much has been said about the celebrated opening graveyard sequence (cf. the account in Karel Reisz's *The Techniques of Film Editing*[25]), but in this context I am concerned with its use of space. The child running along a path through the marshes is dwarfed by the lowering sky, threatened by creaking boughs and, later, gravestones, and by the rising wind. The spectator's apprehension for Pip has been thus aroused when, as he moves leftward, a rough hand shoots out from the left edge of the screen and grabs him, confirming one's sense of the ominous potential of the off-screen space. It is not only the off-screen space beyond the frame's edges which seems charged with menace, but also 'the space behind the set or some object in it'.[26] In this case, such objects include the church wall, thick trees, trunks, and tombstones, surfaces for concealment which conspire with the noises (wind, creaking boughs) that belong to those other areas of off-screen space to create the tension of the sequence. Also, the low-angled shots (e.g. of the boughs, seen from Pip's point of view), Pip's anxious looks (off right, then front, then up) which direct *our* looks, and the rapid cutting (25 shots linked by cuts and flanked by two long shots of the marshes, linked by dissolves, all in 3.44 minutes) collaborate with the use of off-screen space to produce a uniquely unsettling opening. The fact that the segment begins with Pip's running, in extreme long shot, from left to right along the path through the marshes and ends with his running, in a similar shot, in the opposite direction, means, in realistic terms, only that he is now running home. In terms of how one responds to the use of screen space, it is hard to resist the sense that

[25] Karel Reisz, *The Techniques of Film Editing*, (Focal Press: London, 1953), 237–41.

[26] Noel Burch, *The Theory of Film Practice*, trans. H. R. Lane (Secker and Warburg (Cinema Two): London, 1973), 17.

this later shot is a metaphor for the way his life's direction has been (or will be) changed by this meeting.

(ii) Two-thirds of the way through the film (segment 34), Magwitch returns on a night of tempestuous storm to seek out Pip in his rooms at the Temple. When Pip opens the door, this farouche figure fills the screen, and, a little later, Pip is seated, in spatial terms at a disadvantage, as Magwitch towers over him to question him about the source of his fortune. This situation is then reversed to establish his benignity as he kneels before the 'gentleman' he has 'made'. As well, Pip's encounters with Pumblechook and Mrs Joe as they put before him the prospect of Satis House, with Miss Havisham herself, with Jaggers, first at Satis House, later at the forge, then at his London office, are further examples of Lean's use of screen space to show Pip, at crucial moments of his life, dominated by the purposes of others.

These examples are sufficient to suggest how the spectator is encouraged by the use of screen space to view these figures—awesome, grotesque, dominant—as they appear to Pip. Because the film wants us to see Pip as adopting as far as possible the function of the novel's first-person narrator, it follows that the impressions of such figures are likely to be stronger than those of Pip: it is his function to respond to their idiosyncrasies, and the film achieves in this respect a Dickensian larger-than-lifeness for its parade of bizarre figures. However, his continuing presence is the cause of thematic integration. In so far as the film appears to have sought a cinematic equivalent for the novel's first-person narration, it has done so by ensuring that, as far as possible (i.e. almost to the point of coinciding), its diegesis is described by the extent and limits of Pip's knowledge and viewpoint.

To conclude this discussion of the film's evident attempt to retain Pip as its centre of consciousness, there is another sense in which a film does both more and less than a first-person narrator can. As I have argued, almost all of what we see is either witnessed by Pip or is known to him at a later stage. There is, however, another order of information—ideological, historically specific—which is not, generally, consciously seen by the present Pip or remarked on by the reflecting Pip, but is 'seen' by the camera's narrating eye. To this extent, the first-person perspective of the film must always be compromised by the mise-en-scène: matters that either the young Pip or the older narrating voice could simply take for granted and not mention in the novel (e.g. details relating to the period and place) are necessarily given an objective life of their own by the film.

First-person narration: problems of adaptation

What Lean's film offers, then, is not a first-person narration as the novel does, but an enunciatory strategy which goes a long way towards ensuring parallelism between Pip's and the audience's knowledge. This constitutes not a *transfer* of the novel's 'signifiers of narrativity' (Barthes's term) but an *adaptation* in terms of what the screen can, in its classical fictional mode, approximate in this respect. If one considers some of the key functions of the narrating Pip, one will be aware of fields in which adaptation is required by the film-maker who, like Lean, is clearly interested in respecting a classic text even as he recreates it in a new medium. Such functions include:

(*a*) the rendering of Pip's thoughts, feelings, and sensations;
(*b*) the interrelation of past and present, which is a continuing element of the narration;
(*c*) the frequently ironic awareness on the narrator's part of discrepancies between events, characters, even remarks, as they appear superficially, and how the narrator interprets them.

(*a*) It would be generally held that film is less precise than the discursive mode of the novel in conveying *inner processes* and Lean's film is no exception. When Pip's voice-over expresses his youthful shame at his own snobbery (when Joe visits him in London), the effect is textually thin compared with what the novel's narrator can intimate as he recalls his younger self on these two occasions. Just before Joe's arrival (chapter 27), the narrating Pip confides to the reader: 'Let me confess exactly, with what feelings I looked forward to Joe's coming':

Not with pleasure, though I was bound to him by so many ties; no; with considerable disturbance, some mortification, and a keen sense of incongruity. If I could have kept him away by paying money, I certainly would have paid money. My greatest reassurance was that he was coming to Barnard's Inn, not to Hammersmith, and consequently would not fall in Bentley Drummle's way. I had little objection to his being seen by Herbert or his father, for both of whom I had a respect; but I had the sharpest sensitiveness as to his being seen by Drummle, whom I held in contempt. So, throughout life, our worst weaknesses and meannesses are usually committed for the sake of the people whom we most despise. (pp. 219–20)

Compare this with the previously quoted words from the film's voice-over as the younger Pip stands at his window. This is a fair example to choose since it is not one of the novel's extended reflective-descriptive passages, only diffusely related to a stage in Pip's career, but a commentary which enacts his thoughts and feelings on a particular, dramatically rendered occasion. The film's voice-over offers: a bridging comment between Pip's reading of Biddy's letter and the arrival of Joe, untypically dressed in town clothes; the single thought uppermost in Pip's mind ('If I could have paid money . . .') at the time, a sentence taken directly from the novel; and a baldly summarizing account of his development to this point. The novel is at once more supply discriminating (on the nature of Pip's snobbery: *vide* his reference to Herbert and Drummle) and more generalizing ('So throughout our life . . .'). The film's voice-over cannot afford—certainly, does not allow—more commentary than is strictly necessary to introduce the scene and provide an emotional context for it.

(b) In *the interrelation of past and present*, the novel is effortlessly able to draw comparisons between the young Pip and his older narrating self, so that, though the whole narrative is given in the past tense, one has no trouble in distinguishing the 'present' of the novel's discourse (itself, of course, a sort of immediate past) and the 'past' of its story. In the film when everything is *happening* (as opposed to having *happened*), such comparisons must be made by other means. As Alain Silver has perceptively noted (and used two frame enlargements to support his claim), 'Lean forges his own link with Pip's childhood through . . . a single medium close shot of the grown Pip reclining on a slope and tugging at the grass in exactly the same position he assumed as a boy when Estella first caused his dissatisfaction.'[27] In the earlier shot, he has been confiding to Biddy, 'I want to be a gentleman on her [Estella's] account'; in the latter shot, as if Lean wants the spectator to connect Pip's present situation to that earlier unhappiness he says, in answer to Biddy, 'I don't think I shall [marry]'. The adaptor forges the link through the power of mise-en-scène since he is essentially denied the discursive faculty of the novelist (and his narrator) to recall an earlier occasion directly.[28]

(c) Similarly, the *ironic awareness* of his younger self's inadequacies also belongs to the reflective/discursive element of the narrator's voice, and resists dramatization. Since adaptation proper inevitably involves dramatization, the rendering into a mode of execution as well as of representation, it is not surprising that it is the externals of appearance and behaviour which the camera records and not the sense of the narrator's providing an exegesis upon those externals. For instance, in the matter of Pip and Herbert's mounting debts, the film (segment 27) offers a close-up of a 'Memorandum of Debts' and of the pens writing away, followed by a medium close-up of Pip and Herbert adding up the figures, before the scene dissolves to Jaggers's office. The film transfers the novel's cardinal function—the drawing up of the memorandum—but in the processes of adaptation proper, it compresses a whole generalizing account of a period of Pip's life into one occasion and into two shots. The film quite omits the irony implied in the commentary which accompanies the episode in the novel, as in:

The sound of our pens going refreshed us exceedingly, insomuch that I sometimes found it difficult to distinguish between this edifying business proceeding and actually paying money. In point of meritorious character, the two things seemed about equal. (p. 279)

---

[27] Silver, 'Untranquil Light', 151. See also Richard Winnington, 'Critical Survey', 18.

[28] John Mills recalled how Lean got Wager 'to do particular hand movements which I repeated later on', in Brian McFarlane (ed.) *Sixty Voices* (BFI Publishing: London, 1992), 172.

The film *shows* whereas the novel both shows and *tells*, and the irony here is in the telling.

Adaptation and 'the writing'

The points made above all relate to particular functions of the narrating voice of the novel and how the film must either ignore or adapt such functions. Though much of the film's dialogue is transferred directly from the novel, the processes of *adaptation proper* will be necessary to give the spectator a sense of such atmospherically disparate settings as the bleak and lonely marshes and churchyard, the eerie Satis House, and the constricting forge. The film may transfer the setting (i.e. the *idea* of marsh, Satis House, and forge) but the realization of these settings, not only in their physical reality but in their atmospheric and metaphoric significance, is a matter of set design, sound, lighting, camera angle and movement, and so on. That is, it is a matter of how Lean's directorial style works to create such illusions. There is major work of adaptation involved here: the writing can never tell us all about a scene, whereas the film is forced to fill its settings, as it fills its frame, with the paraphernalia of the world in which its action is set, creating a visual replacement for effects achieved by the writing.

One aspect of 'the writing' (in Barthes's somewhat mysterious term) which calls for particular notice in regard to Dickens is his use of tropes of various kinds. The cinema has shown varying capacity for rendering a range of literary figures, suggesting that, if metaphor is difficult, at least in classic realist cinema, and simile impossible, other tropes such as personification, synecdoche, and metonymy are more susceptible to cinematic technique. In considering Lean's directorial style in relation to Dickens's novelistic style in the Special Focus of this chapter, I shall look more closely at the way cinema deals with this question. The Metzian classification of cinematic tropes into metaphor and metonymy[29] (i.e. those which function, respectively, paradigmatically, and syntagmatically) seem to provide a more profitable way of considering the question. The transfer of literary tropes, or the finding of visual equivalents for them, is a limited enterprise, but Metz suggests that cinema achieves its own figurative language.

SPECIAL FOCUS

James Agee begins his review of the film with: '*Great Expectations* does for Dickens what *Henry V* [i.e. Olivier's] did for Shakespeare', then, after, quali-

[29] Christian Metz, *The Imaginary Signifier*, trans. B. Brewster *et al.* (Indiana University Press: Bloomingdale, 1977), 174–80.

fying this praise, concedes that 'the film is never less than graceful, tasteful, and intelligent, and some of it is better than that'.[30] Agee is beginning to talk here about the film's style, and his three complimentary adjectives seem to me fair up to a point but not adequately to allow for those boldnesses of style which are the true source of the film's hold on the mind, both in viewing and in recollection.

It is not that Lean is, in general, a bold stylist but in what are, arguably, his two finest films—*Brief Encounter* and *Great Expectations*, both made in 1946— he has shown a willingness to move away from his literary sources. This willingness is displayed in a striking compositional sense, in a capacity for rendering the subjectivity of experience in a medium not often amenable to this, and a control over the cinema's metonymic and metaphoric resources. If Lean may be said to have declined into the impersonality of the screen epic in recent decades, in the 1940s his style exhibited a more interesting mixture of the discreet and the Gothic. The latter, manifested particularly in his treatment of Magwitch and Miss Havisham, might have served him in rendering the omitted Orlick, that 'free-ranging agent of chaos'.[31] My interest here is to focus on how, in certain key respects, a pre-eminently visual medium goes to work on a literary text noted for *its* visual power—and to suggest that 'visual' means something different in the two. The comparison is the more interesting here because Lean's characteristic restraint seems in many ways at odds with the flamboyance of the author he is adapting. The style of a director and his control over other collaborators must always be significant in governing the nature of an adaptation. I wish to foreground the issue here, not merely to compare Dickens with Lean and Cineguild but to draw attention to some distinctions between what is open, stylistically, to the two media in rendering a largely common body of narrative events.

Realism and symbolism

Q. D. Leavis, writing of the novel, draws attention to 'the gradual and often imperceptible movement from everyday experience to an implicitly symbolic but plausibly real experience which then shades into one overtly unrealistic'.[32] This movement between the realistic and the symbolic is pervasively characteristic of Dickens's style in this novel. The final paragraph of each of the three major parts of the novel is as good an example as any: in each case rooted in the realistic (Pip's departure from the village, awaking after the night of Magwitch's return, and leaving the ruins of Satis House with Estella), there is an effortless commingling of the observations of the

[30] James Agee, from *Nation*, 19 July 1947, in *Agee on Film* (McDowell Oblonsky: New York, 1958), 266–7.

[31] Neil Sinyard, *Filming Literature: The Art of Screen Adaptation* (Croom Helm: London, 1986), 119.

[32] Leavis, 'How We Must Read *Great Expectations*', 391.

real world with an awareness of the symbolic value of those observations. 'And the mists had all solemnly risen now, and the world lay spread before me' (p. 162), at the end of Part I, is the simplest example of this fluid interaction of the real and the symbolic. In relation to characters (e.g. Jaggers's repeated hand-washing) and places (e.g. Wemmick's 'castle' or Satis House itself), Dickens, using that mobility of imagination with which he endows the older, narrating Pip, makes us aware successively—and sometimes simultaneously—of the physical reality and its symbolic significance.

How can the screen which can show us only what is presented to the camera's lens imbue the physical with symbolic significance? As one very familiar with the film, I find it hard to be sure how far on a single or first viewing a spectator might be aware of the symbolic functions I now discern in moments such as the following:

(a) Magwitch's floundering in the mud of the marshes as the soldiers close in—both a striking moment physically and an intimation of his place in the social scheme of things,[33] not to mention, as a psychoanalytic account might, how it seems to stand in palpable terms for an act of psychic repression on Pip's part as the object of his terror slithers helplessly before drifting into the night with his captors;

(b) the meeting of young Pip and Estella with Jaggers on the stairs at Satis House where Jaggers (in medium shot) towers above the children in both of whose lives he is the agent of manipulation; and

(c) the wild night sky which ushers in Magwitch's return, which, in turn, shatters the snug warmth of Pip's rooms at the Temple.

In these moments, the realistic meaning of the action seems to me to melt into the symbolic, without any of the explicitness which characterizes, say, Pip's tearing down the curtains to let the light into the 'dead house' or the superimposition of the words GREAT EXPECTATIONS over the final shot of Pip and Estella running down the garden path in the sunlight. That is to say, in the earlier examples the symbolic effect is a function of the mise-en-scène, inextricably interwoven into the realist texture, and may perhaps be seen as a visual rendering of the verbal procedures described by Mrs Leavis.

The reflective

Whatever attentions Lean's style lavishes on the creation of atmosphere, its primary duty is the telling of the story, which it does through a series of fast-paced, usually short segments. Of the film's 54 segments, only 14 last for more than three minutes and all but four of these have at least 25 shots. Lean's narrating style was not then one that lingered. The reflective el-

---

[33] Silver ('Untranquil Light', 141) refers to the 'dynamic image of the struggle on the mud flats in which Magwitch sinks into the marsh and literally becomes an extension of it'.

ements of Dickens's style are ruthlessly excised and form virtually no part of Lean's style, except in those previously noted uses of the voice-over which provide a vestigial commentary on certain episodes. In fact, the odd examples of its use (e.g. 'All other swindlers upon earth are nothing to the self-swindlers, and with such pretences did I cheat myself. Surely a curious thing.' Segment 30) seem at odds with the film's more or less headlong narrative style. This is as much a matter of film enunciation in general as of Lean's individual style: film simply favours what can be shown (i.e. appearances, behaviour, actions) over what has to be told. It is therefore not surprising to find that the reflective elements of an author's style do not adapt well to the screen: only so much can be implied in a close-up, for instance, and the spoken commentary must be both skimpier and simpler than a novel may aspire to.

The grotesque

Though *Great Expectations* is one of Dickens's more sober works, the imaginative exuberance is still to be found in those more or less grotesque figures among whom Pip moves (Magwitch, Miss Havisham, Mrs Joe, Joe in his dealings with the language); in his way of imparting life to inanimate objects (such as 'the despotic monster of a four-post bedstead' in the room Pip takes in the Hummums); in the fascination with the obsessive (Wemmick's 'posting' his food, the details of Miss Havisham's reclusive life at Satis House); and in numerous instances of behaviour, from the local detail of, say, Mr Wopsle's great-aunt and her approach to education to whole episodes such as those involving Wemmick's castle. There is great visual power in the dramatizing of these grotesque elements but, as suggested earlier, their meaning is apt to be rhetorically encoded in ways not readily amenable to adaptation to a visual medium. This extract from Pip's first view of Wemmick illustrates what may seem like a rich visual invitation to a film-maker and yet, on closer examination, to offer little in the way of actual physical detail and a good deal of purely verbal energy working towards a sense of the grotesque:

. . . a dry man, rather short in stature, with a square wooden face whose expression seemed to have been imperfectly chipped out with a dull-edged chisel. There were some marks in it that might have been dimples, if the material had been softer and the instrument finer, but which, as it was, were only dints. The chisel had made three or four of these attempts at embellishment over his nose, but had given them up without any effort to smooth them off. (p. 171)

The pleasure in that passage is in Dickens's pursuit of a grotesque idea—that a man's face might have been chiselled out of wood—and in the line of diction that renders it. The film can only cast Ivor Barnard, an actor of thin-lipped severity, whose physical impression is appropriate to his function; the grotesquerie of the novel's description is intransigently tied to a particular use of the language.

This is not to suggest that film, and Lean's film in particular, cannot do the grotesque, but merely to suggest that it will be achieved in different ways. It may derive from framing (Magwitch in Pip's doorway on a wild night; Miss Havisham in medium shot, her throne-like chair, surrounded by decay, intoning 'Broken!' as the clutches her heart), from the previously noted placement of Pip in such a way as to put him at the mercy of horrific or baleful figures, from striking chiaroscuro effects (the marshes and church-yard of the opening, the interiors of Satis House) obtained through lighting contrasts at play in carefully framed compositions. It is, thus, largely a product of manipulation of the mise-en-scène, though sound (the creaking of tree boughs) and cutting (the sudden close-up of a gnarled tree-trunk in the opening scene or of the ship's figurehead in the escape scene) make their contribution. Chiefly, the grotesque effects are concentrated in the first third of the film, in which David Lodge rightly claims that Lean has found 'a visual equivalent for the fantastic Gothic quality of Dickens's imagination'. He goes on to suggest that 'black and white [photography] is appropriate to Dickens's rather grotesque melodramatic imagination and appropriate to the expression of the menace and mystery of the world as it presents itself to a vulnerable, insecure, rather frightened child like Pip'.[34]

Tropes

James Monaco describes the literary trope as 'a logical twist that gives the elements of a sign—the signifier and the signified—a new relationship to each other', as 'the connecting element between denotation and connotation'.[35] All fiction is more or less obtrusively imbued with such usages (metaphor, personification, etc.); Dickens is an author who foregrounds them and part of the 'literariness' of Lean's film is to be located in his finding cinematic equivalents for tropes in their traditional sense. Lean is able to invest, say, the 'two dreadful casts on a shelf' in Jaggers's office and Jaggers's hand-washing with a dilute metaphoric significance. However, these two examples are so clearly perceived as physical realities that, shorn of the verbal reinforcements of the novel, they never really attain the metaphoric weight they achieve in the novel. The personification of trees and stairs, the eclectic anthropomorphism of Pip's early morning run to the convict in the churchyard, may be cited as a successful cinematic rendering of verbally created tropes. In this sequence, voice-over and visual image combine to establish a *distance* be-

---

[34] David Lodge in a lecture given at the National Film Theatre, London, on 22 Feb. 1983, as one of a series entitled 'From the Page to the Screen'.

[35] James Monaco, *How to Read a Film* (Oxford University Press: New York, 1981), 140.

tween object and its function that is necessary for trope, of the literary kind at least, to work. The sequence also offers an example of Lean's attempt (perhaps in emulation of Dickens's style) to imbue inanimate objects with life. As to synecdoche, a shot of St Paul's dome looming up announces the city at large as a new force in Pip's career; Estella's sitting in Miss Havisham's chair, her prayer book on the table beside her, as she tells Pip she enjoys being 'away from the world and its complications', encapsulates a whole reclusive way of life. The latter is entirely an invention of the film and through the details of the shot Lean establishes synecdochically how far Estella has come towards filling the role for which her guardian has prepared her. The flapping inn sign on the deserted river bank (in the pre-escape sequence) and the mouse scurrying out of Miss Havisham's bride cake metonymically evoke, respectively, desolation and decay.

As illustration of the Metzian categories of metonymy (subsuming synecdoche) and metaphor, I shall refer briefly to Lean's use of 'journeys' and his representation of Jaggers respectively. The idea of journey as metaphor (life's journey, etc.) is of course common; in Lean's film, it is used syntagmatically, acquiring thereby a metonymic force. For example, in the film's opening segment, Pip is seen as a small boy making a 'journey' across the marshes and over the church wall to the graveyard. In the syntagma presenting his first visit to Satis House, Pip is wrenched away from his forge background, is (literally) led down the garden path by Estella, and via dark passages and stairs to Miss Havisham's room. His first journey to London, conveyed through a montage of horses, coach, glimpses of countryside, and a map, is a mixture of more conventional usages of metonymy (and synecdoche). His journey down the river with Herbert and Magwitch, in the attempt to help the latter escape, is a key stage in Pip's moral reclamation, despite the failure of its ostensible objective. Each of these 'journeys', by which I mean more or less sustained depictions of movement from one place to another, may be seen as metonymic representations of the whole journey of Pip's career: pieces standing for a larger whole, a series of spatial contiguities united by their connection with a larger referent. Lesser examples of such metonymic usage are the two segments (25 and 33) which rapidly juxtapose shots to signify respectively 'Pip's education' (dancing, fencing, and boxing lessons) and 'London social life' (dancing, archery, skating, assembly ball).

Jaggers's metaphoric significance as agent of manipulation is implied, paradigmatically, in the choices made to present him, variously, as looming over Pip and Estella on the stairs of Satis House (segment 14), as coming between the shadows of Joe and Pip as they work at the forge (segment 17a) and standing over them as they sit at the kitchen table (segment 17b), and as filling the doorway of Miss Havisham's room as she orders Pip to 'love her [Estella]' (segment 31). Jaggers has, of course, some clear-cut narrative functions to perform, but to invest these with metaphoric force Lean has both chosen an actor of idiosyncratically imposing presence (Francis L. Sullivan) and contrived framings which emphasize his power-wielding capacity.

One is never unaware that *Great Expectations* is a stylish film and that its style works towards giving expressive life to a fast-moving narrative. Its style is, nevertheless, less richly varied than the novel's: David Lodge laments the loss of 'descriptions of things and people and places, moral reflections, jokes, instances of bits of comic or poignant human behaviour which are cherished for their own sake' and which are omitted 'because they do not contribute to the advancement of the narrative as such'.[36] (This comment recalls Robert Scholes's more general assertion that: 'In a novel, . . . much of the language is busy with description and reflection, which must be eliminated in a cinematic translation'.[37]) However, though the Cineguild publicists stressed the (sometimes absurd[38]) lengths to which the film-makers went to ensure authenticity to the period, Lean has not made a period piece stiff with reverence.

His style, with its brilliant command of editing and its integration of elements of mise-en-scène, ensures its own coherence. Time and space are made to work harder than is necessary or even possible in the novel. The stylistic richness of the latter is partly a product of the greater expansiveness of the mode worked on by a uniquely expansive verbal imagination, whereas Lean's style works towards concentration both in what it chooses to display (i.e. the romantic at the expense of the social) and in the means by which that display is effected.

[36] Lodge, op. cit. n. 34 above.

[37] Robert Scholes, 'Narration and Narrativity in Film' (*Quarterly Review of Film Studies*, Aug. 1976), in Gerald Mast and Marshall Cohen (eds.), *Film Theory and Criticism*, 2nd edn. (Oxford University Press: New York, 1979), 427.

[38] For example, we are told that the coachman who drives Pip to London 'was Mr Dave Jacobs, whose father and grandfather actually drove coaches over this very route' (British Film Institute micro-fiche collection).

Daisy (Cybill Shepherd) enjoys the Punch and Judy show, in company with Winterbourne (Barry Brown), in Peter Bogdanovich's *Daisy Miller*

4

Daisy Miller (1974)

PUBLISHED in *Cornhill Magazine*, 1878, and one of Henry James's early explorations of the 'international situation', *Daisy Miller* was his first popular success. Peter Bogdanovich's 1974 film based on the novella broke his run of popular successes (begun with *The Last Picture Show*, 1972) with a film that neither critics nor public liked, and his career has never recovered commercially.

In terms of 'fidelity', it is possible to make a strong case for Peter Bogdanovich's film as being one of the most rigorously faithful film versions of novels. In examining how far Frederic Raphael's screenplay *transfers* the major cardinal functions of James's narrative and the greater part of his dialogue, a claim for one sort of fidelity can be easily established. In the film's clear additions to the original, another sort—that of authenticity in regard to the period of the novella—can be argued. Both of these will be considered later as appropriate. Also, I am particularly concerned with how the film attempts to adapt the novella's narrational mode. By this, I mean the Jamesian device, variously described by the author and his critics as the use of a 'centre of consciousness', the mode of 'restricted consciousness', and the use of a 'central reflector'.[1] For the narrational mode is crucial to the drama of *Daisy Miller*. As Wayne C. Booth, in his teasingly entitled chapter, 'Authorial Silence', claims, 'the drama of Winterbourne's chilly misunderstanding of her true nature is really more important in the finished tale than Daisy's own actions'.[2] The drama, that is, is essentially inner; it is also, again essentially, shown rather than told. The problem lies in deciding what exactly is being shown.

NARRATIVE AND TRANSFER

Structural Patterns: The Novella

The disruption of a certain complacency

In so far as James's novella is most prominently concerned not with its eponymous heroine but with Winterbourne, its 'central reflector', its

---

[1] Edward R. Branigan (*Point of View in the Cinema* (Mouton: Berlin, 1984)) draws attention to James's 'third-person "reflectors"' and his use of 'the reflecting consciousness of a character', pp. 125, 170.

[2] Wayne C. Booth, *The Rhetoric of Fiction* (University of Chicago Press: Chicago, 1961), 283.

structure is visibly dictated by the disruption of a certain complacency exhibited in the opening scene of the story. He is, we are told, 'an extremely amiable fellow, and universally liked'[3] and has kept many 'youthful friendships' (formed during his education in Geneva) which 'were a source of great satisfaction to him' (p. 9). As he sits in the hotel garden, 'looking about him, rather idly at some of the graceful objects' described previously, he does indeed suggest a figure who, if not necessarily 'booked to make a mistake', seems ripe for some dislocation of his general sense of well-being. Randolph Miller's 'sharp, hard little voice' demanding a lump of sugar ruptures Winterbourne's morning calm in a way that prefigures the more serious and sustained rupture which Daisy herself will occasion by repeatedly offering challenges to his somewhat narrowly formed social views. If by the end of the tale he has understood that Daisy 'would have appreciated one's esteem' (p. 88) and has told his aunt that 'it was on his conscience that he had done her injustice' (p. 88), the irony is that the ruffled complacency enjoined by his *mis*understanding appears to have had no lasting effect. 'Nevertheless, he went back to live in Geneva', the last paragraph begins—back, that is, to where he acquired the cast of thought that made him unequal to a true perception of Daisy.

Oppositions of place and person

Several commentators have pointed to the structural importance in *Daisy Miller* of 'a series of contrasts in atmosphere, scene, and character'.[4] The first two chapters of the novella are set in Vevey, Switzerland, the latter two in Rome, and hovering at the beginning and the end, and in fact pervasive in its influence on Winterbourne, is Geneva.

(i) In Geneva, 'the little Calvinist metropolis' where he had been at school, 'he had become dishabituated to the American tone' (p. 19), and much later, in Rome, as he is arguing with Mrs Walker about Daisy's flirting, he says to her 'I suspect, Mrs Walker, that you and I have lived too long at Geneva!' (p. 63). 'Too long', that is, to respond easily and appropriately to Daisy's openness. When he first meets Daisy, he 'had come from Geneva the day before' (p. 8) and, as already noted, he goes back there to live after Daisy's death, to 'the dark old city at the other end of the lake' (p. 36).

(ii) Vevey has about it, by contrast with both Geneva and Rome, a brightness (the scene there opens on 'a beautiful summer morning') and a freedom from the rigid social constraints we witness in Rome and infer about Geneva. This freedom, as it applies to Winterbourne's acquaintance there with Daisy,

---

[3] Henry James, *Daisy Miller* (1878) (Penguin: Harmondsworth, 1974), 8. (Subsequent references are given in brackets as they occur.)

[4] Charles G. Hoffmann, *The Short Novels of Henry James* (Bookman Associates: New York, 1957), 20.

is partly a matter of Mrs Miller's imbecile incompetence as a traveller and mother; it is also partly because, in Vevey, 'in the month of June, American travellers are extremely numerous; it may be said, indeed, that Vevey assumes at this period some of the characteristics of an American watering-place' (p. 7). It is presented as a place where social conditions so contrast with those of Geneva that a young man might feel at liberty to speak to a young woman and, further to escort her alone to the neighbouring Château de Chillon. Winterbourne behaves in Vevey as he does not feel free to behave in Rome.

(iii) In Rome, where he arrives shortly after Daisy, he has not only his firm-minded, snobbish aunt, Mrs Costello, to pronounce upon the Millers' hopeless vulgarity but a more or less settled society of expatriate Americans, led by his friend Mrs Walker (also formerly of Geneva), to be laying down guidelines of decorum for recklessly innocent young American women. Whereas in Vevey he might accompany Daisy to Chillon with no censure other than his aunt's, in Rome Daisy cannot go walking in the Pincian Gardens by day or visit the Colosseum by night without giving rise to the darkest conjectures on her reputation. The irony is that only the opportunist Roman, Giovanelli, clearly understands her innocence. If Daisy dies of 'Roman fever', this cannot nevertheless be seen as a metaphor for new world innocence crushed by the corruptions of the old; rather, it is the strictures of her compatriots, too long resident in foreign parts and too snobbishly preoccupied with ensuring no taint on their international reputation, who turn a cold shoulder on Daisy.

The *contrasting sets of characters* need little more than listing to draw attention to their structural importance in the tale. The chief contrast—between Winterbourne and Daisy—is adumbrated in their names and articulated through the details of their behaviour: his chilly caution is opposed by her brash heedlessness, his sophistication by her simplicity, his failure to 'read' her correctly by her wish for his 'esteem' and the fact that there is no more to be read than what appears. Also, Winterbourne and Giovanelli are contrasted socially (the impeccably secure with those 'not of the first circles') and emotionally (the inhibited and the fulsome); Mrs Miller and Mrs Walker are contrasted in their notions of social vigilance, though in the end Mrs Walker is as defeated by Daisy's innocence as Mrs Miller has been by her own ineptitude and Daisy's wilfulness; and Mrs Costello and Mrs Miller also represent extremes of concern for propriety, the latter having only the fuzziest idea of what is allowable, while Mrs Costello suffers no such uncertainty.

The narrative creates a series of subtle patterns through the deployment of these contrasts: though the motives between each pair may be contrasted, the outcomes of these are often much less so.

Social occasions

In each of its four chapters, *Daisy Miller* makes use of a series of social occasions which reveal Daisy to Winterbourne (and to the reader) and, in turn, reveal Winterbourne and his confused responses to the reader. The use of these occasions provides evidence for Leon Edel's claim that 'The earlier James—the one who became famous on both sides of the Atlantic with this little story of Daisy—was addicted largely to the recording of external action, allowing the characters to develop before us through the things they say and do.'[5] Elsewhere, Edel writes of *Daisy Miller*: 'There is no lingering, no explaining; the story moves objectively with quiet incident to its conclusion.'[6] Both these comments draw attention to the most filmable aspect of the novella: its preference for showing rather than telling.

The chief social occasions which it shows are: Winterbourne's meeting with Randolph, then with Daisy, in the garden of the 'Trois Couronnes' (chapter 1); his visit to his aunt, Mrs Costello; the evening meeting in the garden with Daisy and, later, Mrs Miller, interrupted by the arrival of the courier, Eugenio; the visit to Chillon; a further brief visit with Mrs Costello (chapter 2); a visit with Mrs Costello in Rome; Mrs Walker's 'at home'; the walk in the Pincian gardens (Winterbourne and Daisy meet Giovanelli), interrupted by the appearance of Mrs Walker's carriage (chapter 3); Mrs Walker's evening party at which she snubs Daisy; Winterbourne and Mrs Costello's visit to St Peter's, where they see Daisy and Giovanelli wandering about; Winterbourne's meeting with Daisy and Giovanelli in the Palace of the Caesars; his coming upon them again in the Colosseum at midnight; and Daisy's funeral (chapter 4). There are some minor linking sequences and a few brief summarizing accounts (e.g. of Winterbourne's several visits to the Millers' Rome hotel), but essentially the narrative is conducted through the presentation of behaviour on the occasions listed, with a minimum of explanation and a maximum of showing.

Again some obvious contrasts are set up: between, for instance, the unchaperoned jaunt to Chillon, which attracts no more obloquy than Mrs Costello's sniffy dismissal of the enterprise, and the midnight visit to the Colosseum which ruins Daisy's reputation and leads to her death. The point is that the narrative of *Daisy Miller* displays itself through a series of contrasts at various levels, and that contrast is at the heart of its meaning.

Structural Patterns: The Film

It is generally true to say that Bogdanovich has followed the larger movements of the novella and articulated these through comparable sets of oppositions and social occasions.

---

[5] Leon Edel, 'Introduction', *Henry James: Selected Fiction* (E. P. Dutton: New York, 1953), pp. x–xi.
[6] Leon Edel, *The Life of Henry James*, i: 1843–89 (Penguin Books: Harmondsworth, 1977), 516.

The structuring notion of *a disruption to Winterbourne's complacency* is foregrounded in the film by the use Bogdanovich makes in the film's opening sequence of the child, Randolph (James McMurtry), replacing James's opening descriptive account of Vevey and the 'Trois Couronnes'. The camera pans down from the hotel ceiling, past balconies and carpeted corridors, coming to rest on a close-up of closed double doors, through which appears a hand removing shoes left out for cleaning. Randolph emerges and switches shoes up and down the corridor, then slides down the banister, lifting someone's alpenstock from a container at the foot of the stairs as staff look on discreetly. The effect is, as Kathleen Murray has noted, that 'Daisy Miller's little brother spreads disorder and impropriety as though to herald the more serious breaches of Old World protocol that his sister will eventually perpetrate'.[7] Randolph subsequently appears in the garden before Winterbourne (Barry Brown) and observes guests exchanging shoes across neighbouring balconies. His work of disruption proceeds when he accosts Winterbourne, seated at his table with coffee and newspaper, with his demand for sugar. Winterbourne's early morning calm is disturbed by Randolph's importunity, prefiguring the way in which the whole complacent tenor of his life is to be disrupted by Daisy (Cybill Shepherd). Randolph's trick with the shoes is wholly Bogdanovich's invention (he claims that Orson Welles suggested beginning with the boy[8]), but by starting in this way he does not subvert the novella's large structural pattern; he merely announces it comically. The film ends with Winterbourne alone at Daisy's graveside, with no reference to his returning to Geneva. This small but important break with the novella's structural pattern leaves the viewer with a stronger sense of disrupted complacency than James does.

Oppositions of place and person

Bogdanovich's film is actually set in Vevey and Rome and the power of the mise-en-scène is such as to render some sharp contrasts between the two: between the soft light of the lakeside town and the brightness of the Roman spring; between the leafy greenness of the Vevey exteriors and the formality of the Pincian Gardens, the forecourt of St Peter's, and the ornamental pool and gardens of the Palace of the Caesars. Bogdanovich and his art director, Ferdinando Scarfiotti, have maintained a firm control over these two major settings and over the contrasts they offer between relative social freedom and social oppressiveness. What they do not—and perhaps cannot—achieve through the mise-en-scène is that sense of how Geneva and what it stands for provides, in the novella, a key to understanding Winterbourne's behaviour.

---

[7] Kathleen Murray, '*Daisy Miller*: An International Episode', in Gerald Peary and Roger Shatzkin (eds.), *The Classic American Novel and the Movies* (Frederick Ungar Publishing Co.: New York, 1977), 91.

[8] Welles is quoted in an interview with Bogdanovich in Henry James, *Daisy Miller* (Warner Paperback: New York, 1974), 14.

The film chooses not to show Geneva and the scattered references to it are unable to render the sort of perception of its influence made explicit in the following:

In Geneva, as he [Winterbourne] had been perfectly aware, a young man was not at liberty to speak to a young unmarried lady except under certain rarely recurring conditions; but here, at Vevey, what conditions could be better than these?—a pretty American girl coming and standing in front of you in a garden. (p. 12)

It is the element of 'telling' rather than 'showing' there that eludes the film-maker; there is no way in which Bogdanovich could so economically have made clear the distinction between the two places and, consequently, the structural effect of Winterbourne's Geneva background is largely effaced—along with his final return there—from the film's narrative.

The *oppositions of persons* noted in the novella, and the narrative functions arising from them, are in essence retained in the film. Mrs Miller's (Cloris Leachman) maternal inadequacy is again contrasted with both the rigorous discrimination of Mrs Costello (Mildred Natwick) and Mrs Walker's (Eileen Brennan) concern for the proprieties of American behaviour in Rome. Such contrasts are underlined by the physical qualities of the actresses and by the way they are costumed: the fussy angularities of Cloris Leachman's Mrs Miller are accentuated by frilly dresses in the lighter colours which recall Daisy's and contrast with facial expressions of considerable firmness and costumes of more vivid and sophisticated style (for Mrs Walker) or of darker, more severe style (for Mrs Costello). And the contrast of Daisy herself, in terms of attitude and behaviour, is similarly underlined. Exquisitely dressed (by John Furness) in pale pinks, whites, and blues, she is made almost to reflect light, in ways that contrast with Mrs Walker's deep greens and reds that seem to draw light into herself rather than to radiate it. Among the men, the sombre formalities of Eugenio (George Morfogen) and the discreet correctness of Winterbourne's dress and manner are in marked opposition to the florid touches in appearance of Giovanelli (Duilio del Prete), and in each case these descriptions chime with their narrative functions, especially in relation to Daisy.

All the major *social occasions* through which the novella's narrative is displayed are retained in the film. There are minor omissions, additions, and alterations of setting which are worth noting chiefly to draw attention to the way in which the film adheres to the narrative outline of the original. The omissions (e.g. Winterbourne's brief meeting with his aunt after the excursion to Chillon, end of chapter 2) are inconsequential. The major additions are Daisy and Winterbourne's stopping at a Punch and Judy show in the Pincio and the scene in which Giovanelli and Daisy, in the Millers' Roman hotel sitting-room, play and sing for Winterbourne (a key scene, to be discussed later). The segments set in the hydropathic baths and at the Opera alter the novella's setting without changing its narrative functions. In general, Bogdanovich and Raphael have resisted the temptation to expand the action of the novella in terms of those occasions which make up the narrative, and have maintained the structure in terms of its overall movement and of its deployment through a series of events and contrasts.

Transfer of Narrative Functions

Perhaps the novella, too short to demand of the film-maker the drastic excisions invariably required by the film version of a full-length novel and too long to need the invention of new episodes which the transposition of a short story into a full-length film is likely to require, is the most congenial fictional form for the 'faithful' adaptor. *Daisy Miller* is a very interesting case in point: almost everything that can be transferred has been; many hostile reviews which the film received suggest that, on the level of adaptation proper, something other than faithful translation has occurred. My first task, then, is to be as exact as possible about what has been transferred.

Major cardinal functions

In terms of Barthes's 'cardinal functions' (or Chatman's 'kernels'), it is easy to establish the 'hinge-points' of *Daisy Miller*'s narrative. The major cardinal functions of the novella may be listed as follows:

1. Winterbourne has come from Geneva to Vevey →
2. He meets Daisy Miller →
3. In conversation, he invites her to the Château de Chillon →
4. She considers the invitation but is interrupted before accepting →
5. Winterbourne asks his aunt if he may present Daisy to her →
6. She refuses and is shocked at the proposed trip to Chillon →
7. He repeats his invitation →
8. Daisy accepts →
9. They visit Chillon →
10. They talk of his going back to Geneva and their re-meeting in Rome →
11. Winterbourne arrives in Rome in January →
12. He re-meets Daisy at Mrs Walker's apartment →
13. Winterbourne leaves Mrs Walker's apartment to accompany Daisy to the Pincian Gardens →
14. They meet Daisy's Italian friend, Giovanelli →
15. Mrs Walker tries to persuade Daisy to leave the Pincio with her →
16. Daisy, refusing, goes off with Giovanelli →
17. Mrs Walker orders Winterbourne to accompany her →

18. Mrs Walker tells him of Daisy's 'scandalous' behaviour →
19. Winterbourne leaves Mrs Walker to rejoin Daisy and Giovanelli →
20. He sees them, presumably kissing, hidden behind her parasol →
21. He leaves without their seeing him -->
22. They re-meet at Mrs Walker's party →
23. Mrs Walker snubs Daisy as she leaves →
24. Daisy goes everywhere with Giovanelli →
25. Winterbourne comes upon them at the Colosseum by night →
26. He loses esteem for her, and she catches 'Roman fever' →
27. Daisy dies →
28. Giovanelli at her funeral proclaims her 'innocence' to Winterbourne →
29. Winterbourne leaves Rome →
30. He rejoins his aunt in Vevey →
31. He goes back to live in Geneva.

Comments

- All of these major cardinal functions (as well as many lesser ones, e.g. Winterbourne's first meeting with Randolph) are transferred intact from novella to film, with the exception of the last.
- The settings for these major cardinal functions, in both time and place, remain those of the novella except in the case of 5 and 6, which take place not in Mrs Costello's apartment, but in the medicinal baths, and 30, which is conveyed by a conversation on the sound-track between Winterbourne and his aunt as he stands at Daisy's graveside.
- The order in which the major cardinal functions occurs is the same in novella and film.
- Two important characters—Mrs Miller and the courier, Eugenio—are not mentioned in the list above since their actions do not produce major effects upon the narrative's course.
- A list such as the one above may be seen as a bare-bones account of the action of the narrative, indicating merely the essential sequence of cause-and-effect-related elements we expect to find in narrative fiction. (The arrows are a crude means of indicating causality as well as sequence; the broken arrow after 21 indicates a connection which is largely sequential, causality more diffuse than elsewhere.)

In the case of *Daisy Miller*, then, if the film offers a notably different experience from the novel, it will do so essentially at levels other than that of cardinal functions or 'story'. The discrepancy noted (i.e. in relation to the endings of the two texts) will no doubt account for a difference of flavour or emphasis. That the film's Winterbourne should be left subdued and solitary at Daisy's grave points to a difference between Bogdanovich's and James's views of what effect Daisy has had on Winterbourne's life. Nowhere else, however, has the film-maker omitted a major cardinal function or, indeed, added one.

Character functions

If one follows the Proppian distinction between the functions of characters and their attributes and motivations, it is clear that Bogdanovich's film has transferred those functions almost intact. For example, Daisy remains the heroine who dies; Winterbourne the hero who is a puzzled observer rather than a participant; Mrs Walker's function is initially that of helper before she rejects Daisy; Giovanelli can be defined as adventurer who causes trouble for Daisy; and so on. Only one new character of even the slightest significance has been created—that of Charles (Nicholas Jones), Winterbourne's former school-friend and Mrs Walker's companion—but the chief function he performs is transferred from the novel. It is that of informant: it is he who, in the segment at the Opera, tells Winterbourne that Daisy has caught Roman fever, whereas in the novella this function is performed by unnamed informants (p. 86). This is the only significant re-attribution of a character function in the film.

However, if Propp notes that functions of characters readily survive successive tellings of a tale, he also draws attention to one of the ways in which a retelling may differ from an earlier version. 'Motivations often add to a tale a completely distinctive, vivid colouring, but nevertheless motivations belong to the most inconstant and unstable elements of the tale.'[9] In *Daisy Miller*, in which James has favoured showing over telling and in which what one knows of other characters is largely governed by the perceptions of a central reflector, elements of 'instability' or 'imprecision' in matters of motivations are more likely to be foregrounded than in omniscient storytelling. The most obvious case is that of Mrs Walker, whose functions are certainly transferred from the novella where, in fact, her motivation does seem a little obscure. In his interview with Jan Dawson, Bogdanovich has said: 'I found her difficult to accept because she seemed rather unmotivated except for her social reasons. . . . So I've changed her. In the way I've cast it and the way she's played, she's rather heavily motivated sexually. She's quite attracted to Winterbourne.'[10]

Perhaps this shift in motivation accounts for critic John Simon's complaint that 'Eileen Brennan lacks upper-class hauteur as Mrs Walker'.[11] Or for John

[9] V. Propp, *Morphology of the Folktale*, trans. Laurence Scott (University of Texas Press: Austin 1968), 21.

[10] Jan Dawson, 'The Continental Divide: Filming Henry James', *Sight and Sound*, 43/1 (Winter 1973–4), 15.

[11] John Simon, 'Jacobin—Not Jacobite', in *Reverse Angle* (Clarkson N Potter, Inc.: New York, 1981), 155.

C. Shields's reading of the change in her presentation: 'Mrs Walker, in James
a well-meaning self-appointed instructor of moral conduct for young ladies
abroad, has become in the film a social butterfly . . . who has entered the
eclipse of middle age and who sees Daisy as a formidable usurper of the
limelight'.[12] This curious, even absurd, interpretation is quoted, along with
Simon's and Bogdanovich's own comment, to draw attention to the comparative difficulty in establishing motivations and to ensure corresponding
accounts of these from any two readers. What the characters *do* may be clear
enough and readily transferable from novel to film, especially from a fiction
such as *Daisy Miller* which stresses *showing*. Since film *shows* more than even
a novel of this kind can, it is at this point that such aspects of mise-en-scène
as facial expression may complicate the question of motivation further in the
sense of offering signifiers not available to the novelist. (Seven years earlier,
the author of the screenplay, Frederic Raphael, had written, in a caustic piece
on relations between film-writing and novel-writing: 'The obsession with
story, with telling, gets in the way constantly of the film-maker's proper art,
which is showing.'[13]) As noted earlier, the ambiguity of Daisy's motivation is
central to Winterbourne's puzzlement: for all that James shows her behaviour, by maintaining Winterbourne as his centre of consciousness, he leaves
her motivation in doubt. In both texts, Giovanelli's final pronouncement
fails to dispel earlier uncertainties. In the film, the characters may perform
the same functions as in the novella; in at least one case, the motivation
appears to have been changed and, in another, the original uncertainty
makes transference unlikely.

Informants

In the case of *Daisy Miller*, the film retains all the names of the characters,
their place in society though this is obviously less specific data than their
names, and such 'attachments' as Mrs Costello's hypochondria, Randolph's
outspoken xenophobia, Winterbourne's Geneva background, and Eugenio's
profession as 'courier'. The places in which the action occurs are faithfully
transferred (Vevey, Chillon, Rome—the Pincio, etc.), though, inevitably,
there is in such transfer an element of *adaptation proper*, since the exercise of
cinematic codes renders such places in ways that do more than merely
inform. That is, the shift to a different signifying system may alter signified
as well as signifier: the word (e.g. 'St Peter's') and the visual image of the
actual place may well set up different connotations despite denotative
equivalences. Some settings have been added but the only one which has

---

[12] John C. Shields, '*Daisy Miller*: Bogdanovich's Film and James's Nouvelle', *Literature/Film Quarterly*,
11/2 (1983), 108.

[13] Frederic Raphael, Introduction to *Two for the Road* (Jonathan Cape: London, 1967), 30.

been both transferred and notably adapted is the cemetery. James records that: 'Daisy's grave was in the little Protestant cemetery, in an angle of the wall of imperial Rome, beneath the cypresses and the thick spring flowers' (p. 87). Bogdanovich transfers the setting of 'cemetery' but, curiously, ignores the Jamesian details and their connotations in favour perhaps of exciting a different kind of pathos: Daisy is buried, and Winterbourne is left standing alone, in a large, open graveyard, quite devoid of the suggestion of a little Protestant ghetto of the dead.

Dialogue

The *dialogue* of Raphael's screenplay is taken overwhelmingly from the novella. For the most part, the actors are given the exact words spoken by the characters in the original, and sometimes reported speech is converted into dialogue, as when Daisy prattles on to Winterbourne about the hotels in Europe, her Paris dresses, etc. (cf. p. 18 in novella). Even so, though the actual words spoken in a novel may seem to invite easy transfer, as soon as they *are* transferred to 'a code of execution',[14] in Barthes's term, they become susceptible to a range of potentially defamiliarizing factors. In the case of Daisy, the words she speaks in the film are transferred with remarkable fidelity from the novella. However, in assessing its impact, the viewer-listener is influenced as well by the timbre of Cybill Shepherd's voice, the speed of her delivery, the inflections she brings to particular lines and the monotone effect she brings to many, her pauses (sometimes idiosyncratic), the facial expressions, stance, and gestures that accompany the words, the way she is framed from shot to shot, whether she is shot in close-up or medium shot, and so on. All of these factors, in varying combinations, provide a more complex mediation between actress/character and audience than does a sentence such as this from the novella: 'She was very quiet, she sat in a charming tranquil attitude; but her lips and her eyes were constantly moving' (p. 17). Further, in the linear, verbal art, such an account cannot be registered at the same time as the dialogue whereas while we listen to the film's Daisy talk we are constantly aware of those other factors, inseparable from 'a code of execution'. As a result, the element of *transfer* is powerfully overlaid with those elements more properly designated *adaptation*, and this is true in varying but usually lesser degree with the transfer of informants. These two elements—spoken dialogue and informants—may be seen as having as much to do with enunciation as with narrative; it is their potential for transfer which leads me to include them here.

[14] Roland Barthes, *S/Z*, trans. Richard Miller (Hill and Wang: New York, 1974), 80.

ENUNCIATION AND ADAPTATION

Narrational Mode: The Novella

The implied author

The implied author of *Daisy Miller* is a very unobtrusive first-person narrator. In fact, this narrative use of the first person is so unobtrusive that one tends to think of the novella as being a species of omniscient story-telling. There are scarcely more than half a dozen usages of 'I' or 'our' in the novella's metalanguage, and their effect is that of a discreetly confiding voice. The pronoun occurs four times in the paragraph introducing Winterbourne and then disappears for fifty pages, leading the reader to suppose that, the scene's having been set and Winterbourne's having been put before him, the implied author's work is largely done. When in mid chapter 3, one comes across a reference to 'our two friends' (i.e. Daisy and Winterbourne), one is a little surprised to be reminded that 'someone' knows more than Winterbourne or the reader about what is going forward. The point of the foregoing is to establish the extent of obvious authorial intervention.

There is a slightly teasing sense at the beginning and end of the novella that the implied author does not know everything about Winterbourne (e.g. the exact nature of his dealings with the lady in Geneva). However, James's 'I' in *Daisy Miller* is not one of Booth's 'dramatized narrators', 'radically different from the implied author who creates him'.[15] His function is sometimes to create a picture, such as that of Vevey which opens the novella or of 'that beautiful abode of flowering desolation known as the Palace of the Caesars' (p. 77). Sometimes, there is a lightly characterizing irony which sharpens one's sense of a narrational presence, as in this account of Winterbourne's aunt: 'Mrs Costello was a widow with a fortune; a person of much distinction, who frequently intimated that, if she were not so dreadfully liable to sick-headaches, she would probably have left a deeper impress upon her time' (p. 24). The observations contained there are obviously available to Winterbourne but the last clause ('she would probably . . .') belongs to an order of ironic perception not elsewhere associated with him.

Once Winterbourne had been introduced—as 'a young American, who, two or three years ago, sat in the garden of the Trois Couronnes, looking about him, rather idly, . . .'—his perceptions become the chief source of the reader's information. The implied author seems almost to withdraw, as if to ensure that the reader will share Winterbourne's vantage-point in relation to the ensuing action of the novella.

---

[15] Booth, *Rhetoric of Fiction*, 152.

The 'central reflector'

The essential narrative mode of *Daisy Miller* is that which employs a 'central reflector' or a 'centre of consciousness', through whom the narrative is filtered. The effect is to create *a drama of restricted consciousness*, diminishing the sense of authorial mediation, so that the reader is aware of having at his disposal only—or, at least, chiefly—the insights and perceptions of a plainly fallible reflecting presence. Though, as Edward Branigan has noted, 'for a critic to speak of "third person reflectors" in the fiction of Henry James . . . is already a way of asserting the existence of a larger, implicit narrational context which frames the characters'.[16]

In the case of *Daisy Miller*, the drama is as much to be located in Winterbourne's misunderstanding as in the 'tragedy' of Daisy. From the moment that Winterbourne settles himself to drink his coffee in the garden of the hotel, virtually everything that happens is revealed to the reader as it is to him, not merely physically but also in terms of what he makes of it. That is, the reader sees, for example, not merely 'a pretty American girl coming and standing in front of you in a garden', but is encouraged also to share his uncertainty in interpreting her sociability: 'Was she simply a pretty girl from New York State—were they all like that, the pretty girls who had a good deal of gentlemen's society? Or was she also a designing, an audacious, an unscrupulous young person? Winterbourne had lost his instinct in this matter, and his reason could not help him' (p. 19). Though the narrative is given in the third person, we are by now firmly within Winterbourne's responding consciousness. So much so, in fact, that one commentator, Stanley Geist, has written: 'A rich, pretty, "typical" American girl on tour of Europe stops over at Vevey and has with *the narrator of the tale* [my italics] what appears to be a flirtation.'[17] Geist's comment is either a mistake that grows out of a sense of Winterbourne as the tale's 'centre of consciousness' or a shorthand way of designating that particular mode of narration referred to by Booth as follows: 'But it was not until authors had discovered the full uses of the third-person reflector that they could effectively show a narrator changing as he *narrates*.'[18]

It is important to be as exact as possible about Winterbourne's narrational status since it so signally governs our response to *Daisy Miller*. His misunderstanding of Daisy's conduct is largely comic and this fact acts as a brake on what might have been a reader's tendency to regard her fate as tragic. The fact that she is 'shown' to us largely as she appears to Winterbourne has a curiously distancing effect on our view of Daisy herself because our more immediate point of identification is with the confused observer-narrator-

[16] Branigan, *Point of View*, 186.
[17] Stanley Geist, 'Portraits from a Family Album: *Daisy Miller*', Hudson Review, 5/2 (Summer 1952), 203.
[18] Booth, *Rhetoric of Fiction*, 157.

participant, with Winterbourne himself. As Booth judiciously notes: 'His slow and ready suspicions are admirably suited to make us aware of the pathos of Daisy, without giving our awareness too much emotional force.'[19]

In examining Bogdanovich's film version, I shall suggest that Daisy's drama, externally presented, as it were, is more susceptible to filming than the drama of Winterbourne's confused and developing consciousness, which is of its nature an inner one.

Narrational Mode: The Film

What becomes of the implied author?

The unobtrusive 'I' of the implied author of the novella is wholly dispensed with. There is no attempt at authorial voice-over and there is no reason why there should be: James's 'I' is in no sense a dramatized character. The only time in which any kind of voice-over is used is in the final scene at Daisy's graveside, when the sound-track records the novella's final conversation between Winterbourne and his aunt. However, this aural 'flash-forward' does not perform the function of 'authorial' voice-over of the kind associated with John Mills's Pip in *Great Expectations*. Perhaps the film's nearest approach to carrying out the functions of the implied author is in the rare objective shots (discussed below) which establish a setting and which correspond to the descriptive element of the narrator's role.

What becomes of the 'central reflector'?

As a drama of *restricted consciousness*, *Daisy Miller* requires the would-be-faithful film-maker (Bogdanovich appears to be one) to keep Winterbourne's view of the action in the forefront of the viewer's attention. He chooses a number of formal ways of doing so. *Daisy Miller* is a film of 400 shots,[20] an unusually small number for a feature film (cf. *The Scarlet Letter*'s 957), and analysis of these reveals that Winterbourne has 116 point-of-view shots, almost invariably followed by shots of him looking. Further, as if to reinforce the centrality of his consciousness, his point-of-view shots are frequently *bracketed* by shots of him looking; for example, in the morning segment in the hotel garden, in which there are 41 shots, 9 of Winterbourne's point-of-view shots are flanked by close-ups of him (twice in two-shots with Daisy). In a further 45 he appears in profile or less (sometimes back of head) while another character appears full-face, so that his implied gaze acts as a focus for

---

[19] Booth, *Rhetoric of Fiction*, 283.

[20] A more detailed account of the type and function of shots is given later in this chapter. See Appendix 4 for shot-by-shot summary.

the viewer's gaze; and from the time he appears in the garden, there are remarkably few objective shots in which he does not appear.

Even when his point-of-view forms part of a shot–reverse shot alternation, the object of his gaze does not necessarily return that gaze. For instance, in the scene in which he, later joined by Mrs Costello, observes Daisy and Giovanelli as they wander about St Peter's, they remain unaware that he is observing them, as the camera alternates between the watcher and the watched. Watchfulness and observation, looking for clues to understanding, may be seen as a key to the film's presentation of Winterbourne, as it is in the novella.

Perhaps even more closely analogous to James's use of a 'central reflector' are those shots in which Winterbourne appears at the edge of the frame looking 'up-screen' as it were, guiding the viewer's eye to the source of his own attention. The term 'up-screen' suggests an analogy with the three-dimensional theatrical performance in which, in order to highlight a particular actor at a given moment, it is common for actors nearer the front of the stage to turn 'up-stage' to observe him/her. Whereas the novel's linearity can achieve this effect by suppressing other presences, those other modes resort to means of directing audience gaze to the centre of attention. Whereas the point-of-view shot may just as easily be compared with first-person narration, the shot in which the protagonist whose stance we are asked to share appears at the edge of the screen suggests an analogy with the way James appears to be viewing the action of the novella over Winterbourne's shoulder. In the film, we see, in such shots, what Winterbourne sees but we also see *him* as well: we and the camera are looking, sometimes literally, over his shoulder. For instance, Winterbourne, down left of frame, with back of head to camera, looks up at Daisy who faces the camera full-face in close-up, as he tells her: 'I'm puzzled if you want to know'; his—and our—gaze is directed at her face for clues about how to 'read' it. In such shots, Bogdanovich appears to have found a visual analogy for a particular literary mode of narration.

The third way in which Bogdanovich works to render the novella's restricted vision of the action is by an austere limiting of 'objective' shots after Winterbourne has been introduced. Prior to this time there are placing shots of the hotel's interior and exterior, comparable in function to James's long opening descriptive paragraph. Afterwards, there are perhaps not more than a dozen clearly objective shots: that is, shots which represent neither Winterbourne's point of view nor anyone else's, and these tend to be in the interests of establishing a change in time and place. For instance, the evening scene at the 'Trois Couronnes' is introduced by a shot of the hotel's exterior before the camera cuts to Winterbourne coming out the front door; there are two front-door views of the Millers' Rome hotel held for a moment before Winterbourne appears in the street and enters; and there are objective shots of a carriage in a midnight street near the Colosseum which ushers in Winterbourne's discovery of Daisy and Giovanelli within. Elsewhere there are 'suppressed' point-of-view shots which are presented as objective (e.g. the first shot of Mrs Walker in her salon, the opera singer in close-up) but which are subsequently revealed to be from Winterbourne's point of view.

What I have tried to suggest is how 'Bogdanovich's technique establishes Winterbourne as the film's "central consciousness"',[21] as J. J. Liggera (without providing any gloss on the remark) has claimed. What Liggera claims seems to me true and demonstrable in the terms in which I have argued, but this is not to say that, despite such procedures, Bogdanovich can necessarily make the viewer privy to Winterbourne's thought processes in the way that the novella does. It does, however, argue for Bogdanovich's commitment to the novella's mode of narration and an unusually determined attempt to realize this in visual terms. Having stressed the predominance of Winterbourne's point-of-view shots and those 'over-the-shoulder' shots which guide the viewer's line of vision to comprehend Winterbourne's, it still has to be claimed that, along with the film's incapacity to render his thoughts directly, goes another matter in which the stylistic analogy breaks down. However assiduously Bogdanovich makes us share Winterbourne's point of view, the latter is inevitably compromised by the screen's necessarily concrete rendering of what he sees. Daisy and everything else that Winterbourne's gaze falls on have an objective life of their own which, for any given viewer, may not have the same connotations as they have for Winterbourne. Where the denotative material has to be rendered in the physical terms of moving images, the film-maker can be sure of everyone's physically seeing the same thing but cannot be sure of everyone's responding to it as Winterbourne does. The novella, with its linking commentary, forces us to limit our conceptions by insisting more firmly than the film can on what Winterbourne is making of what he sees. Reader and Winterbourne will each have quite different physical views of Daisy and the rest, but hard as the film tries to preserve the novella's 'centre of consciousness' approach the film-maker cannot be as sure that the viewer will share the protagonist's assessment. The range of critical response to Cybill Shepherd's Daisy attests to this: Liggera finds her 'radiant';[22] Gordon Gow dismisses her as nothing 'deeper than a pretty little flibbertigibbet, of whose chatter one tires';[23] Jay Cocks disliked the 'taunting sexual hostility'[24] she projects; and Shields claims that she 'comes across more as a *femme fatale* weaving her web about an

[21] J. J. Liggera, '"She Would Have Appreciated One's Esteem": Peter Bogdanovich's *Daisy Miller*', *Literature/Film Quarterly*, 9/1 (1981), 16.

[22] Ibid. 18.

[23] Gordon Gow, 'Daisy Miller', *Films and Filming*, 21/2 (Nov. 1974), 33.

[24] Jay Cocks, 'Culture Shock: *Daisy Miller*', *Time*, 103/22 (3 June 1974), 66.

ingenuous victim than James's young lady of innocent charm and delight'.[25] Confronted with the identical moving image and its aural accompaniment, these four views suggest responses to Daisy markedly different from each other's and (in at least three cases, necessarily) from Winterbourne's.

However, since the restricted consciousness approach works to avoid authoritative intervention by an author, the fact that many viewers may assess what they see differently from each other and from the protagonist is actually another way in which film and novella work analogically. The viewer may see what Winterbourne sees without being any more certain than he is of how to interpret it; at least until reaching Giovanelli's graveside pronouncement. In this sense there is a parallel between the film's showing and the novella's showing (i.e. essentially Daisy's behaviour). The parallel does not, however, extend so readily to that other element of the novella's showing (i.e. Winterbourne's puzzlement). The film can show us Winterbourne apparently thinking, but not, as the novella can, the nature of those thought processes.

There is one further, diegetic means by which Bogdanovich seeks to install Winterbourne as the film's centre of consciousness and that is by ending most major sequences with Winterbourne left standing (usually alone) as other figures (usually including Daisy) go off. His first meeting with Daisy ends by her leaving with the courier, Eugenio, while Winterbourne remains pensively in the garden watching their retreat. At the very end, he is left alone observing the mourners disappear from Daisy's graveside; this is followed by a close-up of his face, after which the camera pulls back slowly to leave him watching, solitary, in a long shot from which the colour gradually fades to white. What Bogdanovich has dramatized in this way is not merely James's narrative mode of the restricted consciousness but the potential loneliness of the inhibited observer who withholds affection and 'esteem' for fear of the object's being unworthy.

Film and 'the writing'

What the film irrevocably loses is the distinctive Jamesian voice that characterizes the novella's metalanguage, even though in this case that voice is for the most part subordinated to dramatizing Winterbourne's own thought processes. Even though James largely eschews the authoritative intervention of the omniscient novelist, the reader is still aware of the discriminatory, sometimes ironic mind of the implied author at work behind what are essentially Winterbourne's reflections. Whether or not a film-maker wants to be faithful to the original in this regard, he will be working in a much more uncertain area (than that of, say, the cardinal functions of the plot) and he

[25] Shields, *Daisy Miller*, 108.

will necessarily be engaged in intricate processes of adaptation. These processes involve the interplay of mise-en-scène and montage, of those codes
specific to the cinema and those more broadly cultural.

Enunciation, adaptation, and the codes

In considering how adaptation proper, as distinct from transfer, is used to
create meaning in the film version of *Daisy Miller* (i.e. at the level of *enunciation*), I shall consider first how those codes specific to cinema work to
manufacture, in a different signifying system, narrative and affective responses frequently similar to those produced by the novel, sometimes notably dissimilar. Secondly, I shall draw attention to ways in which the cinema
integrates these codes with others not specific to cinema but powerfully
influential in creating its effects.

Codes relating to cinematic punctuation

(a) Bogdanovich's film contains 400 shots and in all but two cases these are
separated by cuts. The two exceptions are: (i) between segments 4 and 5 (see
Appendix 4), where a dissolve is used to indicate the passage of several hours
between Winterbourne's meeting with his aunt and his evening meeting
with Daisy when he must tell her his aunt refuses to meet her; and (ii)
between segments 8 and 9, to indicate a gap of some months in time and a
shift from Vevey to Rome, when a fade is used. However, there are other
comparable breaks in time and changes in location (though less major than
that between Vevey and Rome) and these are not marked by dissolves or
fades. There may be some element of stylistic inconsistency here, but the
effect of linking not merely shots but sequences as well by cuts produces a
remarkably coherent, smooth-flowing effect, heightening the effect and importance of the *series of events* in which the narrative is displayed. Further, by
the 1970s, the dissolve and the fade were no longer used pervasively as they
had been in the 1940s and 1950s, when they conveyed not merely major shifts
in time and space, but, as well, particularly lyrical effects and narrative
nuance (cf. *Random Harvest*). As Barry Salt has written, in relation to the
1960s: 'Dissolves and other special forms of shot transition had always been
the site of ambiguity of meaning, so when films came to be made with cuts
as the only form of shot transition there was an increase in the potential
ambiguity of the cut.'[26] My point here is that Bogdanovich's preferred editing
procedure is not just a matter of response to the material of *Daisy Miller* but
a function of the cinematic practice of the time, and this must always be a
significant, extra-literary determinant in the adaptation process.

[26] Barry Salt, *Film Style and Technology: History and Analysis* (Starwood: London, 1983), 346–7.

(b) Several further points need to be made about the function and effect of cutting as virtually the only editing technique: (i) During several scenes of tensely conflicting interests, there is a good deal of rapid *alternation* between speakers (e.g. between Mrs Walker and Winterbourne in the carriage during the segment set in the Pincio, there is an exchange of ten quick shots as she tries to win him to her view of Daisy). (ii) Though segments almost invariably finish on cuts, these cuts most often succeed long-held shots, especially on Winterbourne as he watches others walk away or on his point of view of their retreat (e.g. segments 3, 4, 11, 14 (with Mrs Costello)). In some ways, the long-held shot plus cut has superseded effects of the fade and the dissolve. (iii) Cutting is kept to a minimum during certain key segments, in which long takes, marked by much tracking and panning and striking depth of field, are used to place and establish characters in their environments. The two segments in Mrs Walker's house are notable examples. At her afternoon reception (segment 10), there are only two shots, in which tracking and panning, and the use of mirrors to permit depth of field, create a remarkable sense of fluid movement at the same time as highlighting the key figures. And in the much longer segment (12) of the evening party, there are only seventeen shots in 6.53 minutes. Here, the depth of field, again increased by the use of mirrors, abetted by the graceful tracks and pans, gives a clear sense of a populous gathering in which several relationships are being furthered (invoking Welles and the ball scene in *The Magnificent Ambersons*).

The insistence on the cut to the virtual exclusion of other editing possibilities ends by reinforcing the swift poignancy of Daisy's short career. There is nothing gently reflective about Bogdanovich's Daisy (or James's) and the film's constant movement, dramatized in the tracking and panning within shots, and the pauseless cutting between sequences constitute a true adaptation of a brief, heedless life. Again, it is doubtful if the same can be said about the effectiveness of these procedures in dramatizing Winterbourne's inner confusion. The film has in this respect made its choice—if indeed the choice was open to it.

Codes relating to properties of the shot

(a) *Length of shot*. In the discussion on cutting above, I draw attention to examples of long takes which, interspersed with series of rapid alternation, contribute to the film's rhythmic pattern. A film of conventional length (92 minutes) but of only 400 shots and with considerable use of various kinds of rapid alternation must clearly also make more use of the long take than was common in the 1970s. Barry Salt claims that:

the trend towards the use of short Average Shot Lengths has continued and consolidated [i.e. in the 1970s]. Average Shot Lengths of 4 seconds or less are now fairly common, and hardly any ordinary commercial films have A.S.L.s longer than 9 seconds. Long Average Shot Lengths are now almost exclusively associated with high artistic ambition . . . the long take continues to be the standard mode in European art movies; in fact, the higher the pretensions, the longer the take.[27]

The Average Shot Length of *Daisy Miller* is a revealing 13.8 seconds and the film's general unpopularity with audiences may perhaps be partly attributed to its being at odds with prevailing preferences for a faster tempo. Further, it has, in Salt's term, 'high artistic ambition' by comparison with the director's earlier films (i.e. in adapting a literary classic); and, further still, much more so than his earlier films, *Daisy Miller* offers evidence that 'his sensibility is more European than American; his painterly style comes from his father's love of the French Impressionists'.[28]

There is no gratuitous lingering over the merely picturesque, but Bogdanovich knows when a point is better made by keeping the camera still or by graceful movement within the shot and when a tightening of tension is likely to be effected by a series of very brief shots. The latter occur notably in alternations between speakers or between watcher and watched or between other contrasts of narrative importance. A key example is the segment in the Pincian Gardens (11) which, with 89 shots, has 30 more than any other. This segment, centrally placed in the film, begins with Winterbourne escorting Daisy to the Pincio and ends with his watching her and Giovanelli, presumably kissing, behind her parasol. In between, tensions grow between Winterbourne and Daisy, Daisy and Mrs Walker, Winterbourne and Mrs Walker and the whole segment is crucial dramatically as being the cause of Mrs Walker's subsequent snubbing of Daisy, who is thereafter thrown more into Giovanelli's company, culminating in the fatal nocturnal visit to the Colosseum. The kind of drama being enacted in the Pincio segment requires a preponderance of rapid cutting to establish its tensions, but there is one shot, the twentieth, which lasts for 39 seconds and in this, following the enjoyment of the Punch and Judy show, there is a notable relaxation in the relationship between Daisy and Winterbourne. Her simple enjoyment of the show has eased Winterbourne's stiffness and the ease is maintained throughout tracking shots until it is broken by Daisy's insistence on joining Giovanelli.

There are at least twenty-two shots which last for more than 30 seconds and a dozen for more than a minute. It is worth considering the enunciatory functions of some of these long-held shots. For example, they are used:

(i) *to establish new settings*, such as the exterior of the 'Trois Couronnes' and Randolph's observation of it (45 seconds), or Mrs Costello's apartment in Rome and Winterbourne's restlessness in it (65 seconds);

(ii) *to introduce a character*, such as Mrs Costello in the medicinal baths, where the setting is also new (43 seconds), or Mrs Walker in her Rome salon (1 minute 6 seconds);

[27] Barry Salt, 349.   [28] Liggera, ' "She Would Have Appreciated One's Esteem" ', 18.

(iii) *to provide narrative 'fillers'*, such as when Winterbourne and his friend Charles, in the carriage at night, discuss their future plans and Daisy's behaviour (1 minute 9 seconds), and, most movingly and discreetly, the shot (61 seconds) which records the information of Daisy's death. In the latter, the camera follows Winterbourne along the street, through the hotel door, up the stairs until, as seen through the lace curtain on the door, he stops half-way, drops the hand carrying flowers, comes down the stairs and out the door, while the camera stays on the closed door. The same narrative information is transferred as in James's brief sentence, and its enunciation achieves a visual pathos and restraint comparable with the verbally achieved effect;

(iv) *to establish connections in a confined space*, as in the two social occasions at Mrs Walker's home. The longest shot in the film (4 minutes 12 seconds) at the afternoon At Home, connects Winterbourne first with Randolph, then with Daisy, then with Mrs Miller as Mrs Walker takes Daisy off, though the two remain visible in the mirrors before they come to rejoin the others, and the shot finishes on a disapproving close-up of Mrs Walker as she observes the departure of Winterbourne and Daisy.

(b) *Camera distance and angle*. These two aspects of the framing of the image, which produce 'a *certain vantage point* onto the material within the image',[29] are exercised by Bogdanovich so as to heighten certain narrative points.

There are just over 200 close-ups in the film; that is, almost half the shots of the film. The incidence is sufficient to point to the director's concern with faces (there are, of course, some close-ups of objects rather than faces), as if somehow the truth of the characters' behaviour could be established through a close scrutiny of faces. Very often, as in Winterbourne's characteristic watchfulness, a puzzled uncertainty is reflected, sometimes melting into a touching access of pleasure, or in Mrs Walker's often enigmatic close-ups an ambiguity of motive is suggested.

Medium shots are most often used in those sequences or segments in which the relationship of characters to their environment is important. For instance, in the visit to Chillon, the sense of happy venturesomeness as Daisy and Winterbourne wind about its ancient rooms and cloisters is rendered almost wholly through tracking shots of medium distance. The camera moves into close-up only when the rapport is broken as Daisy begins to chide Winterbourne for his proposed return to Geneva, and the contrast of his inhibition and her brash openness is presented in seven reverse-angle shots.

---

[29] David Bordwell and Kristin Thompson, *Film Art: An Introduction* (Addison-Wesley Publishing Co.: Reading, Mass., 1979), 109.

The shift from medium shot to close-up enunciates change in emotional atmosphere.

Similarly, the very few long shots are also emotionally charged. For instance, the long shot of Chillon Castle, subsequently identified as a point-of-view shot belonging to Daisy and Winterbourne, imbues the place with a misty romantic promise appropriate to the outset of the expedition. The shots of the castle which close the short segment of the carriage journey away from it, first as viewed by Daisy looking back through the rear window of the carriage and, two shots later, objectively viewed, now endow it with a sense of sadness. In leaving the castle in silent huffiness with Winterbourne, Daisy has left behind a lost opportunity for happiness.

As to angle of shot, the fact that for the most part Bogdanovich favours the 'straight-on' angle draws particular attention to those few occasions when he uses a high- or low-angle shot. The film begins and ends with high-angle shots, the former involving a slow vertical pan of the interior of the 'Trois Couronnes', the latter gradually isolating Winterbourne at Daisy's grave. The opening shot, and the one which ushers in the next segment in the garden with another vertical pan, this time of the exterior of the hotel, establishes the discreet luxury of the international watering-place in which the expatriate Winterbourne is so complacently at home. The final shot, by contrast, begins on a close-up of him, then pulls back and up to reveal him quite solitary. However, angle of shot rarely seems in *Daisy Miller* a major enunciatory element.

Codes integrated in the mise-en-scène and on the sound-track

Without wishing to attempt a full, detailed account of all those codes (e.g. visual, linguistic, broadly cultural) which inform mise-en-scène and soundtrack, several elements of *Daisy Miller* call for special attention in so far as they are crucial to the processes of adaptation proper (i.e. to the film's enunciation). By this, I mean essentially that they reinforce those contrasts which are at the heart of the novella's meaning and which Bogdanovich has sought to adapt to film.

(*a*) *Lighting*: The film contrasts the dappled Renoiresque softness of the Vevey exteriors with the bright light of the Roman spring, and the opulent brightness of Mrs Walker's artificially lit salon with the pale blues and shadows of the interior of the Colosseum, where Daisy is finally 'sacrificed' as a result of the coldness of the treatment meted out to her at Mrs Walker's party.

(*b*) *Setting*: Fifty years ago, *Daisy Miller* might have been filmed entirely in the studio; by 1974, location shooting was taken for granted. Bogdanovich has filmed in the actual locations named in the novella but has for the most part scrupulously resisted the temptation of the merely pictorial. His exteriors reflect broadly a contrast between Vevey and Rome in matters of formality; his interiors reflect the personalities of their occupants (Mrs Walker's mirror-dominated rooms, the subdued dignity of Mrs Costello's).

(c) *Language codes*: Daisy's rapid speech and her accent (perhaps indeed 'a good thousand miles south of Schenectady'[30]) establishes her as rawly American, in contrast with the deliberateness of Mrs Costello's East Coast propriety and Mrs Walker's measured severities. In Winterbourne's speech, as in Mrs Walker's, American-ness has been overlaid with internationalism, so that, in his opening encounter with the grating-voiced Randolph, the latter has trouble in identifying Winterbourne's nationality. Both he and Mrs Walker 'have lived too long in Geneva', a fact of considerable dramatic importance at least partly signified through manipulation of language codes. Of course it is not just a matter of accent or timbre but of diction as well and, whereas Daisy's tumble of words seems scarcely to reflect choice, the careful tones of a Mrs Walker or a Mrs Costello give utterance to words selected for particular effect.

(d) *Non-linguistic sound codes*: The use of music is especially important here. Against the massed weight of Mozart, Bach, Haydn, Verdi, *et al.*, signifiers of European high culture as surely as the Colosseum signifies its cruelty, are posed two American folk-songs: 'Pop Goes the Weasel' and 'When You and I Were Young, Maggie'. The latter acquires a haunting thematic significance when it is played on the sound-track over the grave of a girl who was never anything *but* young. The social and cultural contrasts reinforced by the music are obvious.

(e) *Cultural codes*: As to more broadly based cultural codes, I have already adverted to ways in which Bogdanovich has used contrasts in costume, bearing, and décor to establish the oppositions which are at the core of both novella and film. James gives virtually no information about costume, for example; it is an element of adaptation rather than of transference, then, which leads Bogdanovich to dress Daisy persistently in lacy pastels, pale blues, and pinks, which set her off from Mrs Walker's more sophisticated styles and more vivid hues.

To conclude, one short, charming sequence (segment 15) pulls together those codes relating to the mise-en-scène with those of soundtrack and montage and in the process encapsulates a good deal of the film's meaning. Significantly it is a sequence invented for the film. After several fruitless visits to the Millers' hotel (filmed in a way that recalls the vain, repeated visits, in a similar cause, paid by Eugene Morgan to the Amberson house in Welles's film), Winterbourne one afternoon finds Daisy there, entertaining Giovanelli at the piano. Opening the door as Daisy calls 'Avanti',

---

[30] Jonathan Rosenbaum, '*Daisy Miller*', *Sight and Sound*, 43/4 (Autumn 1974), 247.

Winterbourne's point of view takes in the scene. Invited to come in and sit down, he listens first to Giovanelli sing 'Pop Goes the Weasel' as Daisy plays, speeding up the tempo to the point of absurdity, then to Daisy sing 'Maggie'. In narrative terms, the sequence is not especially important. Thematically, however, it establishes in visual and aural terms the cultural contrast at the heart of the story.

The sheer guilelessness of Daisy is signified by her invitation to Winterbourne to enter and to sit by the piano, her engaging imperiousness in the series of commands to Winterbourne ('Don't just stand there. Bring that chair over and sit down', 'Hurry up, Mr Winterbourne', etc.) interspersed with chatter about where her mother and brother are. In an opulent Roman hotel room, with pale green walls and gilt panelling, graceful crimson curtains hung in flounces over the two large windows which flank the piano, heavy red-velvet chairs with gilt woodwork, and handsome flower vases, a pretty girl stands and sings a simple, sentimental American folk-song. As she does, Bogdanovich at first cuts between her, surrounded by the light of the window, and Winterbourne's face, framed by the heavy gilt of the chair. The slight pomposity of his expression melts at the unaffected charm of the picture before him, and the camera then stays on Daisy until she finishes the song. She sings with no special distinction, perhaps not even with a proper sense of the meaning of the words, but the performance is nevertheless perfectly *right*: that is, the singer and mortality seem at this moment so remote from each other that a more 'acted' version of the song about old age would be less, not more, poignant. The cultural conflict of the New World and the Old is effortlessly established through the visual contrast of Daisy and her setting, and emotionally the scene says a good deal about the relationship between Daisy and Winterbourne. She offers him affection (love?) and he fails to read her correctly. Whether or not the scene is 'Jamesian', it renders cinematically some of James's central concerns and is truly an example of adaptation proper, of using the resources of film to arrive at a thematic and affective content that recalls the earlier mode without 'copying' it. Only Jonathan Baumbach among reviewers seems wholly to have appreciated this 'exceptional sequence', claiming that 'in it we glimpse the fragile bravado of her [Daisy's] peculiarly American innocence and her character gains new focus for us'.[31]

SPECIAL FOCUS: THE LIMITS OF FIDELITY

Bogdanovich's *Daisy Miller* offers a very instructive case-study because of the kind of fidelity to which it has aspired—and because of the near-uniform

---

[31] Jonathan Baumbach, 'Europe in the Movies', *Partisan Review*, 41/3 (1974), 451.

hostility of its critical reception. It is ironic to note at this stage that James himself sought to adapt *Daisy Miller* into theatrical form,[32] and received even more opprobrium than Bogdanovich. And, one might add, and with more reason; for James filled out the novella with several foolish intrigues and fashioned a happy ending for Daisy and Winterbourne, in both of these changes drawing on the conventions of less rigorous literary modes.

Fidelity to the Text

In spite of Bogdanovich's published disclaimer of reverential intentions ('I don't want to spend too much time worrying about Henry James. Except to take whatever I can from the story that I like'[33]), the film does, as I have shown, hew very close to the original. Even Bogdanovich, in the same interview, allows that 'on the surface I think we've been very faithful to the story'. In view of the film's retention of the novella's major incidents (and most of its minor ones), of most of its dialogue, of all its named characters, and of its specific settings, that seems an understatement. Further, though he claims that: 'The thing that interests me *least* is what James saw in it', I have shown, in my analysis of the film's narrational mode, that he has sought and substantially reproduced the point of view of the original. That is, through his use of Winterbourne's physical point of view and his placement in the frame on many occasions, he has sought to focus the viewer's attention on the events in a cinematic way that has appreciable parallels with James's own methods.

Fidelity to the text is not measured merely by what is retained and how that is presented but also by the extent and nature of inventions and departures from the original. In a chapter-by-chapter comparison, the inventions for the film can be summarized as follows:

Chapter 1: Randolph's shoe-swapping trick comically foreshadows the theme of American brashness confronting and disrupting European decorums.

Chapter 2: Apart from a moment's play with Winterbourne's hat on the boat to Chillon (fulfilling a similar function to Randolph's trick), the only major invention is a striking change of setting (see below).

Chapter 3: The two episodes comprising this chapter are retained intact, with two minor additions. The Punch and Judy show is used to contrast Daisy's easy delight with Winterbourne's comparative stiffness; and there are two brief, enigmatic long shots of a woman in white observing Winterbourne as he stands with Daisy at the show, and of his returning her glance. Liggera's account of this latter invention draws attention to the fact

[32] Henry James, *Daisy Miller: A Comedy in Three Acts* (1882), in William T. Stafford (ed.), *James's Daisy Miller: The Story, The Play, The Critics* (Charles Scribner's Sons: New York, 1953).

[33] Dawson, 'Continental Divide', 14.

that she is 'an older, more mature woman, a knowing woman' and that at this point Daisy also catches Winterbourne's eye, 'but there is a world of difference between these looks. One is flirtatious; the other is lustful. But Winterbourne can respond to neither. He is too caught between cultures to advance towards either European decadence or American innocence.'[34] The explanation is attractive and thematically coherent, but the shots of the woman are too fleeting and too distant to be other than puzzling.

Chapter 4: The character of Charles, Winterbourne's former school-friend and Mrs Walker's companion, performs some of the functions attributed to an unnamed friend in the novella and also suggests an effeteness which may be Winterbourne's eventual fate. The singing sequence is discussed at the end of the previous section; and the Opera sequence provides occasion for acquainting Winterbourne with information about Daisy that is given in a few summarizing statements in the original.

There is a very high level of fidelity to the words of the novella's dialogue, so high in fact that deviations from it tend to be unduly obvious to one who knows the original well. When Mrs Costello expresses her disgust with the Millers and their courier, she finishes in the novella by saying: 'He sits with them in the garden, in the evening. I think he smokes' (p. 266). In the film the phrase 'in their faces' is added: not much, maybe, but a tiny crudification of the kind that perhaps grates on the Jamesian purist, though justifiable in reinforcing for the 1970s audience the sense of social violation implied. Reviewers have drawn attention to added anachronisms (e.g. Daisy's 'I like just hanging about'), to the script's allowing Giovanelli a few mildly comic lapses in his command of English, to Daisy's use of 'quaint' rather than 'pretty' in describing the Colosseum by moonlight (it 'makes her innocence seem more moronic than charming', claims one[35]). Most of these complaints seem to me quibbles in the light of the overriding fidelity to the words of the original. More arguable are some of the inflections given to those words; but 'arguable' is exactly what they are: that is, whether or not an actor's reading of a particular piece of dialogue coincides with a listener's expectations must always be uncertain, at the mercy of so many diverse subjectivities.

Though the film is largely 'faithful' on the levels of incident, dialogue, setting, and character, and though nothing of narrative consequence is omitted, except the novella's final statement of Winterbourne's return to Geneva, the 'fidelity' critics clearly have something more in mind than this kind of scrupulous transfer of the transferable. What their dissatisfaction comes down to seems to be a sense that the illusion of reality created by the film does not coincide with their perception of the illusion of reality created by the novella. They write as though the latter were somehow *fixed* and that it

---

[34] Liggera, ' "She Would Have Appreciated One's Esteem" ', 20.
[35] Rosenbaum, '*Daisy Miller*', 247.

is merely obtuse of the film-maker not to have noticed this and reproduced it in the new medium. Further, in the case of *Daisy Miller*, dissatisfaction must be essentially located in their perception of the processes of *adaptation proper*, for it is in these that the film-maker's own proclivities, the constraints of the industry and art-form in which he works, and his own individual reading of the original (as distinct from that of his critics) make themselves felt.

When one considers the critical reception given to Bogdanovich's film, one is struck by the way the objections, on the basis of fidelity-related issues, are couched in terms of amorphous, ill-defined disapproval. The following are some samples: 'a literary adaptation which reveals a fine contempt for literary subtlety',[36] chides Dawson; Sandra Hall considers that 'The screenplay . . . is boringly faithful to James's slight story',[37] while Simon claims that 'a novella in particular runs the danger of inadequate additions [when filmed]',[38] prior to listing a few trivial examples; Cocks complains of, *inter alia*, 'the numbing literalness' of the film at the expense of James's 'nuance and inference';[39] David Shipman insists that 'James's subtleties are entirely lost';[40] Shields believes that 'Bogdanovich's rendition of the story shows at best a tenuous relationship to James's conception';[41] and Rosenbaum finds it 'neither fish nor fowl: too indifferent to Jamesian nuance to qualify as appreciation, too faithful (in terms of the over-all plotting and dialogue . . .) to gain credence as an attack on the original'.[42]

The fact that one writer finds 'boringly faithful' a film which another sees as having only 'a tenuous relation' to the original while yet another finds it 'too faithful' suggests that there is no clear consensus about what 'faithful' means in this discourse. Faithful to what? To events, characters, some vague notion of the 'spirit' or 'conception' of the original: that is, to matters of varying degrees of ascertainable, objective truth in relation to the original? As to the other comments, one might reasonably ask whether 'literary subtlety' has any necessary place in a film (whether or not it is derived from a novel) or whether James's means of establishing 'nuance and inference' (i.e. purely *verbal* means) are likely to be a film-maker's means. And if James's 'subtleties are entirely lost', this is not surprising, again since they are wholly verbal in their rendering. If the film is to be subtle, to work through 'nuance and inference' (presumably the writer means 'implication'), it will need to find cinematic ways to do so.

The point of adducing a bunch of representative reviews is to draw attention to the depressing fuzziness and the unpondered subjectivity of the

---

[36] Jan Dawson, '*Daisy Miller, Monthly Film Bulletin*, British Film Institute, 41/489 (Oct. 1974), 222.

[37] Sandra Hall, 'Directors in a double take', *Bulletin*, 96 (17 Aug. 1974), 39.

[38] Simon, *Reverse Angle*, 154.

[39] Cocks, 'Culture Shock', 66.

[40] David Shipman, *The Story of Cinema*, vol. ii (Hodder and Stoughton: London, 1984), 1213.

[41] Shields, '*Daisy Miller*', 106.   [42] Rosenbaum, '*Daisy Miller*', 274.

prevalent critical response to the film adaptation in general and to *Daisy Miller* in particular. It is castigated for being both too faithful and too little faithful without any clear sense of the writers' having reflected on what they mean by the term, or of their having discriminated between those novelistic elements to which fidelity is possible (whether or not it is desirable) and those to which it is not. Rosenbaum's 'neither fish nor fowl' dismissal implies that one or other approach might have succeeded, but that there is no hope of artistic success if a film-maker elects to transfer what he chooses (from what he can) while using this as a basis for creating his own (perfectly respectable) work of art. Fidelity, it needs to be stressed, cannot profitably be used as an evaluative criterion; it can be no more than a descriptive term to designate loosely a certain kind of adaptation.

None of the foregoing is meant to suggest that there is anything inherently culpable in a film-maker's wish to recreate as nearly as he can, in cinematic form, a work which has its origins in another medium. In writing of the film's closing segments, with its 'sense of waste and lost [*sic*], an irrevocable past unspent, the shame of having wilfully misperceived the object of his love', Baumbach writes: 'It is James's theme, and Bogdanovich seems peculiarly alive to it as if it were a shared vision they had arrived at by separate routes.'[43] That seems to me not merely true of this film but a wise statement of a perfectly legitimate goal for a film-maker *and* a recognition that the path by which it is arrived at (i.e. through a quite different signifying system) will look notably different. It may also be read as understanding a distinction between what may be transferred (from 'a shared vision' one may infer the underlying narrative pattern) and what must be adapted (those 'separate routes').

Fidelity to Period and Place

No amount of attention to authentic re-creation of the period in which a novel is set or filming it in the actual locations in which the novel's events are placed will guarantee the sort of textual fidelity to which the would-be-faithful adaptor aspires. Nevertheless, whether a film is derived from a novel or not, if it is in a predominantly realist mode the viewer will not normally welcome a jarring anachronism or an obviously inaccurate representation of place. On these counts, Bogdanovich's film is essentially a faithful transposition of *Daisy Miller*.

As to period, he has adhered to the mores of the novella in so far as these are conveyed by dialogue, with the very few (perhaps) anachronistic touches indicated. Exactly when a young woman might have begun to say: 'I like just hanging around', I cannot be sure, and the moment passes in the film

---

[43] Baumbach, 'Europe in the Movies', 451.

without disrupting my sense of the period, perhaps because it seems to belong to Cybill Shepherd's Daisy, whether or not it would seem appropriate to James's. Bogdanovich claims that the songs, 'Maggie' and 'Pop Goes the Weasel', are authentically of that period. Certainly, they are used to admirable *dramatic* effect in the sequence described above, and that seems a higher order of authenticity.

With regard to settings, Bogdanovich had 'permission to shoot the story's authentic locations (including the Pincio and Colosseum in Rome, the Château de Chillon, and the exclusive Hotel des Trois Couronnes in Vevey)'.[44] On a visit to Vevey, I discovered that Bogdanovich's fidelity in the use of the Château de Chillon in fact belongs to a period twenty years later than that in which James's novella is set. Its complete restoration was only begun in 1897 by architect Albert Naef. As to the Hotel des Trois Couronnes, the memoirs of its late owner describe how, for the film, 'Des mètres cubes de gravier, recourant le dallage moderne, furent déversés sur la terrasse; des candélabres d'époque replacèrent pour quelques semaines les modernes réverbères . . .',[45] along with further recollection of the changes made in the interest of authenticity of period setting. So much for fidelity to time and place. However, Bogdanovich has used the contrast between the Swiss and Roman settings in such a way as to underline certain narrative contrasts which are also to be found in the novella. The most contentious departure from the original is in the use of the medicinal baths as a setting for Winterbourne's first conversation with his aunt, Mrs Costello. Again, Bogdanovich justifies an invention of his own, saying: 'The mixed bathing is authentically of the period. And they're not really underdressed; they are even more absurd-looking because they are dressed so much'.[46] As Mrs Costello and Winterbourne talk, a tea-tray floats between them and another tray with a silver vase of flowers drifts by: it is comic, but there is also a propriety about it which is in keeping with Mrs Costello's stringent social code. It may be argued that our sense of her propriety is strengthened if she can appear dignified, even magisterial, in so bizarre a setting.

There is, however, a more important point at issue here than whether or not the setting enhances or detracts from the film's presentment of Mrs Costello, or even than whether or not it is authentically of the period. James was not writing a period piece in *Daisy Miller*, so that many details of time and place could be taken for granted. When such details are rendered in visual images a century later, they run the risk of seeming, as Daisy herself might have said, 'quaint'. That is, they draw attention to themselves as exhibiting a kind of authenticity which is not at the heart of the experience

[44] Dawson, "Continental Divide', 14.

[45] Marcel Herminjard, *Souvenirs d'un hôtelier veveysan* (Imprimerie Sauberlin & Pfeiffer SA: Vevey, 1976).

[46] Dawson, 'Continental Divide', 15.

of the original text. The baths may be authentically of the period but not of James. This setting represents the most extreme example in the film of that concern for period details which draws attention to itself. This is fidelity of a different order from that which is at stake in most discussions of how closely the film provides an experience equivalent to the reading of the novel.

Whatever Bogdanovich's stated intentions, the final effect of his *Daisy Miller* is one that preserves much of the narrative and affective life of the original in a careful, sometimes independent transposition into another medium. It seems to me a prime example of what the faithful film version may achieve—and of the limits to fidelity inevitable in seeking to make such a transposition.

Danny (Juliette Lewis), Leigh (Jessica Lange), and Sam Bowden in the final moments
of Martin Scorsese's *Cape Fear*

5

Cape Fear (1991)

W H E N John MacDonald's book *The Executioners* was reprinted in the wake of Martin Scorsese's 1991 film adaptation, the book's cover bore in large print the name under which the film appeared—*Cape Fear*. The original title was given in letters approximately one-quarter the height of the film's name. It is, of course, by no means uncommon, indeed is almost mandatory, for the film version of a book to lead to republication of the original, usually with a cover illustration from the film, and the legend, 'Now a major motion picture'. What is unusual is for the film so completely to obliterate the identity of the novel in the way of *Cape Fear* in relation to *The Executioners*. In fact, MacDonald's novel has been filmed twice: in 1991 by Scorsese, and in 1961 by J. Lee-Thompson, both times for Universal Pictures.

The Special Focus for this case-study will be the effect of significant time-lapse between the appearance of a novel and its film version, and in this instance the study is particularly interesting in view of the fact that the novel was first filmed only four years after it appeared in 1957 and then refilmed thirty years later. In some ways, Scorsese's film is as much a remake of Lee-Thompson's film as it is a version of MacDonald's novel, as detailed analysis of plotting will reveal; ideologically, though, Scorsese's film is light years from either. It is a film of 1991, rather than a 'faithful' rendering of a novel written thirty-odd years before.

MacDonald is the prolific author of many thrillers, perhaps best known for the Travis McGee series of private eye detective fictions, and very accomplished within his chosen genre. Scorsese, with an infinitely darker view of human behaviour, and no doubt with a sense of how the world has moved on and older certainties been undermined, has fashioned a film which works both as a chilling melodrama *and as* a study of the gaping cracks which have appeared in the structures of middle-class life since then.

NARRATIVE AND TRANSFER

Structural Patterns: The Novel

Story and plot order

The Executioners is essentially linear in its structure, with no more than a handful of minor 'flashbacks' to fill in important elements of background information. In terms of Bordwell and Thompson's distinction between story and plot,[1] the earliest events which the novel records are:

(a) the meeting of Sam Bowden and his wife Carol as college students (chapter 5[2]) and their subsequent wartime marriage (whereas the earliest *plot* event is the disruption of the Bowdens' happy beach holiday by the return of Cady);

(b) Cady's rape of a girl in Australia during the war and Sam's witnessing of this, which is responsible for Cady's being sent to prison (chapter 1, pp. 5–10);

(c) Cady's post-gaol career, including the return to humiliate the wife who had divorced him when he was in gaol.

(a) is narrated omnisciently, as a formal dip into the past, and is placed after Cady has sought to frighten Sam by telling him how he has ill-treated his ex-wife. It is placed at a time when Sam's fear for *his* family has been wound up, so that the flashback is made to seem like his memory of how their happy family had begun with that meeting in late 1942.

(b) is given through Sam's account to Carol as they lie at ease on the beach after a picnic lunch when Cady has already resurfaced in his life. That is, crucial material from the past is presented through Sam's own recollections, as if it, like Cady himself, represented some sort of 'return of the repressed'. In a very brief flashback and in answer to Sam's narrative, Carol also recounts an experience of the recent unnerving appearance of a strange man, whom she now believes to be Cady and whom she had seen sitting on their fence, while their dog Marilyn barked at him (p. 11). In other words, Cady is first filtered to the reader through the eyes of those he has come to torment and prey on, rather than objectively.

(c) is told in two parts. The first, and very much the briefer, is by Charlie Hooper, 'our bright young city attorney' (p. 13), who provides Sam a report on Cady's movements since his release from a Kansas prison the previous September, concluding that there is 'Nothing out of line' in Cady's post-prison period (pp. 17–18). The second is by Cady himself as he forces Sam to listen, taunting him by the comparison of his own wrecked married life and the child he doesn't know with Sam's apparently rewarding family life (pp. 64–6). The implied threat of revenge is not lost on Sam.

Apart from these short, necessary excursions into the past, the novel's structure unfolds on strictly linear principles, story and plot distinctions otherwise minimal. I draw attention to this point here in order to highlight certain departures from this procedure in Scorsese's film.

---

[1] David Bordwell and Kristin Thompson, *Film Art: An Introduction*, 4th edn. (McGraw Hill: New York, 1993), 65.

[2] John MacDonald, *The Executioners* (1957) (Penguin Books,: Harmondsworth, 1991), 74–82. (Subsequent references are given in brackets as they occur.)

Overall structuring pattern

To invoke Barthes's narrative codes, the 'hermeneutic' of *The Executioners*,[3] the question or puzzle which gives shape to the whole structure of the work, is something like this: what will be the effect on a comfortable, perhaps complacent middle-class family when a vengeful figure from the husband's past suddenly reappears after fourteen years? In psychoanalytic terms, there is a strong suggestion of the return of the repressed, of the surfacing to the consciousness of some creature of the id.

The concept of a placid, seemingly secure family or community about to be tested by the unwanted invasion of some alien and threatening presence is by no means uncommon. MacDonald wastes no time in introducing the disruptive presence; when the novel opens, Sam Bowden is already aware of a threat and is trying, 'almost with desperation, to tell himself that all was right with his particular world. Everything was fine' (pp. 1–2).

All that follows is dictated by Cady's invasion of Sam's 'particular world'. Sam is forced to take steps to secure his family against the threat of Cady, and the difficulty of doing so is compounded by the limits to which the law can help him. The novel stresses Sam as a somewhat idealistic upholder of the processes of the law: he is viewed in his legal firm as the one who is protected from 'some parts of the business' with which the other partners 'dirty [their] hands' (p. 90): he will be pushed into using non-legal methods to deal with the threat of Cady when it is clear that there are no grounds for his arrest. Sam is thus working on two fronts: he is seeking means to remove the threat of Cady; and he is busy getting his family out of harm's way, so that he can act against Cady without the emotional distraction of his family's safety. Cady's death, partly as a result of Sam's bullet, is a matter of 'savage satisfaction' (p. 208).

The overall structural pattern, then, could be summarized as follows: harmony, disruption, dealing with disruption, eliminating disruptive force, restoration of harmony, where harmony is equated with middle-class family life and disruption is embodied in the violent, revenge-seeking, animalistic Cady.

Structuring oppositions

Sam's daughter, Nancy, has been taught by her English teacher that 'good fiction is good because it has character development in it that shows that nobody is completely good and nobody is completely evil. And in bad fiction the heroes are a hundred per cent heroic and the villains are a hundred per cent bad. But I think that man [Cady] is all bad' (p. 69). Nancy's teacher's willingness to categorize is probably misplaced, but there is not a lot of

---

[3] Roland Barthes, *S/Z*, trans. Richard Miller (Hill and Wang: New York, 1974), 84.

evidence to suggest that MacDonald would be radically opposed to it. The polarities, about which his novel is constructed, are not seen as problematic in his scheme. There may be a suggestion that the middle-class paradigm of the Bowden ménage is potentially fragile, vulnerable to external invasion, but that doesn't lead either the Bowdens or the implied author seriously to question its essential rightness and soundness. At the end, the suburban couple walk down to the beach hand in hand: 'A handsome, mild and civilised couple, with no visible taint of violence, no lingering marks of a dreadful fear' (p. 214). There is no suggestion of a reexamination of the nature of the way they live, only a sense of *fear*'s having been dispelled. The other pole—the monster from without and below—is represented as 'all bad'.

Structural Patterns: The Film

Story and plot

The essential linearity of the novel is compromised by the way in which the events of the film are flanked by the voice-over comments of Sam's daughter Danny. The effect of this procedure is a dual one: first, it gives the entire film the status of a flashback; and, second, it casts some unsettling light on the reliability of the events of the plot, an impression intensified by Danny's final voice-over. Here she talks about 'dreams' and not letting Cady into them, saying that the family never spoke to each other about him. Within the confines of these verbal book-ends, the events which make up the plot follow the novel's linear structure.

Unlike in the novel, Cady is introduced 'objectively': we see him for the first time doing push-ups in his prison cell, just prior to his release, rather than being given his story as it is recalled by Sam. The effect of this is to confer on Cady a character status equal to that of Sam, from the outset; he is physically there in the film's present before anything is known about him, instead of being part of someone else's possibly fallible, partial recollection. The details of his imprisonment and post-prison career are gradually allowed to filter through (see segments 8, 11, 17). There is no equivalent to the novel's 'flashback' in chapter 5, which records the meeting and early married life of the Bowdens. Such an account would not be in the interests of the ideological slant of the Bowden/Cady conflict in this version of the story.

Overall structuring pattern

Scorsese retains the basic 'story' events of the novel, though manipulating them to somewhat different ends, as will be shown. Sam Bowden (Nick Nolte) is still responsible for Cady's (Robert De Niro) having been sent to gaol, though the circumstances, including Sam's involvement as Cady's counsel, have been altered. The arrival of Cady in the town of New Essex, when released from prison, still constitutes a threat to the Bowden family and home; and, as in the novel, lawyer Sam is pushed into seeking out non-legal means to restrain Cady. When these means prove futile, Sam removes his wife and daughter to the film's eponymous hideaway, to which Cady follows him,[4] and this leads to a prolonged battle for survival and the death of Cady. The overall pattern is the same, despite minor differences of plotting: the two texts are constructed upon the disruption of the status quo by a vengeful intruder, who is eventually thwarted. If the film feels like a very different experience from the novel (or indeed from the 1961 film), that difference will be largely located at other levels of the narrative.

Transfer of Narrative Functions

Major cardinal functions

As is so often the case, certainly in mainstream cinema, most of the Barthesian cardinal functions, those 'hinge-points' or 'risky moments' of narrative, have been retained. The most basic events in the plot of both novel and film can be summarized as follows:

- arrival of Max Cady, seeking revenge
- the disruption of Sam Bowden's family, home, and professional life
- the vanquishing of the avenger.

Within this bare framework, common to novel and film, the narrative unfolds through the operation of its cardinal functions, connected both sequentially and consequentially, and carrying out the function designated by Barthes in his 1974 taxonomy as the 'proairetic', glossed by one critic as 'the code that gives us the series of actions upon which the narrative is constructed".[5]

Novel

In MacDonald's novel, the following may be designated the major cardinal functions, given in the order in which they appear in the *story's* chronology:

1. Sam Bowden witnesses Cady's crime in wartime Australia.
2. Cady is sent to prison for fourteen years.
3. Cady acquires powerful desire for revenge on Sam.

---

[4] In fact, Cady not so much 'follows' the Bowdens to Cape Fear as 'accompanies' them, by strapping himself to the underside of their station wagon.

[5] Robin Wood, 'Notes for a Reading of *I Walked with a Zombie*', *CineAction!*, 3/4 (Winter 1986), 8.

4. Cady tracks Sam down on release from prison.
5. Sam tries vainly to have the threat of Cady removed.
6. Sam engages private detective Sievers to report on Cady's movements.
7. Sievers, finding nothing illegal, recommends 'work[ing] him over'.
8. Sam refuses to go outside the law to deal with Cady.
9. Cady poisons the Bowdens' dog.
10. Sam takes steps—shooting practice, keeping family busy with boat, etc.
11. Cady tries to frighten Sam with tale of revenge on ex-wife.
12. Sam fails to get comfort or serious help from police or from legal partner.
13. Sam asks Sievers to use tougher measures.
14. Cady is arrested after a fight with three thugs sent to beat him up, and gaoled for thirty days.
15. Sam uses this time to get family out of town, and to try to get case moving against Cady.
16. Sam fails to persuade Bessie, whom Cady has attacked, to help.
17. Cady, out of gaol, shoots Sam's son Bucky at summer camp and causes car accident for his wife Carol.
18. Sam wants to murder Cady.
19. Sam and Carol devise plan to lure Cady to the house.
20. Plan goes awry: Cady attacks Carol and kills Corporal Kersek, the young policeman detailed to help Sam.
21. Sam wounds Cady, who later dies.
22. The Bowden family is reunited.

The above list may not be comprehensive, but I would argue that to remove any of them would be to effect serious changes in the outcome of the narrative. Each of the above is of course surrounded by minor cardinal functions (to list all of which would be unwieldy) and by catalysers which help to embed the major functions listed in a persuasive existential reality. Take, for instance, function (19): the action it refers to is led up to by a series of moves which have led to an increasing sense of powerlessness on Sam's part; to Carol's outburst to Police Captain Dutton, which leads to the seconding of Kersek to the case; and there are complicated arrangements, with the status of 'catalysers', involved in setting the trap for Cady. And in (20), the cause–effect chain is partly propelled by a series of minor cardinal functions which account, for example, for why Sam is delayed in appearing on the scene of Cady's arrival at his house, and with such catalysers as the way Sam 'lowered himself hastily through the trap door, found the rungs of the ladder with his toes' (p. 194), small actions connected to each other sequentially, rather than consequentially.

Film

In Scorsese's film, the causality implied in the above list is maintained, as indeed are almost all of the major cardinal functions. There are, however, several points worth noting in this respect.

- Though function (2) above—'Cady is sent to prison for 14 years'—is retained, and though it is still the result of Sam's intervention, the nature of that intervention is significantly different in the film. In the novel, Cady is sent to prison on the basis of Sam's testimony; in the film, he is gaoled at least partly because Sam, as his Counsellor, has suppressed evidence which might have substantially reduced his sentence. In other words, the same effect is produced by a mutated version of the cause, and the reason for this change is important on an ideological level, as will be shown presently.
- Function (17) is omitted; in the film, Sam has only one child, a daughter, the 14-year-old Danny (Juliette Lewis), an object of Cady's threats, but not ultimately of actual violence; and the car accident is also omitted. By the comparable stage of the film, Cady's threats are directed more generally at the family at large, and at anyone (the cook, Kersek) who comes between him and his plans.
- Functions (15) and (19), (20), (21)—Sam's arrangements to secure his family and to get rid of the menace of Cady—are all subsumed in the film's final move to Cape Fear. Here, on the Bowdens' houseboat, Cady threatens to rape Sam's wife, Leigh (Jessica Lange), and daughter and knocks Sam overboard. There is a long segment (48) of sustained violence on the river, before Sam ultimately vanquishes Cady and the family is left huddling together, having just barely survived not merely Cady's threat to their lives but also the essential fragility of the bonds between them.
- Functions (6), (7), and (13) involve Sievers in the novel, whereas (20) introduces a new character, Kersek. The film retains the functions they perform in the novel but assigns them all to one character called Kersek. Further, the function involving the death of Kersek is placed significantly earlier in the film: that is, the attempt to lure Cady into the Bowdens' house to give a legitimate reason to kill him leads to the death of Kersek, but *not* of Cady. He is saved in the film for a major showdown with Sam in the remoteness of Cape Fear.
- In function (16) in the novel, Sam fails to persuade the woman whom Cady has beaten up to help; she is a stranger to him with no other role in the novel than to be a minor victim of Cady's brutality. In the film, Sam has been having an affair with the woman and this both motivates Cady's horrific treatment of her and seriously compromises Sam's hero role.

- The meeting between Cady and Sam's daughter, Danny, in her school's drama theatre (segment 33) is an invention of the film. It is very important in thematic terms, as a key scene in Cady's attempt to corrupt Sam's family life and for what it says about Danny's burgeoning sexuality, a matter treated with sitcom levity for the most part in the novel. It is one of the longest segments in the film, but it is an elaboration of one of the book's motifs rather than the introduction of a new major cardinal function. In both texts, the threat to Sam's child/children, especially to his adolescent daughter, is an element in Cady's revenge plans; the film chooses to foreground this more forcibly than the novel, and especially (though not only) in the segment referred to.

Overall, then, there is a close parallel between the cardinal functions which carry the action in the novel and those in the film. Sometimes, as indicated, these appear in different orders in the two texts, and sometimes the motivations for the actions vary from one text to the other. However, in terms of the pattern of narrative development which shapes the film as a whole, as distinct from the cardinal functions of varying degrees of importance within individual segments, there is considerable correspondence. The social and affective discrepancies between the two texts will generally be located at other levels of the texts, sometimes at the level of the catalysers which surround the cardinal functions or kernels, but more significantly at the level of enunciation, through the exercise of those strategies peculiar to the medium in question.

Character functions

In the Proppian sense of character functions, *The Executioners* offers a clearer differentiation between Hero and Villain. MacDonald's Sam Bowden is almost archetypally the good man: father, husband, upholder and servant of the law; Cady is by contrast wholly evil. From Propp's list of 'The Functions of the Dramatis Personae', it is clear that the behaviour of Cady adheres to the following which are attributed to the villain:

IV. The Villain Makes an Attempt at Reconnaissance[6] (the success of the attempt has led Cady to New Essex).
V. The Villain Receives Information About his Victim[7] (Cady has found out where Sam lives, and details about his family).
VIII. The Villain Causes Harm or Injury to a Member of a Family[8] (Cady shoots at and wounds Sam's son).

[6] V. Propp, *Morphology of the Folktale* (1928), trans. Laurence Scott (University of Texas Press: Austin, 1968), 28.
[7] Ibid.   [8] Ibid. 30.

Sam, unequivocally the Hero, conforms in his actions to several of the Proppian functions associated with the Hero:

II. An Interdiction is Addressed to the Hero[9] (Sam's own respect for the law prohibits him from adopting illegal means of dealing with Cady at first).

III. The Interdiction is Violated[10] (under pressure of Cady's threat to his family, Sam goes against the Interdiction and allows Sievers to arrange to have Cady beaten up).

The Villain–Hero binarism is very considerably blurred in Scorsese's film. Cady may still seem clearly the Villain, but the film forces us to examine his motivations in more detail than the novel does. He performs those character functions listed above, though the 'harm or injury' he does to Sam's family is more diffuse than in the novel: he kills the family dog in both, but in the film he offers sexual threat to Sam's wife and daughter ('both attracted to and intimidated by his menacing sexuality', as one reviewer notes[11]) without actually violating either, kills the cook and the policeman, Kersek, and does considerable punishing damage to Sam himself in the long-drawn-out fight at the end. However, Sam is far less identifiable as the Hero. He is engaged in an extra-marital affair with a law clerk, Lori (Illeanna Douglas), on whom Cady inflicts hideous damage, a violation paralleled in the novel by his beating up of the barfly Bessie; like her, Lori refuses to testify against Cady. In Scorsese's film and its world-view, Sam has violated several of the codes that seemed sacrosanct in the novel: unfaithful to his wife, disloyal to his mistress, unsettled by his daughter's sexuality, willing to watch while thugs—at his instigation—belabour Cady with chains. If Sam eventually vanquishes Cady in the film as he does in the novel, the contest is not one between unambiguous good and evil.

To invoke the Freudian configuration of id-ego-superego, so often underlying the development of film melodrama, it is by no means unproblematic to typify Cady as the id rampant and Sam as the superego-influenced good man. Cady may, in the film and the novel, be seen as some sort of monster from the id, though the film allows us less comfort in such a view than the novel does; the film's Sam is in almost as much danger from his own id impulses as he is from Cady. From this approach, the psychoanalytic patterns at work in shaping the narrative reveal less congruency between the novel and the film than is true of any of the other case-studies in this book. I shall suggest, in the Special Focus for this chapter, that this shift is likely to be crucially connected to the time-lapse between the publication of the novel and the appearance of the film.

[9] Ibid. 26.   [10] Ibid. 27.
[11] Angela McRobbie, 'Cape Fear', Sight and Sound, NS, 1/11 (Mar. 1992), 40.

ENUNCIATION AND ADAPTATION

Narrational Mode: The Novel

The narrating voice

John D. MacDonald's novel is unfolded, for the most part, in an unaccented third-person prose, serviceable rather than distinctive, a vehicle for the business in hand. It is at its most efficient when it is describing the processes at work on some particular occasion, and is able to catch quite sharp physical impressions in doing so. Here, almost at random, is Sam Bowden last thing at night:

> He turned off the lights, started to lock the front door and then opened it again and went out into the front yard, strolled down toward the road. Rain had washed the air clean, and it had the smell of June and the promise of summer. The stars looked small and high and newly polished. He heard the dwindling snarl of a truck on Route 18 and, after it died, the remote song of a dog on a far-off farm across the valley. A mosquito whined in his ear and he waved it away. (p. 33)

The plainness of the opening statements of activity and the exactness of the sensuous notations of the night are indicative of a prose style which knows its place in the telling of a story about a dangerous intruder in a sort of paradise.

The short paragraphs which follow suggest two discursive tendencies of the style which are, at least arguably, less successful: first, the tendency to abstraction; and, second, the way in which the implied narrator is apt to drift off into Sam's voice and sensibility.

> The night was dark and the sky was high, and the world was a very large place. And a man was almost excessively small, puny and vulnerable. His brood was abed.
> Cady lived somewhere in this night, breathing the darkness.
> He slapped at the mosquito and walked back across the damp grass to the house, locked up, and went up to bed.

Scorsese, it will be seen, allows his Sam no such privileged access to the narrational mode. The reflection on man's place in the scheme of things jars both because it has a whiff of the pretentious and because it is also perfunctory in the context of the novel as a whole. The brief sentence, 'His brood was abed', in the patriarchal whimsy of 'brood' and the archaism of 'abed', is a minor example of the self-conscious tone which characterizes Sam's way of speaking to his family and which is allowed to infiltrate the novel's discursive prose. That MacDonald allows it to do so may be seen as indicating his unequivocal alignment with Sam. With, that is, the Sam of the first page who 'lay on the beach . . . and tried to tell himself that all was right with his particular world' (pp. 1–2).

Dialogue

In the matter of dialogue, there is a similar distinction to be drawn. At its best in the crisp exchanges between Sam and either colleagues or Cady or Sievers, it is seriously undermined in the exchanges between Sam and his wife or his children. These are characterized by an archness which would not have been out of place in a 1950s situation comedy, such as *Father Knows Best*—as, of course, he does, in both the novel and the 1961 film version. Having just discussed daughter Nancy's new boyfriend, Sam tells wife Carol that he thinks 'a very unusual crop of kids is coming along. Good kids, but strange':

'They make me feel like a doddering degenerate. . . . Now stop listening to me and we will sit in this stagy dusk and listen to bugs.'
'To myriad insects, please.'
'You can tell temperature from crickets.'
'So you have told me a hundred times.'
'Another sign of senility. Banality and repetitiousness. And forgetfulness, because I never can remember the formula you use on a cricket.' (p. 108)

Earlier, after Nancy has dismissed a schoolmate (and rival for her ex-boyfriend) as 'an utterly rancid little thing', she claims:

'I'm in no sweat.'
'Now there is an enchantingly feminine expression.' [Sam replies]
'Everybody says that,' she said pityingly. (p. 26)

The entire discourse in which the family's middle-class cosiness is created is peppered with this kind of debilitating facetiousness. Perhaps in 1957 the idea of wives' calling their husbands 'Samuel' in comic exasperation and of husbands' addressing their wives as 'Woman' with mock-paternal authority was a shorthand signifier of the kind of domesticity to which Cady represents such a threat. Several decades later, one finds it difficult to read without wincing. The 1961 film is virtually devoid of attempts at humour: Gregory Peck's Sam is not at all given to the jocose; and such playfulness would be entirely out of place in the domestic scene of the 1991 version.

Oppositions spelt out

MacDonald, both through his implied narrator and through dialogue, enunciates clearly a clash of Good and Evil. Despite some suggestion of complacency about the Bowdens' happiness and despite the suppressed misgivings of Sam's 'free indirect discourse',[12] the most that the narrator/MacDonald would seem to concede is the potential fragility of such happiness, and the vulnerability of the protagonists to fear. At the end, they are 'A handsome,

---

[12] In the sense used by David Bordwell, *Narration in the Fiction Film* (Methuen: London, 1985), 19.

mild and civilised couple, with no visible taint of violence, no lingering marks of a dreadful fear' (p. 214). Sam and Carol are back on the beach where they began, exchanging sexual innuendo with the same arch wholesomeness that has ever been their verbal stock in trade. The rightness of their version of the Good is never seriously questioned. Similarly, the concept of Cady as implacable Evil is accepted as unproblematic: the threat to the Bowdens is entirely external, entirely embodied in the menacing figure of Cady. Nowhere in the novel's narrational mode—not in what MacCabe has called the 'object discourses' of the characters or the 'metalanguage'[13] which teaches us how to read those discourses—is there any attempt to solicit sympathetic understanding for Cady. It is not clear how far MacDonald envisages Cady as a version of Freud's 'return of the repressed'; the setting of the rape which Sam witnessed is Australia: i.e. far away in place as well as time; in fact 'down under'. However, he is clearly conceived as a threat to middle-class paradise, and, indeed, in ideological terms, the whole novel is unequivocally middle-class in its values. Anyone outside the charmed circle that encompasses, say, home, profession, boat club (even the more democratic one the Bowdens have opted for) and summer camps, whether Cady or Bessie, the woman in Nicholson's bar, is summarily disposed of in moral terms.

In short, I should claim that what keeps one's attention in the novel is essentially the narrative pull of what-happens-next. There is no real distinction or distinctiveness in the narrational mode. MacDonald's strategy is to initiate briskly the plot device of the intruder in paradise and to ensure the swift rendering of its results. He is less effective—and no doubt less interested—in creating a convincingly textured world for all this to happen in. It is part of the strength of Scorsese's narrational mode, of his exercise of the enunciatory strategies of the cinema, that he provides exactly this.

Narrational Mode: The Film

The narrating voice

Scorsese's film begins and ends with the narrating voice of Sam's daughter, no longer called Nancy but given the more sophisticated name of Danielle. (It is interesting to note that only Cady calls her by her full name, as if acknowledging her maturity.) In terms of narration, voice-over is film's nearest equivalent to a novel's discursive prose, but, as we have seen in the chapter on *Great Expectations*, it can never be more than intermittent and its function will inevitably be less influential on how we read the film text than even the least obviously 'characterized' narrating voice in a novel. In Scorsese's *Cape Fear*, the 'book-ending' effect of Danielle's voice-over, which,

[13] Colin MacCabe, 'Realism and the Cinema: Notes on some Brechtian Theses', *Screen*, 15/2 (Summer 1974), 10.

in the opening segment, gives way to her physical presence on the screen, exercises a powerful and provocative effect as one considers in hindsight the implications of what one has seen.

In the opening segment, after the shadow of a man over water which then turns red, there is a close-up of eyes as in a photographic negative, followed by the eyes in 'positive' colour, then seen as belonging to Danielle. What is heard, first on the sound-track and then as attributable to Danielle, is the following:

MY REMINISCENCE: I always thought that for such a lovely river the name was mystifying—Cape Fear—when the only thing to fear on those enchanted summer nights was that the magic would end and that real life would come crashing in.

The juxtaposition of the man's shadow and Danielle's eyes signifies a direct connection between them: that the still amorphous threat of the shadowy figure will be directed towards the owner of the eyes and voice. The spoken 'reminiscence', suggestive of a high school essay, also has the effect of attaching the ensuing narrative to the speaker. Though we may forget this for most of the next couple of hours, the final voice-over forces us to reconsider what has happened in the context of Danny's perception of it:

We never spoke about what happened, at least not to each other. Fear, I suppose, that to remember his name or what he did would mean letting him into our dreams. I hardly dream about him any more, but things will never be the way they were before he came, but that's all right, because if you hang on to the past you die a little every day. And for myself, I'd rather live.

The film ends on the same series of shots on which it began, the implication being that this is Danny's story.

The opening and closing segments of a film are patently privileged narrational sites; if they foreground a character in this particular way, viewers will quite properly allow this to influence their reading of the film. Commentators have not been slow to seize upon this enunciatory shift; Cady may still represent the return of Sam's repressed, but the film not only explicitly posits Danny as the key focus of his vengeful attentions; it also insists on the tenuous, illusory nature of the family as the centre of a dream world. Pam Cook, writing of the way the film represents its women as partly drawn to the rapist, claims that 'Scorsese's most controversial move in this respect is to bracket the main action with the narrative voice of Danielle': 'This ruse shifts the bases considerably. If Cady is conjured up by Danielle, then the threat to the family comes, not from an intruder, but from within.'[14] Cook's argument continues that Danielle 'calls up Cady as a defence against her incestuous desire for Sam, and as a wish to find an escape route out of the claustrophobic confines of the Bowden family nexus'. There is plenty of

---

[14] Pam Cook, 'Scorsese's Masquerade', *Sight and Sound*, NS, 1/12 (Apr. 1992), 15.

evidence in the film to support the contention that Danny is oppressed by her family situation, that there are intimations of repressed incest between her and Sam, and that she responds, part-fearfully part-willingly, to Cady's address to her adolescent sexuality. However, I suspect that Cook goes too far when she writes of 'the director's delegation of the narrator's role to Danielle'. The 'narrator's role' is not to be so easily assigned.

Narration in the fiction film is much more complex than such a remark suggests: in talking about the narrational stance of a film, we need to pay attention to all its enunciatory strategies, not just to the most obvious one of voice-over. It is simplistic, on the basis of the narrating voice we hear at the start and the finish of the film, to read the film as 'a teenage girl's fantasy'. Elsewhere, Rose Capp has been alert to this danger: while allowing that Danny's 'reminiscences are a veritable litany of hysterical associations', Capp also claims that 'Scorsese's film is equally a drama of paternal incestuous desire shared by the father figures, Bowden and Cady'.[15]

At this point, my aim is to do no more than draw attention to the crucial placing of the voice-over, to insist that it needs to be listened to in the context of the film as a whole, and to dissociate it entirely from the voice of the implied narrator in the novel. When the latter violates the spirit of omniscience, it does so most endemically through its intermittent assumption of Sam's thought processes.

What becomes of the discursive prose?

When one considers how the film provides an equivalent for the novel's discursive prose, for its 'metalanguage', one must turn, not merely, or even mainly, to the use of voice-over, but to those cinematic strategies of mise-en-scène, editing, and sound-track. It is essentially through their deployment that the film will create the world of the Bowdens and Cady's invasion of this world. These disparate worlds are crucial elements in any reading of the film, even if the differences between the protagonists of each are less clear-cut than they are in the novel.

In terms of mise-en-scène, the film will seek to distinguish these two elements in matters such as setting, lighting, costume, actors' facial expression and body language, and camera placement and movement. Segment 3 introduces the Bowdens' house, exterior and interior, displaying its affluence through such signifiers as size of façade, employment of a servant, its interior spaciousness, including a studio for Leigh, who works as a designer for an advertising agency (in itself a signifier of the professional middle class to which the Bowdens belong). In segment 9, set a couple of nights later, the setting is again the home, this time shown to have a grand piano among its

[15] Rose Capp, 'Cape Fear: Whose Fantasy Marty?', *Metro Magazine*, 19 (Winter 1992), 15.

furnishings. This segment is also partly set in Sam and Leigh's bedroom, as spacious and elegantly appointed as we would by now anticipate. By comparison with the novel which highlights the Bowdens' soul-searching when they took on a house larger than they had intended, and then worked hard to make a home of it, the film simply places them in an ambience of middle-class affluence which is taken for granted.

Segment 9 repays special attention because it is the occasion of Cady's first intrusion in the domestic world of the Bowdens. After Sam and Leigh have finished love-making (in an atmosphere of faintly bickering sensuality), the frame is filled with first their hands, then their faces joined in a photographic negative effect which recalls the eyes of the opening segment. It also anticipates the 'negative' appearance of Cady in their bedroom in segment 45(*b*), as a figment of Sam's nightmare. In segment 9, however, Cady is there in a 'positive' image. Leigh wakes, automatically goes to her dressing-table and makes up her face, then goes to the window to look at the fireworks display, the light from which reveals Cady sitting on their front fence. The juxtaposition of the make-up, the fireworks, and the image of Cady is too suggestive to be overlooked; it is as though Leigh has subconsciously prepared herself for Cady. Further, in this segment, the screen is twice suffused in a block of colour, first yellow, then red, a strategy which seems to suggest a lapsing into pure emotion and sensuality,[16] which is appropriate to the almost oneiric effect of Leigh's movements, an effect intensified by the fact that Cady has disappeared when Sam goes to look for him. This episode in some senses replaces the account given by Carol in chapter 1 of the novel of 'a man sitting on our stone wall, facing the house' (p. 11), but the film locates the intrusion of Cady on the Bowdens' domestic territory in dramatically and sensuously much more complex terms. This complexity of enunciation is merely suggested in my foregoing account.

Regarding the hermeneutically central concept of Cady's intrusion in a middle-class world, however embattled, the episode in the cinema,[17] in segment 5, is crucial and created strikingly in terms of mise-en-scène. The segment is introduced by a medium close-up of the back of Cady's head and shoulders. The aura of menace attaching to this figure is intensified by a wild maniacal laugh and by the huge cigar in whose smoke he is cocooned and which he ignites (in obvious sexual symbolism) with a lighter in the shape of a woman's bikini-clad torso. The Bowdens, as yet unaware of Cady's presence in New Essex, are sitting in the row behind him; Cady is from the first encoded as a disruptive force in their lives, offering in this segment affronts to their senses of sight, sound, and smell. His behaviour forces them to leave in a way that foreshadows the more calamitous disruptions to follow.

[16] This strategy is also employed by Scorsese in his 1993 adaptation of *The Age of Innocence*.

[17] The film they are watching is, aptly enough, the comic horror film, *Problem Child*, directed by Dennis Dugan, 1990.

Through settings and locations, through costume and key objects, the film is constantly putting before us the two worlds of the Bowdens and Cady. The affluence of the Bowden house is contrasted with, first, the austere prison cell (hung with posters of Stalin among others) in which we first see Cady doing the push-ups that help to make him so physically formidable an opponent, and, later, Lori's commonplace lodgings or the bleakness of the car park in which Sam's plan to have Cady beaten up comes unstuck. But if the film makes us as aware as the novel of the difference between Cady's and Sam's circumstances, morally, as we have seen, it is much more likely to blur the novel's Manichean polarities. 'Now you and I will truly be the same', Cady taunts Sam in segment 48: Sam, like Cady, is now threatened with 'loss of freedom, loss of humanity'. Sam, in subverting legal procedures and standards to secure a long gaol term for Cady, has placed himself beyond the law as surely as Cady has, and it is this which is the crux of Cady's revenge. For what he sees as public treachery, he plans to exact private vengeance. An overhead shot of the Bowdens' houseboat heaving about in the storm at Cape Fear assumes major metaphoric significance in this respect: it becomes a visual statement for the frailty of the Bowdens' middle-class world—private and professional—which collapses almost terminally under Cady's threat.

The film seems to me so much richer texturally than the novel that it would be easy to prolong the discussion of how Scorsese's control of mise-en-scène, abetted by Elmer Bernstein's reworking of the 1961 Bernard Herrmann score and by Thelma Schoonmaker's often brutal editing, goes about the work of establishing the Bowden world and Cady's threat to it. Some of these aspects of the film's enunciation will be addressed in the Special Focus section of this chapter, since they offer explicit evidence for the effect of time-lapse between novel and film. The provocative dressing and facial expression of Bowden's daughter, especially in the 'Black Forest' scene in the school's drama theatre, is a long way from the wholesome teenager envisaged by MacDonald.

Schoonmaker's editing works to often striking effect as it cuts from one segment to another. The cut is the only editing device employed, and it is generally used in the interests of a swift-flowing narrative sequence. On perhaps a dozen occasions, though, it colludes with mise-en-scène, sound and camera placement to jolt, or even shock, the viewer into awareness of a particular connection. At least twice the linking of disparate moments by a cut is given heightened emphasis by sound. First, between segments 6 and 7, the scene of the apparently harmonious nuclear family in the ice-cream parlour gives way to Sam and his mistress on the squash court, this latter ushered in by the thwack of the ball against a wall as the cut is made, and acting as a criticism of Sam's obvious duplicity. Second, between segments 39 and 40, the Judge's gavel, as he dismisses Sam's request for a restraining order (it is awarded to Cady instead), coincides with the cut after which Sam bursts into Kersek's office to ask for a gun. Such effects, not necessarily subtle, contribute a good deal to the film's visceral charge as well as underlining motifs important to its overall thematic pattern: the decent middle classes and their little deceptions; the upholder of the law who allows himself to be pushed beyond it.

In several other instances, very telling cuts are made between long shots and close-ups: between the close-up of the office telephone as Sam receives an urgent message from Leigh (segment 14) to a shot of him at the wheel of his car, speeding home to the news of Cady's latest outrage; from a relatively long-held shot of the exterior of Lori's house, showing Cady in silhouette as he beats her (segment 20), to an extreme close-up of Sam's fingers testing the keys of the family's piano; from Lieutenant Elgar (Robert Mitchum) in medium shot regarding Sam with wry drollery to Sam in his car then to close-ups of Sam's hands securing his house. Each of these makes a clear contrast between the Bowdens' increasingly embattled house and the largely indifferent world beyond it.

In place of MacDonald's discursive prose, with its largely unproblematic evocation of Southern middle-class life, Scorsese manipulates the enunciatory strategies of film in such a way as to show that world as perilously near to rotting within. The implied author behind the camera takes a much bleaker and blacker view of the world Cady disrupts than does his counterpart in *The Executioners*.

SPECIAL FOCUS

As we have seen in the preceding case-studies, the time-lapse between the publication of the novel and the production of the film version is apt to be influential on how the original text is rendered in its transposition to the screen. So far, this has been noted more or less in passing. In this chapter, I shall focus on the kinds of difference of emphasis to be found in Scorsese's film made thirty-four years after the appearance of MacDonald's novel—and thirty years after J. Lee-Thompson's film version. The time-lapse accounts for ideological shifts, for changes in censorship strictures, and for variations in aesthetic climate. The intertextuality of Scorsese's film is richer for us today in ways which were not available to readers and viewers in the late 1950s / early 1960s. It obviously includes the two precursor texts, but a good deal else besides.

At the time of the novel and the first film version, the ideal of the middle-class family was still more or less intact. Novels, plays, television series, and films might draw upon disturbance within the family circle, but the *ideal* itself was not really questioned. A term like 'dysfunctional', so regularly attached to the word 'family' nowadays, was barely invented; the disparate concepts of 'nuclear' and 'extended' families gained currency only in the late 1960s/early 1970s; the recognition and acceptance of other kinds of domestic arrangements (for instance, one-parent families, *de facto* relationships, same-sex partnerships): these, and other variants, meant that the scrubbed, whole-some, middle-class family, with father, mother, two or three children, and, possibly, faithful family retainer, had by 1990 lost a great deal of its imagistic potency. Not only was it simply no longer a fact that most people lived in this idealized set-up, but also the hegemonic pressures (as in politicians' attempts to drum up support for family values) at work to pretend that it did seemed increasingly ineffectual.

As noted earlier, MacDonald's novel offers the spectacle of the family under threat, but only from without—from the wild card Cady, not from any sense of inner division. This sense of happy rightness about what the Bowdens have going for them, still intact after the threat of Cady has been removed, is emphasized by the way teenage Nancy Bowden has attracted the attentions of a suitable young man called Tommy, and looks all set to reproduce her own version of the Bowden family pattern in a few years. Tommy calls Sam 'Sir' and is the very picture of responsible young manhood in the making. The nuclear family will be safe in the hands of Tommy and Nancy. Lee-Thompson's film reduces the Bowden family from five to three, dispensing with the sons, perhaps as a way of stressing that Cady (Robert Mitchum) above all represents a threat to the *women* of the Bowden family. However, he maintains the sanitized image of family life offered by the novel. I do not mean that his film fails to be disturbing: indeed many contemporary reviewers commented on its 'unpleasant', even 'nasty' over-tones:[18] in his depiction of the domestic life of Sam and Peggy Bowden (Gregory Peck and Polly Bergen) and daughter Nancy (Lori Martin), he acquiesces in the novel's idealization. The film's Nancy is a little younger than the novel's, which makes the prospect of her being the object of Cady's revenge notably unpleasant: this Nancy is some way from the dating high school girl of the novel, and further still from her sexually knowing counter-part in Scorsese's film. The latter, indeed, often seems to be working as a commentary on the earlier film, as if Scorsese expects the viewer to be familiar with it, if not with the novel. *His* version of the Bowden family has come a long, dishevelled way from either MacDonald's or Lee-Thompson's. This new Sam (Nick Nolte) has had affairs in the past and these, we learn from acrimonious discussion between him and his wife, have involved coun-selling to save the tattered marriage. When the film opens he is currently

---

[18] *Sight and Sound*, reporting it as 'The film of 161 reputed cuts', summed it up as 'Efficiently nasty, nastily efficient', in 'A Guide to Current Film', 32/1 (Winter 1962–3), 52.

involved with a young woman, named Lori, perhaps in an intertextual gesture to Lori Martin (Nancy in the earlier film), signifying her as a substitute for the incestuous urges he feels for his nubile daughter. This family is held together by the most fragile bonds, each living in what seems to be a separate mini-world. The threat of Cady doesn't bring them together: following the death of their dog, Sam and Leigh (a name more sophisticated than Carol, as she was in the book, or Peggy, as in the earlier film?) scream at each other with a readiness that suggests hostility was always near the surface, and daughter Danny runs out of the room in distress (segment 15); and Danny and Sam are noisily at odds when Sam questions her about her meeting with Cady, sex-based anger rising quickly to the surface in a way unthinkable in either of the earlier texts. The family values underlying such television series as *Father Knows Best* (1954–59), *Hazel* (1961–5), and *The Brady Bunch* (1969–73) are represented as entirely unproblematic; they would be spoofed later on (cf. *Soap* (1977–80)) or updated in their domestic arrangements (cf. *Roseanne*, in the late 1980s and into the 1990s). The 1961 film of *Cape Fear* doesn't even begin to suggest the kinds of critique of middle-class family life offered by the 1950s films of Douglas Sirk (e.g. *All I Desire*, *There's Always Tomorrow*) or Vincente Minnelli (e.g. *Home from the Hill*). It is ideologically a very conservative film, more so even than MacDonald's novel, which implies, if not criticism, at least the vulnerability of the Bowdens' happiness.

In the matter of censorship, to anyone who has been observing the cinema during the last forty years, it will be apparent what sweeping changes have occurred in what is deemed permissible on the screen, particularly in the areas of sexuality and violence. I do not propose to go into a lot of detail about legislation, available in works which cover the key years of change (the 1960s and 1970s).[19] From Otto Preminger's defiance of the Production Code by releasing his innocuous comedy *The Moon is Blue* in 1954 without its Seal, denied because of the use of words such as 'seduce' and 'virgin', to mainstream 1990s films when major stars (e.g. Sharon Stone) appear nude and frequently simulate a wide range of sexual activity (e.g. *Body of Evidence*, *Basic Instinct*), there has been a general loosening of strictures about what is or is not acceptable in the representation of sexual matters. The 1961 *Cape Fear* suggests a powerful sense of sexual threat in Robert Mitchum's performance as Cady, slouching his way into New Essex and the Bowdens' lives, but it is entirely aseptic in its depiction of Peggy Bowden or daughter Nancy. They would not have been out of place in *The Brady Bunch*. Between Sam and Peggy there is no suggestion of sexuality, not even of the playful kind to

---

[19] See such works as John Trevelyan's *What the Censor Saw* (Michael Joseph: London, 1973), which has a chapter on 'The American Scene'; James C. Robertson's *The Hidden Cinema: British Film Censorship in Action 1913–1972* (Routledge: London, 1989); and Leonard J. Leff and Jerold L. Simons's *The Dame in the Kimono: Hollywood Censorship and the Production Code from the 1920s to the 1960s* (Weidenfeld and Nicolson: London, 1990).

be found in MacDonald's novel. Perhaps the presence of Gregory Peck ensures this. Apart from his role as Lewt in *Duel in the Sun* (1947), Peck's persona has always seemed devoid of sexual intent. In Scorsese's film there is a powerful erotic charge to certain scenes, though they are by no means as visually explicit as many to be found in mainstream films of the 1980s and 1990s. Nevertheless, the sexual element in Cady's revenge is quite overt. In the drama theatre segment he seduces Danielle to the point of her allowing him the symbolic penetration of his finger in her mouth, whereas in 1961 he merely terrifies Nancy by chasing her in the deserted school. On the houseboat in the final segment, Cady is about to rape Leigh, who has in fact tried to persuade him to take her rather than Danielle, so that in both women, for whatever reason, there is, in their dealings with Cady, an element of complicity unthinkable in either the MacDonald or Lee-Thompson versions thirty-odd years earlier. And unthinkable is the word for the incestuous overtones in the scenes between Sam and Danielle: in segment 36, when Sam questions her about Cady ('Did he touch you?'), he tells her brusquely to put some clothes on, reminding her that she is not a child any more. In fact, operating under the pressure of suppressed incestuous desire, Sam treats Danielle with less understanding and more roughly than Cady has done.

If a great deal more candour and explicitness is now acceptable in the cinema's representation of sexual matters than was the case in 1957 or 1961, the same is certainly true about the graphic depiction of violence. Films such as *The Wild Bunch* (1969), *Soldier Blue* (1970), and *A Clockwork Orange* (1971) seem in retrospect to have been examples of a watershed period in which violence became a much more overt element in commercial film-making. These and other films like them attracted a good deal of notoriety in their time for their realistic blood-letting, coupled as it often was (e.g. in *Bonnie and Clyde*, 1967, and *Straw Dogs*, 1971) with strongly erotic content. The realistic representation of violence is a commonplace of contemporary cinema and Scorsese's *Cape Fear* avails itself of this freedom. Scorsese himself, in such films as *Taxi Driver* (1975) and *The Goodfellas* (1989), both starring Robert De Niro, has been a major exponent of this freedom. Such episodes in *Cape Fear* include Cady's attack on Lori Singer (after handcuffing her, he bites her cheek—segment 20), or the garotting of Kersek in the Bowdens' kitchen, with Sam slipping in his blood (see segment 45(*c*)), or the long final segment which takes place on the houseboat. It is not my intention to assess the place and function of violence in the film (Pam Cook discusses it from the point of view of gender politics[20]); I want here simply to draw attention to the effect of the time-lapse between the antecedent texts and Scorsese's film. Whatever one's moral attitude to the film's violence, whether or not one agrees with Cook that it is directed 'feminophobically', what is beyond question is

---

[20] Cook, 'Scorsese's Masquerade'.

that, as an adaptation of the novel or a remake of the earlier film, any reading of Scorsese's film will be wide of the mark if it does not take specific cognizance of what is allowable *now* and was not *then*. And what is allowable in the cinema is always intricately connected to changing social mores; that is, a sort of unofficial censorship code operates, in big-budget film-making certainly, which ensures that public morality in its hegemonic aspects will not be outraged—at least not so as to threaten the box-office.

In terms of aesthetic climate, it is true to say that there has been an enormously increased interest in and respect for melodrama as a mode in the decades preceding Scorsese's film. Much of this attention has been directed towards the play of psychological patterns in *family* melodrama: one thinks of such work as Peter Brooks's and Robert Heilman's books on literary and theatrical melodrama, and, specifically on film melodrama, that of such critics as Thomas Elsaesser and Christine Gledhill.[21] When Lee-Thompson was filming *The Executioners* as *Cape Fear* in 1961, melodrama was still viewed as an inferior mode and the adjective 'melodramatic' was almost inevitably used as a pejorative term, implying excess of every kind as if that were in itself to be deplored. In a curious way, Scorsese's *Cape Fear*, though characterized by stylistic excess of every kind (in matters of editing, colour, shock cutting, in its insistence on the vivid representation of violent action and its results), blurs the central binary opposition as neither of its predecessors does. The Bowdens on the one hand and Cady on the other represent for MacDonald and Lee-Thompson that 'clear-cut designing, usually a dichotomising, of existence, with divisions between the good and the evil, the weak and the strong, victors and victims, the human and the inhuman' which Brook finds characteristic of melodrama.[22] From my earlier discussion, it will be clear that by 1991 Scorsese was no longer positing these immiscible opposites and the inevitable victory of the 'positives' as a source of middle-class comfort. In a sense, his film benefits critically from (just as it also reflects in its content and style) the rehabilitation of melodrama in recent decades, but at the same time it undermines some of the old certainties of the mode. When the Bowdens slip around in the mud at the end of the film, they are victors but only just, and they have been greatly, perhaps terminally, damaged in the struggle. They were certainly not well equipped for the struggle: 'I'd like to know how strong we are . . . or how weak', Leigh says as they wait to trap Cady in the house. The outcome of the 1991 film cannot leave her feeling very confident.

[21] See Peter Brooks, *The Melodramatic Imagination: Balzac, Henry James, Melodrama and the Mode of Excess* (Yale University Press: New Haven, 1976); Robert Heilman, *Tragedy and Melodrama: Versions of Experience* (University of Washington Press: Seattle, 1965); Thomas Elsaesser, 'Tales of Sound and Fury: Observations on the Family Melodrama' in *Monogram*, 4 (1972), and reprinted in Christine Gledhill's *Home is Where the Heart is* (BFI Publishing: London, 1987).

[22] Brooks, *Melodramatic Imagination*, 22.

The purpose of the Special Focus in this case-study is to make clear that, in several important ways, *Cape Fear* is a film version of a novel which takes advantage of a range of climatic shifts since the novel appeared, and to that extent it offers a critical commentary on the novel and on the earlier film version. These two texts are crucial elements of the 1991 film's intertextuality: to watch it knowing MacDonald's novel and Lee-Thompson's film is to be very much aware of the changes wrought by time in our view of mainstream social and sexual values in the intervening years. Those earlier texts, based on more or less the same events, now seem remote in the mores they espouse; awareness of them can make the reading of the recent film a richer experience, offering a perspective and resonance denied to those unfamiliar with them. In relation to the earlier film, Scorsese, in his film-literate way, seems determined that the film antecedent at least will be in the viewer's mind. J. Hoberman has aptly claimed that: 'The new *Cape Fear* oscillates between a critique of the original and a variation on a common text: it's a choreographed hall-of-mirrors, an orchestrated echo chamber.'[23] As has been much noted, the stars of the earlier film, Gregory Peck (Bowden) and Robert Mitchum (Cady) are knowingly cast in the recent film in supporting roles which reverse their original personae: Peck is now a corrupt criminal lawyer and Mitchum is the local chief of police. The film is also perhaps being playful about other famous roles played by these actors: Peck's Oscar-winning southern liberal lawyer in *To Kill a Mockingbird* (1963) and Mitchum's memorably mad preacher/murderer (with Love and Hate tattooed on his knuckles) in *The Night of the Hunter* (1955). Further, Martin Balsam, the police chief in 1961, is now the judge. These casting permutations may well be more than mere playfulness; they can also be read as a way of signifying that the lines separating the old melodramatic polarities are now irrevocably blurred. That the film's intertextual references are quite self-conscious on Scorsese's part may also be argued by reference to the film's crediting of James R. Webb's original screenplay as one of its sources and to its use of Bernard Herrmann's 1961 score, though those more musically alert than I may agree that: '[Elmer] Bernstein's adaptation illustrates the pitfalls of attempting to adapt to a new film a score so carefully tailored to another narrative'.[24]

In all the other case-studies in this book, I have suggested that the time elapsing between the appearances of a novel and the film based on it will have important effects on the nature of the film. The alternative to such effects would be not so much adaptation as embalmment of the original, a process not likely to conduce to exciting work in the new medium.

[23] J. Hoberman, 'Sacred and Profane', *Sight and Sound*, 1/20 (Feb. 1992), 11.

[24] Graham Bruce, 'Double Score: Bernard Herrmann's Music for *Cape Fear* 1961 and 1991', *Metro Magazine*, 96 (Summer 1993–4), 14.

Scorsese's *Cape Fear*, more strikingly than most, illustrates the differences that the intervening years might make—in what an enterprising film-maker might do with a precursor novel and in what audiences a generation later are prepared to accept.

.

Conclusion

IN view of the nearly sixty years of writing about the adaptation of novels into film, writing across a broad critical range (see Bibliography), it is depressing to find at what a limited, tentative stage the discourse has remained. The relationship between a film and its precursor novel is a topic on which everyone feels free to comment while rarely evincing any concomitant need to explore the complex network of connections between the two texts.

It seems to me that the study of adaptation has been inhibited and blurred by three chief approaches:

    (*a*) the near-fixation with the issue of fidelity;
    (*b*) the reliance on an individual, impressionistic sense of what the two texts are like; and
    (*c*) the implied sense of the novel's supremacy or, the other side of this particular coin, the sense that a film is a film and there is no point in considering it as an adaptation.

Each of these calls for brief, summarizing comments here, though each has been canvassed at various points in the foregoing chapters.

The issue of fidelity

A distinction should be drawn here between directorial intentions and critical appraisal. A film-maker who admires a novel may legitimately feel challenged to represent in audio-visual images as close a correspondence as he can to his own personal response to what that novel has created in purely verbal terms. James Ivory's film version of E. M. Forster's *A Room with a View* (1986) seems in fact to foreground its intentions in this respect. Its episodes are introduced by intertitles which produce Forster's playful chapter headings ('Lying to George', etc.) and which suggest a knowing, sophisticated reworking of the use of summarizing intertitles in such silent adaptations as the Cecil Hepworth–Thomas Bentley version of *David Copperfield* (1913). Ivory's decision to use such intertitles (no longer the necessity they were in 1913) signifies an explicit relation to the precursor text. However, though he may seem to invite attention to this aspect of his film's intertextuality, there are other aspects to which the alert critic might address himself: for example, to the film's place in the Merchant–Ivory *œuvre*, with its predilection for cross-cultural reference; to its status as a piece of cultivated 'art cinema'; to its discourse on 'Englishness'; and to questions of the film's own distinctive tone and atmosphere. It is one thing for the film-maker to make an 'effort, successful or not, to preserve intact [the novel's] essential contents and emphases',[1] in Kracauer's words; quite another for the critic to limit his view of the film to its comparative success in this respect.

Reliance on individual, impressionistic comparisons

What I mean here is the absence of a methodology for arriving at more rigorous, objective statements about what has gone on in the process of transposing a text created in one medium into a text in a very different medium. It has been the modest aim of this study to see if any apparatus might be found to replace the reliance on one's subjective response to the two texts as a basis for establishing similarities and differences between them. In spite of the limitations enjoined by the choice of any five texts as case-studies, I believe it has been shown possible to draw some useful conclusions about the processes involved in novel-to-film adaptation and about critical procedures in dealing with these. Broadly, a distinction has been made between those novelistic elements which can be *transferred* and those which require *adaptation proper*, the former essentially concerned with *narrative*, which functions irrespective of medium, and the latter with *enunciation*, which calls for consideration of two different signifying systems. By narrative is meant a series of (more or less) causally connected events working towards the illumination of a larger, underlying pattern which shapes the whole work, while enunciation comprehends all those elements of the work responsible for the display of this narrative.

Since this distinction is so elementary, it is surprising not to find it invoked in the discourse on adaptation as a means of systematizing what is possible—what in fact has *happened*—in the process. Of course much of one's pleasure in reading novel or film *is* subjective; my point is that such responses will be so variable as to offer no firm basis for examining the present problem. Without some attempt to sort out (i) what *may* be transferred from what will necessarily require adaptation proper, (ii) what *has* been transferred from among what may be, and (iii) what kinds of correspondences may exist between the '*functional equivalents*'[2] (Bordwell's term) available to novelist and film-maker, one is not likely to talk about the *kind* of adaptation.

In relation to the points listed above, I have made clear elsewhere the basis for the distinction referred to in (i). The taxonomies proposed by Barthes in his 1966 essay on the structural analysis of narratives, and by Seymour

---

[1] Siegfried Kracauer, *Theory of Film* (Oxford University Press (A Galaxy Book): New York, 1960), 239.

[2] David Bordwell, in Bordwell *et al.*, *The Classical Hollywood Cinema* (Routledge and Kegan Paul: London, 1985), 5.

Chatman in his 1978 study of narrative structure in fiction and film, use different terminologies but preserve the basic distinction between those narrative elements which function independently of medium (Barthes's 'cardinal functions' and 'catalysers', Chatman's 'kernels' and 'satellites') and those such as character, atmosphere, tone, point of view[3] (vague enough terms, certainly), which are intransigently tied to the medium which displays them. One does not expect that newspaper reviewing of films (perhaps the most widely read writing about film?) will explicitly embrace such a theoretical position. However, even at that level, with all its exigencies, let alone in more expansive discourse, it should be possible to imply a distinction that would preclude the display of *mere* subjectivity. An awareness that some elements are more likely than others to survive transfer could deflect reviewers and critics from pointlessly chastising a film for not reproducing their sense of the original text.

As to (ii) above, it may be argued that a first step towards establishing the *kind* of adaptation a film-maker has produced is to see how far he has chosen to transfer what is susceptible to transfer. Among the five case-studies chosen here, spanning over sixty years of cinema, it is instructive to find how closely the film-makers have adhered to the original text at a level of major cardinal functions. And the more one thinks of other films derived from popular and/or classic novels (Karel Reisz's *The French Lieutenant's Woman* (1981), David Lean's *A Passage to India* (1984), James Ivory's *Howard's End* (1992), three fairly recent examples), the more it appears that at this level there is a marked degree of transfer. Certainly film will need to select from among a novel's cardinal functions and sometimes it may feel a need to create new ones of its own; but the incidence of actual distortion at this level is much rarer than the general dissatisfaction expressed with adaptations would lead one to expect. When the film-maker chooses radically to alter such key plot elements (e.g. Lean's changed endings for *Great Expectations* or *A Passage to India*), the effects are apt to be striking and interesting in so far as they reflect on the way the film-maker is *using* his source material.

When one speaks of 'functional equivalents', (iii) above, one is inevitably on shakier ground than in discussing cardinal functions. The kinds of choices available to novelists in matters such as narrating pronoun, tense, diction, relation of dialogue to discursive prose, and sentence structure (i.e. to aspects of enunciation) are not necessarily open to the film-maker. For the latter, choices must be made about matters relating to mise-en-scène (lighting, colour, actors, camera angles, etc.), to editing procedures (cuts, dissolves, fades, etc.), and to sound-track. In discussing the functional equivalents available to the film-maker, Bordwell (using the example of cues for a flashback) indicates how several devices, such as the close-up and the

---

[3] See Edward R. Branigan, *Point of View in the Cinema* (Mouton: Berlin, 1984), for detailed, sophisticated discussion of this narrational element.

dissolve, may appear together.[4] Here, in matters of enunciation, the capabilities of two quite separate signifying systems are called into play. Once it is accepted that transfer is not possible at this level, it is nevertheless possible to be reasonably systematic about the ways in which the film-maker has sought to present narrational elements so as to reproduce certain thematic and affective elements of the novel. If, that is, he has *chosen* to do so as distinct from favouring a more radical approach to the original. He may retain the novel's major cardinal functions while exercising the film's signifying system in such a way as to give a different emphasis. The serious study of adaptation will seek to establish at what level such shifts of emphasis are produced and by what means. This will certainly be more useful work than looking for audio-visual equivalents for effects produced in a wholly verbal system.

Two unhelpful critical attitudes

The fidelity critics, at whatever level of intellectual distinction, inevitably premiss their reading and evaluation of the film on the implied primacy of the novel. There is no need here to document further the prevalence of this bias. The opposite approach is that which simply insists on the film's autonomy and leaves it at that. Such an approach may well advocate a proper respect for the film's autonomy, but it ignores the continuing interest that exists in the convergence among the arts. The present study accepts the facts of a shifting relationship between film and novel and of the long-established process of adaptation of novels into film. It seems better not simply to dismiss such interest as irrelevant but to try to find it a focus and a methodology.

PROSPECTS AND PROCEDURES

Guidelines for investigation

My purpose has not been to arrive at comparative evaluations of novel and film, a surely pointless enterprise, but to try to establish some guidelines for exploring the different natures of the experiences by the two related texts. By distinguishing between transfer (i.e. of certain narrative functions) and adaptation proper (i.e. aspects of enunciation), and by recognizing certain 'grey' areas (e.g. dialogue, 'informants', which draw on both processes), I believe it is possible to discuss what kind of adaptation has been made. That is to say, one can with some degree of objectivity distinguish the literal-minded translation from those adaptations which, more or less radically, rework their

---

[4] Bordwell *et al.*, *Classical Hollywood Cinema*, 5.

source material. In fact, of course, all adaptations rework the source novel in the sense that film's signifying system will inevitably enjoin paradigmatic choices of a kind largely unavailable to novelists. The most obvious departures from the earlier text will be at the level of the major cardinal functions. There will be other departures, less easy to pinpoint, in matters of Barthesian 'indices', those more pervasively operating functions which lead us to construct notions of, say, character and atmosphere.

Categories of adaptations

The procedures followed in this study are intended to help discriminate among kinds of adaptation: they reveal, for example, that the film of *Daisy Miller* stands in much closer relationship to James's novella than does the film of *Random Harvest* to James Hilton's novel. On the evidence of the films Bogdanovich appears to have sought cinematic means for rendering James's narrational procedures, whereas MGM simply jettisoned Hilton's. My chosen case-studies do not include a really radical adaptation nor do they include the film version of a post-modernist novel; however, I believe the procedures I have followed would enable one to establish the nature and degree of the relationship any narrative film bears to the novel it is derived from: that is, to arrive at classification of films adapted from novels from the point of view of their use of their source material.

Theory and adaptation

To date there has been very little attempt to construct any theoretical basis for the study of literature–film adaptation. While the phenomenon has attracted so much attention, it has never seemed a major interest of those film theoreticians who have done so much to promote the understanding of how film narrative and narration work. Seymour Chatman's valuable study of narrative structure in film and fiction (1978) stops short of applying its insights to adaptation itself, though it is perhaps the most sustained attempt at a rigorous comparison between the two narrative media. Barthes's structural analysis of narratives has been very useful to my study of adaptation though his work is essentially addressed to literary texts, with no more than the odd comment on cinematic narrative. On the other hand, there is now a substantial and growing body of theoretical work on the nature of film narrative and how the viewer constructs his sense of that narrative. The British journal *Screen* (e.g. in Stephen Heath's analysis of *Touch of Evil*[5]) and David Bordwell's *Narration and the Fiction Film* are important instances of such writing. In relation to both the novel and the film, that is, one finds

---

[5] Stephen Heath, 'Film and System: Terms of Analysis', *Screen*, 16/1, 2 (Spring and Summer 1975).

valuable theoretical insights into the process of narration and enunciation, but not, as far as I am aware, evidence of this sort of attention to the processes of adaptation from novel to film. The exception is Monica Lauritzen's book-length study of the BBC's television serial version of Jane Austen's *Emma* which makes use of various theoretical approaches to illuminate a single case-study.[6]

One of the areas in which potentially interesting work remains to be done is the study of the varying susceptibility of different kinds of novel to adaptation. There are plenty of incidental perceptions about which novels adapt 'better' than others but no sustained treatment of how matters such as a novel's length, its narrational mode, its characteristic diction (degrees of abstraction or concretization, use of trope, etc.), or the relative weight of dialogue and discursive prose might bear on the processes of adaptation. I have touched on all these matters in earlier chapters, but any one of them deserves a full study. My own study (cf. chapters on *Great Expectations* and *Daisy Miller*) of the curious effect of trying to achieve on film an equivalent for the novels' first-person narration and 'restricted consciousness' approach, respectively, suggests that attempts to duplicate a novel's narrational mode on film may be doomed.

The question of what happens to a novel's narrational mode in the transposition to film is one which requires major study. It opens up the whole issue of the effect of the cinema's institutional mode of representation on the display of a narrative derived from a text in a different medium. It has seemed to me comparatively easy to assess how far a film has chosen to reproduce those elements of a novel to which are applied the term 'narrative': the sequence of events, the functions performed by characters, the overall structural motifs (journey, search, etc.), the relationship of events and episodes to that comprehensive structure, and the psychological and/or mythic patterns which underlie them. The extent to which the film-maker has sought to preserve these narrative elements is a necessary starting-point for the student of adaptation to establish. However, the more taxing and more engrossing work lies in exploring how the film-maker, influenced by his reading of the novel and by the screen's enunciatory capacities and techniques, as well as by other pressures which have to do with neither, has chosen to display these narrative elements.

It is not easy to identify objectively correspondences between the two systems of enunciation, but it is important to attempt to do so if one is concerned with how the essential work of adaptation proper has been carried out and in what ways the film-maker has sought either to reproduce cinematically certain novelistic effects or to inscribe the film with his own distinctive interpretation. The characteristic use of certain editing techniques

[6] Monica Lauritzen, *Jane Austen's 'Emma' on Television*, Gothenburg Studies in English, 48 (Acta Universitatis Gothoburgensis: Gothenburg, 1981).

(the pervasive dissolves in *Random Harvest*, the all-but-exclusive cutting in *Daisy Miller*); the use of devices such as voice-over, the recurrent point-of-view shot, the frame composition (all working to keep Pip as a central narrating protagonist in *Great Expectations*); the screen's capacity for alternating between events occurring simultaneously at different places and its general reliance on processes of alternation; the tension that is set up between on-screen and off-screen space; the decisions that are made about matters of mise-en-scène, music, and other sound effects: all these, and more, operating in varying combinations, constitute elements of the film's enunciatory system. And it is a system inevitably more complex than that which obtains in novels, if only in the sense that the paradigmatic choices required of the film-maker embrace several codes (e.g. lighting, music, camera angle) at any given moment. It is possible by close attention to particular corresponding scenes from novel and film to see what the film-maker has achieved by way of equivalence or how he has departed from the original. Such attention is not only possible but important if one is to avoid the unproductive impressionism that undermines so much of the writing about adaptation.

EXTRA-NOVELISTIC INFLUENCES

Prevailing cinematic practice

A film scholar such as Barry Salt[7] has shown clearly—has indeed quantified—one's impression of changing cinematic practice, in regard to (for example) such matters as average shot length and use of various editing procedures. On the basis of his researches he has sought to make discriminations about characteristic film styles at different periods. My point in referring here to work of this kind is to suggest that any narrative film—adaptation or not—will be made within the prevailing parameters of the cinema, within certain cinematic traditions. This is not to say that a film-maker may not consciously aim to extend, test, or subvert such parameters and traditions, but that these need to be kept in mind in assessing the achievement of the director of an adaptation. His concern is as much with the exercise of cinematic practice as with his view of the original text. The critic who fails adequately to address the former is guilty of undervaluing the film's cultural autonomy as well as of failing to understand the processes by which the novel has been transposed to film. A film is not merely (perhaps not even primarily) an adaptation; it is also a film of its time and this fact will bear on the kind of adaptation it is.

[7] Barry Salt, *Film Style and Technology: History and Analysis* (Starwood: London, 1983).

Further, this aspect of the film's production need not be a matter of casual impressionism. The preceding case-studies have suggested a more objective approach to the processes and kinds of adaptation. It is possible, as Salt has shown, to be exact about use of such techniques as rapid cutting and the long take, camera movements, and so on, and the serious study of adaptation stands to gain from such attention, corresponding as it does to certain kinds of close reading of literary texts. This is not to suggest that such attention will eradicate the subjective element of one's response (probably neither possible nor desirable), and Salt himself has not done so. However, not to attend to such matters is to relegate the discussion of adaptation to a subjective, vaguely comparative study of 'content', as if the latter had a life of its own distinct from the cinematic norms of the period and from a cinematic tradition that, in a much shorter time than the novel, has thrown up its own masters.

The modified structuralist approach I have brought to the question of narrative transfer from novel to film can clearly take us only so far; it is more complex, but possible, to examine how far the film has sought and/or achieves an audio-visual enunciation that corresponds with or notably differs from the novel's verbal style. What I am suggesting is that unless one is prepared to pay detailed attention to such matters of enunciation one's comments on the way the adaptation has been effected will remain impressionistic.

Other elements of intertextuality

Attention to the ways in which influences, not all of them literary, may bear on the film version of a novel points to one of the potentially most rewarding approaches to the processes of transition. The fact that the effect on the spectator of other texts (literary, cinematic, non-fictional) and of other pressures (e.g. genre conventions, auteurist predilections, studio style, 'industry' matters such as use of certain stars, let alone extra-cinematic influences such as the prevailing ideological climate) is not readily susceptible to the quantifying possibilities referred to above does not mean that the critic of adaptation can afford to ignore them. The procedures I have been suggesting, in relation to narrative transfer and to a shift in enunciatory modes as a result of change of medium, offer, I believe, a sound basis for the study of any adaptation of novel into film. However, in the case of any particular example, the pressures and influences listed above (and discussed elsewhere in this study) will require consideration.

It is clearly unrewarding to treat the role of the precursor text with equal priority in considering all adaptations: whereas Bogdanovich's *Daisy Miller* clearly invites comparison with James, it seems to me that *Random Harvest*, now, if not in 1942, survives as the triumphant product of a particular studio

(MGM) and a particular genre (romantic melodrama) rather than as an adaptation. When the novel is an established 'classic', the film version will inevitably attract critical attention from the point of view of how far it reworks the original, and such attention is potentially illuminating of both texts if it is not premissed on the notion of the novel's inviolability. The popular novel, whose popularity may be tied to a particular time, is apt to become no more than a dimly recollected item in the film's intertextuality. Perhaps, as a result, films derived from such culturally less privileged sources are more likely to survive on their own merits than as adaptations.

If my last point is sound, it is likely to be at least partly because at the level of 'writing' (*écriture* in Barthes's term) the film version is less constrained by a distinguished predecessor. The novel is a verbal medium and films too are written but it is usual (and most often right) to regard the director as the chief author of a film. Directors, and sometimes producers (e.g. Val Lewton) and studios (e.g. MGM in relation to *Random Harvest*), can be shown to have their own *écriture*, to inscribe films with their own signature as it were. In the case of the adaptation, this signature is more able to emerge strongly if the film's author is not awed by the novelist's inscribed presence. Whereas the novelist's signature is entirely a matter of verbal manipulation, that of the filmmaker (whether director, writer, producer, or even studio) will be the product of a signifying system in which the visual almost invariably dominates the perceptions of its viewer, taking precedence over the aural.

The relations between novel and film remain endlessly interesting and open to exploration, partly by virtue of their basis in words, partly because the film's enunciation necessarily involves much more than words. That they both exist as texts, as documents, in the way that a stage performance does not, means that both are amenable to close, sustained study. However, what they have in common is perhaps less important in the study of adaptation than what separates them. Narrative seems to me to offer the best and most obvious starting-point for comparative study, but it is at the level of enunciation—the means by which narrative is displayed and organized— that most rigour is needed to offset the lure of mere subjectivism. This study offers procedures for considering such distinctions on lines more systematic than those which have been commonly followed.

APPENDIX I

The Scarlet Letter: Segmentation and Shot Analysis

Segment and Image	Link	Titles

1. *Opening Credits*
  (a) LILLIAN GISH in *THE SCARLET LETTER*
  (b) Directed by VICTOR SEASTROM (i.e. SJÖSTRÖM)
  (c) Cast
		1. Here is recorded a stark episode in the lives of a stern, unforgiving people; a story of bigotry uncurbed and its train of sorrow, shame and tragedy.
		2. Puritan Boston on a Sabbath Day in June . . .

2. (a) Flowers (roses) in bloom.	CUT	

(b) Bells tolling.
    Pillory.
    Barred door.
    Figure in barred room moves to reveal wood plaque round neck saying DRUNK in close-up (CU).
	DISSOLVE	

(c) Another figure emerging from jail door (by rose bush). Pan L. to show people going to church, past pillory.	DISSOLVE	
(d) Bells tolling.	CUT	
(e) Children in Puritan garb.	DISSOLVE	
(f) Adults in Puritan garb.	CUT	
(g) Long shot of Puritan procession.	CUT	
(h) Interior of church—figures moving in foreground, still figure at back.	CUT	
(i) Close-up of minister receiving large book from parishioner, then turning away; parishioner disappears.		
		3. The Reverend Arthur Dimmesdale
(j) Dimmesdale in profile, backlit to give aureole effect—reading.	CUT	
(k) Two Puritans with staves in medium CU, joined by two others.	CUT	
(l) Dimmesdale in medium CU, holding book, looking off R. at the four Puritans, then turns to face almost front-on.	CUT	
(m) Two old men looking at a third who has plaque around neck A WANTON GOSPELLER. Track in to CU of GOSPELLER sign.	CUT	
(n) Dimmesdale and three churchwardens: Dimmesdale looking away from them out front; they at him. Dimmesdale exits R. from frame, watched by three wardens.	CUT	
(o) GOSPELLER joined by Dimmesdale who talks compassionately to him.		

Segment and Image	Link	Titles
		4. 'I pray that God will help me to explain the point which thou hast disputed with the Elder on Lecture Day . . .' (D)
(*p*) Dimmesdale and GOSPELLER in medium CU. Dimmesdale puts hand on his shoulder as he looks down in shame.		
		5. '. . . and make thee one with us again in spirit' (D)
(*q*) Medium CU of Dimmesdale and GOSPELLER, latter now facing Dimmesdale in profile. Dimmesdale leaves GOSPELLER, watching as he goes.	CUT	
(*r*) Pulpit entrance; warden smiling near it, stops Dimmesdale to talk to him.		
		6. 'A Purse for thy good works Master D' (ch. warden)
(*s*) Medium shot of warden passing over purse.		
		7. 'It comes as a gift from our hearts. We thank God every day for thy ministry' (warden)
(*t*) Medium shot of warden and Dimmesdale in profile in conversation. Warden moves away leaving Dimmesdale alone in frame.		
		8. His Worship, the Governor of the Colony.
(*u*) Long shot of Governor coming down aisle between bell-ringers and congregation.	CUT	
3. (*a*) Sign Heſter Prynne (CU) Ye Seamſtreſs	DISSOLVE	
(*b*) Medium CU of Hester in lacy white clothes, ribbons, etc., in each hand a bonnet she is testing for colour against her dress.	CUT	
(*c*) Hester going to and standing before wall sampler.	CUT	
(*d*) CU of sampler saying VANITY IS AN EVIL DISEASE.	CUT	
(*e*) Hester looking at sampler with mixed feelings. Hand reaches to lift it. Drops it. Relifts.	CUT	
(*f*) Close up of Hester's face in mirror (under sampler) as she tries on bonnets.	CUT	
(*g*) Medium shot of Hester considering bonnets and looking in mirror, then off apprehensively.	CUT	
(*h*) Bells ringing.	CUT	
(*i*) Hester apprehensive in CU.	CUT	
(*j*) Reflection of shot of light swinging (like pendulum) back and forth past window and over dark interior walls, then window again.	CUT	

Segment and Image	Link	Titles
(k) Close up of Hester who turns in profile to find source of light.	CUT	
(l) Object of her gaze—i.e. the mirror in CU.	CUT	
(m) Exterior—Puritans walking in pairs past cottage and coming to halt.	CUT	
(n) Interior—Hester in medium CU, pulling sampler over mirror.	CUT	
(o) Hester on other side of room—then uncovers bird in cage.	CUT	
(p) Exterior—Puritans looking shocked.	CUT	
(q) Interior—CU of bird in cage singing.	CUT	
(r) Exterior—Puritans in medium CU looking shocked.		

9. 'Hester Prynne's bird singing on the Lord's Day! What is Boston coming to?' (Hibbins)

(s) Giles, at L., rebukes Hibbins for malice.		

10. 'Must thou always be a tabby cat, Mistress Hibbins?'

(t) Puritan on R. side of Hibbins rushes off.	CUT	
(u) Him chalking across Hester's door, then turning away.	CUT	
(v) Hester in medium CU holding bird, out of cage. Bird flies off. Hester puts hands to face in fear.	CUT	
(w) Hibbins in CU—bird settles on her hat.	CUT	
(x) Giles and Hibbins in medium CU.	CUT	
(y) Bird escaping over wooden fence.	CUT	
(z) Hester runs off in pursuit to woods, losing her hat by gate.	CUT	
(a2) Medium shot of Puritans: Hibbins talking at R. of centre, Giles (at L. of centre) looking off after Hester.		

11. 'Tis against the law to run and skip on the Sabbath! The minister must be told' (Hibbins)

(b2) Giles rounds on Hibbins and all march off.	CUT	
4. (a) Hester running into woods (CUT on action).	CUT	
(b) Bird in another part of woods.	CUT	
(c) Bells in CU.		
(d) Giles trying to stop Hibbins as she marches down church aisles. She pulls herself clear and marches on as he watches.	CUT	
(e) Medium CU of Dimmesdale talking to Governor as Hibbins's silhouette appears at L. of scene.	CUT	

12. 'It distresses me to gossip Master Dimmes., but—' (Hibbins)

(f) CU of Hibbins telling, looking pleased.	CUT	
(g) CU of Dimmesdale looking distressed.	CUT	
(h) CU of Giles looking cross.	CUT	
(i) CU of Hibbins, triumphant.	CUT	
(j) Three elders listening, sitting in pew, straining to hear.	CUT	

Segment and Image	Link	Titles
(k) CU of Hibbins in full flight.	CUT	
(l) Medium CU of Dimmesdale and Governor.		
		13. 'Hester Prynne must be punished' (Gov.)
(m) Ditto.	CUT	
(n) Full-length shot of Hester running in woods.	CUT	
(o) Medium CU as she tries to catch bird.	CUT	
(p) Sunny clearing in woods—bird flies through (Hester's point of view (p.o.v.)).	CUT	
(q) Medium CU of Hester—hair streaming, waterfall, Hester jumping up and down; suddenly stops.	CUT	
(r) Church bells ringing in CU, then stop.	CUT	
(s) Hester apprehensive in medium shot, runs L. out of frame.	CUT	
(t) Hester in long shot enters frame R., runs diagonally across bottom.	CUT	
5. (a) Interior of church. Dimmesdale mounts pulpit in long shot.	CUT	
(b) Congregation—church warden walking in aisle.	CUT	
(c) CU of Giles singing, then sneezing.	CUT	
(d) Medium CU of warden, turning to prod Giles with staff.	CUT	
(e) CU of Giles being hit on head with staff.	CUT	
(f) Warden reprimanding Giles.	CUT	
		14. 'Control thy wanton sneezing Master Giles!' (Warden)
(g) Ditto.	CUT	
(h) Giles in medium CU, sneezing and being hit again.	CUT	
(i) Warden looking balefully at him as he stands in aisle.	CUT	
(j) Giles looking sheepish.	CUT	
6. (a) Exterior of church. Hester arriving, going up steps, explaining to men at entrance.	CUT	
(b) Interior, as Hester goes through door.	CUT	
(c) CU of Dimmesdale.	CUT	
(d) CU of Hester.	CUT	
(e) Long shot of Hester from Dimmesdale's p.o.v. as she comes down aisle.	CUT	
(f) Hester in medium CU, trying to scuttle into pew, sitting.	CUT	
(g) Dimmesdale in medium CU, hands on pulpit, pointing to Hester, indicating her to come before pulpit.	CUT	
(h) Long shot of Hester, walking down aisle, looking downcast.	CUT	
(i) CU of Giles, looking compassionate.	CUT	
(j) Hester (rear seen from Giles's p.o.v.) approaching pulpit.	CUT	

Segment and Image	Link	Titles
(*k*) Dimmesdale in CU, pointing at Hester.		
		15. 'Hester Prynne, thou hast profaned God's holy day' (D)
(*l*) Ditto.	CUT	
(*m*) CU of Hester, downcast (from Dimmesdale's p.o.v.)	CUT	
(*n*) CU of Dimmesdale, gesturing at Hester.	CUT	
(*o*) CU of Hester.	CUT	
(*p*) CU of Dimmesdale, raising hand.	CUT	
(*q*) CU of Hester, eyes still down, then raised.	CUT	
(*r*) CU of Dimmesdale, hand still raised.	CUT	
(*s*) CU of Hester, eyes gleaming with tears.	CUT	
(*t*) CU of Dimmesdale, lowering hand, looking more tenderly.	CUT	
(*u*) CU of Hester, looking up at Dimmesdale.	CUT	
(*v*) CU of Dimmesdale, looking worried, under influence of Hester's beauty. Points again.		
		16. 'Take heed, therefore! If ye sin, ye must pay—there is no escape!' (D)
(*w*) Ditto.	CUT	
(*x*) Three elders in pew, looking grave.	CUT	
(*y*) Another part of congregation, including Hibbins.	CUT	
(*z*) CU of Hester.	CUT	
(*a2*) CU of Dimmesdale, hands clasping edges of book, looking tense, pointing again.	CUT	
(*b2*) CU of Giles looking sad/cross.	CUT	
(*c2*) Medium long shot (Giles's p.o.v.) of Hester's back view as she stands before and below pulpit and Dimmesdale.	CUT	
(*d2*) CU of Giles glaring off R.	CUT	
(*e2*) CU of Hibbins looking pleased with self.	CUT	
(*f2*) CU of Giles rubbing nose at Hibbins.	CUT	
(*g2*) CU of Hibbins looking still more smug.	CUT	
(*h2*) CU of Giles grimacing at Hibbins and being hit on head again.	FADE OUT / IN	
7. (*a*) Exterior—long shot of square with cows going off L., dignitaries off R., leaving Hester in stocks L. in middle.	DISSOLVE	
(*b*) CU of wooden notice saying FOR RUNNING & PLAYING ON YE SABBATH. Bird perched on this.	DISSOLVE	
(*c*) Medium CU of Hester in stocks beneath notice.	CUT	
(*d*) CU of Hester in stocks.	CUT	
(*e*) Long shot of Dimmesdale coming out of doorway and picket gate, looking off R.	CUT	
(*f*) Dimmesdale arriving at stocks, standing sympathetically above Hester.	CUT	
(*g*) Two dignitaries noticing and discussing this.	CUT	

Segment and Image	Link	Titles
(h) Dimmesdale running off R., leaving Hester in stocks.	CUT	
(i) Giles outside barber's as Hibbins passes—grimaces and heckles her, and she, having passed, returns to argue with him.		
		17. 'Behold what thy gabbling tongue hast done—old crow!' (G)
(j) Long shot of Giles pointing out to Hibbins the results of her malice (i.e. stocks).	CUT	
(k) Medium shot of Dimmesdale bringing water to (R. of) Hester.	CUT	
(l) CU of Hester drinking as he holds cup and wipes her lips with bonnet strings. Touches her arm tenderly.		
		18. 'I did not dream the Committee would mete out further punishment to thee' (D)
(m) CU of Dimmesdale, looking to L. (i.e. to Hester).	CUT	
(n) CU of Hester looking slightly R. (i.e. not quite *at* him).		
		19. 'It matters not—since the order came not from thee' (H)
(o) Medium CU, two-shot of Hester and Dimmesdale.	CUT	
(p) Two dignitaries talking as they observe.	CUT	
(q) Medium shot of Dimmesdale releasing Hester from stocks.	CUT	
(r) Giles and Hibbins, she looking displeased, outside shop. She goes off L. as Giles calls after her.		
		20. 'Wood-pussy!' (G)
(s) Giles still observing.	CUT	
(t) Dimmesdale and Hester walking off (Giles's p.o.v.).	CUT	
(u) Giles smiling outside shop, waiting; turns to slap assistant for not attending to hair-rinsing.	CUT	
(v) Medium shot of back view of Hester and Dimmesdale walking—her cottage, talking, missing her gate, stop, go back, Dimmesdale stops to talk again, shakes hands at gate. She points.	CUT	
(w) CU of bird sitting *on* cage.	CUT	
(x) Medium CU of Hester and Dimmesdale, she pointing to bird.	CUT	
(y) Medium CU of Hester by cage, grabbing and reproving bird, joined by Dimmesdale.	CUT	
(z) CU of Dimmesdale in profile, facing R.	CUT	
(a2) CU of Hester, facing slightly L.	CUT	
(b2) CU of Dimmesdale in profile, facing R.	CUT	
(c2) Two-shot of Dimmesdale and Hester with bird.	CUT	

Segment and Image	Link	Titles
(d2) Dimmesdale and Hester standing; he gives warning.	CUT	
		21. 'Hester, I hope thou hast learned a great lesson' (D)
(e2) Ditto.		
(f2) Hester kisses Dimmesdale's hand (he touches spot) and he goes.	CUT	
(g2) Medium long shot as Hester watches him go through gate.	CUT	
(h2) Rear view (Hester's p.o.v.) of Dimmesdale walking away and out of sight behind bushes.	CUT	
(i2) Medium shot of Hester, hands folded, watching.	CUT	
(j2) Dimmesdale returning from behind bushes to look back.	CUT	
(k2) Medium CU of Hester still looking at him.	CUT	
(l2) Medium CU of Dimmesdale—looks thoughtful, then disappears.	CUT	
(m2) Medium CU of Hester, wistful, goes inside.	FADE OUT / IN	

8.	(a) Book cover in CU: Ye RECORDS of Ye LAWS & STATUTES of Ye COLONIE. Hands unlock book and turn its pages.	DISSOLVE	
	(b) Governor in medium shot reading and turning pages.	CUT	
	(c) CU of page: '*Laws for Washing*. Undergarments of women are immodest tho' necessary/They must be washed in secret and hidden from masculine eyes'	CUT	
	(d) Long shot of communal washing at forest stream.	DISSOLVE	
	(e) Medium CU of three women washing and talking.	CUT	
	(f) Medium shot of Hester alone in patch of light, doing washing.	DISSOLVE	
	(g) Medium CU of Hester, wringing out garment. Goes off screen.	CUT	
	(h) Hester entering frame to hang panties on clothes-line.	CUT	
	(i) CU of male legs going past.	CUT	
	(j) Medium shot of Hester, listening to steps.	CUT	
	(k) Dimmesdale enters frame reading, in little clearing.	CUT	
	(l) Hester removes panties from line and runs off.	CUT	
	(m) Dimmesdale in medium shot.	CUT	
	(n) Hester running off (from Dimmesdale's p.o.v.).	CUT	
	(o) Hester hiding behind bushes, panties behind back.	CUT	
	(p) Dimmesdale looking for her.	CUT	

Segment and Image	Link	Titles
(q) Hester hiding behind bush—long shot.	CUT	
(r) Dimmesdale in medium CU, calling out.		
		22. 'Woman, whoever thou art—stop!' (D)
(s) Ditto.		
(t) Hester hiding behind bush.	CUT	
(u) Medium CU of Dimmesdale—leaves frame.	CUT	
(v) Long shot of Dimmesdale going behind bush, he at L., Hester at R. of bush.	CUT	
(w) CU of Hester behind bush, panties behind her back.	CUT	
(x) CU of Dimmesdale from behind.	CUT	
(y) Long shot—Hester and Dimmesdale meet in front of bush.	CUT	
(z) Medium CU of Dimmesdale and Hester.		
		23. 'Again thou has been doing wrong! What are thou hiding?' (D)
(a2) Ditto.		
(b2) CU of Hester backing away, panties behind back.	CUT	
(c2) Medium CU of Dimmesdale watching her.	CUT	
(d2) CU of Hester.	CUT	
(e2) CU of Dimmesdale.	CUT	
(f2) Two-shot of Hester and Dimmesdale (he at R.).	CUT	
(g2) CU of Hester's hands behind back holding panties.	CUT	
(h2) Two-shot as Dimmesdale grabs her arm, turns her to reveal panties.	CUT	
(i2) CU of panties.	CUT	
(j2) Medium CU—two-shot, then move in to closer shot, he thoughtful, she suppressing smile. Dimmesdale makes to read book and exits, Hester watches him go.	CUT	
(k2) Long shot of sunlit road in woods, as Dimmesdale enters bottom L.	CUT	
(l2) Medium CU of Hester who throws panties away.	CUT	
(m2) CU of panties on bush.	CUT	
(n2) CU of Hester as she goes to follow Dimmesdale.	CUT	
(o2) Long shot of Dimmesdale on path. Hester's head at bottom frame, pursuing.	DISSOLVE	
(p2) CU of Hester's legs catching up to Dimmesdale's on path. Forward track with rear view of Dimmesdale and Hester on path. Stops—Dimmesdale with book, Hester addresses him. Turn and move towards camera which tracks as they come down path—camera.		
		24. 'It would be pleasant, sir, to walk beside thee and hear thee condemn me for my sins' (H)

Segment and Image	Link	Titles
(*q2*) Medium CU of Dimmesdale and Hester. He closes book, takes her hand, looks at her intently, clasps book again, walks off as she watches then runs.	CUT	
(*r2*) Medium long shot, rear view, as Hester catches up to Dimmesdale, on path again: camera tracks them out of sight, stops, waits until they re-emerge and go off R.	CUT	
(*s2*) Medium long shot. Sunny clearing. Hester and Dimmesdale enter hand in hand, exit R. Camera stays on empty clearing, then pans L. to panties on bush in medium shot.	FADE OUT / IN	

9. | (*a*) Reflection of white and dark figure in water. Ripples gradually reveal Dimmesdale and Hester. | CUT | |
(*b*) Medium CU of Dimmesdale and Hester sitting by stream, close together; then Dimmesdale moves apart a bit, worried.		25. 'I have told thee my thoughts—thou dost say they are sinful—but why?' (H)
(*c*) Ditto—Dimmesdale turns to look at her as she looks partly at him.	CUT	
(*d*) Ditto—Dimmesdale turns to Hester, takes her in arms, turns away, she leans to him.	CUT	
(*e*) Full-length shot as he stands looking down at her.	CUT	
(*f*) Medium CU of Hester.	CUT	
(*g*) Medium shot as Dimmesdale kneels by Hester.	CUT	
(*h*) CU of Dimmesdale in profile.	CUT	
(*i*) CU of Hester, front on.	CUT	
(*j*) Two-shot (new angle) as Dimmesdale goes to embrace Hester, half obscured by bushes.	CUT	
(*k*) CU of Dimmesdale in profile.	CUT	
(*l*) Medium CU of Hester looking reflective.	CUT	
(*m*) CU of Dimmesdale, in profile, talking.		27. 'Hester, I have fought against it—but I love thee' (D)
(*n*) Ditto.	CUT	
(*o*) CU of Hester.	CUT	
(*p*) Two-shot as Dimmesdale and Hester embrace.	CUT	

10. | (*a*) CU of *Laws of Ye Courtship* 'Engaged couples must conduct their courtship through long speaking Tubes and not until after their marriage may ye speaking Tube be laid aside and lips meet in chaste and restrained Caress'. | CUT | |
| (*b*) Medium shot of man sitting by fire with book. | CUT | |

Segment and Image	Link	Titles
(c) CU of Giles in profile talking into tube. Pan to other end of tube where fiancée sits. CU of fiancée. Pan to Giles listening, smiling, and talking. Pan to fiancée (NB different reaction).	CUT	
(d) Father by fire, looking at pair.	CUT	
(e) Medium shot of Giles and fiancée at table.	CUT	
(f) Exterior—snow. Crier goes past.		28. 'Nine o'clock and all's well. Go to your homes' (Crier)
(g) Ditto.	CUT	
(h) Interior—father and mother at fire.	CUT	
(i) Doorway—Giles and fiancée say goodnight. She helps with coat.	CUT	
(j) Different angle as door opens. Giles embraces her. Scream.	CUT	
(k) Mother and father, outraged, by fire.	CUT	
(l) Outraged fiancée.	CUT	
(m) Fiancée joins mother by fire.	CUT	
(n) Giles aghast at door—father joins him.	CUT	
(o) Mother and daughter at fireplace.		29. 'Father! I will not be wed to a man of such unbridled passions' (fiancée)
(p) Ditto.		
(q) Father pushes Giles out door.	CUT	
(r) Exterior—Giles in snow; more falls on him from eaves.	CUT	
(s) Interior—Father inside door.	CUT	
(t) Exterior—Giles sitting in snow.	CUT	
11. (a) Interior of Hester's cottage: she is by fire R.	CUT	
(b) Exterior snow scene: Dimmesdale arriving.	CUT	
(c) Interior, as at (a)—Hester goes to door.	CUT	
(d) Rear view of Hester going to door, spinning wheel shadow against wall, then on her back. Opens door, admits Dimmesdale. Embrace, then break.	CUT	
(e) View of fire. Hester moves needlework. Dimmesdale enters frame R.	CUT	
(f) Medium CU of Dimmesdale and Hester, she behind chair.	CUT	
(g) CU of Dimmesdale in profile, looking R.		30. 'The Governor is sending me to England with a message for the King' (D)
(h) Ditto.	CUT	
(i) Medium CU of Hester receiving news gravely (front on).	CUT	
(j) CU of Dimmesdale in profile—pan to Dimmesdale joining Hester and embracing (medium CU).		31. 'Now thou canst refuse me no longer. Thou art going with me— as my wife' (D)

Segment and Image	Link	Titles
(k) Ditto—Hester looks grave and breaks away.	CUT	
(l) CU of Hester.	CUT	
(m) Medium shot of Hester, turned away.	CUT	
(n) Dimmesdale watching her in medium CU. Goes to join her.	CUT	
(o) Medium CU of Dimmesdale and Hester, he pleading, she anguished.		
		32. 'I cannot marry thee' (H)
(p) Ditto: more talk, he kisses her on forehead, she still anguished, turns head away. Pleading from Dimmesdale. Pan as Hester goes L. to chest on floor, kneels by it, and opens it.	CUT	
(q) CU of Dimmesdale in profile, staring wildly. Pan to Hester seated by chest. Dimmesdale joins her.	CUT	
(r) CU of Hester, downcast. Opens hand to show ring.	CUT	
(s) CU of Dimmesdale in profile, anguished.	CUT	
(t) CU of ring on Hester's hand.	CUT	
(u) CU of Dimmesdale in profile, anguished.	CUT	
(v) CU of Hester, still kneeling, restores ring to hand as a camera pulls back a bit, hands clasped penitently.		
		33. 'My wedding ring . . .' (H)
(w) Ditto.		
(x) CU of Dimmesdale in profile—talking hard at Hester.		
(y) CU of Hester fidding with ring.		
(z) Medium CU of Dimmesdale in profile, berating her.		
		34. 'Another man's wife!—in my heart thou hast been my wife . . . *My wife!*' (D)
(a2) Ditto.	CUT	
(b2) Hester looking up beseechingly.	CUT	
(c2) CU of Dimmesdale in profile, demented.	CUT	
(d2) Dimmesdale grappling with Hester, still kneeling.		
		35. 'I loved thee so . . . I feared to tell thee lest thou turn from me entirely' (H)
(e2) Ditto. Dimmesdale has Hester by her wrists, their eyes locked.	CUT	
(f2) Dimmesdale breaks away. Camera pulls back.	CUT	
(g2) Hester moves off R.—Dimmesdale at fire (head in hand).	CUT	
(h2) Hester enters from L., faces front.		
		36. 'On the day I left England, my father forced me to marry a wealthy surgeon' (H)
(i2) Medium CU of Hester.	CUT	
(j2) Dimmesdale seated at fire, looking down.	CUT	

Segment and Image	Link	Titles
(*k*2) Medium CU of Hester talking to him.		
		37. 'When his estates were settled he left England but these years have brought no news of him.' (H)
(*l*2) Ditto.		
		38. 'I have never been a wife to him—I loved him not and told him so.' (H)
(*m*2) Ditto.	CUT	
(*n*2) Dimmesdale by fire, head down, turns to look at Hester, wild-eyed.	CUT	
(*o*2) Medium CU of Hester.	CUT	
(*p*2) Medium CU of Dimmesdale at fire, facing her.	CUT	
(*q*2) Hester comes to stand *behind* him, looking the stronger. Dimmesdale rises and stands with back to her.	CUT	
(*r*2) Other side of room by door.	CUT	
(*s*2) Hester by chairs. Pan as Hester runs to Dimmesdale by fire. She begs him to forgive her.		
		39. 'I cannot live without thy forgiveness' (H)
(*t*2) Medium CU embracing—he kisses her.	CUT	
(*u*2) Snowy exterior. Crier appears.		
		40. 'Lights out! All's well' (Crier)
(*v*2) Ditto.	CUT	
(*w*2) Interior. Entrance in shadows L. Candle out.	CUT	
(*x*2) Exterior. Crier in snow.	CUT	
(*y*2) Interior. Embrace. They go apart. Firelight on chair as they embrace L.	CUT	
(*z*2) Exterior. Dimmesdale goes into snow, down path.	CUT	
(*a*3) Hester inside looking through doorway after Dimmesdale.	CUT	
(*b*3) Hester running across room.	CUT	
(*c*3) Hester through door down path.	CUT	
(*d*3) Interior—Hester against door 'pinioned' by spinning wheel shadow. Pan as she moves to fire, walks up and down room.	FADE	
		41. It was summer again.
12. (*a*) Small lighted square in centre of dark screen. A barred window. Camera pulls back till window fills screen, revealing crowd outside. Bars.	DISSOLVE	
(*b*) Unobstructed view of crowd and scaffold.	CUT	
(*c*) CU of Hibbins and other talking. Giles, behind, snarls.		
		42. 'Cockroach!' (G)
(*d*) Two gossips pull apart at this and Giles goes off.	CUT	
(*e*) Giles goes off on stairs and looks back.	CUT	

Segment and Image	Link	Titles
(f) Hibbins and gossip.	CUT	
(g) Interior—Governor. Messenger brings news.		
		43. 'Master Dimmesdale hath returned' (Messenger)
(h) Governor joined by other dignitaries on balcony. All face off R. at Dimmesdale's approach.	CUT	
(i) Long shot of balcony of town hall.	CUT	
(j) Crowd below. Scaffold. Watching Dimmesdale's approach.	CUT	
(k) Dignitaries watching.	CUT	
(l) Crowd—Dimmesdale's arrival (on horseback).	CUT	
13. (a) Interior—table, books, dignitaries in medium CU.	CUT	
(b) Door opening and Dimmesdale's entry—taking off cloak.		
		44. 'The ship arrived at Salem a week earlier than we expected' (D)
(c) Dimmesdale removing cloak in medium CU.	CUT	
(d) Dignitaries greeting him. He looks jubilant.		
		45. 'I bring good news. Our petition was granted by the King' (D)
(e) Ditto.	CUT	
(f) Exterior. Crowd—jail—scaffold where drummer mounts.	CUT	
(g) Interior. Dimmesdale asking what's up, goes off.	CUT	
(h) Exterior—balcony. Dimmesdale emerges in long shot.	CUT	
(i) Crowd below (Dimmesdale's p.o.v.)	CUT	
(j) Dimmesdale watching crowd, turns to dignitaries.	CUT	
(k) CU of Dimmesdale.	CUT	
(l) CU of Governor, talking to Dimmesdale.		
		46. 'Hester Prynne is to be punished on the scaffold' (Gov.)
(m) CU of Dimmesdale, horrified.		
		47. 'Hester Prynne! What hath she done?' (D)
(n) Ditto.	CUT	
(o) CU of Governor in explanation.	CUT	
(p) CU of Dimmesdale—hand to head in horror.	CUT	
(q) Long shot of crowd. Drummer on scaffold.	CUT	
(r) Dimmesdale in CU, then pan as he moves off L., watched by others; camera stops on Governor and Beadle.	CUT	
(s) Interior. Dimmesdale exits from here.	CUT	

Segment and Image	Link	Titles
(*t*) Governor and dignitary talking in medium CU.	CUT	
		48. 'Truly a man of God. He hath compassion for the blackest sinner' (Gov.)
(*u*) Ditto.	CUT	
14. (*a*) Interior of jail—Hester sitting R., by cradle (just seen).	CUT	
(*b*) Exterior of jail door as Dimmesdale walks through crowd, up steps and enters.	CUT	
(*c*) Interior. Hester in medium CU.	CUT	
(*d*) Medium CU of Dimmesdale inside jail.	CUT	
(*e*) Hester seated.	CUT	
(*f*) Dimmesdale talking to her.	CUT	
(*g*) CU of Dimmesdale talking to her, looking down.	CUT	
(*h*) Hester seated, talking up to him.	CUT	
(*i*) CU of baby in cradle.	CUT	
(*j*) CU of Dimmesdale.	CUT	
(*k*) Medium CU of Hester who stands.	CUT	
(*l*) Dimmesdale moves her, takes her arm, kneels by her, and is then below frame.	CUT	
(*m*) CU of Hester who comforts him.	CUT	
(*n*) Medium CU of Hester standing by him and bending over to comfort him.		
		49. 'Thou shall not be branded alone. Together we must stand, thou and I' (D)
(*o*) Medium CU—Dimmesdale pleading at R. of Hester seated, he kneels.		
		50. 'I am the guilty one, Hester. I must share thy punishment' (D)
(*p*) Ditto—as she puts hand up to stop his talk.		
		51. 'And make me suffer doubly? To know that I have helped destroy thee?' (H)
(*q*) CU of Hester.	CUT	
(*r*) CU of Dimmesdale, in pleading profile.	CUT	
(*s*) CU of Hester.		
		52. 'Thou hast no right to tear down the ideals of thy followers who look to thee for guidance. I shall have comfort in beholding thy life of devotion and service' (H)
(*t*) Ditto.	CUT	
(*u*) CU of Dimmesdale in profile, looks up, then front, down in anguish, then up at Hester.	CUT	
(*v*) Hester in CU.		
		53. 'Atone! Atone for both of us with thy good works' (H)

Segment and Image	Link	Titles
(w) Medium two-shot. Hester pleading, Dimmesdale still kneeling by her, holding and shaking her hands. He stands and moves away R. (long-held shot).	CUT	
(x) Medium shot of Dimmesdale by wall.	CUT	
(y) Hester, still seated, stands.	CUT	
(z) Hester moves to L. of Dimmesdale (she is centre of light at entrance).		54. 'We may never see each other again but I will have comfort in beholding thy life of devotion & service' (H)
(a2) Medium CU of Dimmesdale and Hester, his hands on her arm. She turns and breaks away.	CUT	
(b2) Hester goes to sit, hands folded.	CUT	
(c2) Door opening, Beadle appears L., holds door open.	CUT	
(d2) CU of Dimmesdale, aghast.	CUT	
(e2) Medium CU of Hester still seated.	CUT	
(f2) CU of Dimmesdale, eyes lowered in pain, turns and exits L. as camera follows him. Beadle turns to Hester.	CUT	
(g2) Hester still seated. Hand at breast. Camera follows as she stands and goes to child.	CUT	
15. (a) Exterior—balcony, dignitaries joined by Dimmesdale, centre.	CUT	
(b) Crowd below; drummer leaves platform.	CUT	
(c) Dimmesdale in medium CU on balcony.	CUT	
(d) Puritan (who gave purse) and wife in crowd, talking.		55. 'How our dear minister suffers with the guilty one' (Puritan)
(e) Ditto (medium CU).	CUT	
(f) Jail door—Beadle enters from inside.	CUT	
(g) Medium CU of Dimmesdale on balcony.	CUT	
(h) Jail door—Beadle moves to L. of frame as Hester appears with child in medium CU.	CUT	
(i) Medium CU of Dimmesdale, looking deranged.	CUT	
(j) Medium CU of Hester.	CUT	
(k) Medium CU of Puritan and wife in crowd.	CUT	
(l) Medium CU of three women in crowd.	CUT	
(m) Medium CU of Hibbins in crowd, Giles moves behind her.	CUT	
(n) Medium shot of Hester and child at jail door.	CUT	
(o) Crowd, from Hester's p.o.v.	CUT	
(p) Long shot of Hester, crowd at edges as she starts to move.	CUT	
(q) Hester, preceded by drummer, moves through crowd, long shot.	CUT	

Segment and Image	Link	Titles
(r) Children watching.	CUT	
(s) Hester walking with dignity.	CUT	
(t) Medium CU of Giles snarling at Hibbins.	CUT	
(u) Medium CU of Hester with child.	CUT	
(v) Crowd, close, watching her, side on at scaffold as she enters frame and mounts scaffold.	CUT	
(w) Crowd in long shot, watching as she reaches top of scaffold—balcony visible.	CUT	
(x) Dimmesdale watching, with others, from balcony.	CUT	
(y) Medium CU of Hester and child.	CUT	
(z) CU of Dimmesdale, demented.	CUT	
(a2) Medium CU of Hester with child.	CUT	
(b2) CU of Dimmesdale, demented.	CUT	
(c2) CU of Hester—looking at Dimmesdale (?).	CUT	
(d2) CU of Dimmesdale, demented, looking R. (at Hester?).	CUT	
(e2) CU of Governor.	CUT	
		56. 'The charge of her soul hath been with thee. Exhort her to name her fellow sinner' (Gov.)
(f2) Ditto.	CUT	
(g2) Medium CU of Dimmesdale.	CUT	
(h2) CU of Hester, listening to Dimmesdale.	CUT	
(i2) Medium CU of Dimmesdale, begging, hand on breast.	CUT	
(j2) CU of Hester.	CUT	
(k2) Medium shot of Dimmesdale on balcony, Governor at his R.	CUT	
(l2) Long shot of crowd, with scaffold centre.	CUT	
(m2) CU of Dimmesdale, anguished.		
		57. 'Hester Prynne I charge thee to speak out the name of thy fellow sinner' (D)
(n2) Ditto.	CUT	
(o2) CU of Hester, looking at Dimmesdale, directly, firmly, no fear	CUT	
(p2) CU of Dimmesdale, pleading, eyes and mouth wide.		
		58. 'Be not silent from any mistaken pity or tenderness for him. Speak out his name' (D)
(q2) Ditto.	CUT	
(r2) CU of Hester, nodding head.	CUT	
(s2) Puritan (of purse) and wife in crowd, piously yapping.	CUT	
(t2) CU of Dimmesdale.		
		59. 'It would be far better for him to stand on thy pedestal of shame than hide a guilty heart through life' (D)
(u2) CU of Dimmesdale pleading still more vigorously.	CUT	

Segment and Image	Link	Titles
(*v2*) CU of Hester, firm.		
		60. 'I will never betray him. I love him—and I will always love him' (H)
(*w2*) Ditto.	CUT	
(*x2*) CU of Dimmesdale, still pleading, frantic.	CUT	
(*y2*) CU of Hester, speaking.		
		61. 'And would that I might endure his agony as well as my own' (H)
(*z2*) Ditto.	CUT	
(*a3*) CU of Dimmesdale imploring.	CUT	
(*b3*) CU of Hester.	CUT	
(*c3*) CU of Hibbins and woman in crowd.	CUT	
(*d3*) Dimmesdale seated, with Governor by him.	CUT	
(*e3*) CU of Governor.		
		62. 'Reveal the brand of shame' (Gov.)
(*f3*) CU of Dimmesdale, distraught, looking at Hester.	CUT	
(*g3*) CU of Hester, front on.	CUT	
(*h3*) Puritan (purse) and woman in crowd.	CUT	
(*i3*) Two Puritan women in crowd.	CUT	
(*j3*) CU of Hester holding child.	CUT	
(*k3*) CU of Dimmesdale distraught.	CUT	
(*l3*) CU of the Scarlet Letter.	CUT	
(*m3*) Two Puritan women—one points, Hibbins calls out.		
		63. 'Adultress!' (Hibbins)
(*n3*) Ditto—points, now sniggers to Hibbins.	CUT	
(*o3*) Medium CU of Hester with child and scarlet letter visible.	CUT	
(*p3*) Two women in crowd, pointing.	CUT	
(*q3*) CU of Hester dignified.	CUT	
(*r3*) Puritan (purse) man and women in crowd now snarling at Hester; crowd behind, too, yelling.	CUT	
(*s3*) Medium CU of Dimmesdale, anguished, eyes shut, head down.	CUT	
(*t3*) Medium CU of Hester, child and scarlet letter.	CUT	
(*u3*) CU of baby's head in shawls.	DISSOLVE	
(*v3*) Medium shot of Hester with child on scaffold, surrounded by staves, crowd behind, heads in front. Light on scaffold.	FADE OUT/IN	
16. (*a*) Interior. Medium. CU Dimmesdale, hand on heart. Inside jail—by cradle. He looks wildly about. Goes off L., as camera pans.	CUT	
(*b*) Hester seated by cradle. Medium shot. Touches letter on breast.	CUT	
(*c*) Medium shot of Dimmesdale, hand going to heart.	CUT	

Segment and Image	Link	Titles
(d) CU of Hester's face (madonna-like) with child's head which she kisses.	CUT	
(e) Figures with lamps seen appearing at window.	CUT	
(f) Dimmesdale goes to look out window.	CUT	
(g) Dimmesdale, in medium CU, looking out window.	CUT	
(h) View from rear of small crowd outside, looking.	CUT	
(i) Interior—Hester putting child in cradle.	CUT	
(j) Exterior—rear view of crowd moving in through doorway.	CUT	
(k) Interior—Hester kneeling at cradle, looks up as they enter.	CUT	
(l) Face at barred window of cell door.	CUT	
(m) Hester, fearful, kneeling at cradle.	CUT	
(n) Cell door opens, dignitary opens and enters, followed by Hibbins and others.	CUT	
(o) Medium CU of Hester at cradle, light on face and cradle blanket.	CUT	
(p) Medium shot of intruders facing Hester.	CUT	
(q) Medium CU of Hester at cradle, looking up.	CUT	
(r) Medium CU of Beadle and Hibbins (smug), exchange places.		
		64. 'We have decided thy child shall be taken from thee and brought up by a Christian woman' (B)
(s) Ditto. Hibbins turns to glare at Hester.	CUT	
(t) Medium CU of Hester—hands go protectively to cradle.	CUT	
(u) Medium CU of Beadle and Hibbins.	CUT	
(v) Medium CU of Hester standing, looking down at cradle, wide-eyed, pleading, moves—Beadle.	CUT	
(w) Hester before Beadle, pleading, looking at cradle.		
		65. 'I pray thee—any punishment but that! I cannot give thee my child' (H)
(x) Ditto. Hester takes Beadle's arm. Hibbins looks on. Hester distraught goes off L.	CUT	
(y) Hester enters from R. to plead with other Puritan.	CUT	
(z) Beadle and Hibbins point at cradle.	CUT	
(a2) Medium CU of Hester, she turns.	CUT	
(b2) Beadle at cradle.	CUT	
(c2) Hester in CU, shouting, goes R.	CUT	
(d2) Beadle bending over cradle as Hester enters frame, pushes him aside, bends and picks up child, hugs it, defying Beadle and others. Looks round wildly. Off R.	CUT	
(e2) Hester enters L. of frame, tigerish defence of child.	CUT	

Segment and Image	Link	Titles
(*f2*) Medium CU of Beadle.	CUT	
(*g2*) Medium CU of Hester, grasping child to her.	CUT	
(*h2*) Beadle looking serious.	CUT	
(*i2*) Medium CU of Hester, turns away from camera, turns back, looking for escape.	CUT	
(*j2*) CU of Beadle looking grim.	CUT	
(*k2*) Hibbins and others looking on. Crowd parts as Dimmesdale enters.	CUT	
(*l2*) CU of Hester and child; she implores Dimmesdale.	CUT	
(*m2*) Medium CU of Dimmesdale looking about.	CUT	
(*n2*) CU of Beadle.	CUT	
(*o2*) Medium shot of Dimmesdale, centre, women to each side. Leaves frame L.	CUT	
(*p2*) Dimmesdale enters frame R., stands by Hester protectively.	CUT	
(*q2*) Medium CU of Beadle—flanked.	CUT	
(*r2*) Medium CU of Hibbins—flanked.		66. 'Wouldst thou protect the brat of the Devil—un-baptized and damned?' (H)
(*s2*) Medium CU, Hester and Dimmesdale.	CUT	
(*t2*) Hibbins flanked by yapping crones.	CUT	
(*u2*) Medium CU Hester and Dimmesdale, he looks front.		67. 'Before God thy child shall have a name—and I will baptize her!' (D)
(*v2*) Ditto.	CUT	
(*w2*) Medium CU, Hibbins and crones, outraged.	CUT	
(*x2*) Medium CU, Dimmesdale and Hester, he silences crones.	CUT	
(*y2*) Hibbins and crones silenced.	CUT	
(*z2*) Medium CU of Dimmesdale; he leaves frame R., Hester watches.	CUT	
(*a3*) Medium CU, Hibbins's and crones' eyes follow him.	CUT	
(*b3*) Dimmesdale puts table by Hester standing with child.	CUT	
(*c3*) Medium CU of Beadle.	CUT	
(*d3*) Medium CU of Hester and Dimmesdale who takes child from her tenderly, looks at her, then at child.	CUT	
(*e3*) Hibbins and crones watch outraged as Dimmesdale holds child.	CUT	
(*f3*) Medium CU as Dimmesdale removes blanket from child's face, its hand plays with his collar.		68. 'What wilt thou name her?' (D)
(*g3*) Ditto.	CUT	
(*h3*) CU of Hester, brightly lit.		

Segment and Image	Link	Titles
		69. 'Pearl—for she is indeed a pearl of great price' (H)
(i3) Ditto.	CUT	
(j3) Dimmesdale holding child, searching its face, its hand on him.		
		70. 'I baptize thee Pearl in the name of the Father, the Son and the Holy Ghost' (D)
(k3) Ditto.	CUT	
(l3) Hibbins and crones looking on in outrage.	CUT	
(m3) Medium CU as Dimmesdale gives child back to Hester.	CUT	
(n3) Medium CU of Beadle—takes off hat for prayer.	CUT	
(o3) Hibbins and others forced to bow heads.	CUT	
(p3) Long shot of Puritans, cradle; Hester and Dimmesdale in corner of room (new set-up)—Dimmesdale praying, hands clasped.	FADE	
17. (a) Exterior of cottage. CU of lighted sandy path, hand drawing scarlet letter.	CUT	
(b) CU of Pearl as little girl.	CUT	
(c) CU of Hester, sewing.	CUT	
(d) Medium CU of Pearl, laughing, wringing hands in pleasure.	CUT	
(e) CU of Hester.	CUT	
(f) CU of scarlet letter in sand.	CUT	
(g) Hester looking at it, her own scarlet letter clear.	CUT	
(h) Pearl laughing, hands in air.	CUT	
(i) Hester, looking grave, lowers needle, goes on sewing.	CUT	
(j) Pearl, laughing, runs off R.	CUT	
(k) Pearl enters frame L. to sit on Hester's knee, centre frame.		
		71. Outcasts—shunned and despised. But Hester's happy child reflected the hope that still lay in the mother's heart.
(l) Interior. Hester nursing and kissing Pearl. Pearl kisses her and runs off.	CUT	
(m) Pearl at window looking out.	CUT	
(n) Medium CU of Hester.	CUT	
(o) Dimmesdale seen (by Hester) through doorway, walking by cottage.	CUT	
(p) Medium CU of Hester looking out.	CUT	
(q) Dimmesdale looks up, sees her face.	CUT	
(r) Medium CU of Hester.	CUT	
(s) Medium CU of Dimmesdale with book in hand, over heart, looks sadly at Hester.	CUT	
(t) Hester looking off-screen, smiling.	CUT	
(u) Medium CU of Dimmesdale (in broad hat) looking off.	CUT	
(v) Empty road, wheel marks, tree stumps (long shot).	CUT	

Segment and Image	Link	Titles
(w) Medium CU of Dimmesdale, goes off L.	CUT	
(x) Hester looking off-screen.	CUT	
(y) Dimmesdale on path going away, forced to move aside by horse and cart. Goes on his way.	CUT	
(z) Hester watching as he goes.	CUT	
(a2) Pearl watching at other window turns to Hester.	CUT	
		72. 'Mother, why does the minister put his hand over his heart?' (P)
(b2) Ditto—mocking the hand-on-heart gesture.	CUT	
(c2) Medium CU of Hester, sadly.	CUT	
(d2) Long shot of room, Hester at table, Pearl runs from window to hug Hester and then exits L.	CUT	
18. (a) Exterior, Pearl outside door on step, looking off.	CUT	
(b) Pearl's p.o.v.: children near cottage gateway, stop to mock Pearl.	CUT	
(c) Pearl comes down steps and runs towards them.	CUT	
(d) Pearl at gate joins them in frame; they point and sneer at her, run away L. as she watches.	CUT	
(e) Pearl's p.o.v. of them hiding behind bushes.	CUT	
(f) Pearl watching, then stepping on to path beyond gate, looking off R.	CUT	
(g) Pearl's p.o.v.—four Puritans walking past (Hibbins and woman in front, men behind), off R.	CUT	
(h) Pearl at gate, watching, curtseying. They stop on L. of frame then go off.	CUT	
(i) Medium shot, Puritan stops a little past gate.		
		73. 'Stay! I would question the brat as to her soul' (Puritan grey-beard)
(j) Grey-beard (with fish) exits L.	CUT	
(k) Grey-beard enters R. to talk to Pearl.		
		74. 'Tell me—who created thee?' (Elder)
(l) Elder in medium CU.	CUT	
(m) Medium CU of Pearl answering.		
		75. 'My mother picked me from a rose bush' (P)
(n) Ditto.	CUT	
(o) Medium CU of elder, looks off R.	CUT	
(p) Medium CU of Hibbins and crone looking outraged at each other, then off L.	CUT	
(q) Medium shot of elder and Pearl. Elder leaves frame L.	CUT	
(r) Three other Puritans (medium shot) looking L., joined by elder who points at Pearl.		

Segment and Image	Link	Titles
		76. 'Heard ye ever such blasphemy! She is possessed by the devil' (Elder)
(s) Ditto—gossip, then off R.	CUT	
(t) Children emerging from bush, pick up mud and start to throw.	CUT	
(u) Medium CU of Puritan who turns, gets mud on dress.	CUT	
(v) Children picking up more mud.	CUT	
(w) Pearl fending off mud, then throwing some.	CUT	
(x) Children throwing more mud.	CUT	
(y) Pearl looking very bespattered, throwing mud.	CUT	
(z) Hester appears in doorway.	CUT	
(a2) (New angle) Pearl behind fence (doll thrown away) and other children over fence. Mutual mud throwing.	CUT	
(b2) Hester comes down path in medium shot.	CUT	
(c2) Children running away, long shot.	CUT	
(d2) Hester joins Pearl at wall, Pearl is covered in mud.	CUT	
(e2) One child emerges (medium shot), picks up and throws mud.	CUT	
(f2) CU of Hester and Pearl.	CUT	
(g2) Boy throwing mud.	CUT	
(h2) Medium CU of mud hitting Hester's bodice.	CUT	
(i2) Boy runs away behind bushes.	CUT	
(j2) Medium CU of Hester and Pearl. Hester trying to comfort Pearl carries her inside, kicking wildly.	CUT	
19. (a) Medium long shot of Dimmesdale, centre of group of Puritans outside church.		
		77. 'Thou art ill, reverend sir. We are frightened by thy weakness' (Puritan)
(b) Ditto.		78. 'Spare thyself, Master Dimmesdale. We could ill afford to lose thee' (Puritan)
(c) Ditto. People milling round Dimmesdale (touches head of child). Four Puritans (Hibbins, etc.) bustle up R., miming outrage.	CUT	
(d) Medium CU of Hibbins and elder.		
		79. 'Every time I pass the house I put a curse upon that child of sin' (Hibbins)
(e) Ditto.	CUT	
(f) Medium CU of Dimmesdale, distraught, clutching heart in collapse, people help him. Turns to go in.	CUT	
(g) Medium shot of Dimmesdale's going off, with Puritans solicitously watching. As he exits into church, they fall to talking.	CUT	

Segment and Image	Link	Titles

(h) Interior of church—Dimmesdale goes up aisle.

80. The tortured heart—doubly tortured by the love and veneration of his people.

20. (a) Interior. Dimmesdale seated by stone fireplace, looking into fire. Dimmesdale is centre frame. Medium shot. — DISSOLVE

(b) Medium CU of Dimmesdale looking into fire, holding poker. — CUT

(c) CU of poker, red-hot, in fire. — CUT

(d) Medium CU of Dimmesdale, looking at fire, picking up poker, applying it to his heart.

81. And Hester—never in all the bitter, lonely years had she felt so helpless.

21. (a) Interior—Hester's cottage. Pan from table to bed as she goes to soothe Pearl. Long shot. — DISSOLVE

(b) CU of Pearl with Hester. — CUT

(c) As Hester stands, agitated, by bed, she looks wildly around, runs off L. — CUT

(d) Hester enters frame R., on other side of room. Looks distraught, leaves frame L. — CUT

(e) Hester enters frame R., goes to cloak behind door, dons it, opens door, turns R. and leaves frame R. — CUT

(f) Pearl's bed. Hester enters from L., goes to bed, makes Pearl secure (chair by bed), leaves frame L. — CUT

(g) Doorway lit, Hester enters frame R. and opens door. — CUT

(h) Exterior. Hester runs through village, through frame, off R. — CUT

22. (a) Interior of Council room. Long shot (Indians, dignitaries, Giles with Indian). — CUT

(b) CU of Giles with Indian. Giles points. — CUT

(c) Beadle standing with stranger (Chillingworth) sitting. — CUT

(d) Medium CU of Governor behind table. — CUT

(e) Beadle, and stranger who rises and leaves frame L. — CUT

(f) Long shot of room as stranger goes to stand before Governor. — CUT

(g) Medium CU of Governor and stranger addressing him. Chillingworth turns to face audience, a black-bearded, sinister man, of piercing eye. Tells story.

82. 'Our boat was wrecked on the coast and I was held prisoner by the Indians for seven years' (C)

(h) CU of Chillingworth, centre frame, eyes gradually turn away. — CUT

Segment and Image	Link	Titles
(*i*) CU of Governor listening to story.	CUT	
(*j*) CU of Chillingworth.		
		83. 'If your colony will ransom me, my skill will repay you. In England, I was a physician of some renown' (C)
(*k*) Ditto.	CUT	
(*l*) Medium shot of audience (guards). Hester breaks through to front and is restrained.	CUT	
(*m*) Giles and Indian in medium CU watching her.	CUT	
(*n*) CU of Chillingworth.	CUT	
(*o*) Medium shot of Hester, restrained, pleading.	CUT	
(*p*) CU of Chillingworth, recognizing Hester.	CUT	
(*q*) Medium CU of Hester, breaking free from holding hands.	CUT	
(*r*) CU of Chillingworth, watching.	CUT	
(*s*) Medium CU of Hester, still struggling.	CUT	
(*t*) Medium CU of Giles. Hester enters frame L., joins Chillingworth and pleads with him.		
		84. 'Come with me Giles. My child! My child!' (H)
(*u*) CU of Chillingworth, shocked at mention of child.	CUT	
(*v*) Medium CU of Hester pleading with Giles.	CUT	
(*w*) CU of Chillingworth (penetrating eyes).	CUT	
(*x*) Medium CU of Hester and Giles.	CUT	
(*y*) Two-shot of Governor and Chillingworth, Governor behind desk.	CUT	
(*z*) Hester pulls Giles off L.	CUT	
(*a2*) Two-shot of Governor and Chillingworth.	CUT	
(*b2*) View of crowd in room. Chillingworth comes into frame behind them and talks to them.	CUT	
(*c2*) Governor behind desk. Chillingworth comes before desk again.	CUT	
(*d2*) Changed angle of desk as Governor gives Chillingworth pen to sign with.	CUT	
(*e2*) CU of Chillingworth writing Roger Pr . . .	CUT	
(*f2*) CU of Chillingworth's face, looking down as he writes.	CUT	
(*g2*) CU of writing, changing Pr to Chillingworth.	CUT	
(*h2*) Same angle of Governor and Chillingworth as in (*d2*).	CUT	
23. (*a*) Interior Hester's cottage. Hester and Giles bending over Pearl.	CUT	
(*b*) CU of Giles standing.	CUT	
(*c*) CU of Hester pleading with him.	CUT	
(*d*) CU of Giles.	CUT	
(*e*) CU of Hester, pleading.	CUT	
(*f*) CU of Giles.	CUT	

Segment and Image	Link	Titles
(g) CU of Hester, pleading.	CUT	
(h) Two-shot of Hester and Giles, she urging him to go.		
		85. 'Go for the minister! Tell him my child is dying!' (H)
(i) Ditto. Hester points Giles to door and he goes off leaving her in frame, distraught.	CUT	
(j) Giles at door, going out.	CUT	
(k) Hester inside, anguished, turns to kneel by child.	CUT	
(l) Exterior—Giles runs off R. Someone out there (Chillingworth and Beadle) watch Giles pass.	CUT	
(m) Interior long shot of Hester by child. Picks child up. Leaves frame L.	CUT	
(n) Doorway—Hester and child enter frame R. and go to door.	CUT	
(o) Hester takes child back to bed.	CUT	
(p) Exterior—dim. Chillingworth arrives at door.	CUT	
(q) Hester, by Pearl's bed, stands.	CUT	
(r) Exterior—Chillingworth knocking at door.	CUT	
(s) Medium CU of Hester with Pearl, looks round at knocking.	CUT	
(t) Exterior—dim.	CUT	
(u) Hester with child, runs off frame L.	CUT	
(v) Doorway—Hester enters frame R., runs to door.	CUT	
(w) Hester from door, looking out in shock—head of visitor from rear, at bottom of frame.	CUT	
(x) CU of Chillingworth who removes hat.	CUT	
(y) Medium CU of Hester, hands up as if warding him off.	CUT	
(z) Chillingworth enters doorway, seen from within, shuts door.	CUT	
24. (a) Medium CU of Hester, shocked.		
		86. 'Thou hast come back from the dead' (H)
(b) CU of Chillingworth	CUT	
(c) CU of Hester, hands to mouth.	CUT	
(d) CU of Pearl in bed.	CUT	
(e) Hester looking at Pearl in anxiety.	CUT	
(f) Hester at Pearl's bedside.	CUT	
(g) Medium shot of Chillingworth who puts things on table and exits frame R.	CUT	
(h) Chillingworth joins Hester at Pearl's bedside—medium shot.		
		87. 'Better that such a child should die' (C)
(i) Ditto. Chillingworth moves off L.	CUT	
(j) Chillingworth at table, opening bag.	CUT	
(k) CU of Hester, watching him in fear.	CUT	

Segment and Image	Link	Titles
(*l*) Medium CU of Chillingworth preparing medicine at table.	CUT	
(*m*) CU of Hester watching.	CUT	
(*n*) Chillingworth shaking medicine, leaves frame R.	CUT	
(*o*) Chillingworth rejoins Hester by Pearl's bed; Hester stands as if to defend child.	CUT	
(*p*) CU of Chillingworth.	CUT	
(*q*) CU of Hester.		88. 'Wouldst thou avenge thyself on an innocent child?' (H)
(*r*) Ditto.	CUT	
(*s*) CU of Chillingworth.		89. 'Dost think a vengeance so shallow would satisfy me?' (C)
(*t*) Ditto.	CUT	
(*u*) CU of Hester, reaching for mug.	CUT	
(*v*) CU of Chillingworth.	CUT	
(*w*) CU of Hester, drinks from mug.	CUT	
(*x*) CU of Chillingworth.	CUT	
(*y*) CU of Hester—turns to bed and gives Pearl to drink.	CUT	
(*z*) CU of Chillingworth watching.	CUT	
(*a2*) Chillingworth joins Hester by bed.	CUT	
(*b2*) Chillingworth at table.	CUT	
(*c2*) CU of Hester at bed.	CUT	
(*d2*) CU of Chillingworth facing R.	CUT	
(*e2*) CU of Hester at bed, child soothed, Hester smiles.	CUT	
(*f2*) CU of Chillingworth, moves R.	CUT	
(*g2*) Chillingworth joins Hester at bed, bends over bed. Hester backs away L.	CUT	
(*h2*) Hester backs R. into frame, in CU watching Chillingworth.	CUT	
(*i2*) CU of Chillingworth at bed, turns to speak to Hester.		90. 'Calm thy fear. She will live' (C)
(*j2*) Medium CU of Hester—gratitude, relief, hand-wringing.	CUT	
(*k2*) CU of Chillingworth.		91. 'Hester Prynne. Who is the father of this child?' (C)
(*l2*) Ditto.	CUT	
(*m2*) CU of Hester.	CUT	
(*n2*) CU of Chillingworth—gets up and leaves frame L.	CUT	
(*o2*) Two-shot of Hester and Chillingworth standing as he seems to threaten her, some struggle.	CUT	
(*p2*) Exterior. Dim. A figure approaching.	CUT	
(*q2*) Interior—two-shot of Hester and Chillingworth—they move apart.	CUT	
(*r2*) Chillingworth back by bedside.	CUT	

Segment and Image	Link	Titles
(s2) Exterior—Dimmesdale approaching.	CUT	
(t2) Interior—Hester rushes to door—off frame L.	CUT	
25. (a) Door—Dimmesdale rushes in.		92. 'Hester! Our child' (D)
(b) Dimmesdale by door. Hester joins him, puts hand over mouth.	CUT	
(c) Chillingworth turns at bed to look.	CUT	
(d) Hester and Dimmesdale in two-shot.	CUT	
(e) Chillingworth facing them.	CUT	
(f) Hester and Dimmesdale in two-shot.	CUT	
(g) Chillingworth facing them.	CUT	
(h) Chillingworth stands.	CUT	
(i) Dimmesdale and Hester embracing.	CUT	93. 'Who is that man?' (D)
(j) Ditto.	CUT	
(k) CU of Chillingworth, looking at them.		94. 'I am her husband' (C)
(l) Chillingworth in medium CU.	CUT	
(m) Medium CU of Dimmesdale and Hester, she facing him, Dimmesdale looks off anguished.	CUT	
(n) Medium CU of Chillingworth—full CU.	CUT	
(o) CU of Dimmesdale and Hester.	CUT	
(p) CU of Chillingworth.		95. 'Thou art the man! I had not thought to find thee so soon!' (C)
(q) Dimmesdale holding Hester. Chillingworth approaches R. and joins them in three-shot. Dimmesdale leaves frame L.	CUT	
(r) Medium CU of Dimmesdale, hand on breast. Hester comes to stand before him, light on bodice and scarlet letter.	CUT	
(s) CU of Chillingworth.	CUT	
(t) Medium CU of Dimmesdale and Hester (as for r).	CUT	
(u) CU of Chillingworth.		96. 'I will not betray thy guilty secret' (C)
(v) Ditto.	CUT	
(w) Two-shot of Dimmesdale and Hester (medium CU).	CUT	
(x) CU of Chillingworth, putting on coat.		97. 'My revenge will be infinite' (C)
(y) Ditto.	CUT	
(z) Two-shot of Dimmesdale and Hester.	CUT	
(a2) Medium CU of Chillingworth, picking up things at table, putting on hat, leaves frame L.	CUT	
(b2) Doorway lit—Chillingworth enters frame R., goes to door, opens it and exits.	CUT	

Segment and Image	Link	Titles
(c2) Two-shot of Dimmesdale and Hester, she talking at him, he beyond speech.	CUT	
(d2) Exterior as seen through open door, distant light.	CUT	
(e2) Two-shot of Dimmesdale and Hester, he looks demented.	CUT	
(f2) Dim exterior—Chillingworth going away.	CUT	
(g2) Pearl in bed.	CUT	
(h2) CU of Dimmesdale in anguish.	CUT	
(i2) CU of Hester.	CUT	
(j2) Hester goes to comfort Dimmesdale.		
		98. 'Do not lose heart—the world is wide—leave this place of suffering' (H)
(k2) Two-shot of Hester talking to Dimmesdale.		
		99. Days of indecision—and wretchedness—At last a way seemed open—
26. (a) Exterior. Medium shot of Pearl, by brook, playing with flowers.	CUT	
(b) Long shot of Hester and Dimmesdale lying, facing each other on grass, at distance from Pearl.	CUT	
(c) Pearl laughing and calling, runs off.	CUT	
(d) Hester and Dimmesdale as before.	CUT	
(e) Medium shot of Chillingworth watching them, unobserved in bushes.	CUT	
(f) Hester and Dimmesdale as before.	CUT	
(g) Medium CU of Hester sitting up.	CUT	
		100. 'A Spanish ship sails tomorrow after the election festival. I have seen the captain and secured passages.' (H)
(h) Ditto.	CUT	
(i) Medium CU of Dimmesdale, worried.	CUT	
(j) Medium CU of Hester, happy.		
		101. 'Across the seas—there is happiness to be enjoyed, good to be done—' (H)
(k) CU of Hester, joyous, arms outspread.	CUT	
(l) Medium CU of Dimmesdale.		
		102. 'I am too ill—too broken. I lack the courage to venture alone' (D)
(m) Ditto. Medium CU, sombre, lies down, head on hands.	CUT	
(n) CU of Hester talking.		
		103. 'We shall be with thee' (H)
(o) Ditto.	CUT	
(p) Medium CU of Dimmesdale, lying, raises head, looks L. at Hester.	CUT	
(q) CU of Hester, pulls off scarlet letter.		

Segment and Image	Link	Titles
		104. 'With this symbol I undo the past and make it as if it had never been!' (H)
(r) Hester throws letter, reveals whiteness of bodice.	CUT	
(s) CU of Dimmesdale, in profile watching.	CUT	
(t) CU of Hester, takes bonnet off.	CUT	
(u) CU of Dimmesdale, rises, goes off L.	CUT	
(v) Dimmesdale joining Hester, strokes her hair, embraces her.	CUT	
(w) CU of embrace, he kisses her hair.	CUT	
(x) Medium CU of Chillingworth in bushes, watching.	CUT	
(y) Two-shot of happy Dimmesdale and Hester, little hand from bottom of frame restores scarlet letter to Hester's bodice.	CUT	
(z) CU of Pearl at Hester's side, then runs off R.	CUT	
(a2) Two-shot of Hester and Dimmesdale, pensively watching Pearl as she goes, turn to each other.	CUT	
27. (a) Hibbins seated by fire. Long shot of interior.	CUT	
(b) CU of Giles, by window looking in.	CUT	
(c) Exterior—Giles at window, moving away.	CUT	
(d) A bit of illuminated path (from Giles's p.o.v.).	CUT	
(e) Giles at window again, then moving away.	CUT	
(f) Giles entering at door (from interior p.o.v.).	CUT	
(g) Giles comes to stand R. of sleeping Hibbins—long shot. He takes shawl from her.	CUT	
(h) Giles, other side of room, puts on Hibbins's cap and shawl, looks at her.	CUT	
(i) Medium CU of Hibbins as she stirs.	CUT	
(j) Giles finishes donning her clothes.	CUT	
(k) Exterior. Governor and Beadle in medium long shot.	CUT	
(l) CU of Giles, disguised as Hibbins.		
		105. 'Breathe it not to a soul—the Gov. is an old nincompoop' (G)
(m) Medium CU of Governor and Beadle.	CUT	
(n) CU rear view of Giles's head, from Governor's p.o.v.	CUT	
(o) Medium CU of Governor and Beadle.	CUT	
(p) CU rear view of Governor's head (see (n)).		
		106. '—and the Beadle is a parrot in petticoats!' (G)
(q) Ditto.	CUT	
(r) Medium CU of Governor and Beadle.	CUT	
(s) CU of Giles, inside, laughing.	CUT	
(t) Medium CU of Governor and Beadle.		

Segment and Image	Link	Titles
		107. 'I'll finish Mistress Hibbins for this! She shall be ducked by Giles!' (Gov.)
(*u*) Medium CU of Hibbins by fire.	CUT	
(*v*) CU of Giles, laughing.	CUT	
(*w*) Governor and Beadle as before, move off L.	CUT	
(*x*) CU of Giles, laughing.	CUT	
(*y*) Giles to Hibbins by fire, restores shawl.	CUT	
28. (*a*) Interior—Dimmesdale is packing.	CUT	
(*b*) Interior—Hester packing	FADE	
		108. On the morrow—Election Day—the one day in the Puritan's year when gaiety was not an offence.
(*c*) Medium CU of Giles tying Hibbins to end of dunking pole. Pan as Giles walks to other end of pole.	CUT	
(*d*) Long shot of pole, pool, crowd.	CUT	
(*e*) Medium CU of Hibbins's end of pole. Crowd laughing.	CUT	
(*f*) Medium CU of Giles at his end of pole.	CUT	
(*g*) Medium CU of Hibbins being raised and lowered on pole.	CUT	
(*h*) Medium CU of Giles.	CUT	
(*i*) Long shot of pole, pool, etc., swinging pole round so that Hibbins is over pool. First ducking.	CUT	
(*j*) Long shot of crowd drinking and laughing.	CUT	
(*k*) Long shot of Hibbins's end of pole, from side.	CUT	
(*l*) Long shot of crowd at Giles's end.	CUT	
(*m*) Medium CU of Hibbins going down, up and down again into pool.	CUT	
(*n*) Medium shot of Indians watching.	CUT	
(*o*) Medium CU of Giles pulling pole down.	CUT	
(*p*) CU of Hibbins in air.		
		109. 'I am wrongly accused! Never hath my tongue been given to gossip!' (Hibbins)
(*q*) Ditto.	CUT	
(*r*) Giles's end of pole.	CUT	
(*s*) Medium CU of Beadle watching.		
		110. 'Falsehood. Her tongue hath wagged like the tail of a dog. Duck her again!' (B)
(*t*) Ditto.	CUT	
(*u*) Medium CU of Giles and others at his end of pole.	CUT	
(*v*) Medium CU of Hibbins, going into pool again.	CUT	
(*w*) Medium CU of Giles's end again.	CUT	
(*x*) Hibbins in pool again.	CUT	

Segment and Image	Link	Titles
(y) Change of angle to reveal whole pond, pole in water, crowd behind pool (cf. (*d*)). Shaking Hibbins dry, turning pole over land again.	DISSOLVE	
29. (*a*) Two drums being beaten. Camera tracks before them.	CUT	
(*b*) Medium CU of three trumpeters.	DISSOLVE	
(*c*) Long shot of scaffold in circle of light— Pearl and Hester stand by it, separated from crowd. Band comes down from top R.		
(*d*) Band marches in front of scaffold—L. frame, turning to pass Hester and Pearl.	CUT	
(*e*) Medium CU of Pearl and Hester. Pearl points.	DISSOLVE	
(*f*) Procession; elders, then Governor and other dignitaries in long shot. Hibbins gets in Governor's way.	CUT	
(*g*) Medium CU of Pearl and Hester— Chillingworth passes them.	CUT	
(*h*) Crowd scene—Chillingworth goes through it.	CUT	
(*i*) CU of Hester seeing him, alarmed.	CUT	
(*j*) Crowd scene—Chillingworth goes through it.	CUT	
(*k*) CU of Hester watching him.	CUT	
(*l*) Crowd scene. Marching: Dimmesdale comes into frame and into medium CU.	CUT	
(*m*) CU of Hester.	CUT	
(*n*) Medium shot of Dimmesdale, marching, looking at Hester.	CUT	
(*o*) CU of Hester, looking at Dimmesdale.	CUT	
(*p*) Medium shot of Dimmesdale, marching, looking at Hester.	CUT	
(*q*) Long shot of Dimmesdale, in clear area before scaffold, at low centre. Hester and Pearl up L. by scaffold; Dimmesdale and marchers go off low L., crowd mills around.	CUT	
(*r*) Front of church as procession goes in; staves in foreground.	CUT	
(*s*) Scaffold at centre of crowd who surge towards church.	CUT	
(*t*) Medium CU of Chillingworth and Spanish captain.		III. 'We sail tonight on the flood tide—the wind is favourable' (Sp. Capt.)
(*u*) Ditto.	CUT	
(*v*) Crowd from behind. Elder looks around.	CUT	
(*w*) Exterior of church door. Crowd pushes through.	CUT	
(*x*) Beadle from inside, holds them off.	CUT	
(*y*) Pearl and Hester at foot of scaffold in deserted square.	CUT	

Segment and Image	Link	Titles
(z) Rear view of crowd peering at church door.	CUT	
30. (a) Interior of church—packed, sea of faces.	CUT	
(b) Hester and Pearl at scaffold and crowd from p.o.v. of church steps.	CUT	
(c) CU of Hester.	CUT	
(d) Interior of church—long shot of Dimmesdale in pulpit.	CUT	
(e) CU of Dimmesdale.	CUT	
(f) CU of Chillingworth.	CUT	
(g) CU of Dimmesdale.	CUT	
(h) CU of Chillingworth.	CUT	
(i) CU of Dimmesdale.	CUT	
(j) CU of congregation.	CUT	
(k) CU of Hester (exterior).	CUT	
(l) CU of Dimmesdale.		112. 'Purge yourselves of intolerance! Judge not—for only the eyes of God may see into the heart of a sinner' (D)
(m) Ditto. Dimmesdale is eloquent, arms raised.	CUT	
(n) CU of Chillingworth glaring.	CUT	
(o) CU of Dimmesdale, hands up.	CUT	
(p) Hester and Pearl at scaffold, and crowd.	CUT	
(q) Interior—Dimmesdale in long shot over congregation.	CUT	
(r) Exterior—looking to church door.	CUT	
(s) Long shot of scaffold and crowd milling back.	CUT	
(t) Medium CU of Hester and Pearl, people pass them.	CUT	
(u) Crowd talking. Medium shot of three women.		113. 'An inspired sermon! Never hath he spoken so eloquently!' (Woman)
(v) Ditto.	CUT	
(w) CU of Pearl and Hester.		114. 'When are we going on the ship mother?' (P)
(x) Ditto.	CUT	
(y) Long shot of crowd, scaffold at centre.	CUT	
(z) Interior—Dimmesdale with Governor.	CUT	
(a2) Exterior—row of drummers.	CUT	
(b2) Another view of crowd.	CUT	
(c2) CU of Pearl and Hester.	CUT	
(d2) Row of drummers.	CUT	
(e2) Interior—Dimmesdale with Governor.	CUT	
(f2) Governor etc. go down the aisle.	CUT	
(g2) Medium CU of Dimmesdale, looks off L., turns up to pulpit, head down.	CUT	
(h2) Medium CU of Chillingworth.	CUT	
(i2) Dimmesdale in semi-collapse, back to screen. Governor returns.	CUT	

Segment and Image	Link	Titles
(*j*2) Medium CU of Chillingworth.	CUT	
(*k*2) Governor/Dimmesdale/Chillingworth before pulpit, Giles and Chillingworth helping Dimmesdale.	CUT	
(*l*2) Exterior—drummers.	CUT	
(*m*2) Crowd, scaffold.	CUT	
(*n*2) Crowd again, different angle.	CUT	
(*o*2) Interior. Governor at centre.	CUT	
(*p*2) Medium CU Dimmesdale and Chillingworth.		
		115. 'The ship that takes thee and Hester away takes *me*!' (C)
(*q*2) CU of Dimmesdale, horrified.	CUT	
(*r*2) Exterior—Hester and Pearl with Spanish captain in medium CU by scaffold.		
		116. 'Yes, everything is ready. Come on board at sunset' (Capt.)
(*s*2) Ditto. Then Captain goes off R.	CUT	
(*t*2) Interior—CU of Dimmesdale, horrified.	CUT	
(*u*2) CU of Chillingworth.		
		117. 'Dost think thou shalt ever have happiness? *I shall always follow thee!*' (C)
(*v*2) Two-shot of Dimmesdale and Chillingworth (medium CU). Dimmesdale looks off front.	CUT	
(*w*2) Exterior—dignitaries emerge from church.	CUT	
(*x*2) Interior—medium shot of Dimmesdale and Chillingworth in church. Dimmesdale exits.	CUT	
(*y*2) Exterior—crowd. Scaffold to L.	CUT	
(*z*2) Interior—medium shot of Dimmesdale walking down aisle.	CUT	
31. (*a*) Exterior—crowd. Scaffold to L.	CUT	
(*b*) Crowd. Different shot. Jubilant as—	CUT	
(*c*) Dimmesdale appears (medium CU) on church steps, hand on heart.	CUT	
(*d*) CU of Hester and Pearl, smiling, then not.	CUT	
(*e*) CU of Dimmesdale.	CUT	
(*f*) Crowd cheering Dimmesdale.	CUT	
(*g*) CU of Hester.	CUT	
(*h*) Crowd, including Governor in foreground, looking anxious—Dimmesdale.	CUT	
(*i*) Medium CU of Dimmesdale at church door.	CUT	
(*j*) CU of Hester.	CUT	
(*k*) CU of Dimmesdale.	CUT	
(*l*) CU of Hester, hand to mouth in fear.	CUT	
(*m*) CU of Dimmesdale, face down, grave. Chillingworth over shoulder.	CUT	
(*n*) CU of Hester, wide-eyed.	CUT	
(*o*) Medium CU of Dimmesdale, Chillingworth visible over shoulder.	CUT	
(*p*) Scaffold, pillory in silhouette.	CUT	

Segment and Image	Link	Titles
(q) Medium CU of Dimmesdale; Chillingworth behind, hand on Dimmesdale's arm looking up at him. Dimmesdale clenches fist.	CUT	
(r) CU of Hester wide-eyed. Scarlet letter obvious.	CUT	
(s) Medium shot of Dimmesdale walking forward, away from church (pulpit in background). Chillingworth watching.	CUT	
(t) Long shot of Dimmesdale walking through parted crowd from church steps. Hand on heart.	CUT	
(u) Hester and scarlet letter in CU.	CUT	
(v) Dimmesdale at scaffold steps, mounting, camera tilts up as he reaches top.	CUT	
(w) CU of Hester, fearful.	CUT	
(x) Dimmesdale on scaffold facing crowd—arms spread.		118. 'People of New England. At last! At last! I stand where I should have stood five years hence—with Hester Prynne' (D)
(y) Ditto.	CUT	
(z) CU of Hester.	CUT	
(a2) Crowd looking up, Governor in front centre.	CUT	
(b2) CU of Hester, goes off frame below.	CUT	
(c2) Dimmesdale on scaffold, arms still spread. Hester runs up, arms round him.	CUT	
(d2) CU of Governor who looks up.	CUT	
(e2) Medium CU of Dimmesdale and Hester. He sinks to knees, hands on her.	CUT	
(f2) Medium CU of watching crowd.	CUT	
(g2) Medium CU of Dimmesdale and Hester as she turns to crowd.		119. 'Believe him not! His mind is unbalanced by his illness. He accuses himself falsely' (H)
(h2) Ditto. Hester wild-eyed, Dimmesdale more peaceful.	CUT	
(i2) Medium CU of Governor and Beadle looking up.	CUT	
(j2) CU of Dimmesdale kneeling at Hester's bosom, facing crowd.	CUT	
(k2) Crowd, hats being put on.	CUT	
(l2) Medium CU of Dimmesdale and Hester below pillory, crowd at edges. Dimmesdale stands, starts talking to crowd.		120. 'Hear me! Ye have shuddered at Hester's scarlet letter while *my* brand of sin and infamy is hidden! Behold it!' (D)
(m2) CU of Dimmesdale who rips open shirt, reveals A.	CUT	

Segment and Image	Link	Titles
(n2) CU of Hester—scarlet letter clear.	CUT	
(o2) Extreme CU of Dimmesdale's A.	CUT	
(p2) Governor and Beadle, looking up.	CUT	
(q2) CU of Hester, hands raised.	CUT	
(r2) CU of Dimmesdale, hands hold shirt open to show A.	CUT	
(s2) Giles in medium CU in crowd.	CUT	
(t2) Two-shot of Dimmesdale (L.) and Hester (R.). Dimmesdale collapses. Hester takes him in her arms.	CUT	
(u2) Hester turning Dimmesdale to R.	CUT	
(v2) Hester and Dimmesdale, medium CU, pietà pose.	CUT	
(w2) Medium CU of Chillingworth watching.	CUT	
(x2) CU of Hester and Dimmesdale, she in grief looking around, calling out to Giles.	CUT	
(y2) Crowd. Giles runs off; fiancée comes forward a little, struck by what she has seen.	CUT	
(z2) Hester and Dimmesdale in CU. She talks to him as he looks at her.	CUT	
(a3) Medium CU of crowd.	CUT	
(b3) CU of Hester kissing Dimmesdale's hand which strokes her face.		121. 'I love thee so—I cannot face life without thee!' (H)
(c3) Ditto.	CUT	
(d3) CU of Dimmesdale—Hester's arm around his neck L.		122. 'That is as God wills—and God is merciful' (D)
(e3) Ditto.	CUT	
(f3) CU of Hester with Dimmesdale's hand in hers.	CUT	
(g3) CU of Dimmesdale's hand at scarlet letter.	CUT	
(h3) CU of Dimmesdale.	CUT	
(i3) Extreme CU of Dimmesdale's fingers on letter pulling it away.	CUT	
(j3) CU of hand putting letter on own chest. Hand falls.	CUT	
(k3) CU of Dimmesdale's face.	CUT	
(l3) CU of Governor—eyes closed and lowered.	CUT	
(m3) CU of Dimmesdale, raising eyes.	CUT	
(n3) CU of Hester and Dimmesdale.		123. 'Is not this a better freedom than any we have dreamed of?' (D)
(o3) Ditto. Hester talks to and kisses him. Realizes he's dead and pulls away in grief.	CUT	
(p3) Medium CU. Giles (in crowd) returns with mug to stand by fiancée.	CUT	
(q3) CU of Hester and Dimmesdale.	CUT	

Segment and Image	Link	Titles
(*r*3) Giles's fiancée restrains him from going up, he turns to look at her, puts his hand on hers which is on his arm. Looks of understanding. Look at scaffold.	CUT	
(*s*3) CU of Hester and Dimmesdale.	CUT	
(*t*3) Long shot of crowd watching. Governor in front centre. Crowd removes hats, bows heads.		
(*u*3) CU of Hester looking up.	DISSOLVE	
(*v*3) Long shot of scaffold small in centre, surrounded by crowd.	THE END	

APPENDIX 2

Random Harvest: Segmentation

Segment		Link
1. *Credits*	Names on white satin.	
	Apple-blossom. 'O perfect love' on sound-track (12 dissolves).	DISSOLVE
2. *Asylum*	(*a*) Exterior—camera tracks down pathway to asylum. Voice-over on sound-track.	DISSOLVE
	(*b*) Interior—psychiatrist, Benet, with elderly couple, Mr and Mrs Lloyd.	
	(*c*) Interior—Benet, with Smith, etc. in ward.	DISSOLVE
	(*d*) Interior—Waiting-room. Smith is joined by the Lloyds. He is not their son.	DISSOLVE
3. *Melbridge*	(*a*) Exterior—hospital façade. Smith leaves.	DISSOLVE
	(*b*) Exterior—Melbridge Cable works archway. Crowds. Smith moves through them.	DISSOLVE
	(*c*) Exterior—Melbridge Arms (Biffer's pub). Smith moves on, seeks escape.	CUT
4. *Tobacconist's shop*	Interior. Meeting with Paula.	DISSOLVE
5. *Street/pub/street*	(*a*) Exterior—Smith in crowd again; Paula follows him.	DISSOLVE
	(*b*) Interior—pub: noise and song; Paula and Smith enter. The Biffer is introduced.	CUT
	(*c*) Exterior—Smith and Paula in the street again.	DISSOLVE
6. *Theatre*	(*a*) Interior—Paula's theatre dressing-room. Talks as she changes.	CUT
	(*b*) Interior—small balcony outside dressing-room, overlooking stage. She leaves Smithy there.	CUT
	(*c*) Interior—theatre, stage and auditorium. Paula sings. Crowd swarms on stage. Smithy faints.	DISSOLVE
7. *Hotel*	(*a*) Interior—hotel bedroom. Paula and Biffer watch over Smithy in bed.	FADE
	(*b*) Interior—bar. Theatre company manager Sam speaks to Paula.	DISSOLVE
	(*c*) Interior—stairs. Paula goes up with tray.	DISSOLVE
	(*d*) Interior—bedroom. Paula and Smithy talk.	DISSOLVE
	(*e*) Interior—bar. Paula talks to Sam about Smithy, as asylum attendant enters, looking for escapee.	DISSOLVE
	(*f*) Interior—bedroom. Paula tells Smithy he'll have to return to asylum, then changes her mind and tells him to hurry.	CUT
	(*g*) Interior—stairs. Paula and Smithy exit by back stairs.	CUT
	(*h*) Interior—bar. Paula pays and confides in Biffer.	CUT
	(*i*) Exterior—alley behind pub. Smithy has laid out Sam.	DISSOLVE
8. *Train journey*	(*a*) Exterior—Train speeds through countryside.	DISSOLVE
	(*b*) Interior—Smithy and Paula in train compartment.	DISSOLVE
	(*c*) Exterior—long shot of train. Smoke.	DISSOLVE
9. *Countryside*	Exterior—Paula and Smithy observe misty hill.	DISSOLVE

Segment		Link
10. *Inn*	(a) Interior—country inn lobby. Paula and Smithy enter. Landlady and doctor come down stairs.	CUT
	(b) Interior—inn phone booth. Paula talks to Biffer.	CUT
	(c) Interior—pub. Biffer tells Paula that Sam is all right.	CUT
	(d) Interior—inn phone booth. Paula laughs in relief.	CUT
	(e) Interior—inn lobby. Paula and Smithy by the fire.	CUT
	(f) Interior—landlady on stairs calls up.	DISSOLVE
11. *Countryside*	Exterior—beside stream. Smithy is sleeping. Paula arrives with letter. Proposal.	DISSOLVE
12. *Wedding day*	(a) Interior—church. Wedding.	DISSOLVE
	(b) Exterior—cottage viewed from bridge (NB always from the same angle). Spring scene. Car arrives, lets out Smithy and Paula. Farewells to doctor and vicar.	DISSOLVE
13. *Cottage/married life*	(a) Exterior—cottage in winter. Milkman and Smithy—talk of child expected.	DISSOLVE
	(b) Exterior—cottage at night.	DISSOLVE
	(c) Interior—cottage at night. Smithy by fire.	DISSOLVE
	(d) Interior—cottage at morning. Smithy asleep, wakened by Doctor, announcing birth of son.	DISSOLVE
	(e) Interior—Registry Office. Smithy registers son.	DISSOLVE
	(f) Exterior—cottage. Smithy cycles in.	DISSOLVE
	(g) Interior—cottage. Smithy is greeted by nurse.	CUT
	(h) Interior—cottage. Bedroom. Smithy gives Paula necklace. Vicar arrives with telegram.	DISSOLVE
	(i) Interior—cottage. Close-up of suitcase.	FADE OUT/ FADE IN
14. *Liverpool*	Exterior—hotel doorway. Smithy comes out, walks through streets (2 DISSOLVES) until he is knocked down by car.	DISSOLVE
15. *War*	Exterior—flashback to battlefield. Shells bursting, etc.	DISSOLVE
16. *Liverpool/train*	(a) Interior—chemist's shop. Smithy 'becomes' Charles Rainier.	DISSOLVE
	(b) Exterior—Liverpool street. Rainier walking.	DISSOLVE
	(c) Exterior—train leaving station.	DISSOLVE
	(d) Exterior—train travelling through countryside.	DISSOLVE
17. *Arrival at Random Hall*	(a) Exterior—RANDOM HALL plaque on gate, car arrives.	DISSOLVE
	(b) Exterior—keeper's gate.	DISSOLVE
	(c) Exterior—Rainier at door of lodge.	CUT
	(d) Interior—lodge-keeper's sitting-room.	FADE OUT/ FADE IN
18. *Random Hall—later*	(a) Interior—family breakfast at Random Hall.	DISSOLVE
	(b) Exterior—Rainier farewells family, talks to Kitty.	DISSOLVE
	(c) Interior—Rainier at piano, then talking to Seldon.	FADE OUT/ FADE IN
19. *Kitty–Charles relationship*	(a) Interior—Cambridge. Kitty on window-seat, writing to Charles.	DISSOLVE
	(b) Interior—photo of Kitty in academic dress (DISSOLVE TO) photo of Kitty in evening dress.	DISSOLVE
	(c) Interior—Rainier's office. He enters and finds Kitty there.	DISSOLVE
	(d) Interior—restaurant. Charles proposes to Kitty. Dr Benet is there; Charles reacts to Benet's voice.	DISSOLVE

Segment		Link
20. *Office*	Interior—Charles's office. Enter 'Miss Hanson' (Paula), his secretary. Talk of her past, of Melbridge Cable Works, of Charles's impending marriage.	DISSOLVE
21. *End of Paula's marriage*	(a) Interior—Benet's sitting-room. Paula is there.	DISSOLVE
	(b) Interior—lawyer's office. Paula discusses Smithy's disappearance.	DISSOLVE
	(c) Interior—judge's chambers. Marriage dissolved. Ends on close-up of Paula.	DISSOLVE
22. *Garden/chapel*	(a) Exterior—Random Hall garden. Charles and Kitty walking.	DISSOLVE
	(b) Interior—chapel. Wedding preparations for Charles and Kitty.	FADE OUT/ FADE IN
23. *Office*	Interior—Charles's office. Discussion of his disappearance.	DISSOLVE
24. *Liverpool*	(a) Interior—Liverpool hotel. Charles is joined by Miss Hanson.	DISSOLVE
	(b) Interior—Liverpool. 'Northern Hotel': suitcase lid open. Charles fails to identify it.	FADE OUT/ FADE IN
25. *Charles–Margaret relationship*	(a) Exterior—long shot of Houses of Parliament.	DISSOLVE
	(b) Interior—Parliament. Tea-room. Charles proposes to Miss Hanson.	DISSOLVE
	(c) Interior—Paula's sitting-room, with Benet. Charles telephones for her answer.	FADE OUT/ FADE IN
26. *Theatre*	(a) Interior—theatre. Rainiers in box.	DISSOLVE
	(b) Theatre—matrons discussing them.	DISSOLVE
	(c) Theatre—Rainiers in box.	FADE OUT/ FADE IN
27. *Insert*	Close-up of invitation.	DISSOLVE
28. *Random Hall*	(a) Interior—Random Hall. Chandeliers.	DISSOLVE
	(b) Interior—dancing couples; others watching as Paula dances with Prime Minister.	DISSOLVE
	(c) Interior—Paula's sitting-room after reception.	CUT
	(d) Interior—Paula's bedroom.	FADE OUT/ FADE IN
29. *Railway platform*	Exterior—large railway station. Charles farewells his wife. Harrison brings itinerary.	DISSOLVE
30. *Melbridge*	(a) Exterior—Melbridge Cable Works archway. Night.	DISSOLVE
	(b) Exterior—Melbridge—Charles and Harrison in street.	CUT
	(c) Interior—Melbridge Arms. Charles and Harrison drink.	DISSOLVE
	(d) Exterior—street. Charles and Harrison walking.	DISSOLVE
	(e) Interior—tobacconist's shop.	CUT
	(f) Exterior—street. Charles and Harrison walking, talk with taxi driver about hospitals.	DISSOLVE
	(g) Exterior—Melbridge County Asylum archway.	DISSOLVE
31. *Inn*	(a) Interior—Paula's face at window	CUT
	(b) Interior—inn lobby: talk of Mrs Deventer.	DISSOLVE
32. *Cottage*	Exterior. Charles approaches. Joined by Paula whom he now recognizes.	

THE END

Great Expectations: Segmentation

Segment		Length mins./secs.	No. of shots	End-of-sequence editing
1. *Credits*	On plain background, 'old-fashioned' print. John Mills and Valerie Hobson in Great Expectations *by Charles Dickens*			
2. *Pages of novel*	Adult Pip reads first paragraph on sound-track.	0.18	1	DISSOLVE
3. *Marshes*	(a) Pip runs along path to churchyard. (b) Meeting with convict (Magwitch). (c) Pip runs home.	3.44	25	CUT
4. *House*	(a) (*Kitchen*) Joe warns Pip that Mrs Joe is 'on the rampage'. (b) Mrs Joe beats Pip. Meal-time. Talk of convicts and hulks. (c) (*Pip's bedroom*) Pip in bed, fully clothed. (d) (*Kitchen and Forge*) Pip takes food from pantry and file from forge.	3.40	14	CUT
5. *Marshes*	(a) Pip runs through fog to graveyard. (b) Meeting with second convict (Compeyson). (c) Pip gives food etc. to Magwitch, and leaves him filing leg-iron.	3.33	31	DISSOLVE
6. *House*	(a) (*Dining-room*) Christmas dinner; guests. (b) Arrival of officer. (c) (*Forge*) Joe at work.	1.39	17	CUT
7. *Marshes*	(a) Pip and Joe join soldiers searching for convicts. (b) Capture of Magwitch and Compeyson. (c) Magwitch's speech about theft.	3.58	41	FADE OUT/IN
8. *House*	(a) Mrs Joe and Pumblechook arrive with news of Miss Havisham. (b) Pip is scrubbed and sent off with Pumblechook.	1.45	12	DISSOLVE DISSOLVE
9. *Satis House*	(a) Arrival. Estella at window, then gate. (b) Pip is led through dark passages. (c) Meeting with Miss Havisham. (d) Pip is led out, humiliated by Estella.	6.09	32	DISSOLVE

Segment		Length mins./secs.	No. of shots	End-of-sequence editing
10. *House*	Pip in bed, thinks of Estella (voice-over).	0.20	1	FADE OUT/IN
11. *Satis House*	(a) Pocket relations present. (b) Estella slaps Pip's face. (c) Pip wheels Miss Havisham around bridal table. (d) Fight with Herbert Pocket in garden, observed by Estella.	6.52	41	FADE OUT/IN
12. *Marshes*	(*Churchyard*) Mrs Joe's funeral (voice-over).	0.12	1	DISSOLVE
13. *House*	(a) Arrival of Biddy with bag. (b) Pip talks to Biddy about wanting to be a gentleman.	1.09	7	DISSOLVE
14. *Satis House*	(a) Pip meets Jaggers on stairs. (b) Pip wheels Miss Havisham around decayed bridal feast. (c) Estella lets him out. (NB several visits collapsed here (voice-over))	1.09	7	DISSOLVE DISSOLVE
15. *House*	Pip, in bed, thinks of Estella (voice-over).	0.12	1	DISSOLVE
16. *Satis House*	Pip tells Miss Havisham he cannot come again because his apprenticeship starts. Estella is going away.	2.09	2	FADE OUT/IN
17. *House*	(a) (*Forge*) Jaggers interrupts Joe and Pip at work. (b) (*Kitchen*) Jaggers, in house, tells Pip he has 'great expectations'.	3.16	17	DISSOLVE DISSOLVE
18. *Satis House*	(a) Pip dressed as gentleman outside SH. (b) Farewell visit to Miss Havisham.	1.32	8	DISSOLVE
19. *Rochester coach station*	Pip farewells Joe and Biddy. Coach moves off.	0.47	6	DISSOLVE
20. *Journey*	Coach to London: montage of horses, countryside, map.	0.32	7	DISSOLVE
21. *London* (arrival)	(a) St Paul's dome. (b) Pip walks to Jaggers's office.	0.44	5	CUT
22. *Jaggers's office*	(a) Pip meets Wemmick. (b) Jaggers arrives (hand-washing); glimpse of woman (Molly).	2.39	14	DISSOLVE
23. *Streets*	(Long tracking shot as) Wemmick and Pip walk through streets.	0.26	1	DISSOLVE
24. *Barnard's Inn*	(a) Arrival of Pip and Wemmick who then leaves. (b) Herbert and Pip recognize each other.			

Segment		Length mins./secs.	No. of shots	End-of-sequence editing
	(c) Dinner; manners; Miss Havisham's history.	4.42	26	DISSOLVE
25. *London*	Pip's education as a gentleman (a) dancing. (b) fencing. (c) boxing.	0.51	15	DISSOLVE
26. *Jaggers's office*	Pip asks for money.	0.10	1	DISSOLVE
27. *Barnard's Inn*	(a) Pip and Herbert's 'At Home'. (b) Pip and Herbert adding up debts.	0.45	5	DISSOLVE
28. *Jaggers's office*	Pip's birthday; receipt of annual allowance of £500.	2.16	17	FADE OUT/IN
29. *Barnard's Inn*	(a) Pip reads letter from Biddy. (b) Joe's visit and departure (voice-over at start and finish).	3.13	20	DISSOLVE
30. *Journey*	Pip goes to village by coach (voice-over).	0.48	3	FADE OUT/IN
31. *Satis House*	(a) Estella is there with Miss Havisham. (b) Estella and Pip walk in garden. (c) Pip wheels Miss Havisham around room. (d) Jaggers appears.	2.55	10	FADE OUT/IN
32. *London*	(a) (*Coachyard*) Pip meets Estella. (b) (*Tea-room*) Pip and Estella talk ('We are not free . . .').	1.30	5	DISSOLVE
33. *London*	Social life (a) Dancing, archery, skating. (b) Assembly ball—Pip is jealous of Bentley Drummle.	3.19	23	FADE OUT/IN
34. *Temple*	(a) Wild night sky. Rooftops. (b) Pip sitting by fire. (c) Return of Magwitch. (d) Return of Herbert.	6.47	36	FADE OUT/IN
35. *Jaggers's office*	(a) Discussion of Pip's benefactor. (b) Mass hanging outside window.	2.13	16	DISSOLVE
36. *Temple*	Pip and Herbert talk of rescuing Magwitch.	0.26	1	DISSOLVE
37. *Rochester coach station*	Meeting between Pip and Drummle.	0.56	3	DISSOLVE
38. *Satis House*	(a) Pip with Miss Havisham and Estella who is to marry Drummle. (b) Pip tries to rescue Miss Havisham from fire.	5.54	38	DISSOLVE
39. *Temple*	(*Exterior*) Gateman gives Pip Wemmick's message: 'DON'T GO HOME'.	0.25	4	DISSOLVE

Segment		Length mins./secs.	No. of shots	End-of-sequence editing
40. *Walworth*	Wemmick's House—Aged P.—Wemmick and Pip discuss Magwitch's escape.	2.01	16	DISSOLVE
41. *Riverside House*	Pip, Herbert, and Magwitch discuss escape.	1.10	7	FADE OUT/IN
42. *Shipping office*	(*Exterior*) Herbert goes to make enquiries (voice-over).	0.12	1	CUT
43. *River*	Training and practice for escape (voice-over).	1.27	10	DISSOLVE
44. *Shipping office*	(*Exterior*) Herbert goes in observed by Compeyson.	0.11	1	FADE OUT/IN
45. *River*	Pip, Herbert, and Magwitch go down river. Magwitch talks of lost child and how Pip has replaced her.	2.41	24	FADE OUT/IN
46. *Ship Inn*	Pip and Herbert see two men examining the escape boat.	1.00	6	FADE OUT/IN
47. *River*	Escape attempt fails. Pip saves Magwitch's life.	3.22	53	DISSOLVE
48. *Courtroom*	Sentence passed on Magwitch (and others).	0.49	4	DISSOLVE
49. *Jaggers's office*	(a) Jaggers's oblique account of Estella's parentage. (b) Molly's face seen for first time.	3.32	22	DISSOLVE
50. *Prison infirmary*	Pip at Magwitch's bedside. Tells him of Estella. Death of Magwitch.	2.18	4	DISSOLVE
51. *London*	(*Streets*) Pip wanders, feverish, through crowds. A 'montage' of places, finishing in bedroom.	0.57	6	FADE OUT/IN (very slow)
52. *House*	Pip's old bedroom; Joe looking after him.	2.26	10	DISSOLVE
53. *Marshes*	Joe and Biddy (married) and Pip on river bank. Talk of Estella (voice-over).	0.46	3	DISSOLVE
54. *Satis House*	(a) Exterior—FOR SALE. (b) Pip walks through passages. (c) Re-meeting with Estella—tearing down curtains. (d) Exterior—Pip and Estella leave together. 'GREAT EXPECTATIONS' superimposed on final shot, before credits and THE END.	5.34	34	FADE OUT

APPENDIX 4

Daisy Miller: Segmentation and Shot Analysis

Segment	Editing
1. *Opening Credits*	
(a) The Director's Company Presents	All on pale, yellow-
(b) A Peter Bogdanovich Production	green background.
(c) Based on the story by HENRY JAMES	Cross-bars faded in.
(d) *Daisy Miller*	
2. *Early Morning—interior—Vevey*	
(a) Camera pans down (tilts) from ceiling, past balconies, to cleaners on ground floor. (Crane shot of cleaners.)	CUT
(b) Balconies—clock striking.	CUT
(c) Different view of balconies.	CUT
(d) Carpeted hall, shoes outside doors.	CUT
(e) Different view of corridor.	CUT
(f) Close-up (CU) of double doors, voices behind CU of hand removing shoes. (Track in and down to shoes. Camera tilts up.) Boy (Randolph) appears, answers unseen questioner.	CUT
(g) Porter on balcony above (Randolph's point of view (p.o.v.)).	CUT
(h) Corridor as Randolph switches shoes (camera tracks).	CUT
(i) Randolph slides down banisters.	CUT
(j) Further down banisters to foyer. Randolph takes alpenstock from container.	CUT
3. *Morning—exterior—garden of 'Les Trois Couronnes'*	
(a) Front view of 'Les Trois Couronnes'. People sitting in garden.	Vertical pan down, ends on CU.
CU of Randolph.	CUT
(b) View of lake (Randolph's p.o.v.).	CUT
(c) CU of Randolph.	CUT
(d) People exchanging shoes on exterior balconies. (Randolph's p.o.v.)	CUT
(e) CU of Randolph.	CUT
(f) Man (Winterbourne) arrives with paper, picks up handkerchief for lady, goes to table, sits centre screen (Randolph's p.o.v.).	CUT
(g) CU of Randolph.	CUT
(h) Winterbourne reading at table.	CUT
(i) CU of Randolph.	CUT
(j) Randolph approaches Winterbourne (viewed over Winterbourne's shoulder) and asks for sugar.	CUT
(k) Winterbourne puts down paper.	CUT
(l) Two-shot of Randolph and Winterbourne at table (trick with sugar lump).	CUT
(m) CU of Randolph's hand, holding teeth.	CUT
(n) Two-shot of Randolph and Winterbourne as people walk past them. Pan to CU of Winterbourne as Randolph leaves frame.	CUT
(o) Girl in white dress approaching through trees (Winterbourne's p.o.v.).	CUT
(p) CU of Winterbourne watching her.	CUT
(q) Randolph at fountain, planning to squirt girl.	CUT

Segment	Editing
(r) CU of Winterbourne watching.	CUT
(s) Girl (Daisy) walking towards Randolph and Winterbourne (forward tracking, depth of field).	CUT
(t) Daisy still walking, talks as she passes Randolph.	CUT
(u) CU of Winterbourne as Daisy approaches. Exchange of looks.	CUT
(v) Daisy walks to balustrade, stops, looks out (tracking).	CUT
(w) Winterbourne turns to look at her, joined by Randolph.	CUT
(x) CU of Daisy as she turns to look at Winterbourne.	CUT
(y) CU of Winterbourne, half-smiling at Daisy.	CUT
(z) Daisy turns back to look at lake.	CUT
(a2) CU of Winterbourne who looks away.	CUT
(b2) Randolph returns on alpenstock, falls. Winterbourne and Daisy in discussion as he joins her at balustrade. Two-shot of Daisy and Winterbourne, then Winterbourne in profile looking at Daisy full on; final track brings Daisy into CU (Winterbourne's p.o.v.).	CUT
(c2) CU of Winterbourne, looking off L.	CUT
(d2) CU of Daisy, looking off R. She walks to balustrade, followed by Winterbourne (tracking). They stop in medium shot. Talk of visiting Chillon.	CUT
(e2) Courier, Eugenio, appears from trees. Walks towards them.	CUT
(f2) CU of Daisy and Winterbourne.	CUT
(g2) CU of Eugenio, asking for Randolph.	CUT
(h2) CU of Daisy and Winterbourne.	CUT
(i2) CU of Eugenio, asking about Chillon arrangements.	CUT
(j2) Two-shot—Daisy and Winterbourne looking at each other, Winterbourne turns away from Eugenio. Daisy leaves frame as Winterbourne turns front.	CUT
(k2) CU of Eugenio—turns and walks off with Daisy.	CUT
(l2) Medium CU of Winterbourne, watching them go.	CUT
(m2) Medium shot of Eugenio and Daisy, as Randolph jumps out at them.	CUT
(n2) CU of Winterbourne, watching.	CUT
(o2) Eugenio, Daisy, and Randolph move off (Winterbourne's p.o.v.).	CUT

4. *Afternoon—interior—hydropathic baths*

Segment	Editing
(a) Woman, Mrs Costello, in CU. Winterbourne in baths, too; tea-tray between them. Talk of Millers. (Camera tracks back and pans slightly R.)	CUT
(b) CU of Mrs Costello (profile) looking up at Winterbourne (R. of frame).	CUT
(c) CU of Mrs Costello (front on) looking down at Winterbourne (profile).	CUT
(d) CU of Mrs Costello (profile) looking up at Winterbourne (front on).	CUT
(e) CU of Mrs Costello and Winterbourne (both profile). Tray between them. Camera stays on them.	CUT
(f) CU of Mrs Costello (front on), looking down at Winterbourne (rear head).	CUT
(g) CU of Mrs Costello (rear head), looking up at Winterbourne (front on).	CUT
(h) CU of Mrs Costello (front on), looking off, Winterbourne (rear head). 'Well she's just as I supposed' (Mrs Costello).	CUT
(i) CU of Mrs Costello, moving off, past Winterbourne and looking back at him. Medium CU of chess players in foreground, as Winterbourne goes off after Mrs Costello.	CUT
(j) Winterbourne and Mrs Costello put on bath robes. Mrs Costello declines to meet Daisy.	CUT

Segment	Editing
(*k*) CU of Mrs Costello (front on), looking down to Winterbourne (rear head).	CUT
(*l*) Mrs Costello at low R. (profile), looking up at Winterbourne (front on) as he strokes moustache.	CUT
(*m*) CU of Mrs Costello.	CUT
(*n*) CU of Winterbourne, looking off slightly R.	CUT
(*o*) CU of Mrs Costello who turns to leave, with attendant (camera tracking).	CUT
(*p*) CU of Winterbourne, watching her.	DISSOLVE

5. *Night—exterior—garden of 'Les Trois Couronnes'*

Segment	Editing
(*a*) Medium long shot of façade of hotel. Music.	CUT
(*b*) Medium long shot of Winterbourne entering from interior to look out.	CUT
(*c*) Medium long shot of Daisy, walking along balustrade; stops and speaks to Winterbourne (tracking).	CUT
(*d*) CU of Winterbourne replying.	CUT
(*e*) Medium CU of Daisy, joined by Winterbourne. They walk together (tracking). Stop on CU of Daisy ('She doesn't want to meet me'), then more walking.	CUT
(*f*) Medium shot of Mrs Miller walking in shadows.	CUT
(*g*) CU of Winterbourne and Daisy.	CUT
(*h*) Medium shot of Mrs Miller, not quite approaching.	CUT
(*i*) CU of Winterbourne and Daisy.	CUT
(*j*) Daisy enters frame behind mother at balustrade; Winterbourne joins them at R. Tracking, as Daisy leads off, followed by Winterbourne and Mrs Miller, then stops with Winterbourne and Mrs Miller in medium CU.	CUT
(*k*) Medium shot of Daisy, flanked by back views of Winterbourne and Mrs Miller till all three meet in medium CU.	CUT
(*l*) Eugenio emerges from shadows to announce time.	CUT
(*m*) Medium CU of Winterbourne, Daisy, and Mrs Miller, looking towards Eugenio.	CUT
(*n*) Medium CU of Eugenio, smoking.	CUT
(*o*) Medium CU of Winterbourne, Daisy, and Mrs Miller. Tracking back as Eugenio enters frame to take Mrs Miller off, as Daisy and Winterbourne talk in CU. (Daisy is front on, looking down at Winterbourne, rear head.) Daisy goes to join Eugenio and Mrs Miller.	CUT
(*p*) CU of Winterbourne, watching them go. Tracking as he walks.	CUT
(*q*) Randolph in tree addresses Winterbourne (medium CU), who walks off, followed by camera.	CUT
(*r*) CU of Randolph in tree. Points stick.	MATCH CUT

6. *Day—exterior—boat journey to Chillon*

Segment	Editing
(*a*) CU of boat funnel.	CUT
(*b*) Daisy and Winterbourne running down steps.	CUT
(*c*) Gangway of boat being moved; Daisy and Winterbourne just reach it in time.	CUT
(*d*) Medium CU of Daisy and Winterbourne on board.	CUT
(*e*) CU of Daisy (front on), looking down at Winterbourne (rear head).	CUT
(*f*) Long shot (tracking) of boat moving off.	CUT
(*g*) Long shot of castle, gradually coming nearer.	CUT
(*h*) Medium CU of Daisy and Winterbourne on boat deck; tracking in until CU. (Play with Winterbourne's hat.)	CUT

Segment	Editing
(*i*) CU of Daisy at L. (front on), looking down at Winterbourne (rear head).	CUT
(*j*) CU of Daisy (rear head), looking up at Winterbourne (front on).	CUT
(*k*) CU of Daisy (front on), looking down at Winterbourne (rear head).	CUT

7. *Day—exteriors and interiors—Castle of Chillon*

(*a*) Medium long shot of castle. Daisy and Winterbourne enter frame from bottom, move R. and enter doorway ('Maggie' on sound-track).	CUT
(*b*) Courtyard, man with accordion. Daisy and Winterbourne enter frame L. Guide approaches them.	CUT
(*c*) Another courtyard. Daisy and Winterbourne enter, Winterbourne pays off guide who goes to sit in alcove. (Panning.)	CUT
(*d*) Winterbourne and Daisy enter cloister, talking.	CUT
(*e*) Interior—room with barred window. Daisy and Winterbourne enter and walk about. (Tracking.)	CUT
(*f*) Low-angle shot of Daisy and Winterbourne peering down oubliette.	CUT
(*g*) Exterior—bridge connecting parts of castle. Daisy and Winterbourne walk across and then off to R.	CUT
(*h*) Interior—Daisy and Winterbourne walk through bedroom.	CUT
(*i*) Exterior—high covered balcony. Daisy and Winterbourne walk across it. (Tracking.)	CUT
(*j*) Interior—staircase.	CUT
(*k*) Exterior—wall with window at which Daisy and Winterbourne appear.	CUT
(*l*) Interior—decorated roof of chapel. Vertical pan down to pulpit below window. Daisy goes to pulpit, Winterbourne (down R.) turns back to look.	CUT
(*m*) Exterior—dark cloisters. Daisy and Winterbourne walk along.	CUT
(*n*) Daisy and Winterbourne enter dungeons. Winterbourne (down L.) turns back to watch Daisy standing in sunlight. She comes to join him.	CUT
(*o*) Interior of big room. Camera tracks in to CU of Winterbourne and Daisy.	CUT
(*p*) Stairway—Daisy going down. (Tracking, past guide.)	CUT
(*q*) Exterior—Daisy, then Winterbourne, into CU, talking about his woman friend in Geneva. Tracking, then stop for CU of Daisy (front on), looking down to Winterbourne (rear head).	CUT
(*r*) CU of Daisy down L. (rear head), looking up to Winterbourne (front on).	CUT
(*s*) CU of Daisy (front on), looking down to Winterbourne (rear head).	CUT
(*t*) CU of Winterbourne (front on), looking down to Daisy (rear head).	CUT
(*u*) CU of Daisy (front on), looking down to Winterbourne (rear head).	CUT
(*v*) CU of Winterbourne (front on), looking down to Daisy (rear head).	CUT
(*w*) CU of Daisy (front on), looking down to Winterbourne (rear head). (Camera pulls back to watch them leave.)	CUT

8. *Day—exteriors and interiors—carriage journey*

(*a*) CU of Winterbourne and Daisy in carriage, silent.	CUT
(*b*) Castle and foliage from rear window of carriage as Daisy looks back.	CUT
(*c*) CU of Winterbourne and Daisy in carriage.	CUT
(*d*) Exterior of carriage along muddy road. (Tracking stops on misty view of castle.)	FADE OUT / FADE IN

Segment	Editing
9. *Day—interior—Mrs Costello's apartment, Rome*	
(a) Vista of Rome (St Peter's dome, etc.), from Mrs Costello's window (Winterbourne's p.o.v.). As camera pulls back, Winterbourne closes window, then moves over to Mrs Costello who is having a miniature taken, talking of Daisy the while. Winterbourne turns to face her.	CUT
(b) Medium CU of Mrs Costello, taking salts.	CUT
(c) Winterbourne walks (tracking shot) to take up photo.	CUT
(d) Winterbourne at L. foreground with photo, Mrs Costello at rear. He moves back to and behind her. Talk of Mrs Walker (more tracking).	CUT
(e) Winterbourne walks to look at artist's work (tracking).	CUT
(f) CU of miniature of Mrs Costello's face.	MATCH CUT
10. *Day—interior—Mrs Walker's house, Rome*	
(a) CU of woman (Mrs Walker). Back-tracking reveals she is talking to Winterbourne (R). Mirrors reveal others. She leaves frame to greet the Millers, leaving Winterbourne alone in frame. Further tracking shows the Millers in background, Winterbourne in foreground.	CUT
(b) CU of Daisy as Winterbourne joins her. Camera tracks back as Winterbourne joins Mrs Miller and Randolph and Mrs Walker takes Daisy off.	
Camera tracks gently until Winterbourne and Mrs Miller are seated at edges of frame, Mrs Miller and Daisy reflected in mirror behind. Winterbourne looks front at Daisy who is seen in mirror at rear. (CU of Daisy.)	(Much panning and tracking in long take.)
Daisy and Mrs Walker join Winterbourne and Mrs Miller. Talk of Mr Giovanelli, of going to the Pincio, of Roman fever.	
As Daisy and Winterbourne go off L., camera tracks forward to frame Mrs Walker in CU watching them go.	CUT
11. *Day—exterior—streets and Pincian Gardens*	
(a) Daisy says goodbye to Eugenio and goes walking in street with Winterbourne.	CUT
(b) CU of Eugenio watching and smoking.	CUT
(c) Daisy and Winterbourne walking in park as camera tracks them.	CUT
(d) Daisy and Winterbourne walk through park, followed by camera.	CUT
(e) CU of Punch and Judy show.	CUT
(f) Crowd, including Daisy and Winterbourne, watching. Track into Daisy and Winterbourne.	CUT
(g) CU of Punch and Judy show.	CUT
(h) CU of Daisy and Winterbourne, pan to bring Winterbourne into full CU.	CUT
(i) CU of Daisy in profile, watching, laughing, turns to Winterbourne.	CUT
(j) CU of Winterbourne watching her.	CUT
(k) CU of Daisy watching him, turning back to watch show.	CUT
(l) CU of Winterbourne watching her, smiling.	CUT
(m) Medium long shot of woman in white watching (Winterbourne's p.o.v.).	CUT
(n) CU of Winterbourne, eyes averted.	CUT
(o) Medium long shot of woman in white, watching Winterbourne (?).	CUT
(p) CU of Winterbourne, watching.	CUT
(q) CU of Punch and Judy show.	CUT
(r) CU of Daisy (laughing) and Winterbourne (smiling) as they watch.	CUT
(s) CU of Punch and Judy show.	CUT

Segment	Editing
(*t*) Crowd at end of show, clapping; Daisy and Winterbourne walk off, buy candy. Tracking stops on CU of Daisy and Winterbourne as they talk of Giovanelli.	CUT
(*u*) Medium shot of Giovanelli against tree.	CUT
(*v*) CU of Daisy and Winterbourne watching Giovanelli. Winterbourne walks to stand before her at L. ('Do you seriously mean to speak to that thing?')	CUT
(*w*) CU of Daisy (rear head) and Winterbourne (front on) talking down to her.	CUT
(*x*) CU of Daisy (front on), talking down to Winterbourne (rear head).	CUT
(*y*) CU of Daisy (rear head) and Winterbourne (front on) talking down to her.	CUT
(*z*) CU of Daisy (front on), laughing, going off L., watched by Winterbourne (rear head). Daisy walks to meet Giovanelli who comes towards her. (Tracking.)	CUT
(*a2*) Winterbourne stands watching, then goes to join her in medium CU. (Tracking.)	CUT
(*b2*) Long shot of Giovanelli, Daisy, and Winterbourne (Mrs Walker's p.o.v.).	CUT
(*c2*) CU of Mrs Walker in carriage, watching.	CUT
(*d2*) Medium shot of Giovanelli, Daisy, and Winterbourne (Mrs Walker's p.o.v.).	CUT
(*e2*) Mrs Walker, then shot of carriage wall, as it drives off. (Tracking.)	CUT
(*f2*) Giovanelli, Daisy, and Winterbourne (arms linked) in CU, walking. Winterbourne leaves to go to Mrs Walker's carriage (tracking).	CUT
(*g2*) Medium shot of Daisy and Giovanelli (Mrs Walker's p.o.v.).	CUT
(*h2*) CU of Mrs Walker in carriage, Winterbourne (rear head).	CUT
(*i2*) CU of Winterbourne, looking down at Mrs Walker (rear head).	CUT
(*j2*) CU of Mrs Walker (front on), looking down at Winterbourne (rear head).	CUT
(*k2*) CU of Winterbourne (front on), looking down at Mrs Walker (rear head).	CUT
(*l2*) CU of Mrs Walker (front on), Winterbourne turns and goes off, leaving Mrs Walker watching.	CUT
(*m2*) Medium shot of Winterbourne going back to Daisy and Giovanelli. They all move forward.	CUT
(*n2*) Winterbourne, Daisy, and Giovanelli arrive at carriage, Mrs Walker in foreground L. (tracking).	CUT
(*p2*) CU of Mrs Walker talking to Daisy (off L.).	CUT
(*q2*) Winterbourne, Daisy, and Giovanelli in CU talking to Mrs Walker.	CUT
(*r2*) CU of Mrs Walker, trying to persuade Daisy to get in.	CUT
(*s2*) Winterbourne, Daisy, and Giovanelli, standing by carriage.	CUT
(*t2*) CU of Mrs Walker ('It's not the custom here').	CUT
(*u2*) Winterbourne, Daisy, and Giovanelli, standing by carriage.	CUT
(*v2*) CU of Mrs Walker.	CUT
(*w2*) Winterbourne, Daisy, and Giovanelli, standing by carriage.	CUT
(*x2*) CU of Mrs Walker ('You're old enough to be talked about').	CUT
(*y2*) Winterbourne, Daisy, and Giovanelli, standing by carriage.	CUT
(*z2*) CU of Mrs Walker ('Step into my carriage').	CUT
(*a3*) Winterbourne, Daisy, and Giovanelli, standing by carriage, as Daisy refuses.	CUT
(*b3*) CU of Mrs Walker.	CUT
(*c3*) CU of Daisy—pan R. to Giovanelli, then L. to Winterbourne.	CUT
(*d3*) CU of Mrs Walker.	CUT
(*e3*) CU of Winterbourne.	CUT

Segment	Editing
(f3) CU of Daisy, looking at Winterbourne.	CUT
(g3) CU of Winterbourne ('I think you should get into the carriage').	CUT
(h3) CU of Daisy, then Daisy and Giovanelli walk off as camera tracks them.	CUT
(i3) CU of Mrs Walker in carriage, Winterbourne at R.—both looking off ('Get in', she orders).	CUT
(j3) CU of Winterbourne (front on) looking down at Mrs Walker (rear head).	CUT
(k3) CU of Mrs Walker ('Mr Winterbourne, if you don't get in . . .').	CUT
(l3) CU of Winterbourne.	CUT
(m3) CU of Mrs Walker.	CUT
(n3) CU of Winterbourne, who looks off R. behind, then walks off.	CUT
(o3) CU of Mrs Walker watching him go.	CUT
(p3) Medium shot as Daisy and Giovanelli are joined by Winterbourne. She drops his hand as Winterbourne speaks and goes off with Giovanelli.	CUT
(q3) CU of Winterbourne watching them go.	CUT
(r3) Over-shoulder (of Winterbourne) shot as Daisy and Giovanelli go off. Winterbourne looks around and Daisy and Giovanelli walk away from camera.	CUT
(s3) Winterbourne returns to carriage (tracking) and sits beside Mrs Walker.	CUT
(t3) Medium shot of band rotunda as Daisy and Giovanelli approach it. Tracking shot, with overheard conversation of Winterbourne and Mrs Walker.	CUT
(u3) CU of Winterbourne and Mrs Walker in carriage (Winterbourne '. . . perhaps you and I have lived too long in Geneva').	CUT
(v3) CU of Mrs Walker watching him.	CUT
(w3) CU of Winterbourne watching her.	CUT
(x3) CU of Mrs Walker watching him.	CUT
(y3) CU of Winterbourne watching her.	CUT
(z3) CU of Mrs Walker watching him ('Let her alone').	CUT
(a4) CU of Winterbourne watching her.	CUT
(b4) CU of Mrs Walker ('You shouldn't help her to make a scandal').	CUT
(c4) CU of Winterbourne watching her.	CUT
(d4) CU of Mrs Walker looking ahead.	CUT
(e4) CU of Winterbourne.	CUT
(f4) Medium shot of Daisy and Giovanelli walking, as Mrs Walker in carriage suggests Winterbourne rejoin 'the young lady'.	CUT
(g4) CU of carriage—Winterbourne gets out, back to camera; Mrs Walker orders carriage on; Winterbourne looks for Daisy and Giovanelli.	CUT
(h4) Medium shot of Daisy and Giovanelli at balustrade.	CUT
(i4) CU of Winterbourne watching them.	CUT
(j4) Medium shot of Daisy and Giovanelli as they go behind parasol.	CUT
(k4) Medium CU of Winterbourne, watching then backing away.	CUT
(l4) As Winterbourne turns, camera stays on Daisy and Giovanelli.	CUT

12. *Evening—interior—Mrs Walker's house*

Segment	Editing
(a) Winterbourne, Mrs Walker, and friend Charles with Mrs Miller at Mrs Walker's party. Mrs Miller prattles on as Mrs Walker walks away.	CUT
(b) CU of violinist as footman announces Miss Miller. (Pan to entrance.)	CUT
(c) Medium CU of Mrs Walker, Charles, and others who turn at announcement.	CUT

Segment	Editing

 (*d*) Medium shot of Daisy and Giovanelli entering. Winterbourne (in
   mirror) down R.   CUT

 (*e*) Daisy and Giovanelli go to join Mrs Walker, who greets her curtly and
   walks away. Tracking as Daisy goes off with Giovanelli, joins mother,
   then stops on Winterbourne in medium shot, reflected in mirror. CUT

 (*f*) Medium CU of pianist.   CUT

 (*g*) CU of Giovanelli singing.
   Tracking shot of waiter with glasses, stops at Charles and Mrs Walker. CUT

 (*h*) Daisy goes to stand by Winterbourne in CU. They walk off, followed
   by camera, sit and talk. Tracking gives way to long two-shot. CUT

 (*i*) Daisy and Winterbourne stand; she starts clapping in CU. CUT

 (*j*) Medium CU of Giovanelli taken aback at clapping. Tracking as
   Giovanelli walks over to Daisy and Winterbourne. Daisy goes off R.
   with Giovanelli; Winterbourne, in CU, watches them go. CUT

 (*k*) Medium CU of elderly viola player, pan to other musicians, to Mrs
   Miller talking to old man asleep, then to Giovanelli and Daisy sitting
   together in alcove.   CUT

 (*l*) Medium CU of Winterbourne watching Daisy and Giovanelli, then
   joined by Charles and Mrs Walker, who goes off with guests. CUT

 (*m*) Daisy and Giovanelli walk towards Mrs Miller. CUT

 (*n*) CU of Winterbourne watching them. CUT

 (*o*) Mrs Walker farewelling guests, cuts Daisy as Mrs Miller comes up. CUT

 (*p*) CU of Daisy, hurt, as she turns away. CUT

 (*q*) CU of Winterbourne, goes to Mrs Walker ('She never enters my
   drawing-room again'). Two faces in profile. CUT

13. *Day—interior—the Millers' hotel*

 (*a*) CU of bell at hotel desk.   CUT

 (*b*) Medium CU of Winterbourne (rear view) with receptionist. CUT

 (*c*) CU of gloved finger on bell.   CUT

 (*d*) Medium CU of Winterbourne (rear view) with other receptionist. CUT

 (*e*) Medium CU of bellboys sniggering.   CUT

 (*f*) Winterbourne leaves note.   CUT

14. *Day—interior/exterior—St Peter's Cathedral*

 (*a*) Stained glass window (CU). Tracking down to Daisy and Giovanelli
   (medium shot).   CUT

 (*b*) Medium shot of Winterbourne standing by pillar. CUT

 (*c*) Daisy and Giovanelli walking off R.   CUT

 (*d*) Winterbourne watching them.   CUT

 (*e*) Daisy and Giovanelli walking off R.   CUT

 (*f*) Winterbourne watching them.   CUT

 (*g*) Daisy and Giovanelli walking in cathedral. CUT

 (*h*) CU of Winterbourne watching, as Mrs Costello comes behind him. CUT

 (*i*) Daisy and Giovanelli walking.   CUT

 (*j*) CU of Winterbourne and Mrs Costello ('Your mind's on other things').
   Camera lingers on their conversation.   CUT

 (*k*) Daisy and Giovanelli walking.   CUT

 (*l*) Winterbourne and Mrs Costello talking of them. CUT

 (*m*) Daisy and Giovanelli walking a little nearer. CUT

 (*n*) Winterbourne watching them.   CUT

 (*o*) Daisy and Giovanelli walking off L.   CUT

 (*p*) CU of Winterbourne. Tracking as Winterbourne and Mrs Costello
   walk off R.   CUT

Segment	Editing
(q) Daisy and Giovanelli (long shot) go out into the sun; she puts up parasol. (Tracking.)	CUT
(r) Winterbourne and Mrs Costello walking.	CUT
(s) Winterbourne and Mrs Costello emerge from cathedral door.	CUT
(t) Overhead shot of Daisy and Giovanelli in forecourt (Winterbourne's p.o.v.).	CUT
(u) CU of Mrs Costello and Winterbourne.	CUT

15. *Day—interior—the Millers' hotel*

Segment	Editing
(a) Front door, street—Winterbourne passes, comes back, enters.	CUT
(b) Winterbourne enters, goes to desk (tracking).	CUT
(c) Medium CU of Winterbourne at desk. Tracking as he goes from desk and up stairs.	CUT
(d) Medium CU of grinning bellboys.	CUT
(e) Corridor. Winterbourne appears and knocks on door. Music within.	CUT
(f) Medium shot of Daisy and Giovanelli at piano in sitting-room.	CUT
(g) Winterbourne at door ('Am I interrupting?')	CUT
(h) Closer shot of Daisy and Giovanelli at piano.	CUT
(i) Winterbourne at door, flanked by rear head view of Daisy and Giovanelli. Winterbourne brings heavy gilt chair to sit on.	CUT
(j) Giovanelli and Daisy face Winterbourne who is at R. (rear head) in CU.	CUT
(k) Winterbourne sitting down.	CUT
(l) Medium CU of Daisy and Giovanelli at piano.	CUT
(m) CU of Winterbourne watching them.	CUT
(n) CU of Daisy and Giovanelli at piano.	CUT
(o) CU of Winterbourne watching, beginning to smile.	CUT
(p) Giovanelli and Daisy at piano as Giovanelli sings 'Pop Goes the Weasel'.	CUT
(q) CU of Winterbourne watching, smiling.	CUT
(r) Giovanelli and Daisy at piano, he singing as she plays faster.	CUT
(s) CU of Winterbourne watching, smiling.	CUT
(t) Giovanelli and Daisy at piano, faster still.	CUT
(u) CU of Winterbourne clapping.	CUT
(v) Medium CU of Giovanelli and Daisy (Giovanelli offers to play while she sings).	CUT
(w) CU of Winterbourne.	CUT
(x) Giovanelli and Daisy—she stands L.; framed by window, sings 'Maggie'.	CUT
(y) CU of Winterbourne, watching, head slightly to one side.	CUT
(z) CU of Daisy singing.	CUT
(a2) CU of Winterbourne, smiling.	CUT
(b2) Daisy standing, Giovanelli at piano.	CUT
(c2) CU of Winterbourne, smiling and clapping.	CUT
(d2) Medium CU of Winterbourne (rear head) in L. foreground, Giovanelli sitting, and Daisy standing.	CUT
(e2) Mrs Miller entering with parcels; other three with backs to camera.	CUT
(f2) Daisy and Giovanelli watching Winterbourne help Mrs Miller in foregound. Tracking as Winterbourne and Mrs Miller go into next room. (Talk of 'engagement'.) He goes off R.	CUT
(g2) CU of Winterbourne at door; Mrs Miller joins him. Tracking as Mrs Miller goes back into room, into CU.	CUT
(h2) Medium CU of Randolph pretending to be hanged.	CUT
(i2) CU of Mrs Miller who sits.	CUT

Segment	Editing

16. Day—exterior—gardens of Palace of Caesars

    (a) Long shot of Winterbourne walking by ornamental pool.   CUT

    (b) CU of Winterbourne as he hears Daisy call his name.   CUT

    (c) Medium shot of Daisy and Giovanelli coming towards pool.   CUT

    (d) CU of Winterbourne, smiling at her.   CUT

    (e) Daisy approaches Winterbourne; they walk off together (tracking) in CU two-shots. As they stop, he turns to face her.   CUT

    (f) CU of Winterbourne against dark background.   CUT

    (g) CU of Daisy against light background.   CUT

    (h) CU of Winterbourne.   CUT

    (i) CU two-shot, Daisy (front on) and L., Winterbourne (rear head) at R. (Tracking.)   CUT

    (j) CU of Winterbourne.   CUT

    (k) CU two-shot, Daisy (front on) at L., Winterbourne (rear head) at R.   CUT

    (l) CU of Winterbourne ('Yes I do'—i.e. believe she's engaged).   CUT

    (m) Two-shot again. Giovanelli arrives between them. Daisy moves off (tracking shot), says she's not engaged. Giovanelli comes after her.   CUT

    (n) Medium CU of Winterbourne watching them go.   CUT

17. Night—exterior/interior—streets and Colosseum

    (a) Dark street, carriage moving towards camera.   CUT

    (b) Charles and Winterbourne in carriage, talk of Daisy, Geneva, etc.   CUT

    (c) Medium shot of horses moving (tracking), then of Charles in carriage as Winterbourne gets out. Winterbourne in CU as Charles drives off.   CUT

    (d) Triumphal arch. Overhead shot as Winterbourne walks through.   CUT

    (e) CU of Winterbourne's face in low-angle shot.   CUT

    (f) Exterior shot of Colosseum, low-angled.   CUT

    (g) CU of Winterbourne looking at it.   CUT

    (h) Façade of Colosseum and waiting carriage.   CUT

    (i) Medium CU of Winterbourne.   CUT

    (j) Rear view of Winterbourne walking towards Colosseum, low-angled.   CUT

    (k) Interior—Winterbourne enters, passes between columns.   CUT

    (l) Winterbourne enters arena.   CUT

    (m) Long shot of arena as whole.   CUT

    (n) CU of Winterbourne, looking about.   CUT

    (o) Part of interior (Winterbourne's p.o.v.).   CUT

    (p) CU of Winterbourne, looking about, walking. (Tracking.)   CUT

    (q) Part of interior (Winterbourne's p.o.v.).   CUT

    (r) CU of Winterbourne, walking.   CUT

    (s) View of interior, of figures moving. (Tracking.)   CUT

    (t) CU of Winterbourne watching.   CUT

    (u) Interior—Winterbourne enters L. (Tracking.)   CUT

    (v) CU profile of Winterbourne as he hears Daisy's giggle.   CUT

    (w) Long shot of Giovanelli and Daisy.   CUT

    (x) Medium CU of Winterbourne who turns to look at her.   CUT

    (y) Medium shot of Giovanelli and Daisy.   CUT

    (z) CU of Winterbourne, coming very close to camera. He turns, walks back towards camera.   CUT

    (a2) Medium shot of Daisy and Giovanelli, Winterbourne at L. edge of frame.   CUT

    (b2) CU of Daisy and Giovanelli (Winterbourne's p.o.v.).   CUT

    (c2) CU of Winterbourne.   CUT

    (d2) CU of Daisy and Giovanelli ('I never saw anything so quaint').   CUT

    (e2) CU of Winterbourne warning against malaria.   CUT

    (f2) CU of Giovanelli and Daisy (Giovanelli—'. . . for myself I have no fear')   CUT

Segment	Editing
(g2) CU of Winterbourne ('Neither have I—for you!').	CUT
(h2) CU of Giovanelli and Daisy.	CUT
(i2) CU of Winterbourne.	CUT
(j2) CU of Giovanelli and Daisy; Giovanelli walks off behind, Daisy with rose in CU.	CUT
(k2) CU of Winterbourne, walking up to Daisy.	CUT
(l2) Winterbourne joins Daisy in frame; they turn.	CUT
(m2) Daisy and Winterbourne walk off; Giovanelli in CU.	CUT
(n2) CU of Winterbourne.	CUT
(o2) CU of Daisy.	CUT
(p2) CU of Winterbourne.	CUT
(q2) Exterior—Daisy in foreground, Giovanelli with carriage at rear R.	CUT
(r2) CU of Winterbourne.	CUT
(s2) CU of Daisy ('Well, what do you believe now?').	CUT
(t2) CU of Winterbourne ('. . . very little difference whether you're engaged or not').	CUT
(u2) CU of Daisy.	CUT
(v2) CU of Winterbourne.	CUT
(w2) CU of Daisy—Giovanelli takes her arm, leads her away as she looks back at Winterbourne.	CUT
(x2) CU of Winterbourne (Daisy's p.o.v.).	CUT
(y2) Medium shot of Giovanelli leading Daisy to carriage.	CUT
(z2) CU of Winterbourne looking at them.	CUT
(a3) Daisy and Giovanelli getting in carriage (Winterbourne's p.o.v.).	CUT
(b3) CU of Daisy ('I don't care if I have Roman fever or not').	CUT
(c3) CU of Winterbourne watching them leave, very serious.	CUT
(d3) Long shot of Daisy and Giovanelli driving off.	CUT

18. *Night—interior—the Opera*

(a) CU of opera singer.	CUT
(b) Long shot of stage; pan R. to reveal Winterbourne's head and p.o.v. Head in CU profile.	CUT
(c) Liveried doormen in corridor. People emerge at interval.	CUT
(d) Medium CU of members of crowd, as Winterbourne moves through them. Stops when he hears Daisy discussed. Hears someone calling him. (Tracking.)	CUT
(e) Medium CU of Charles waving.	CUT
(f) CU of Winterbourne (front on) joined by Charles (rear head). Talk of Daisy Miller. Tracking, stops on CU of Winterbourne.	CUT
(g) CU of Charles ('The silly girl has caught Roman fever'). Winterbourne has run off.	CUT

19. *Night—interior—the Millers' hotel*

(a) Long overhead shot of Mrs Miller and Randolph in sitting-room.	CUT
(b) CU of Winterbourne also sitting there.	CUT
(c) Eugenio entering with tray (tracking).	CUT
(d) CU of Winterbourne (Eugenio's p.o.v.).	CUT
(e) Eugenio goes out with tray (tracking).	CUT
(f) CU of Winterbourne, anxious.	CUT
(g) Mrs Miller and Doctor crossing room. (Tracking.)	CUT
(h) CU of Winterbourne—crosses room to door. (Tracking.)	CUT
(i) CU of Randolph.	CUT

Segment	Editing

(j) Winterbourne at door R. (profile), looking out where Mrs Miller and Doctor are talking. Doctor leaves. Winterbourne talks to Mrs Miller about Daisy. Mrs Miller (front on) in CU tells Winterbourne (rear head) Daisy's message.   CUT

(k) CU of Winterbourne (front on) looking down at Mrs Miller (rear head) at L.   CUT

(l) Mrs Miller (front on) at L., looking down at Winterbourne (rear head).   CUT

(m) CU of Winterbourne (front on), looking down at Mrs Miller (rear head).   CUT

(n) CU of Mrs Miller (front on), looking down at Winterbourne (rear head) ('She wants you to know she's not engaged').   CUT

(o) CU of Winterbourne listening.   CUT

20. *Day—exterior—the Millers' hotel*
Carriage rounds corner, followed by Winterbourne with flowers. Camera follows him through door and up stairs where he stops half-way. Camera stays on door with lace; Winterbourne comes down stairs, out door. Camera stays on lace.   CUT

21. *Day—exterior—graveside*

(a) Bare ground. Camera tilts up to reveal mourners (Randolph, Mrs Miller, Eugenio, Mrs Walker, Charles, Giovanelli at L. behind him). Camera stays on them. Giovanelli leaves.
Eugenio takes Mrs Miller off. Winterbourne goes to Randolph at L. as camera pulls back and pans L.   CUT

(b) CU of Randolph who turns to look at Winterbourne.   CUT

(c) CU of Winterbourne at R., Randolph (rear head) at L.   CUT

(d) CU of Randolph, accusing look. Randolph walks off.   CUT

(e) CU of Winterbourne.   CUT

(f) Long shot—Winterbourne's p.o.v. as Randolph, etc. walk off through cemetery.   CUT

(g) CU of Winterbourne. Voice-over of Winterbourne talking to Mrs Costello ('I fear I did her an injustice', etc.).
Winterbourne in increasingly long shot as voice-over continues. Camera back-tracking.
Colour fades as 'Maggie' is heard on sound-track.   FADE

22. *Cast*
Cast brought on one by one, named with character's name. Other credits on pale yellow ground as at start.

Cape Fear: Segmentation

Segment	Editing
1. *Credits* (*a*) Over camera panning water, reflecting bird in flight, then close-up of eye, over rippling water, followed by shadow of man appearing over water, which turns red. (*b*) After director's credit, close-up of eyes in the photographic negative, then the eyes in 'positive' colour as belonging to a young girl speaking about the mystifying name, Cape Fear.	
2. *Prison* Max Cady is doing push-ups in his cell, prior to being released.	CUT
3. *Bowden House* Danielle helps maid Graciella with parcels. Then goes in to her mother Leigh who is working on design for her advertising agency.	CUT
4. *Outside Court House* Sam Bowden talks with colleague Tom about outcome of case.	CUT
5. *Cinema* Cady is watching a violent movie, laughing loudly, smoking cigar—smoke causes Bowden family to move.	CUT
6. *Cafe* Danielle tells Sam he should have hit the man. Cady is sitting in car outside café.	CUT
7. *Squash Court* Sam is playing squash with girl Lori to whom he says, 'We're going to stop doing this for a while.'	CUT
8. *Street outside Cafe* Cady reaches out and takes Sam's keys and forces Sam to listen to his account about losing weight in prison, etc. Cady taunts Sam with idea that he may settle down in town, New Essex.	CUT
9. *Bowden House—night* (*a*) Danielle asks Sam to stop tinkering at piano. (*b*) Bedroom—Sam wants them to go away for two weeks but Leigh doesn't want to. Love-making. (Hands, then faces, joined in photographic negative effect.) Later, Leigh gets up, makes up face at mirror, goes to window to look at fireworks, and sees Cady sitting on their fence. (*c*) Sam goes to warn Cady off but he's gone. (*d*) Sam tells Leigh about Cady.	CUT
10. *Bowden House—morning* As he leaves for work, Sam tells Leigh to warn Danny not to go out on her own.	CUT
11. *Broadbent's Office* Sam tells Tom Broadbent about his fears of Cady. Tom thinks he hasn't got much of a harassment case. Sam tells Tom how he 'buried' evidence that might have helped Cady, and tries to justify having done so.	CUT

Segment	Editing

12. *Bowden House*
Leigh asks Danny to come and work with her, tells her not to go outside.   CUT

13. *Street*
Cady accosts Sam in the street, talks of young girl. Sam tries to persuade him he did
his best to defend Cady, got him off rape charge. Sam tries to bribe him to leave.   CUT

14. *Bowden's Office*
Sam gets urgent call from Leigh.   CUT

15. *Car*
Sam drives home frantically.

16. *House*
Leigh talks of a sound of 'screaming' and the death of their dog which has been poisoned.
Leigh and Sam suddenly start shouting at each other and Danny runs out of the room.   CUT

17. *Police Station*
Lieutenant Elgar and Sam observe Cady brought in for identification, through a one-way
mirror. Cady's arms reveal messages—'Vengeance is mine' and 'My Time is at hand',
and other messages tattooed on back and chest.
Elgar tells Sam that he hasn't got enough grounds against Cady.   CUT

18. *Street*
Sam tries to assure Leigh and Danny that 'sooner or later he's [Cady's] going to screw up'.
Street parade for Independence Day. Sam spots Cady watching them across the street.
Sam crosses through parade, pushes Cady to ground. Bystanders hold Sam back.   CUT

19. *Bar Room*
Cady is talking to Lori, who laughs semi-drunkenly with him.   CUT

20. *Bedroom*
Cady and Lori on bed. He handcuffs her, then bites her face and batters her.   CUT

21. *Bowden House*
Sam finds piano wire broken. Phone call from Elgar to say Cady has raped another girl.   CUT

22. *Hospital*
Elgar and Sam walk down hospital corridor to ward where Sam finds the girl is Lori.
Lori doesn't want to go to court and explain.   CUT

23. *Outside Hospital*
Elgar tells Sam that he can't help Sam just because Sam is 'afraid' Cady will rape his wife. CUT

24. *Bowden House*
Montage of Sam slamming doors and windows shut.   CUT

25. *Kersek's Office*
Private investigator Kersek asks Sam his connection with Cady. Kersek will write up a
'risk assessment'.   CUT

26. *Bowden House*
Leigh tries to make fun of Sam having a private investigator on the payroll. Interrupted
by call from Kersek who has information about Cady having broken someone's neck
in prison.   CUT

27. *Cady's Room*
Kersek is talking on car phone outside Cady's lodgings.   CUT

Segment	Editing

28. *Bowden House*
Sam phones Lori, quietly so as not to be overheard. Hangs up when he sees Leigh in doorway; Leigh realizes his infidelities. Danny hears them quarrelling, races to her room. Mutual accusations. Sam tries to assure Leigh that Lori is 'just infatuated' with him, lies to her about their association. Sam ends up sleeping on the sofa. CUT

29. *Bar Room/Outside*
Kersek follows Cady as he leaves bar, warns him to leave town, but Cady is unmoved. CUT

30. *Bowden House*
Cady drives past, gives Leigh dog collar while she is collecting mail. He talks of how her husband has 'betrayed' them both. He drives off as Danny appears. CUT

31. *Car Park*
Kersek reports to Sam no success in nailing Cady, and recommends man who can be hired to beat up Cady.
Sam rejects idea of operating outside law. CUT

32. *Bowden House/Car*
Leigh drops Danny off at school, warns her.

33. *Bowden House/School*
Danny goes downstairs to drama theatre for class. Cady is sitting on stage set.
Danny accepts Cady's offer of a puff of a joint; talks to her about her parents' not wanting her to achieve pleasures of adulthood. Danny begins to realize who Cady is. He asks if he may put his arm around her and she allows him to touch and kiss her. CUT

34. *Bowden House/Kersek's Office*
Phone conversation. Sam tells Kersek he's decided to hire the three guys to beat up Cady. CUT

35. *Restaurant*
Sam comes in and threatens Cady that he will be 'hurt like you never dreamed' if he doesn't get out. CUT

36. *Bowden House*
Sam locks up. Danny tells Sam that Cady 'didn't force himself on me', that he was 'trying to make a connection'. In rage, Sam asks, 'Did he touch you?' CUT

37. *Car Park*
Sam watches as thugs beat up Cady, who then retaliates and overwhelms them. Cady, aware that Sam has been watching, shouts warnings at him. CUT

38. *Sam's Office*
When Sam tries to engage a criminal lawyer Lee Heller to take out a restraining order on Cady, Heller tells him he's been engaged by Cady. CUT

39. *Courtroom*
Heller puts Cady's case before Judge, who grants restraining order to stop Sam from coming within 500 yards of Cady! Heller says he will petition the ABA for Sam's disbarment. CUT

40. *Kersek's Office*
Sam bursts in and asks for a gun. Kersek warns him about killing a man. Kersek proposes luring Cady into their home, believing them to be away, and killing him justifiably. CUT

41. *Bowden House*
Family drives off at nightfall.
Cady follows them to the airport. CUT

Segment	Editing

42. *Airport*
  (a) Sam, watched by Cady, 'farewells' Leigh and Danny, then appears to go to catch flight.
  (b) Cady tries to get information from ticket agent about Sam's movements.   CUT

43. *Bowden House—night*
  (a) The family returns home. Kersek is there, rigging trap for Cady. Danny is angry at idea of setting trap.
  (b) While they wait, Sam reads the Bible. Leigh wants to find out 'how strong we are'.   CUT

44. *Bowden House—morning*
  (a) Danny and Graciella are dealing with the rubbish; Danny finds a copy of Henry Miller's *Sexus* under trash can. She hides book.
  (b) Kersek tells Sam he may have to live with idea of killing a man.   CUT

45. *Bowden House—night*
  (a) Watching *All That Heaven Allows* on television. Kersek says Graciella should 'stay over'.
  (b) Night passes. Sam has nightmare (or is it?), wakes Leigh to say he has 'the weirdest feeling' that Cady is already in the house.
  (c) Cady, dressed in Graciella's clothes, garrottes Kersek in kitchen. Sam emerges calling for Kersek. Leigh sees figure racing across lawn. Discovery of bodies of Kersek and Graciella. Sam slips in Kersek's blood, races outside firing revolver wildly.   CUT

46. *Road/Fruit Stall*
  (a) Family driving along road, tense and silent.
  (b) Sam phones Elgar, who says they are fugitives. Cady is hanging on underneath car.   CUT

47. *Cape Fear*
  (a) Arrival at Cape Fear boat landing.
  (b) Cady unties self from under car, watched by elderly black woman; goes to washroom.
  (c) Sam's boat heads off.   CUT

48. *Lake*
  (a) Boat heads off into stormy sunset. Sam lets down anchor in remote spot.
  (b) As they sit at dinner, squall rocks boat. Sam goes on deck to secure boat, takes revolver. Cady is on the boat and grabs him. Cady cuts them adrift. Cady threatens the women; Danny hurls hot water at him.
  (c) Cady hurls Danny out of kitchen then attacks Leigh, while Danny looks for weapon to use against him. He handcuffs her to pole.
  (d) Sam tries to intervene. Cady kicks him in head. Leigh tries to persuade him to rape her, not Danny.
  (e) Danny hurls inflammable fluid at Cady as he lights cigar. He leaps overboard.
  (f) Boat is heaving about in storm—Cady grabs its rope and gets back on board. Cady tries to drag from Sam details of his defence 14 years earlier; Sam admits he has buried evidence that might have saved Cady.
  (g) Cady orders the women to take off their clothes, just as boat is heaving worse. The women jump off but Cady grabs Sam as he is about to jump. Boat splits apart on rocks. Cady is chained to boat. They fight.
  (h) Cady drowns, singing about 'the promised land' as Sam watches from shore, appalled at the blood on his own hands.
  (i) Leigh and Danny embrace in the mud, joined by Sam.
[Film ends on the same series of shots with which it began, and Danny is heard in voice-over.]
FINAL CREDITS (storm and music on sound-track)
THE END

Filmography

The Scarlet Letter (1926)

Directed by Victor Sjöström.
Produced by Victor Sjöström for Metro-Goldwyn-Mayer.
Screenplay by Frances Marion.
Leading players: Lillian Gish (Hester Prynne), Lars Hanson (Reverend Arthur Dimmesdale), Henry B. Walthall (Roger Prynne), Karl Dane (Giles), Marcelle Corday (Mistress Hibbins), Joyce Coad (Pearl).
Running time: 70 minutes (at 24 feet per second).

Random Harvest (1942)

Directed by Mervyn LeRoy.
Produced by Sidney Franklin for Metro-Goldwyn-Mayer.
Screenplay by Claudine West, George Froeschel, Arthur Wimperis.
Leading players: Ronald Colman (Charles Rainier), Greer Garson (Paula Ridgeway), Susan Peters (Kitty), Philip Dorn (Dr Benet), Reginald Owen (Biffer), Jill Esmond (Lydia), Henry Travers (Dr Sims), Margaret Wycherly (Mrs Deventer), Bramwell Fletcher (Harrison), Arthur Margetson (Chet), Norma Varden (Julia).
Running time: 126 minutes.

Great Expectations (1946)

Directed by David Lean.
Produced by Ronald Neame and Anthony Havelock-Allan for Cineguild (and the J. Arthur Rank Organization).
Screenplay by David Lean, Ronald Neame, Anthony Havelock-Allan, with Kay Walsh and Cecil McGivern.
Leading players: John Mills (Pip, grown up), Valerie Hobson (Estella, grown up), Anthony Wager (Pip, as child), Jean Simmons (Estella, as child), Martita Hunt (Miss Havisham), Bernard Miles (Joe Gargery), Finlay Currie (Magwitch), Alec Guinness (Herbert Pocket), Freda Jackson (Mrs Joe Gargery), Francis L. Sullivan (Jaggers), Ivor Barnard (Wemmick), Eileen Erskine (Biddy).
Running time: 118 minutes.

Daisy Miller (1974)

Directed by Peter Bogdanovich.
Produced by Peter Bogdanovich for Copa de Ora Productions.
Screenplay by Frederic Raphael.
Leading players: Cybill Shepherd (Daisy), Barry Brown (Winterbourne), Cloris Leachman (Mrs Miller), Mildred Natwick (Mrs Costello), Eileen Brennan (Mrs Walker), Duilio del Prete (Giovanelli), James MacMurtry (Randolph), George Morfogen (Eugenio).
Running time: 92 minutes.

Cape Fear (1991)

Directed by Martin Scorsese.
Produced by Barbara de Fina.
Screenplay by Wesley Strick, based on James R. Webb's screenplay and John D. MacDonald's novel.
Leading players: Robert De Niro (Max Cady), Nick Nolte (Sam Bowden), Jessica Lange (Leigh Bowden), Juliette Lewis (Danielle Bowden), Joe Don Baker (Claude Kersek), Robert Mitchum (Lieutenant Elgar), Gregory Peck (Lee Heller), Martin Balsam (Judge), Illeana Douglas (Lori Davis).
Running time: 128 minutes.

Note: The four sound films listed above are all available on video, on familiar labels. *The Scarlet Letter* is not on video as far as I can discover, but 16 mm. prints are available in the UK and the USA.

Bibliography

A. PRIMARY TEXTS

DICKENS, CHARLES, *Great Expectations* (1860) (Thomas Nelson and Sons: Edinburgh (no publication date given, approx. 1960)).

HAWTHORNE, NATHANIEL, *The Scarlet Letter* (1850) (Signet Classics, The New American Library: New York, 1959).

HILTON, JAMES, *Random Harvest* (Grosset and Dunlap: New York, 1941).

JAMES, HENRY, *Daisy Miller* (1878) (Penguin: Harmondsworth, 1974).

MACDONALD, JOHN M., *The Executioners* (1957) (Penguin: Harmondsworth, 1991).

B. SECONDARY REFERENCES

General: Books and Articles on Films and/or Literature and on Adaptation

AMBLER, ERIC, 'Screenwriting: The Novelist and Films', *Journal of the British Film Academy*, 8 (Summer 1956), 9–14, 20.

ANDREW, J. DUDLEY, *The Major Film Theories* (Oxford University Press: New York, 1976).

——'The Well-Worn Muse: Adaptation in Film History and Theory', in S. M. Conger and J. R. Welsch (eds.), *Narrative Strategies* (West Illinois University Press: Macomb, Ill., 1980), 9–17.

Anon., 'Adapting a Story for the Screen', *The Times*, 53/824 (25 Apr. 1957), 3.

ASHEIM, LESTER, 'From Book to Film: Simplification', *Hollywood Quarterly*, 5/3 (Spring 1951), 287–304.

——'From Book to Film: Mass Appeals', *Hollywood Quarterly*, 5/4 (Summer 1951), 334–49.

——'From Book to Film: The Note of Affirmation', *Hollywood Quarterly*, 6/1 (Fall 1951), 54–68.

——'Book to Film: Summary', *Hollywood Quarterly*, 6/3 (Spring 1952), 258–73.

ASTRUC, ALEXANDRE, 'The Birth of a New Avant-Garde: La Caméra-Stylo' (1948); repr. in Peter Graham (ed.), *The New Wave* (Secker and Warburg and the British Film Institute: London, 1968), 17–23.

BARR, CHARLES (ed.), *All our Yesterdays: 90 Years of British Cinema* (British Film Institute Publishing, London, in association with the Museum of Modern Art, New York, 1986).

BARTHES, ROLAND, *Image-Music-Text: Essays Selected and Translated by Stephen Heath* (Fontana/Collins: Glasgow, 1977).

——*S/Z*, trans. Richard Miller (Hill and Wang: New York, 1974).

BATES, H. E., 'It Isn't Like the Book', *Films and Filming*, 5/8 (May 1959), 7.

BAUER, LEDA V., 'The Movies Tackle Literature', *American Mercury*, 14/55 (July 1928), 288–94.

BAZIN, ANDRÉ, 'In Defense of Mixed Cinema', in *What is Cinema?*, vol. i, essays selected and trans. Hugh Gray (University of California Press: Berkeley and Los Angeles, 1967).

BEJA, MORRIS, *Film and Literature* (Longman: New York, 1979).

BELLOUR, RAYMOND, 'The Obvious and the Code', *Screen*, 15/4 (Winter 1974–5), 7–17.

BERGMAN, INGMAR, 'Bergman Discusses Film-Making', introd. to *Four Screenplays of Ingmar Bergman*, trans. Lars Malmstrom and David Kushner (Simon and Schuster: New York, 1960).

BERGSTROM, JANET, 'Alternation, Segmentation, Hypnosis: Interview with Raymond Bellour', *Camera Obscura*, 3–4 (1979), 71–103.

BLUESTONE, GEORGE, *Novels into Film* (University of California Press: Berkeley and Los Angeles, 1957).

——'Word to Image: The Problem of the Filmed Novel', *Quarterly of Film, Radio, and Television*, 11/2 (Winter 1956–7), 171–80.

BODEEN, DEWITT, 'The Adapting Art', *Films in Review*, 14/6 (June–July 1963), 349–56.

BOOTH, WAYNE C., *The Rhetoric of Fiction* (University of Chicago Press: Chicago, 1961).

BORDWELL, DAVID, *Narration in the Fiction Film* (Methuen: London, 1985).

——*et al. The Classical Hollywood Cinema* (Routledge and Kegan Paul: London, 1985).

——and THOMPSON, KRISTIN, *Film Art: An Introduction* (Addison-Wesley: Reading, Mass., 1979).

——, ——*Film Art: An Introduction*/4th edn. (New York: McGraw Hill, 1993) (considerably revises and extends the above).

BOYUM, JOY GOULD, *Double Exposure: Fiction into Film* (New American Library: New York, 1985).

BRANIGAN, EDWARD R., *Point of View in the Cinema: A Theory of Narration and Subjectivity in Classical Film* (Mouton Publishers: Berlin, 1984).

BURCH, NOEL, *The Theory of Film Practice*, trans. Helen R. Lane (Secker and Warburg/ Cinema Two: London, 1973).

BURGESS, ANTHONY, 'On the Hopelessness of Turning Good Books into Films', *New York Times*, 124/42820 (20 Apr. 1975), s. 2, p. 1.

CAUGHIE, JOHN (ed.), *Theories of Authorship: A Reader* (Routledge and Kegan Paul/ British Film Institute: London, 1981).

CHANAN, MICHAEL, *The Dream that Kicks* (Routledge and Kegan Paul: London, 1980).

CHATMAN, SEYMOUR, *Coming to Terms: The Rhetoric of Narrative in Fiction and Film* (Cornell University Press: Ithaca, NY, 1990).

——*Story and Discourse: Narrative Structure in Fiction and Film* (Cornell University Press: Ithaca, NY, 1978).

CHIAROMONTE, NICOLA, 'Priests of the Highbrow Cinema: On Image and Word', *Encounter*, 20/1 (Jan. 1963), 40–5.

COHEN, KEITH, *Film and Fiction: The Dynamics of Exchange* (Yale University Press: New Haven, 1979).

COLLIER, LIONEL, 'This "Adaptation" Business', *Picturegoer*, 14/79 (July 1927), 14–15.

CONGER, SYNDY M., and WELSCH, JANICE R. (eds.), *Narrative Strategies: Original Essays in Film and Prose Fiction* (West Illinois University Press: Macomb, Ill., 1980).

COOK, PAM (ed.), *The Cinema Book* (British Film Institute: London, 1985).

CULLER, JONATHAN, *Structuralist Poetics: Structuralism, Linguistics, and the Study of Literature* (Routledge and Kegan Paul: London, 1975), ch. 9.

DISHER, M. WILLSON, 'Classics into Films', *Fortnightly Review*, NS 124 (Dec. 1928), 784–92.

DITTMAR, LINA, 'Fashioning and Re-fashioning: Framing Narratives in the Novel and Film', *Mosaic*, 16/1–2 (Winter–Spring 1983), 189–203.

DOMARCHI, JEAN, 'Littérature et cinéma', *Cahiers du cinéma*, 3/18 (Dec. 1952), 15–20.

DURGNAT, RAYMOND, 'The Mongrel Muse', in *Films and Feeling* (Faber and Faber: London, 1967), 19–30; repr. in F. H. Marcus (ed.), *Film and Literature* (Chandler Publishers: Scranton, 1971).

EATON, MICK, and NEALE, STEVE (eds.), *Cinema and Semiotics: Screen Reader* 2 (Society for Film and Television: London, 1981).

ECO, UMBERTO, *A Theory of Semiotics* (Indiana University Press: Bloomingdale, 1976), esp. pp. 191–216.

EIDSVICK, CHARLES, *Cineliteracy: Film among the Arts* (Random House: New York, 1978).

EISENSTEIN, SERGEI, 'Dickens, Griffith, and the Film Today', in *Film Form*, ed. and trans. Jan Leyda (Harcourt, Brace: New York, 1949), 195–255.

—— *Notes of a Film Director* (1959) (rev. edn. Dover Publication: New York, 1970).

ELLIS, JOHN, 'The Literary Adaptation: An Introduction', *Screen*, 23/1 (May–June 1982), 3–5.

—— *Visible Fictions—Cinema: Television: Video* (Routledge and Kegan Paul: London, 1982).

ELSAESSER, THOMAS, 'Film and the Novel: Reality and Realism in the Cinema', *Twentieth Century Studies*, 9 (Sept. 1973), 58–62.

FADIMAN, WILLIAM, 'But Compared to the Original', *Films and Filming*, 11/5 (Feb. 1985), 21–3.

FELL, JOHN, *Film and the Narrative Tradition* (University of Oklahoma Press: Norman, 1974).

FOWLER, ROGER, *Linguistics and the Novel* (Methuen: London, 1977).

FOX, JULIAN, 'The Great Story Chase', *Films and Filming*, 26/6 (Mar. 1980), 14–21.

—— 'Through the Roof', *Films and Filming*, 26/7 (Apr. 1980), 12–19 (Part 2 of above).

FRENCH, PHILLIP, 'All the Better Books', *Sight and Sound*, 36/1 (Winter 1966–7), 38–41.

GAUTEUR, CLAUDE, 'De l'adaptation ou . . .' *Image et son*, 186 (July 1965), 12–18.

GENETTE, GÉRARD, 'Time and Narrative in *A la recherche du temps perdu*', in J. Hillis Miller (ed.), *Aspects of Narrative* (Columbia University Press: New York, 1971), 93–118.

GILL, BRENDAN, 'Novels into Movies', *Film Comment*, 13/2 (Mar.–Apr. 1977), 44–5.

GLEDHILL, CHRISTINE (ed.), *Home is Where the Heart is: Studies in Melodrama and the Woman's Film* (BFI Publishing: London, 1987).

GOW, GORDON, 'Novel into Film', *Films and Filming*, 12/8 (May 1966), 19–22.

GRIFFITH, BILL, 'The Tale's the Thing', *ABC Film Review* (Thirteen articles appearing monthly between Jan. 1968 and Feb. 1969).

HAMILTON, IAN, *Writers in Hollywood 1915–1951* (Heinemann: London, 1991).

HARRINGTON, JOHN (ed.), *Film and/as Literature* (Prentice-Hall: Englewood Cliffs, NJ, 1977).

HAWKES, TERENCE, *Structuralism and Semiotics* (Methuen: London, 1977).

HEATH, STEPHEN, 'Film/Cinetext/Text', in M. Eaton and S. Neale (eds.), *Cinema and Semiotics* (Society for Film and Television: London, 1981), 99–124.

—— 'Film and System: Terms of Analysis', Part I, *Screen*, 16/1 (Spring 1975), 7–77; Part II, *Screen*, 16/2 (Summer 1975), 91–113.

HEINICH, NATALIE, 'La Politique des hauteurs', *Cahiers du cinéma*, 306 (Dec. 1979), 16–17.

HENDERSON, BRIAN, 'Tense, Mood, and Voice in Film (Notes after Genette)', *Film Quarterly*, 36/4 (Summer 1983), 4–17.

JACOBS, LEWIS, *The Rise of the American Film* (Harcourt, Brace: New York, 1939).

JAMESON, FREDRIC, *The Prison-House of Language: A Critical Account of Structuralism and Russian Formalism* (Princeton University Press: Princeton, 1972).

JINKS, WILLIAM, *The Celluloid Literature: Film in the Humanities* (Glencoe Press: Riverside, NJ, 1971).

JORGENS, JACK, *Shakespeare on Film* (Indiana University Press: Bloomington, 1977).

KATZ, EPHRAIM, *The International Film Encyclopedia* (Macmillan: London, 1979).

KAUFFMAN, STANLEY, 'Notes on Theatre-and-Film', in *Living Images: Film Comment and Criticism* (Harper and Row: New York, 1975), 353–62.

KERR, PAUL, 'Classic Serials: To Be Continued', *Screen*, 23/1 (May–June 1982), 6–16.

KLEIN, MICHAEL, and PARKER, GILLIAN (eds.), *The English Novel and the Movies* (Frederick Ungar Publishing: New York, 1981).

KRACAUER, SIEGFRIED, *The Theory of Film: The Redemption of Physical Reality* (Oxford University Press: New York, 1960).

LAURITZEN, MONICA, *Jane Austen's 'Emma' on Television* Gothenburg Studies in English 48 (Acta Universitatis Gothoburgensis: Gothenburg, 1981).

LÉVI-STRAUSS, CLAUDE, *Structural Anthropology* (1958), trans. Claire Jacobson and Brooke Grundfest Schoepf (1963) (Penguin Books: Harmondsworth, 1972).

LODGE, DAVID, *Working with Structuralism: Essays and Reviews on Nineteenth- and Twentieth-Century Literature* (Routledge and Kegan Paul: London, 1981).

MACCABE, COLIN, 'Realism and the Cinema: Notes on Some Brechtian Theses', *Screen*, 15/2 (Summer 1974), 7–27.

MACCANN, RICHARD DYER (ed.), *Film: A Montage of Theories* (E. P. Dutton: New York, 1946).

MCCONNELL, FRANK, *Storytelling and Mythmaking* (Oxford University Press: New York, 1979).

—— *The Spoken Seen: Film and the Romantic Imagination* (Johns Hopkins University Press: Baltimore, 1975).

MCDOUGAL, STUART Y., *Made into Movies: From Literature to Film* (Holt Rinehart and Winston: New York, 1985).

MCFARLANE, BRIAN, 'The Australian Literary Adaptation: An Overview', *Literature/Film Quarterly*, 21/2 (1993).

—— *Words and Images: Australian Novels into Film* (Heinemann Publishers Australia: Melbourne, 1983).

MADDOX, R., SILLIPHANT, S., and ISAACS, N. D., *Fiction into Film: A Walk in the Spring Rain* (University of Tennessee Press: Knoxville, 1970).

MAGILL, FRANK, N. (ed.), *Cinema: The Novel into Film* (Salem Press: Pasadena, Calif., 1980).

MARCUS, FRED H. (ed.), *Film and Literature: Contrasts in Media* (Chandler Publishers: Scranton, 1971).

MAST, GERALD, and COHEN, MARSHALL, *Film Theory and Criticism: Introductory Readings* (2nd edn., Oxford University Press: New York, 1979).

MENDILOW, A. A., *Time and the Novel* (Humanities Press: New York, 1972).

METZ, CHRISTIAN, 'Current Problems of Film Theory', in M. Eaton and S. Neale (eds.), *Cinema and Semiotics* (Society for Film and Television: London, 1981), 38–85.

——*Film Language: A Semiotics of the Cinema*, trans. Michael Taylor (Oxford University Press: New York, 1974).

——*The Imaginary Signifier*, trans. Ben Brewster *et al.* (Indiana University Press: Bloomingdale, 1977).

——*Language and Cinema*, trans. Donna Jean Umiker-Sebeok (Mouton: The Hague, 1974).

——'Methodological Propositions for the Analysis of Film', in M. Eaton and S. Neale (eds.), *Cinema and Semiotics* (Society for Film and Television: London, 1981), 86–98.

MICHAELIS, A. R., 'In the Beginning Was the Word: A Comparison between Books and Films', *University Film Journal*, 7 (Spring 1955), 1–6, and 8 (Summer 1955), 10–15.

MILLER, GABRIEL, *Screening the Novel: Rediscovered American Fiction in Film* (Frederick Ungar Publishing: New York, 1980).

MONACO, JAMES, *How to Read a Film: The Art, Technology, Language, History and Theory of Film and Media* (Oxford University Press: New York, 1981).

MORENO, JULIO, 'Subjective Cinema: And the Problem of Film in the First Person', trans. Ray Morrison, *Quarterly of Film, Radio, and Television*, 7/4 (Summer 1953), 341–58.

MORRISSETTE, BRUCE, *Novel and Film: Essays in Two Genres* (University of Chicago Press: Chicago, 1985).

MULVEY, LAURA, 'Visual Pleasure and Narrative Cinema', *Screen*, 16/3 (Autumn 1975), 6–18.

MURRAY, EDWARD, *The Cinematic Imagination* (Frederick Ungar Publishing: New York, 1972).

NICOLL, ALLARDYCE, *Film and Theatre* (George Harrap: London, 1936).

NOWELL-SMITH, GEOFFREY, 'A Note on "History/Discourse"', in J. Caughie (ed.), *Theories of Authorship* (Routledge & Kegan Paul/British Film Institute: London, 1981), 232–41.

ORR, CHRISTOPHER, 'The Discourse on Adaptation', *Wide Angle*, 6/2 (1984), 72–6.

——and NICHOLSON, COLIN (eds.), *Cinema & Fiction 1950–90: New Modes of Adapting* (Edinburgh University Press: Edinburgh, 1992).

PARKINSON, DAVID, *The Graham Greene Film Reader: Mornings in the Dark* (Carcanet: Manchester, 1993).

PEARY, GERALD, and SHATZKIN, ROGER (eds.), *The Classic American Novel and the Movies* (Frederick Ungar Publishing: New York, 1977).

—————(eds.), *The Modern American Novel and the Movies* (Frederick Ungar Publishing: New York, 1978).

PERKINS, V. F., *Film as Film: Understanding and Judging Movies* (Penguin: Harmondsworth, 1972).

PIRIE, DAVID, 'The Novel and the Cinema', in Martin Seymour-Smith (ed.), *Novels and Novelists* (St Martin's Press: New York, 1980), 253–66.

POTAMKIN, H. A., 'Novel into Film: A Case Study of Current Practice', *Close Up*, 8/4 (Dec. 1931), 267–79.

PROPP, V., *Morphology of the Folktale* (1928), trans. Laurence Scott (University of Texas Press: Austin, 1968).

RAPHAEL, FREDERIC, introd. to *Two for the Road* (Jonathan Cape: London, 1967).

READ, HERBERT, 'The Poet and the Film: Towards a Film Aesthetic', *Cinema Quarterly*, 1/4 (Summer 1933), 197–202.

RENTSCHLER, ERIC (ed.), *German Film and Literature: Adaptations and Transformations* (Methuen: New York, 1986).

RICHARDSON, ROBERT, *Literature and Film* (University of Indiana Press: Bloomington, 1969).

ROBBE-GRILLET, ALAIN, introd. to *Last Year at Marienbad*, trans. Richard Howard (Grove Press: New York, 1962).

ROSS, LILLIAN, *Picture* (Doubleday: New York, 1962).

ROUD, RICHARD, 'The Empty Streets', *Sight and Sound*, 26/4 (Spring 1957), 191–5.

——'Two Cents on the Rouble', *Sight and Sound*, 27/5 (Summer 1958), 245–7.

SALT, BARRY, *Film Style and Technology: History and Analysis* (Starwood: London, 1983).

SAMUELS, CHARLES THOMAS, *Mastering the Film and Other Essays*, ed. Laurence Grover (University of Tennessee Press: Knoxville, 1977).

SAUSSURE, FERDINAND DE, 'Course in General Linguistics', in *Cours de linguistique générale*, ed. Charles Bally, Albert Sechehaye, with Albert Riedlinger (1915); repr. in Richard and Fernand de George, *The Structuralists from Marx to Lévi-Strauss* (Anchor Books: New York, 1972), 59–79.

SCHOLES, ROBERT, 'Narration and Narrativity in Film', *Quarterly Review of Film Studies* (Aug. 1957), in G. Mast and M. Cohen, *Film Theory and Criticism* (2nd edn., Oxford University Press: New York, 1979), 417–33.

SINYARD, NEIL, *Filming Literature: The Art of Screen Adaptation* (Croom Helm: London, 1986).

SMITH, SARAH, W. R., 'The Technology of Narrative: Notes on the Esthetics of Nonexistent Fictions', *Mosaic*, 16/1–2 (Winter–Spring 1983), 19–32.

SPIEGEL, ALAN, *Fiction and the Camera Eye: Visual Consciousness in Film and the Modern Novel* (University Press of Virginia: Charlottesville, 1976).

STAFFORD-CLARK, DAVID, *What Freud 'Really' Said* (Penguin Books: Harmondsworth, 1967).

STOLTZFUS, BEN, F., *Alain Robbe-Grillet and the New French Novel* (Southern Illinois University Press: Carbondale, 1964), ch. 6.

STRAUSS, FLORENCE L., 'A Synopsized View of Literature', *Bookman*, 64/4 (Dec. 1926), 455–6.

STURROCK, JOHN (ed.), *Structuralism and Since: From Lévi-Strauss to Derrida* (Oxford University Press: Oxford, 1979).

TARADASH, DANIEL, 'Into Another World', *Films and Filming*, 5/8 (May 1959), 9, 33.

TODOROV, TZVETAN, *The Fantastic: A Structural Approach to a Literary Genre* (The Press of Case Western Reserve University: Cleveland, 1973), ch. 1.

TRUFFAUT, FRANÇOIS, *Hitchcock* (Simon and Schuster: New York, 1966).

WAGNER, GEOFFREY, *The Novel and the Cinema* (Fairleigh Dickinson University Press: Rutherford, NJ, 1975).

WALD, JERRY, 'Screen Adaptation'. *Films in Review*, 5/2 (Feb. 1954), 62–7.

WALPOLE, HUGH, 'Can a Book be Filmed?', *Star* (22 June 1939) (in British Film Institute cuttings file on Adaptation).

WARD, JOHN, 'Alain Robbe-Grillet: The Novelist as Director', *Sight and Sound*, 37/2 (Spring 1968), 86–90.

WATT, IAN, *The Rise of the Novel* (Chatto and Windus: London, 1957), chs. 1, 2.

WILLIAMS, CHRISTOPHER (ed.), *Realism and the Cinema: A Reader* (Routledge and Kegan Paul/British Film Institute: London, 1980).

WILLIAMS, W. E., 'Film and Literature', *Sight and Sound*, 4/156 (Winter 1935–6), 163–5.

WINNINGTON, RICHARD, *Drawn and Quartered* (Saturn Press: London, 1948).

WINSTON, DOUGLAS GARRETT, *The Screenplay as Literature* (Fairleigh Dickinson University Press: Rutherford, NJ, 1973).

WOLLEN, PETER, '*North by North-West*: A Morphological Analysis', *Film Form*, 1 (1976), 20–34.

WOOD, ROBIN, 'Notes for a Reading of *I Walked with a Zombie*', *CineAction!*, 3–4 (Winter 1986), 6–20.

——*Personal Views: Explorations in Film* (Gordon Fraser: London, 1976).

C. REFERENCES RELEVANT TO INDIVIDUAL CASE-STUDIES

1. The Scarlet Letter

ESTRIN, MARK W., '"Triumphant Ignominy" on the Screen', *Literature/Film Quarterly*, 2/2 (Spring 1974), 110–22; repr. (abridged) in G. Peary and R. Shatzkin (eds.), *The Classic American Novel and the Movies* (Frederick Ungar Publishing: New York, 1977).

GISH, LILLIAN, and PINCHOT, ANN, *Mr Griffith, the Movies and Me* (W. H. Allen: London, 1969).

HAWTHORNE, NATHANIEL, preface to *The House of Seven Gables* (1851) (Penguin: Harmondsworth, 1981), 1–3.

HOFFMAN, DANIEL, *Form and Fable in American Fiction* (Oxford University Press (A Galaxy Book: New York, 1965), ch. 9.

JAMES, HENRY, 'Nathaniel Hawthorne' (1897), in Leon Edel (ed.), *The House of Fiction: Essays on the Novel* (Mercury Books: London, 1962), 176–86.

MARX, LEO, foreword to *The Scarlet Letter* (Signet Classics, The New American Library: New York, 1959), pp. vii–xii.

MILNE, TOM, 'The Scarlet Letter', *Monthly Film Bulletin*, British Film Institute, 41/490 (Nov. 1974), 260–1.

PAINE, ALBERT BIGELOW, *Life and Lillian Gish* (Macmillan: New York, 1932).

SHIPMAN, DAVID, *The Story of Cinema*, vol. i (Hodder and Stoughton: London, 1982).

SMITH, JULIAN, 'Hester, Sweet Hester Prynne: *The Scarlet Letter* in the Movie Market Place', *Literature/Film Quarterly*, 2/3 (Summer 1974), 196–206.

2. Random Harvest

(a) Contemporary reviews of the film

Anonymous authors in *Kinematograph Weekly* (Jan. 1943); *Monthly Film Bulletin*, 10/109 (31 Jan. 1943); *Today's Cinema* (1 Jan. 1943).

AGEE, JAMES, *Nation* (26 Dec. 1942); repr. in *Agee on Film* (McDowell Oblonsky: New York, 1958), 266–8.

COLLIER, LIONEL, 'Random Harvest', *Picturegoer*, 12/575 NS (6 Mar. 1943), 12.

LEJEUNE, C. A., 'The Films', *Observer*, 7913 (21 Jan. 1943), 2.

WHITEBAIT, WILLIAM, 'The Movies', *New Statesman*, 25/623 (30 Jan. 1943), 76.

(b) Other works consulted

CAMPBELL, ROBERT JEAN, *A Psychiatric Dictionary* (Oxford University Press: New York, 1981), 546–7, 610–13.

CANHAM, KINGSLEY, 'Mervyn LeRoy: Star-Making, Studio Systems and Style', *The Hollywood Professionals*, vol. v (Tantivy Press: London, 1976), 133–65.

DEMING, BARBARA, *Running away from Myself: A Dream Portrait of America Drawn from the Films of the Forties* (Grossman Publishers: New York, 1969), 72–81.

EAMES, JOHN DOUGLAS, *The MGM Story* (Octopus: London, 1979).

FREUD, SIGMUND, *Introductory Lectures on Psychoanalysis* (Penguin: Harmondsworth, 1974).

——*On Metapsychology* (Penguin: Harmondsworth, 1991).

——*On Sexuality* (Penguin: Harmondsworth, 1991).

——*An Outline of Psycho-analysis*, trans. and ed. James Strachy (Hogarth Press: London, 1973).

HALLIWELL, LESLIE, *The Filmgoer's Companion* (Grafton: London, 1992; 1st pub. Granada: London, 1977).

KNOX, COLLEY (ed.), *For Ever England* (Cassell: London, 1943) (includes Beverley Nichols, 'All These I Love').

LEROY, MERVYN, *Mervyn LeRoy: Take One* (as told to Dick Kleiner) (W. H. Allen: London, 1974).

MCFARLANE, BRIAN, 'Re-shaped for the Screen: *Random Harvest*', *Literature/Film Quarterly*, 17/4 (1989).

MORLEY, SHERIDAN, *Tales from the Hollywood Raj* (Weidenfeld and Nicolson: London, 1983).

QUIRK, LAWRENCE J., *The Great Romantic Films* (Citadel Press, Secaucus, NJ, 1974), 105–7.

RHODE, ERIC, *A History of Cinema* (1976) (repr. Penguin Books: Harmondsworth, 1978).

RICHARDS, JEFFREY, *Visions of Yesterday* (Routledge and Kegan Paul: London, 1973).

RYECROFT, CHARLES, *A Critical Dictionary of Psycho-analysis* (Nelson: London, 1968), 142, 160–1.

TIMS, HILTON, *Emotion Pictures: The 'Women's' Picture, 1930–55* (Columbus Books: London, 1987).

TYLER, PARKER, *Magic and Myth of the Movies* (1947) (repr. Secker and Warburg: London, 1971).

3. **Great Expectations**

AGEE, JAMES, *Agee on Film* (McDowell Oblonsky: New York, 1958), 266–7 (repr. from *Nation*, 19 July 1947).

BUTLER, IVAN, *Cinema in Britain: An Illustrated Survey* (A. S. Barnes: New York, 1973), 163, 165.

Cineguild publicity material, held in British Film Institute (microfiche collection, London).

DE BONA, GUERRIC, 'Doing Time; Undoing Time: Plot Mutations in David Lean's *Great Expectations*', *Literature/Film Quarterly*, 20/1 (1992).

DURGNAT, RAYMOND, *A Mirror for England* (Faber and Faber: London, 1970).

FORSTER, JOHN, *The Life of Dickens* (1872–4) (repr. J. M. Dent: London, 1966).

HOPKINS, CHARLES, '*Great Expectations*', in *Magill's Survey of Cinema: English Language Films*, First Series, vol. ii (Salem Press: Pasadena, Calif., 1980), 685–9.

HOUSE, HUMPHRY, *The Dickens World* (Oxford University Press: London, 1976).

LAMBERT, GAVIN, 'British Films 1947: Survey and Prospect', *Sequence 2* (Winter 1947), 9–14.

LEAVIS, Q. D., 'How We Must Read *Great Expectations*', in F. R. Leavis and Q. D. Leavis, *Dickens the Novelist* (Penguin: Harmondsworth, 1972).

LEJEUNE, C. A., 'Communiqués from the London Film Front', *New York Times*, 96/32, 663 (29 June 1947), s. 2, p. 5.

LODGE, DAVID, Lecture on *Great Expectations* in the series 'From the Page to the Screen', National Film Theatre, London, 22 Feb. 1983.

McFARLANE, BRIAN, 'A Literary Cinema? British Films and British Novels', in Charles Barr (ed.), *All our Yesterdays* (British Film Institute Publishing, London/Museum of Modern Art, New York, 1986).

—— 'David Lean's *Great Expectations*: Meeting Two Challenges', *Literature/Film Quarterly*, 20/1 (1992).

—— *Sixty Voices: Celebrities Recall the Golden Age of British Cinema* (British Film Institute, London, with Monash University, 1992).

McVAY, DOUGLAS, 'Lean: Lover of Life', *Films and Filming*, 5/11 (Aug. 1959).

MOYNAHAN, JULIAN, 'Seeing the Book, Reading the Movie', in M. Klein and G. Parker (eds.), *The English Novel and the Movies* (Frederick Ungar Publishing: New York, 1981), 143–54.

MURPHY, ROBERT, *Realism and Tinsel*: Cinema and Society in Britain 1939–1948 (Routledge: London, 1989).

POOLE, JULIAN, 'Novel–Film; Dickens–Lean: A Study of *Great Expectations* and *Oliver Twist*' (unpublished MA thesis, University of East Anglia, 1979).

PRATLEY, GERALD, *The Cinema of David Lean* (Tantivy Press: London, 1974), 58–71.

REISZ, KAREL, *The Technique of Film Editing* (London: Focal Press, 1953), 237–41.

R. M. 'Great Expectations', *Monthly Film Bulletin*, 13/156 (31 Dec. 1946), 166.

SILVER, ALAIN, 'The Untranquil Light: David Lean's *Great Expectations*', *Literature/Film Quarterly*, 2/2 (Spring 1974), 140–52.

SILVERMAN, STEPHEN M., *David Lean* (Andre Deutsch: London, 1989).

THOMAS, R. GEORGE, *Dickens' 'Great Expectations'* (Edward Arnold: London, 1977).

VERMILYE, JERRY, *The Great British Films* (Citadel Press: Secaucus, NJ, 1978), 102–3.

WINNINGTON, RICHARD, 'Great Expectations', *News Chronicle* (11 Dec. 1946). (In British Film Institute cuttings file on this film.)

—— 'Critical Survey', in *The Penguin Film Review 2* (Penguin: Harmondsworth: 1947), 16–19.

ZAMBRANO, A. L., '*Great Expectations*: Dickens and David Lean', *Literature/Film Quarterly*, 2/2 (Spring 1974), 154–61.

4. Daisy Miller

BAUMBACH, JONATHAN, 'Europe in the Movies', *Partisan Review*, 41/3 (1974), 450–4.

BRADBURY, NICOLA, 'Filming James', *Essays in Criticism*, 29/4 (Oct. 1979), 293–301 (on James Ivory's film of *The Europeans*).

COCKS, JAY, 'Culture Shock: *Daisy Miller*', *Time*, 103/22 (3 June 1974), 66.

DAWSON, JAN, 'The Continental Divide: Filming Henry James', *Sight and Sound*, 43/1 (Winter 1973–4), 14–15; repr. in part as 'An Interview with Peter Bogdanovich', in G. Peary and R. Shatzkin (eds.), *The Classic American Novel and the Movies* (Frederick Ungar Publishing: New York, 1977).

—— '*Daisy Miller*', *Monthly Film Bulletin*, 41/489 (Oct. 1974), 222.

EDEL, LEON, *The Life of Henry James*, i: *1843–89* (Penguin Books: Harmondsworth, 1977).

—— introd. to *Henry James: Selected Fiction* (E. P. Dutton: New York, 1953), pp. x–xi.

GEIST, STANLEY, 'Portraits from a Family Album: *Daisy Miller*', *Hudson Review*, 5/2 (Summer 1952), 203–6.

GOW, GORDON, '*Daisy Miller*', *Films and Filming*, 21/2 (Nov. 1974), 33–4.

HALL, SANDRA, 'Directors in a double take', *Bulletin*, 96 (17 Aug. 1974), 39.

HERMINJARD, MARCEL, *Souvenirs d'un hôtelier veveysan* (Imprimerie Sauberlin & Pfeiffer SA: Vevey, 1976).

HOFFMANN, CHARLES, ['The Two-Part Contrast in *Daisy Miller*'], in *The Short Novels of Henry James* (Bookman Associates: New York, 1957), 20–3; repr. in Stafford, *James's Daisy Miller*.

JAMES, HENRY, *Daisy Miller: A Comedy in Three Acts* (1882); repr. in Stafford, *James's, Daisy Miller*.

LIGGERA, J. J., ' "She Would Have Appreciated One's Esteem": Peter Bogdanovich's *Daisy Miller*', *Literature/Film Quarterly*, 9/1 (1981), 15–21.

MCFARLANE, BRIAN, 'Bogdanovich's *Daisy Miller* and the Limits of Fidelity', *Literature/Film Quarterly*, 19/4 (1991).

MURRAY, KATHLEEN, '*Daisy Miller*: An International Episode', *Movietone News*, 33 (July 1974), 13–16; repr. in G. Peary and R. Shatzkin (eds.), *The Classic American Novel and the Movies* (New York: Frederick Ungar Publishing Co., 1977).

ROSENBAUM, JONATHAN, '*Daisy Miller*', *Sight and Sound*, 43 / 4 (Autumn 1974), 247.

SHIELDS, JOHN C., '*Daisy Miller*: Bogdanovich's Film and James's Nouvelle', *Literature/Film Quarterly*, 11/2 (1983), 105–11.

SHIPMAN, DAVID, *The Story of Cinema*, ii (Hodder and Stoughton: London, 1984).

SIMON, JOHN, 'Jacobin—Not Jacobite' (Aug. 1974), in *Reverse Angle: A Decade of American Films* (Clarkson N. Potter: New York, 1981), 153–5.

STAFFORD, WILLIAM T. (ed.), *James's Daisy Miller: The Story, The Play, The Critics* (Charles Scribner's Sons: New York, 1953).

5. Cape Fear

BISKIND, Peter, 'Slouching toward Hollywood', *Première*, 5/3 (Nov. 1991).

BROOKS, PETER, *The Melodramatic Imagination: Balzac, Henry James, Melodrama and the Mode of Excess* (Yale University Press: New Haven, 1976).

BRUCE, GRAHAM, 'Double Score: Bernard Herrmann's Music for *Cape Fear* 1961 and 1991', *Metro Magazine*, 96 (Summer 1993/4).

CAPP, ROSE, '*Cape Fear*: Whose Fantasy Marty?', *Metro Magazine*, 19 (Winter 1992).

COOK PAM, 'Scorsese's Masquerade', *Sight and Sound*, NS, 1/12 (Apr. 1992).

ELSAESSER, THOMAS, 'Tales of Sound and Fury: Observations on the Family Melodrama', *Monogram*, 4 (1972); repr. in C. Gledhill, *Home is Where the Heart is* (BFI Publishing: London, 1987).

HEILMAN, ROBERT, *Tragedy and Melodrama: Versions of Experience* (University of Washington Press: Seattle, 1965).

HOBERMAN, J., 'Sacred and Profane', *Sight and Sound*, 1/20 (Feb. 1992).

KELLY, MARY PAT, '*Cape Fear*', in *Martin Scorsese: A Journey* (Thunder's Mouth Press: New York, 1991).

KEYSER, LES, *Martin Scorsese* (Twayne: New York, 1992).

LEFF, LEONARD J., and SIMONS, JEROLD L., *The Dame in the Kimono: Hollywood Censorship and the Production Code from the 1920s to the 1960s* (Weidenfeld and Nicolson: London, 1990).

McROBBIE, ANGELA, '*Cape Fear*', *Sight and Sound*, NS, 1/11 (Mar. 1992).

MURRAY, GABRIELLE, '*Cape Fear*: Punishment and Salvation', *Metro Magazine*, 90 (Winter 1992).

ROBERTSON, JAMES C., *The Hidden Cinema: British Film Censorship in Action 1913–1972* (Routledge: London, 1989).

SOLMAN, GREGORY, 'The Bs of Summer', *Film Comment*, 29/4 (July–Aug. 1993).

STONE, JUDY, 'A *Cape Fear* for the '90s', *San Francisco Chronicle* (12, Nov. 1991).

TREVELYAN, JOHN, *What the Censor Saw* (Michael Joseph: London, 1973).

Index